W9-CFO-244

Social History of Africa

"I WILL NOT EAT STONE"

Recent Titles in
Social History of Africa Series
Series Editors: Allen Isaacman and Jean Allman

"I WILL NOT EAT STONE"

A WOMEN'S HISTORY OF COLONIAL ASANTE

Jean Allman
and Victoria Tashjian

HEINEMANN
Portsmouth, NH

JAMES CURREY
Oxford

DAVID PHILIP
Cape Town

DT
507
, A45
2000

Heinemann
A division of Reed Elsevier Inc.
361 Hanover Street
Portsmouth, NH 03801-3912
USA
www.heinemann.com

James Currey Ltd.
73 Botley Road
Oxford OX2 0BS
United Kingdom

David Philip Publishers (Pty) Ltd.
208 Werdmuller Centre
Claremont 7708
Cape Town, South Africa

Offices and agents throughout the world

ISBN 0–325–07001–6 (Heinemann cloth)
ISBN 0–325–07000–8 (Heinemann paper)
ISBN 0–85255–691–8 (James Currey cloth)
ISBN 0–85255–641–1 (James Currey paper)

British Library Cataloguing in Publication Data

Allman, Jean
　I will not eat stone : a women's history of colonial Asante.—(Social history of Africa)
　1. Women, Ashanti—Social conditions　2. Women, Ashanti—History　3. Ghana—Social conditions
　I. Title　II. Tashjian, Victoria
　305.4'88963385'009

　ISBN 0–85255–641–1 (James Currey paper)
　ISBN 0–85255–691–8 (James Currey cloth)

Library of Congress Cataloging-in-Publication Data

Allman, Jean Marie.
　"I will not eat stone" : a women's history of colonial Asante / Jean Allman and Victoria Tashjian.
　　p.　cm.—(Social history of Africa, ISSN 1099-8098)
　Includes bibliographical references and index.
　ISBN 0–325–07001–6 (alk. paper)—ISBN 0–325–07000–8 (pbk : alk. paper)
　1. Women, Ashanti—History. 2. Marriage—Economic aspects—Ghana. 3. Ashanti (African people)—Social conditions. 4. Ashanti (African people)—Economic conditions.
　I. Tashjian, Victoria. II. Title. III. Series.

　DT507.A45 2000
　966.7004'963385—dc21　　　00–024253

Paperback cover photo: Women in the market, ca. 1914. Copyright Basel Mission Archive, QD-30.019.0007. Reprinted with permission.

Printed in the United States of America on acid-free paper.

04 03 02 01 00 SB 1 2 3 4 5 6 7 8 9

Copyright Acknowledgments

The authors and publisher gratefully acknowledge permission to use scattered excerpts from the following material:

Jean M. Allman, "Fathering, Mothering and Making Sense of Ntamoba: Reflections on the Economy of Child-Rearing in Colonial Asante, *Africa: Journal of the International African Institute* 67:2 (1997), 296–321. Reprinted by permission of the International African Institute.

Jean M. Allman, "Adultery and the State in Asante: Reflections on Gender, Class and Power from 1800 to 1950," in *The Cloth of Many Colored Silks: Papers on History and Society, Ghanaian and Islamic, in Honor of Ivor Wilks*, ed. John Hunwick and Nancy Lawler, 27–65 (Evanston, IL: Northwestern University Press, 1996). Reprinted by permission of Northwestern University Press.

Jean M. Allman, "Rounding Up Spinsters: Gender Chaos and Unmarried Women in Colonial Asante," *Journal of African History* 37:2 (1996), 195–214. Reprinted with the permission of Cambridge University Press.

Jean M. Allman, "Making Mothers: Missionaries, Medical Officers and Women's Work in Colonial Asante, 1924–1945," *History Workshop Journal* 38 (1994), 25–48. Reprinted by permission of Oxford University Press.

Victoria B. Tashjian, "'It's Mine' and 'It's Ours' Are Not the Same Thing: Changing Economic Relations between Spouses in Asante," in *The Cloth of Many Colored Silks: Papers on History and Society, Ghanaian and Islamic, in Honor of Ivor Wilks*, ed. John Hunwick and Nancy Lawler, 205–22 (Evanston, IL: Northwestern University Press, 1996). Reprinted by permission of Northwestern University Press.

To our mothers and grandmothers

CONTENTS

ILLUSTRATIONS

ACKNOWLEDGMENTS

As co-authors, we have accumulated many debts over the years—some in common, some individually. Our deepest gratitude goes to the many women and men who shared so freely their stories and reminiscences. The windows they opened for us on to Asante's past made this book possible. We also owe a profound and common debt to our mentor, advisor, and friend, Ivor Wilks, who showed us the importance of those windows. By word and example, he introduced both of us to the study of history and taught us how to listen. In Ghana, we enjoyed the support of many of the same individuals, whose advice, friendship, and assistance made our separate research endeavors possible. We would like to particularly thank Nana Osei Agyeman-Duah, who served as a research assistant and "cultural translator" for both of us, his father, the late Rev. Joseph Agyeman-Duah, and their wonderful extended family, which welcomed us with open arms. We are also grateful to the former director of the Institute of African Studies, Nana Arhin Brempong, whose assistance facilitated our work in more ways than we can recount here. Special thanks are due, in addition, to Selina Opoku-Agyeman, with whom we both shared many a meal in Kumasi, and Kojo Grunshie, one of several supportive staff members at Manhyia Palace who made the day-to-day solitude of archival work in the Record Office much more bearable. It is also important that we recognize the late Asantehene, Nana Opoku Ware II, who, throughout his 29-year reign, saw to it that the doors of Manhyia Record Office were always open to researchers. We are but two of many, Ghanaian and non-Ghanaian, who have benefited from the open scholarly climate he fostered.

The arguments in this book did not develop in isolation, and for that we are extremely grateful. Though none but ourselves bear responsibility for the final content of those arguments, many individuals over the past decade, in both formal and informal discussions, have encouraged us, challenged us, and helped us to glimpse the forest, when all we could see were the trees: Emmanuel Akyeampong, Kojo Amanor, Gareth Austin, Tani Barlow, Susan Porter Benson, Gracia Clark, Anna Davin, Janet Ewald, Steve Feierman, Susan Geiger, Heidi Gengenbach, Sandra Greene, Karen Tranberg Hansen, Nancy Rose Hunt, John Hunwick, Allen Isaacman, Cheryl Johnson-Odim, Robert Kramer, Joshua Lazerson, Takyiwaa Manuh, T. C. McCaskie, Maanda Mulaudzi, Nakanyike Musisi, Agnes Odinga, David Owusu-Ansah, Jane Parpart, Charles Piot, Helena Pohlandt-McCormick, Sita Ranchod-Nilsson, Richard Rathbone, Claire Robertson, David Roediger, John Rowe, Beverly Stoeltje, Luise White, Ivor Wilks, and Larry Yarak. We thank Kefa Otiso for his careful work on our maps. We would also like to single out for special mention Allen Isaacman and the two anonymous readers who collectively managed to push us over the last hurdle in preparing this manuscript.

Neither of our research agendas would have been possible without the financial and practical support of numerous institutions. Northwestern University provided Victoria with fellowships, teaching assistantships, and a Foreign Language and Area Studies Title VI grant during her years as a graduate student in the Department of History. Northwestern also supported her field research through a Dissertation Year Grant awarded by the Graduate School and a Field Research Support Award granted by the Program of African Studies. Through a MacArthur Junior Scholar Award, the John D. and Catherine T. MacArthur Foundation provided the primary support for her field research in Ghana in 1990. More recently, the Faculty Development Fund of St. Norbert College provided generous financial assistance, which allowed her to present preliminary results of her work at several conferences and to conduct research at Rhodes House Library, Oxford, in 1996. In addition to internal support from the University of Missouri (1988–1994) and the University of Minnesota (1994–1999), Jean's research was made possible by funding from the American Council of Learned Societies (1990 Grant-in-Aid), the National Endowment for the Humanities (1991 Fellowship), the Department of Education's Fulbright-Hays Program (1992 Faculty Training Grant), and the Social Science Research Council (1992 Advanced Area Research Fellowship).

We both are indebted to the Institute of African Studies at the University of Ghana for the practical and collegial support we received as research affiliates and to the supportive staff at the following institutions for their invaluable assistance in accessing archival documentation: the African Studies Centre, Cambridge University; the Basel Mission Archives (especially Peter Haenger and Paul Jenkins); Manhyia Record Office, Kumasi; the Methodist Missionary Society (especially M. J. Fox); the National Archives of

Ghana, Accra and Kumasi (especially Cletus Azangweo); the Red Cross Archives, U.K.; Rhodes House, Oxford (especially Alan Bell and Allen Lodge); and the Library of the School of Oriental and African Studies. We are also grateful for the able assistance provided over the years by Hans Panofsky, Dan Britz, and Mette Shayne at the Melville J. Herskovits Memorial Library at Northwestern University.

While many of our debts are common, some are personal and individual. Jean would like to express special thanks to Thomas E. Kyei, who has been endlessly patient with her constant questions over the years—about changes in family life and shifts in Twi language use and meaning. Thanks to his patience and generosity, she is a much more learned student of Asante history. Jean also owes much to friends who have, against all odds, kept her sane over the past decade, especially Sue Benson, Helen Levin, Jeani O'Brien, Jennifer Pierce, and the lively participants in the S.A.B.L.E. seminar. She also wishes to thank her partner, David Roediger, and her two sons—Brendan and Donovan—who by dint of fate had to share a house with this project for nearly a decade. She is grateful that they seldom complained, were always there when she needed them, yet wisely knew when to keep their distance. She also wishes to express her appreciation to her mother and best friend, Peggy Allman, and the other members of her extended family for their ongoing support over the past decade. Her work on this book is dedicated to the memory of her father, John, who taught her the real meaning of *obirεmpɔn* long before she ever traveled to Kumasi.

For their invaluable encouragement and collective sense of humor, Victoria is profoundly grateful to her good friends Janet Phillips Kahla, Diane Legomsky, Karen Lovejoy, and Pamela Podger, to her sisters Liz and Amy Tashjian, and to her parents Armen and Carol Tashjian. She also wishes to thank Judy Butterman and Roger Tangri who, by opening their house in Accra to her on numerous occasions, provided a much-appreciated home away from home as well as exuberant friendship and hospitality. Her young daughter, Allegra, whose arrival coincided with the writing of this book, has led her to think about its focal points, mothering and marriage, in entirely new ways. Her work on this book is dedicated to her co-conspirator and traveling companion, Bob Kramer, whose unstinting and unconditional support has meant everything.

Together we wish to conclude by thanking the Basel Mission, the Methodist Missionary Society, and the Bodleian Library, Oxford, for granting us the rights to reproduce photographs from their superb collections, and the journals and presses who generously gave permission for us to include here excerpts from previously published material.

GLOSSARY OF TWI TERMS

aberewa	old woman
abusua	matrilineal family
adidi sika	"chop money"
adwadifoɔ	retail traders
Asantehemaa	queenmother of Asante
Asantehene	king of Asante
aseda	thanksgiving
aware deɛ	marriage things
ayefare sika	adultery compensation
ayerefa	adultery; the taking of someone's wife
batafoɔ	state traders, but can also refer to private traders
bɔ asɔn	to seduce
gyae aware	to divorce
kunu	husband
mmerante	youngmen
mogya (**or** *bogya*)	blood
mpaafoɔ	hawkers
nkwankwaa	youngmen or commoners
ntoro	spiritual identity inherited from one's father
ɔhemaa	queenmother, pl. *ahemaa*
ɔkyeame	linguist or king's spokesman
ɔman	state or territorial division, pl. *aman*

ɔmanhene	chief of territorial division, pl. *amanhene*
sika	money
tan	to parent or nurture
tiri nsa	"head drink"
tiri sika	"head money"
ware	to marry
yere	wife

Map 1 Colonial Ghana
Source: Survey Department, Gold Coast, Accra, 1927.

Map 2 Asante
Source: Survey Department, Gold Coast, 1927.

BY WAY OF INTRODUCTION

BEGINNINGS

This book had two very different, though concurrent, beginnings nearly a decade ago. Victoria Tashjian set out as a graduate student at Northwestern University to explore marriage in rural Asante during the first decades of the twentieth century, when the development of extensive cash cropping and the monetization of the economy led to far-reaching changes in the value of land and labor. Because of the web of productive and reproductive interests that lay at the heart of conjugal relationships in Asante, Tashjian saw marriage as a very useful prism through which to understand the profound economic changes of the early twentieth century.[1] Meanwhile, Jean Allman was drawn by a set of very similar concerns to a study of mothering and childrearing in Asante. She sought to understand the nonbiological ways motherhood was constructed in this matrilineal society by examining, historically, women as producers and reproducers. For Allman, mothering seemed to provide a unique lens through which to explore changes in family structure, in the land and labor requirements of production, and in the sexual division of labor, particularly during the tumultuous early decades of the twentieth century.

Though our respective projects shared much common ground and our initial concerns overlapped in significant ways, we worked separately for several years. Tashjian conducted her fieldwork in Asante in 1990. After a short preliminary visit in 1989, Allman completed the bulk of her fieldwork in 1992.[2] We shared insights whenever we had occasion to meet, but we sought desperately to avoid substantive overlap in our work. We would like to think that this had very little to do with defining or defending academic turf—that most unfortunate, though pervasive, affliction of those who find themselves competing for jobs, grants, or publishers in today's academic "market"—

and more to do with our shared recognition that we were at different career stages and faced very different sets of expectations, especially regarding individual and collaborative work. While this strategy made sense initially, it seemed increasingly cumbersome and artificial after Tashjian completed her dissertation on marriage and divorce in Asante in 1995 and both of us had presented and/or published papers based on our respective areas of interest. If we spent much of the first half of the decade thinking about how our work differed, we had the luxury, after 1996, of thinking about how and where it overlapped. By 1997, it was clear to both of us that we each had pieces of a very large and complex puzzle, and that by putting our respective pieces together we could develop a much more comprehensive understanding of women's lives than either of us could ever hope to achieve alone. And so, a dialogue began through which we thought about the connections in our work and their broader implications for understanding the lived experiences of Asante women during the colonial period. We pondered what we had been taught and what we had learned from the scores of elderly Asante women and men who shared their stories and reminiscences with us. Our dialogue thus grew into collaboration, and collaboration into the work that now lies before you.

In its most general contours, this book explores the ways in which Asante women, as wives and mothers, shaped and were shaped by the colonial world in which they lived. By focusing on conjugal production and reproduction, on women as both producers and reproducers, we seek to understand how broader social and economic forces—cash cropping, trade, the monetization of the economy, British colonial rule, and missions—recast the terrain of domestic struggle in Asante and how ordinary women and men, in turn, negotiated that ever-shifting landscape. Like Elizabeth Schmidt, we are convinced that any historical analysis "that neglects the area of domestic struggle, the lives of women, and their critical contribution to production and biological and social reproduction misconceives the society as a whole and presents a distorted view of the entire historical process."[3] By centering our analysis on Asante women as both producers and reproducers, we hope not only to avoid misconceptions and distortions but also to provide at least some of the building blocks for constructing a broader social history of a society whose past has largely been understood in terms of the state, political evolution, trade, and the careers of political elites.

We have subtitled our work "A Women's History of Colonial Asante," and that perhaps requires some explanation and at least two caveats. It is not "women's history" in the sense that we ignore or marginalize the experiences of men. We have chosen the subtitle "a women's history" because we believe it captures our efforts to make women visible and to center their experiences in a gendered history of colonial Asante.[4] Our chronological indicator in the subtitle may also require clarification. By "colonial Asante" we wish only to delineate the book's primary chronological parameters, not to privilege British colonial rule as the defining factor in understanding women's lives during the first half of the twentieth century. Ours is not a history of colonialism; nor can women's lived experiences in the first decades of the twentieth century be explained with sole reference to those external forces—political structures, globalization of the capitalist economy, Christian missions—that are so often and so neatly packaged as "colonialism." Indeed, much that we discovered in this women's history defied a colonial chronology. As we listened in the 1990s to stories about the early twentieth century, we often found ourselves reaching back into the early nineteenth century in order to make sense of both continuity and change. In short, the women's history presented here is bracketed, but not defined, by British colonial rule.

COLLABORATING ON COMMON GROUND: SOURCES AND METHOD

That our work seemed to blend easily and productively was due in no small part to the common [back]ground we shared, even in the very early stages, when we were first conceptualizing our respective research agendas. We both studied with Ivor Wilks at Northwestern University (though some six years apart) and spent a good portion of our graduate careers immersed in the ways and byways of Asante's precolonial past. There we were exposed to a rich historical scholarship on the eighteenth and nineteenth centuries, which has few parallels in the history of precolonial Africa south of the Sahara. Yet much of that scholarship has been concerned with the state—its evolution, its economic underpinnings, its ruling elites, and its ideological legitimations.[5] With a few important exceptions, women and/or gender did not figure prominently in this precolonial historiography,[6] nor had this historiography informed or generated much of a discussion about Asante's colonial past, gendered or not.[7] Although colonial-era ethnographers like R. S. Rattray (1910s–1920s) and Meyer Fortes (1940s) paid careful attention to women's roles, and their works influenced in many other ways the contours of Asante's precolonial historiography, their concern with marriage, childrearing, and reproduction did not have a substantial impact.[8] We were thus both challenged early on by a precolonial historiography that, for the most part, marginalized women (especially commoners), by an extensive colonial ethnography that had much to say about women and social reproduction but was not particularly attentive to historical change, and, finally, by a comparatively underdeveloped historiography for Asante's colonial period.

As we began to conceptualize our separate research agendas, our ideas were not only shaped by both the substantive richness *and* the lacunae of Asante historiography but also by the burgeoning feminist scholarship on Ghana as a whole in the late 1970s and 1980s. Much of this literature was produced by anthropologists, political scientists, and sociologists who were concerned with women and gender in contemporary Ghana, although with few exceptions their analyses were informed by some discussion of Ghana's colonial or precolonial past. Authors of many of the most important of these feminist analyses in the 1970s–1980s contributed to Christine Oppong's pathbreaking *Female and Male in West Africa*, published in 1983.[9] While early feminist scholarship on Ghana was dominated by nonhistorians, there were several important exceptions. Claire Robertson's work, including the award-winning 1984 monograph *Sharing the Same Bowl: A Socioeconomic History of Women and Class in Accra, Ghana*, along with important articles by Agnes Akosua Aidoo, Penelope Roberts, and others, put women's history on Ghana's historiographical map.[10]

Yet, by and large, this small but important corpus of Ghanaian women's history did not develop in dialogue with the historiography on precolonial Asante; nor was that historiography shaped to any important degree by the emergence of feminist scholarship in the 1980s.[11] The chasm between the two, however, did begin to narrow in the early 1990s as we were conducting our research. In many ways, Kwame Arhin's work in the 1970s and 1980s seemed to set the stage for bridging the gap, though he would probably be the first to disclaim any status as a women's historian. Although Arhin is an anthropologist by training, his work has always been profoundly historical and central to the development of Asante's rich precolonial historiography. At the same time, it has explored questions of gender, particularly in production, addressed the political and military roles of Asante women, and, most recently, explored the gendered impact of monetization on social life in Asante.[12]

Arhin's work thus facilitated the first productive dialogue between feminist scholars and historians of precolonial Asante, though interestingly, it has largely been a dialogue with feminist anthropologists and political scientists, not with women's historians. For example, significant sections of Gwendolyn Mikell's important monograph, *Cocoa and Chaos in Ghana* (1989), draw heavily on the precolonial historiography of Asante and bring those insights to bear on a gendered analysis of cocoa and kinship in Ghana's colonial and postcolonial periods. Beverly Grier's influential article on women in the development of cash crop agriculture in colonial Ghana is also firmly grounded in that historiography, as is Gracia Clark's recent study of women traders in Kumasi's Central Market and Takyiwaa Manuh's insightful account of shifts in marriage and funeral exchanges from the colonial period to the present.[13]

If recent feminist scholarship on Ghana has sought dialogue with and drawn insights from Asante's rich precolonial historiography, there is also some evidence that women's history and questions of gender have begun to shape that historiography, though perhaps in less dramatic ways.[14] For example, Wilks's "She Who Blazed a Trail: Akyaa Yikwan of Asante" (1988) and T. C. McCaskie's "*Konnurokusem*: Kinship and Family in the History of the *Oyoko Kɔkɔɔ* Dynasty of Kumase" (1995) gender our understanding of power and its articulations in precolonial Asante.[15] Emmanuel Akyeampong's work, including *Drink, Power, and Cultural Change*, makes important contributions to Asante's historiography by speaking both to that rich precolonial historiography and to broader feminist and social history scholarship on Ghana.[16] But in a number of ways, Gareth Austin has done most to narrow the chasm between Asante's precolonial historiography and gender/women's history. In form and content, his work posits the outlines of an Asante historiography capable both of transcending the great divide between the colonial and precolonial periods and of making sense of the profound ways in which gender, as well as rank, class, and place, shaped lived experience. Though grounded in the precolonial historiography of Asante, Austin's work brings nineteenth-century insights to bear on the twentieth century and demonstrates how different that past can look if we move beyond the world of male political elites and affairs of the state to the very gendered world of ordinary farmers and traders.[17]

As both of us began to put our separate thoughts on paper, we thus shared a very similar agenda. Although focusing broadly on women, gender, and social change in the twentieth century, we sought to draw from Asante's rich precolonial historiography. Inspired by the broader Ghanaian feminist scholarship of the 1980s, we also sought to situate our work in dialogue with the growing body of literature, by Austin, Mikell, Grier, and others, which was narrowing the scholarly chasm we had encountered as graduate students in the 1980s. By the time our formal collaboration began, we thus shared very similar intellectual genealogies. As historians, we both wanted to write women's history, but a women's history of Asante that stood in productive dialogue with a range of scholarship on Ghana's recent and more distant pasts.

In addition to having similarly situated our respective projects in a rich, multidisciplinary secondary literature, we both benefited from a large body of primary archival material. This documentation not only provided detailed, though largely exterior, views of politics, economics, and social change from the late nineteenth century through the Second World War, but yielded quite extraordinary insights into women's historical subjectivity. In addition to examining government records in the National Archives (Accra and Kumasi) and in the Public Record Office (London), we both spent months working through many of the 600 bound volumes of customary court records housed at Manhyia Record Office in Kumasi. The very earliest of these volumes contain cases heard before British officials in the first years of colonial rule (1907–1910), but the vast majority record cases tried before Asante's chiefs, both before and subsequent to the Native Jurisdiction Ordinance of 1924, as well as after the consolidation of indirect rule and the restoration of the Asante Confederacy Council in 1935.[18]

Several scholars have discussed the methodological and theoretical problems posed by the utilization of such cases in historical reconstruction. Like them, we were challenged in a number of ways by Manhyia's court documentation—from the very physical labor of putting volumes in order in an underutilized nongovernmental archive, to the problems of situating court cases in a broader social context, to the limitations posed by transcripts that were written on the spot by a court clerk who was listening to Twi and transcribing in English.[19] But the depth and richness of this body of documentation for the social history of Asante far outweighed the difficulties. Both women and men appeared as plaintiffs and defendants in these cases, and their testimony, as well as the courts' rulings, provided an important window on to contests over marriage, divorce, inheritance, childrearing, and land ownership. It was, moreover, through careful reading in these volumes over the breadth of the colonial period that chronologies of subtle and not-so-subtle change began to appear and that we came to appreciate the extent of the crisis in gender relations that shook Asante in the 1920s and 1930s. It was a crisis widely evidenced in the courts by some women's refusal to marry, by chiefs in several towns ordering the detention of unmarried women, by contentious child custody cases, and by the dramatic upsurge in the number of divorce, adultery, and inheritance cases—the latter often pitting wives against deceased husbands' matrikin in struggles over the ownership of cocoa farms. The minutes and correspondence of the Asante Confederacy Council and the Kumasi State Council, also housed at Manhyia, provided wonderful insight into how Asante's chiefs perceived this crisis and what actions they were willing to take in order to contain it.

Because of Allman's interests in mothering, childrearing, and social welfare initiatives, she also consulted the archives of a range of organizations involved with the colonial government in those initiatives, including the papers of the Methodist Missionary Society (both the Women's Work and Wesleyan sections), the Basel Mission Society, and the British Red Cross. Her particular interest in the encounters between European women missionaries and Asante mothers led to a close reading of the correspondence of women missionaries sent to Asante from the 1920s to the 1940s. This approach not only gave her an interior view of the women missionaries and helped her to understand the kind of cultural baggage they brought with them to Asante, it also provided a strategy for getting at counter-narratives of the mission process and social welfare initiatives through interviews. By spending time in the very places women missionaries had worked and by interviewing elderly women who well remembered their early encounters with representatives of the Women's Work section of the Methodist Mission, Allman was able to read one very specific encounter from the perspective of both missionary and "missionized."

Indeed, for both of us, the memories and reminiscences of elderly Asante women and men were the most important sources for our work. The oral portion of Tashjian's research, from January to December 1990, focused primarily on the rural villages of Oyoko (15 kilometers south of Kumasi) and Mamponten (12 kilometers north), where she interviewed both women and men of the oldest generation (born roughly between 1900 and 1925). She chose Oyoko and Mamponten because they had been founded by the same woman, Kyerew Akenten, and thus both fell under the authority of the Oyoko Clan.[20] Political differences between the two, then, were minimal. Because legal disputes coming from Mamponten and Oyoko were heard in the Oyokohene's Native Court, both had close ties to Kumasi's courts. Tashjian thus based herself in Kumasi not only because its location midway between Oyoko and Mamponten minimized travel time but because it facilitated her work with court records at Manhyia Record Office and allowed her to move back and forth between interviewing and archival work on a near-daily basis. The proximity of the two villages to Kumasi also allowed for the exploration of a broad range of occupations that were available in areas nearer to the city's large markets. That people farmed cocoa in Oyoko but not in Mamponten provided an important point of comparison regarding the impact of cocoa on conjugal relations. Finally, because relatives of her research assistant, Nana Osei Agyeman-Duah, lived in both villages, Tashjian was welcomed by both communities and her research path was smoothed considerably.

Tashjian's interviews were conducted in Twi with the assistance of Nana Osei Agyeman-Duah and then transcribed into English. (Transcripts have been deposited in the Herskovits Library, Northwestern University.) Her interviews centered primarily on marriage, particularly on the economic relationships between spouses and the changes that followed the rapid expansion of the cocoa industry and the broadened commoditization of consumer goods in the first half of the twentieth century. She combined a set of standard questions with a more open-ended interviewing approach. After gathering basic information about a person's age, number of marriages, number of children, and hometown, she moved on to more detailed questions, which focused on the types of work a person had been engaged in and on the connections between work, money, and marriage. These last sets of questions usually launched the open-ended portion of the discussion, for people's reminiscences led in a multiplicity of unanticipated directions, as new issues and themes emerged concerning what it meant to be married, how one married, how one divorced, and who owned what and why. Tashjian's approach allowed elderly Asante women and men who were, of course, the primary players in marriage rather than peripheral observers, to identify what they understood as significant change and to explain why that change was important. Because her work drew on customary court cases as well as the reminiscences of elderly Asante, Tashjian was able to draw critical comparisons between the actions of Kumasi's native courts and the actions of elders in rural villages. Courts and rural elders often chose to address in markedly different ways the new social dilemmas faced by the first colonized generation, such as the disposition, following death or divorce, of cocoa farms made jointly by husbands and wives. By reading court cases against oral reminiscences and vice versa, Tashjian was able to ask questions of each and bring her two main bodies of evidence into direct dialogue.

Although the divergences she found between rural villagers and Kumasi courts proved to be central to her understanding of historical processes, Tashjian had not anticipated such variance. Her preliminary research into conjugality in Asante had drawn upon descriptions in the secondary ethnographic literature and on a limited number of native court case transcripts available at Northwestern University. Based on these sources, she concluded that marriage could be neatly defined and demarcated according to a set definition to which Asantes uniformly adhered. In fact, she persisted with this definition until one early interview pulled her up short. As Tashjian discussed marriage with Kwabena Manu of Mamponten, time and again he told her he had been married several times, although according to Tashjian's understanding of marriage, none of his unions seemed to qualify. Finally, after many repetitions and what must have seemed a stubborn obtuseness on her part, Tashjian grasped the essential point Manu was making. Not only could marriage occur in stages over time, it could also be defined by the wishes of the families involved and follow no set pattern of ritual. The realization that commoner marriage was a much more fluid process than the conjugal institution ruled on by Kumasi's courts led Tashjian to a wide-ranging comparison of court versus commoner practice.

In many ways, Allman's oral research with elder Asantes from January through November 1992 and during the summers of 1993, 1995, and 1996 paralleled Tashjian's in method, if not in scope. Allman was also interested in the reminiscences of Asante's oldest citizens, but with a focus on the meanings and makings of mothering and childrearing (though questions concerning marriage and conjugal production also came into play). With Kumasi as a base, Allman initially planned an interview schedule that included the

Ashanti New Town area of Kumasi (highly urban), suburban Tafo (two kilo-meters northeast), and the rural towns of Effiduasi and Asokore (40 and 42 kilometers northeast, respectively). Her goal was to get at a range of set-tings and experiences that might have shaped childrearing. She quickly learned, however, that the boundaries between urban, suburban, and rural were extremely fluid in the life histories of those to whom she spoke. An elderly woman in Kumasi, for example, was just as likely to have spent most of her life in a small cocoa farming village, while her counterpart in Asokore was just as likely to have spent most of her productive years as a trader in Kumasi. But this particular set of locations did allow her to collect quite specific reminiscences about Methodist women missionaries who were ac-tive in all four locations and to move from one area to another via the web of connections among current Women's Fellowship groups, as church lead-ers in one town provided contacts and in some cases letters of introduction to another.

While Tashjian's oral research focused on both women and men, Allman's centered primarily on women in 1992, though in subsequent research trips, as she became increasingly intrigued by what seemed to be the shifting and rather ambiguous roles of fathers, she included more men in her interview schedules. She also added Agogo (70 kilometers east of Kumasi) as a re-search site in order to situate a portion of her work in an area extensively studied by Meyer Fortes during the Ashanti Social Survey of the 1940s.[21] Most of her discussions with elderly women and men were conducted in Twi with the assistance of Nana Osei Agyeman-Duah, whom she had known since 1977 and with whom she had worked closely on her dissertation re-search in the mid-1980s. (English transcriptions of her interviews are also on deposit at Northwestern University's Herskovits Library and at the Insti-tute of African Studies Library, University of Ghana.) Like Tashjian, Allman's interviews were not aimed at collecting full life histories. She be-gan with a series of questions regarding age, place of birth, parents' occupa-tions, and other basic identifying information. She then had a set of ques-tions that served as a guide for exploring in an open-ended fashion issues surrounding family life, marrying, and childrearing.

Over time, that guide evolved in quite dramatic ways. Susan Geiger has recently underscored in *TANU Women* the dependence of researchers on the "researched" and the degree to which "research subjects" actively shape the researcher's agenda.[22] Allman's ever-evolving guide is surely evidence of this process. The original guide, based on her own understandings of domestic processes, drew from secondary and archival documentation. Early inter-views in 1992, framed by this question guide, were too often flat and pre-dictable: uninteresting questions generated some uninteresting answers! But the few interesting answers that did surface seemed to suggest a very different set of priorities and to pose new kinds of questions. And so, slowly, the guide evolved. As it did, discussions became far more lively and interesting because the guide increasingly and more effectively engaged with the common themes and experiences people did want to talk about: inheriting (or not inheriting) property from a deceased husband or father, contests over school fees, or discussions of how to properly bathe a baby. For example, most conversations with elderly women, especially outside of Kumasi, often drew a small audience of daughters, granddaughters, and even great-granddaughters. After several occasions in which such an interview changed into a lively intergenerational discussion of the comparative burdens and benefits of raising children at a particular point in time, the question "Who had it rougher . . . ?" worked its way on to the guide. In short, the guide no longer belonged totally to the researcher, though as Geiger also reminds us, "the researcher" is still left with "the final power of translation."[23]

The oral research methodologies we both developed were shaped to a significant degree by the fact that so little had been published on the social history of early twentieth-century Asante when we began our work. Although we were not concerned with accumulating a so-called "fair and representative sampling" of respondents, we both felt a certain urgency about getting at a broad enough range of individuals to enable us to appreciate the complexity and multiplicity of women's experiences in the first decades of colonial rule and begin to differentiate between the common and the exceptional. Issue-focused, open-ended discussions/interviews, rather than full life histories,[24] allowed us to accomplish this, although with some sacrifice of depth for breadth. In the chapters that follow, we introduce and refer to the accounts that were shared with us as "reminiscences," "stories," "recollections," or "memories." They are not quantifiable, social scientific data elicited from Asante's octo- and nonagenarian population; nor are they excerpts from much longer, self-reflective personal narratives constructed in the course of numerous meetings with a few carefully chosen life historians. To call them "reminiscences," "memories," or "stories" is not to devalue their content but merely to capture and recall the context in which they were generated.

Of course, one of the many wonders of listening to those who have lived so long is that their stories can bring you first hand into a world long since gone. They are "bridges between the past and the present."[25] Unfortunately, so many of the elderly women and men who shared their time and stories with us have since traveled to *Asaman*,[26] and with their departure we have lost what Wilks has called our "windows" into the early twentieth century— "living memories" for which there is no substitute. But in the time we spent with these old men and women—time that we wish had come sooner and lasted longer—they brought early colonial Asante to life for us in ways that neither the secondary nor the archival documentation ever could. *Tete ka asɔm*, as the proverb reminds us: "Ancient things remain in the ears."[27]

PROFILE OF A GENERATION

As we thought about the interviews we had conducted and the stories embedded in them, we came to appreciate the particular implications of having interviewed women and men who were born in the first two decades of this century. We began to think about the reminiscences not as oral documents pertaining to the experiences of a rather chronologically amorphous "women and colonialism" but as generationally specific. They spoke to the distinct experiences of a generation of women whose lives differed in many ways from those of their daughters, even though their daughters' lives also fell largely within a colonial chronology. Generation and life cycle thus became important factors in how we conceptualized our work. Although the reminiscences we collected speak to a range of diverse experiences, they also share certain commonalities from which it is possible to derive a sort of generational profile.

That profile is most profoundly marked by the fact that the women and men with whom we spoke were born and came of age precisely in the years when Asante experienced the dramatic transformations fueled by the advent of cocoa. As members of a common generation, they recognized the arrival of cocoa and the growing ascendancy of the cash economy as watershed events affecting their lives. Moreover, they largely experienced those defining economic developments through conjugal relations: women-as-wives provided much of the labor necessary for the creation of cocoa farms, yet men-as-husbands dominated ownership of these farms and therefore controlled the resulting profits. Marriage was thus at the center of stories of Asante's cocoa boom.

Though the stories we heard are not quantifiable, marriage was clearly a universal experience for both women and men. None of the individuals with whom we spoke had never married. Because divorce was (and remains) widely accepted and practiced, women of this generation, on average, married twice over the course of their lives, and in roughly half of those marriages they were co-wives. While many who shared stories with us were members of Christian denominations in the 1990s, few were actively associated with churches before World War II. The overwhelming majority, therefore, married outside the church, according to custom, even though Christian missions were well established in Asante by the time this generation married. Women's marriages were concentrated in their childbearing years. Indeed, it was not uncommon to opt out of marriage (or "retire" from it, as one woman reported in a telling turn of phrase)[28] after menopause. Because they identified childbearing as a central reason for marrying, most women chose to be married, although not necessarily to the same person, for the duration of their childbearing years. They viewed children as a crucial source of security for their old age. Those with whom we spoke bore an average of six children, a third of whom had predeceased their mothers by the 1990s. While Asantes have historically placed great value on childbearing, the demographic devastation wrought by the 1918 influenza pandemic clearly had significant implications for this particular generation in terms of marriage and fecundity.[29] Many recalled the pandemic as a catastrophe that decimated many families and thus intensified pressures to marry and bear children. Ama Brago's experience was probably not atypical: "My mother died in the epidemic, as well as my brother and sister . . . my mother had left me so they needed somebody, so I was given to the man whether I liked it or not. From the way my siblings and mother died, it was feared that if I didn't get a husband to have children with, the family would run out."[30]

In addition to marrying and bearing children, women of this generation expected to work and to be economically self-sufficient, like their mothers and grandmothers before them. Most of the women with whom we spoke were commoners rather than royals—a choice we both made not only because, at least numerically, commoners dominated cocoa farming but also because of our interest in addressing another of the lacunae of Asante historiography, the lived experiences of nonelites. Virtually all of the women we write of here worked as farmers and traders, in addition to performing the domestic labor of cooking, cleaning, and childcare. Although a handful attended some of the first schools set up in Asante by Christian missions, the overwhelming majority did not. They therefore lacked the educational skills that might have provided access to the few jobs that would be deemed appropriate for women in the colonial economy, like nursing or teaching. Their energies were directed at growing the staple starchy food crops of cocoyam and plantain, cultivating the vegetable crops of pepper, onion, tomato, okra, and garden egg (a type of eggplant), and occasionally farming corn, cassava, and yams. Women traded all of these basic food items, as well as fruit, groundnuts, eggs, meat, fish, rice, and salt. They also sold cloth, medicines, firewood, and various imported items, and they cooked and sold prepared foods. Many engaged in crafts, making soap, pots, and brooms, and practiced sewing and midwifery. Last but certainly not least, many worked on cocoa farms, sometimes self-owned but more frequently the property of their husbands.

Traveling in order to work formed something of a leitmotif in the lives of this generation. In some ways, travel was considered valuable in and of itself. As Kofi Owusu of Mamponten explained, "If you don't travel, you will not see the world. It is only when you travel that you come to see the larger perspective of the world. Those who did not were looked down upon. . . . It was only those who were swollen-headed who didn't bother."[31] But most importantly, travel provided opportunities for making money that were simply unavailable within the confines of the village economy. Some women traveled to Kumasi to trade; others traveled to remote rural areas as they followed the cocoa frontier. However, women's responsibility to provide domestic services in marriage, as well as social mores that associated some impropriety with women traveling alone, could circumscribe women's independent mobility. Although many certainly did travel in the course of their own occupations, more frequently women accompanied their husbands and labored for them.

Though travel was a shared experience, it was a decidedly temporary state of affairs for the vast majority of Asante commoners. When people traveled, it was assumed they would return home. As a result, we found no pervasive rural-urban schism demarcating separate rather than shared experiences, which would have divided life stories among the members of this generation into distinct and mutually exclusive categories based on place. Instead, the stories shared with us underscored the importance of thinking about rural communities "as being at a different point along a continuum," as Audrey Smock has written, rather than emphasizing "the contrasts between rural and urban."[32] Indeed, often rural and urban women were one and the same, since traveling to take advantage of economic opportunities meant that most women spent time in both urban and rural settings over the course of their productive years. If the prevalence of traveling made one usual distinction moot in this generational profile, however, it did create another. Although married women and men often resided not with their spouses but with their respective matrikin, married couples who traveled away from family and family homes to either urban areas or remote rural settings were much more likely to share a conjugal home. And distance from matrikin could compound the hardships of many women. In the remoteness of the cocoa frontier or in the urban setting of Kumasi, distance from family meant that women could not easily rely upon mothers, grandmothers, aunts, and sisters who in the past had shared the burdens of childcare.

Indeed, in many ways, hardship and hard work are salient themes in this generational profile. Women not only remembered facing heightened obligations to work for their husbands in what were now cash-earning contexts, but recalled fewer safety nets when faced with unexpected tragedy, like the death of a spouse. Responsibilities for childrearing, including at times the payment of school fees, seemed to fall increasingly on mothers alone, as support from husbands and fathers, as well as brothers and uncles, became far less predictable. That these were remembered as difficult times is not surprising, given the economic transformations of the first decades of this century and women's pivotal role in those transformations as productive and reproductive laborers. Yet as we reflected on the stories shared with us and on the generational profile of those born in the first two decades of the twentieth century, we were most struck by the salience of a different theme. Women of this generation consistently articulated as a lived priority their struggles for economic autonomy. In a rapidly changing world in which productive and reproductive obligations seemed only to heighten while social safety nets vanished, women's stories were stories of struggle—to assert and defend economic independence. That profile of struggle stands at the center of our analysis.

ASANTE WOMEN IN THE HISTORIOGRAPHY OF GENDER AND COLONIALISM IN AFRICA

The book's title, *"I Will Not Eat Stone,"*[33] is intended to capture the resilience and tenacity of this first colonized generation of Asante women—a generation that bore many of the heaviest burdens of colonial rule. Commoner women, as wives and mothers, provided the productive and reproductive labor that fueled much of the economic change of the early twentieth century, while they suffered the social and political consequences of an indirect rule that would increasingly marginalize them as it remapped the terrain of patriarchal power in colonial Asante. While we can trace the growing burden for women of market-oriented conjugal production to the early nineteenth century and the abolition of the transAtlantic slave trade,[34] the impact of rubber toward the end of that century and then the dramatic changes wrought by cocoa in the first decades of the twentieth century exponentially increased that burden. Yet by the 1920s, many Asante women had managed to successfully negotiate their own places within the expanding colonial economy as traders and cocoa farmers in their own right, and to challenge in both direct and indirect ways the shifting terrain of patriarchal power. Their actions, aimed at securing economic autonomy in a monetized world, and the multitude of responses to those actions—by fathers, husbands, brothers, chiefs, district officers, and missions—marked the mid-1920s through the 1930s as an era of gender chaos in colonial Asante. That chaos was met head on in the decade following the formalization of indirect rule in 1935, when chiefs and elders, missionaries, and social welfare officers went to work trying to make dutiful wives and "proper" mothers out of a generation of women who, by official accounts anyway, were nothing short of intractable. That those efforts at asserting control were uneven, episodic, and often limited in scope speaks to the resilience of a generation who refused "to eat stone."

But the experiences of this generation were certainly not unique. A number of works by social historians of Africa concerned with gender, sexuality, reproduction, and colonialism have explored questions and developed gendered chronologies strikingly similar to those presented here.[35] Nearly a decade ago, Margot Lovett, for example, posited a gendered colonial chronology for east, central, and southern Africa that, with a few changes of phrase, might easily have encompassed the experiences of Asante women. She maintained that in the first decades, when

> the local apparatus of colonial rule was not yet fully effective and the future of . . . capitalism was still uncertain, women were able to challenge the developing logic of the underlying processes. . . . Women seized new avenues of power and agency, such as the creation of colonial courts, and also actively constructed other opportunities . . . in order to accumulate surplus, gain autonomy, and exercise control over their own labor power, fertility, and sexuality.[36]

By the 1930s, Lovett argued, women's challenges to colonial production and systems of rule "no longer could be ignored," and the state, working in concert with male elders, began to "develop and impose new forms of control over women."[37] It is not particularly surprising that Lovett noted a similar chronology across much of east, central, and southern Africa given that many of these areas experienced sizable settler populations, the expropriation of vast amounts of land for plantation agriculture, capitalist mining ventures, and the development of large migrant labor systems that tended to gender production male and largely urban, and reproduction rural and female. There was, in short, a profound and shared need throughout much of southern and eastern Africa to exercise firm control over women's mobility and sexuality.[38]

Yet in Asante there was no sizable settler population. Migration in the region was dominated by the movement of male laborers from the Northern Territories to the mines and cocoa farms of Asante, and by the movement of Asante farmers (men and women) into frontier areas to develop new cocoa farms. The rapid spread of cash cropping (largely cocoa) rested on the initiative of small-scale farmers, not on that of settler plantation owners.[39] Production, moreover, was not gendered exclusively male, nor reproduction female. Women's mobility and population decline were never at issue in the same ways they were in many colonial settler states. These striking differences notwithstanding, Asante women still shared with many women of southern and eastern Africa, often of the very same generation, a time of opportunity in the early colonial period when new options to secure economic autonomy were seized and when still fragile configurations of power, state and local, were challenged. An ensuing period of gender chaos was soon followed, typically in the 1930s, by a consolidation of indirect rule, an increased empowerment of local male elites, and concerted attempts to reassert control over unruly women and junior men.

Mahmood Mamdani's recent work, which attacks the notion of South African exceptionalism and argues for a common form—"a decentralized despotism"—among colonial states, would certainly be buttressed by this pervasive chronology, although Mamdani himself is largely silent on the gendered implications of colonial constructions of citizens and subjects.[40] Indeed, we are perhaps not yet at the point where we can, with confidence, speak broadly and comparatively about gendered "transnational processes and hybrid colonial situations."[41] However, Elizabeth Schmidt, in the introduction to her pathbreaking *Peasants, Traders, and Wives*, provides several crucial, though tentative, comparative insights. Noting the central role of women in cash crop production across the continent, she argues that where women were able to retain "control over the products of their labor, they experienced an increase in economic and social status." She further maintains that women's position increasingly deteriorated as "strategic resources" became "concentrated in male hands." And, finally, she makes a direct correlation between male "out-migration" and both a decline in women's status and an increase in women's burden of work.[42] The experiences of Asante women in the first decades of this century—which, at once, present striking parallels and equally striking contrasts with much of the published literature from which Schmidt draws her insights—suggest additional avenues for comparative investigation. That many Asante women lost control of the products of their labor before or during the first two decades of the colonial period and then regained it suggests the importance of exploring not only how women retained control in the colonial period but also under what specific historical conditions they were able to reassert control over labor that had previously been alienated. The Asante material also suggests the importance of understanding the processes through which "strategic resources such as land, labor and cash income" were "concentrated in male hands." While clearly many of those transnational processes were economic—rooted in systems of land ownership and male migration/wage earning—women's experiences in Asante underscore the absolute centrality of the state and mechanisms of indirect rule in widening women's and men's differential access to "strategic resources." Finally, while there was no substantial out-migration of Asante males during the colonial period, women's status clearly declined and their work burdens increased, though perhaps not to the degree that they did in southern Africa. We need to look closely, then, at how and why responsibilities and burdens shifted in the colonial period, even within household economies in which both husbands and wives were present.

As the relevant literature expands and it becomes increasingly possible to draw meaningful comparative insights into the ways in which women shaped and were shaped by the colonial world, we may in fact conclude that Asante women encountered more openings for securing economic autonomy than did women in southern or eastern Africa.[43] If so, then some of the reasons for their enhanced ability to maneuver must surely fall outside of the parameters of colonial rule. Women's roles as mothers and sisters in this tenaciously matrilineal society, as well as the ease with which wives could divorce, meant that Asante women were perhaps better equipped to cope with the rapid and often dislocating changes brought on by colonial rule and the integration of Asante into the world capitalist system as a cash cropping economy. Yet other reasons were clearly grounded in the specifics of the "colonial moment": in the absence of white settlers and of out-migration by men, in the successes of cocoa farmers, in the early feminization of the retail market, and in the relative demographic balance between women and men in both rural and urban areas.[44]

Surely another important aspect of comparative inquiry must be the native court systems through which male elites, empowered by the colonial state, sought to control the sexuality and the reproductive power of African women. Margaret Jean Hay and Marcia Wright's important volume, *African Women and the Law* (1982), set the initial parameters for such a comparison, and subsequent monographs and anthologies have pushed the parameters in exciting new directions.[45] Asante, we argue, has much to contribute to these broader discussions that, heretofore, have focused largely on southern and east Africa and often on areas where there was no large, centralized state before colonial conquest. Were native courts and tribunals places where colonial change was brokered or where continuity with a precolonial past was reinforced? This is an important question that has been addressed in some of the recent studies on colonial courts and the "invention" of custom. Hay and Wright's volume, as well as Martin Chanock's *Law, Custom, and Social Order* and many of the essays collected in Kristin Mann and Richard Roberts' *Law in Colonial Africa*, have emphasized the invention or codification of customary law in the colonial period, in contrast to earlier works by legal anthropologists and legal historians who viewed customary law as the twentieth-century survival of "a really African, local law."[46] For Hay and Wright, "customary law" as articulated by male elders was a blend of "tradition and wishful thinking."[47] In examining the specific formulations of customary law concerning adultery, Chanock writes that "the claims were fed into the court system, where they were given in evidence and 'proved' and from whence they emerged as customary law."[48] Yet in the case of Asante, as we will see, there are quite striking continuities in proceedings and judgments between the precolonial and colonial periods, as well as disjunctures and anomalies.[49]

An alternative to the colonial invention model that goes some way toward explaining the continuities and disjunctures in Asante "custom" is suggested in Sara Berry's recent work. Berry argues that "tradition" and "custom" were always changing and, indeed, continued to change even during the colonial period. Thus, the very fact of ongoing change, from the precolonial through the colonial periods, embodied continuity.[50] Berry's insight regarding the continuity of "custom-in-flux" forces us to look back into the nineteenth century and historicize the basic question. Rather than ask whether or not "custom" was a colonial construct, we need to consider whether there have been particular historical junctures in a society's past at which dynamic processes of flux entered into stasis. As the following chapters seek to demonstrate, "custom" or "tradition" in Asante, for much of the precolonial and colonial periods, was not immutable; it was consistently subject to contestation and to change, as Berry would argue. However, beginning in 1924 and occurring rapidly after 1935, mutability in Asante gave way to stasis.

At least some authors have linked this kind of stasis or the appearance of an "unchanging body of tradition" with the written word. Once customs were written down, Terence Ranger argues, they could no longer change.[51] Yet the causal link posited between writing and rigidity does not fully explain the process in Asante, which was extremely uneven and unfolded in unpredictable ways. The colonial government's restoration of the Asante Confederacy Council in 1935 and its recognition of the Asantehene as the head of Asante, we argue, marked an important watershed by creating a centralized context in which custom could be systematically reformulated as a set of unyielding rules—rules that provided a clear mechanism for social control.[52] Yet some aspects of custom, as we shall see, remained dynamic and mutable well into the 1940s, while other aspects assumed a "petrified" form much earlier. How Asante women negotiated this shifting customary terrain at particular historical moments, by defending older formulations of custom in court or demanding new ones, is a thematic thread running through this book. Their stories underscore the importance of carefully historicizing, over the longue durée, the contested (re)inventions of customary law.

THE CHAPTERS IN BRIEF

The chronological parameters of this book are defined by the generation of women and men who shared their life stories with us; that is, the generation born in the first two decades of the twentieth century. Our focus on domestic struggle—on the shifting terrain of conjugal production and reproduction—is thus largely situated in the 1920s to the 1940s, the years during which this generation married, gave birth, and raised their children. That said, there are certain themes, particularly surrounding testimony and judgments in native court cases, that impelled us to follow the story into the final decade of colonial rule. Moreover, the reminiscences that were shared with us and the women's history we found hidden between the lines of colonial documentation could not be "contained" by a colonial historical narrative. We consistently found ourselves reaching back across the colonial divide into the nineteenth century to make sense of women's lived experiences in the early twentieth century.

Chapter 1 is thus aimed at situating the women of this generation in the broader currents of Asante history. It begins with the premise that their life stories defy existing chronologies of colonialism, which have conflated the experiences of men and women into one ungendered story. It then explores a series of alternative chronologies—of conjugal production, economic change, and monetization; of travel and trade; of courts and custom; and of missions and conversion—that emerge from within the lived experiences of this first colonized generation. While providing important social, economic, and political background for subsequent chapters, chapter 1 also introduces the two strategic entry points through which subsequent chapters move: marrying and childrearing.

Chapter 2 takes on the first of these: marrying. After exploring why women married, it contrasts early anthropological definitions of Asante marriage with perspectives from Asante's first colonized generation. It then explores how the meanings and makings of marriage shifted as a result of the rapid monetization of the economy and increased conjugal production for the market. The fluid, transactional process of marrying, largely defined by families, gave way to a singular notion of marriage, defined by the native courts. By the time this generation married, women were obliged to provide far more labor to their husbands than had their mothers or grandmothers. Such changes are evident not just in personal reminiscences or in divorce statistics but also in the shifting content and meaning of various marrying rituals and in women's efforts to reshape the conjugal terrain by strengthening their economic independence through movement into retail trade and the establishment of their own cocoa farms.

In chapter 3, we turn to our second strategic entry point: childrearing and the changing rights and obligations of mothers and fathers vis-à-vis their children. Just as the expanding cash economy reshaped the meanings of marriage, so too did it recast the terrain of childrearing. Again, fluid relationships based on reciprocity and exchange gave way to essentialized "natural" categories within which were conflated a range of relationships of subordination. During the first decades of the twentieth century, fathers came to assert rights in their free children that, in previous times, could only be claimed by fathers who held their children in pawn. But as money began to articulate "natural" connections between fathers and their children, these children, with their mothers, began to stake claims to the wealth their fathers produced and to challenge the foundations of matrilineal inheritance in Asante.

Chapter 4 moves the discussion from shifting terrains of childrearing and marrying to an exploration of women's conjugal strategies in a world of cash and cocoa. In order to safeguard their precarious positions, women formulated new strategies and redeployed older ones in struggles that were, more than anything, about control over their productive and reproductive labor. The chapter begins by looking at older strategies, especially divorce and seduction, and then at newer ones, which entailed opting out of formal marriage altogether. Many of these newer conjugal strategies suggest both strong parallels with and striking deviations from the social history of women in east and southern Africa.

Finally, chapter 5 examines the concerted attempts by chiefs, male elders, the colonial state, and missions to reassert control over women's productive and reproductive labor in the 1930s by molding proper mothers and dutiful wives. It connects the onset of indirect rule in Asante to the solidification of the partnership between the colonial state and mission societies and then explores how the two functioned as twin efforts to address the gender chaos that had sprung from Asante's expanding cash economy. By exploring the multiple ways in which Asante women shaped and were shaped by a range of initiatives—from fidelity ordinances to missionary instructions on how to bathe their children—the chapter demonstrates the resilience and tenacity of this pivotal generation in the making of twentieth-century Asante.

NOTES

1. For the results of that doctoral research, see "It's Mine and It's Ours Are Not the Same Thing: A History of Marriage in Rural Asante, 1900–1957" (Ph.D. dissertation, Northwestern University, 1995).

2. Additional fieldwork aimed at filling in gaps and fleshing out arguments took place in the summers of 1993, 1995, and 1996.

3. Elizabeth Schmidt, *Peasants, Traders, and Wives: Shona Women in the History of Zimbabwe, 1870–1939* (Portsmouth, NH: Heinemann, 1992), 1.

4. In a recent survey of the scholarship on women and gender in Africa, Nancy Hunt has described the first wave of feminist scholarship as being "focused primarily on the economically productive activities and social agency of African women." A second wave, she argues, has looked at questions of "gender meanings and relations, . . . colonial domesticity, customary law, motherhood, reproduction, sexuality and the body." And, more recently, a third wave has begun to explore "social and institutional identities." Our concern with reproduction, mothering and customary law, and, to a lesser extent, with so-

cial identities situates our work in these second and third waves. Yet, in many ways, the women's history we write of here remains firmly grounded in the concerns of that first wave of feminist scholarship, in no small part because economic struggles were at the very heart of the stories told to us by women born in the first decades of the twentieth century. See Nancy Hunt, "Introduction," special issue on "Gendered Colonialisms in African History," *Gender and History* 8:3 (1996), 324.

5. A full citation of these works is not possible in one note, but a representative sampling would include the following: Kwame Arhin, "Aspects of the Ashanti Northern Trade in the Nineteenth Century," *Africa* 40:4 (1970), 363–73; Arhin, "Rank and Class among the Asante and Fante in the Nineteenth Century," *Africa* 53:1 (1983), 2-22; Arhin, "The Structure of Greater Ashanti (1700–1820)," *Journal of African History* [hereafter, *JAH*] 8:1 (1967), 65–85; Arhin, "Trade, Accumulation and the State in Asante in the Nineteenth Century," *Africa* 60:4 (1990), 524–37; Thomas Lewin, *Asante before the British: The Prempean Years, 1875–1900* (Lawrence: University of Kansas Press, 1978); Thomas C. McCaskie, "Accumulation, Wealth and Belief in Asante History I: To the Close of the Nineteenth Century," *Africa* 53:1 (1983), 23–43; McCaskie, "*Ahyiamu*—'A Place of Meeting': An Essay on Process and Event in the History of the Asante State," *JAH* 25:2 (1984), 169–88; McCaskie, *State and Society in Pre-Colonial Asante* (Cambridge: Cambridge University Press, 1995); David Owusu-Ansah, *Islamic Talismanic Tradition in Nineteenth Century Asante* (Lewiston, NY: Edwin Mellen Press, 1991); Ivor Wilks, *Asante in the Nineteenth Century: The Structure and Evolution of a Political Order* (Cambridge: Cambridge University Press, 1975); Wilks, *Forests of Gold: Essays on the Akan and the Kingdom of Asante* (Athens: Ohio University Press, 1993); Larry Yarak, *Asante and the Dutch, 1744–1873* (Oxford: Clarendon Press, 1990).

6. See, for example, Agnes Akosua Aidoo, "Asante Queen Mothers in Government and Politics in the Nineteenth Century," in Filomina Chioma Steady, ed., *The Black Woman Cross-Culturally* (Rochester, VT: Schenkman, 1981), 65–77; Kwame Arhin, "The Political and Military Roles of Akan Women," in Christine Oppong, ed., *Female and Male in West Africa* (London: Allen and Unwin, 1983), 91–98; Thomas C. McCaskie, "Anti-Witchcraft Cults in Asante: An Essay in the History of an African People," *History in Africa* 8 (1981), 125–54; McCaskie, "State and Society, Marriage and Adultery: Some Considerations toward a Social History of Pre-Colonial Asante," *JAH* 22:4 (1981), 477–94; Ivor Wilks, "Land, Labor, Gold and the Forest Kingdom of Asante: A Model of Early Change," in Wilks, *Forests of Gold*, 41–90, originally published as "Land, Labour, Capital and the Forest Kingdom of Asante," in J. Friedman and M. J. Rowlands, eds., *The Evolution of Social Systems: Proceedings of a Meeting of the Research Seminar in Archaeology and Related Subjects, London University* (Pittsburg, PA: Duckworth, 1977), 487–534; Wilks, "She Who Blazed a Trail: Akyaawa Yikwan of Asante," in P. Romero, ed., *Life Histories of African Women* (London: Ashfield Press, 1988), 113–39, republished in *Forests of Gold*, 329–62.

7. The exceptions include Kwame Arhin, "The Pressure of Cash and Its Political Consequences in Asante in the Colonial Period," *Journal of African Studies* [hereafter, *JAS*] 3:4 (1976), 453–68; Arhin, "Some Asante Views of Colonial Rule: As Seen in the Controversy Relating to Death Duties," *Transactions of the Historical Society of Ghana* 15:1 (1974), 63–84; Gareth Austin, "The Emergence of Capitalist Relations in South Asante Cocoa-Farming, c. 1916–33," *JAH* 28:2 (1987), 259–79; Austin, "Capitalists and Chiefs in the Cocoa Hold-Ups in South Asante, 1927–1938," *International Journal of African Historical Studies* [hereafter, *IJAHS*] 21:1 (1988), 63–95; Thomas C. McCaskie,

"Accumulation, Wealth and Belief II: The Twentieth Century," *Africa* 56:1 (1986), 3–23; William Tordoff, *Ashanti under the Prempehs, 1888–1935* (London: Oxford University Press, 1965).

8. See, for example, Meyer Fortes, "The Ashanti Social Survey: A Preliminary Report," *Rhodes-Livingstone Journal* 6 (1948), 1–37; Fortes, "A Demographic Field Study in Ashanti," in Frank Lorimer, ed., *Culture and Human Fertility* (Paris: UNESCO, 1954); Fortes, "Kinship and Marriage among the Ashanti," in A. R. Radcliffe-Brown and Daryll Forde, eds., *African Systems of Kinship and Marriage* (London: Oxford University Press, 1950), 252–84; R. S. Rattray, *Ashanti* (London: Oxford University Press, 1923); Rattray, *Ashanti Law and Constitution* (London: Oxford University Press, 1929); Rattray, *Religion and Art in Ashanti* (London: Oxford University Press, 1927).

9. Oppong, ed., *Female and Male*, passim. By way of example, see also Lynne Brydon, "Women at Work: Some Changes in Family Structure in Amedzofe-Avatime, Ghana," *Africa* 49:2 (1979), 97–111; Deborah Pellow, *Women in Accra: Options for Autonomy* (Algonac, MI: Reference Publications, 1977). For a thorough listing of much of this literature, see Elizabeth Ardayfio-Schandorf and Kate Kwafo-Akoto, *Women in Ghana: An Annotated Bibliography* (Accra: Woeli Publishing Services for United Nations Population Fund, 1990).

10. See Claire Robertson, *Sharing the Same Bowl: A Socioeconomic History of Women and Class in Accra, Ghana* (Bloomington: Indiana University Press, 1984); Agnes Akosua Aidoo, "Women in the History and Culture of Ghana," *Research Review* (new series) 1:1 (1985), 14–51; Aidoo, "Asante Queen Mothers"; Penelope Roberts, "The State and the Regulation of Marriage: Sefwi Wiawso (Ghana), 1900–40," in H. Afshar, ed., *Women, State, and Ideology: Studies from Africa and Asia* (Albany: State University of New York Press, 1987), 48–69.

11. The breadth of the chasm is evident in McCaskie's 1981 comment on women's history in "State and Society." "The study of women," he wrote, "however laudably motivated, is firmly becalmed in the biological particularism of gender. While some scholars are sensitive to this problem, it remains the case that much work on women effectively marginalizes them as historical actors by divorcing them from any overall historical context." "State and Society," 478. The chasm is certainly not unique to Asante. See, for example, Kristin Mann, *Marrying Well: Marriage, Status and Social Change among the Educated Elite in Colonial Lagos* (Cambridge: Cambridge University Press, 1985), 10; Margaret Jean Hay, "Queens, Prostitutes and Peasants: Historical Perspectives on African Women, 1971–1986," *Canadian Journal of African Studies* [hereafter, *CJAS*] 22:3 (1988), 432; Helen Bradford, "Women, Gender and Colonialism: Rethinking the History of the British Cape Colony and Its Frontier Zones, c. 1806–70," *JAH* 37:3 (1996), 351–70; Hunt, "Introduction," 324.

12. See, for example, Kwame Arhin, "The Economic and Social Significance of Rubber Production and Exchange on the Gold and Ivory Coasts, 1880–1900," *Cahiers D'Etudes Africaines*, 57/58 (1980), 49–62; Arhin, "Gold-mining and Trading among the Ashanti of Ghana," *Journal des Africanistes* 48:1 (1978), 89–100; Arhin, "Monetization and the Asante State," in J. Guyer, ed., *Money Matters: Instability, Values and Social Payments in the Modern History of West African Communities* (Portsmouth, NH: Heinemann, 1995), 97–110; Arhin, "Peasants in 19th-Century Asante," *Current Anthropology* 24:4 (1983), 471–80; and Arhin, "Political and Military Roles."

13. Gwendolyn Mikell, *Cocoa and Chaos in Ghana* (New York: Paragon House, 1989); Mikell, "The State, the Courts, and 'Value': Caught between Matrilineages in Ghana," in Guyer, ed., *Money Matters*, 225–44; Beverly Grier, "Pawns, Porters, and Petty Traders: Women in the Transition to Cash Crop Agriculture in Colonial Ghana," *Signs* 17:2 (1992), 304–28; Gracia Clark, *Onions Are My Husband: Survival and Accumulation by West African Market Women* (Chicago: University of Chicago Press, 1994); Takyiwaa Manuh, "Changes in Marriage and Funeral Exchanges in Asante: A Case Study from Kona, Afigya-Kwabre," in Guyer, ed., *Money Matters*, 188–201.

14. For example, the index to the most recent monograph on precolonial Asante history, McCaskie's *State and Society in Precolonial Asante*, contains no entries for women or gender.

15. Wilks, "She Who Blazed a Trail"; Thomas C. McCaskie, "*Konnurokusem*: Kinship and Family in the History of the *Oyoko Kɔkɔɔ* Dynasty of Kumase," *JAH* 36:3 (1995), 357–89.

16. Emmanuel Akyeampong, *Drink, Power and Cultural Change: A Social History of Alcohol in Ghana, c. 1800 to Recent Times* (Portsmouth, NH: Heinemann, 1996). See also Akyeampong, "Sexuality and Prostitution among the Akan of the Gold Coast, c. 1650–1950," *Past and Present* 156 (1997), 144–73; and Akyeampong and Pashington Obeng, "Spirituality, Gender, and Power in Asante History," *IJAHS* 28:3 (1995), 481–99.

17. In this regard, see especially Gareth Austin, "Between Abolition and *Jihad*: The Asante Response to the Ending of the Atlantic Slave Trade, 1807–1896," in R. Law, ed., *From Slave Trade to "Legitimate" Commerce: The Commercial Transition in Nineteenth Century West Africa* (Cambridge: Cambridge University Press, 1995), 93–118; Austin, "Human Pawning in Asante, 1800–1950: Markets and Coercion, Gender and Cocoa," in T. Falola and P. Lovejoy, eds., *Pawnship in Africa: Debt Bondage in Historical Perspective* (Boulder, CO: Westview Press, 1994), 121–59; Austin, "'No Elders Were Present': Commoners and Private Ownership in Asante, 1807–96," *JAH* 37:1 (1996), 1–30.

18. For a full listing of volumes, see bibliography.

19. See, especially, Kristin Mann and Richard Roberts, "Introduction," in their edited volume, *Law in Colonial Africa* (Portsmouth, NH: Heinemann, 1991), 43–48.

20. A brief account of Kyerew Akenten's life and her role in founding Oyoko and Mamponten can be found in Joseph Agyeman-Duah, *Mamponten Stool History* (Legon, Ghana: Institute of African Studies, University of Ghana, 1963).

21. Much of the research of Thomas Kyei, who worked with Fortes during the Ashanti Social Survey of the 1940s, was also based in Agogo, Kyei's hometown. See Thomas Kyei, *Marriage and Divorce among the Asante: A Study Undertaken in the Course of the Ashanti Social Survey (1945)*: Cambridge African Monographs 14 (Cambridge: African Studies Centre, 1992). Because Agogo was also the site of a large Basel Mission station, Allman hoped to be able to draw some comparisons between Presbyterian and Methodist mission initiatives.

22. See Susan Geiger, *TANU Women: Gender and Culture in the Making of Tanganyikan Nationalism, 1955–1965* (Portsmouth, NH: Heinemann, 1997), xvi and xvi, n. 4 and n. 8. A similar point has recently been made by Barbara Cooper in *Marriage in Maradi: Gender and Culture in Hausa Society, 1900–1989* (Portsmouth, NH: Heinemann, 1997), xviii–xxiv.

23. Geiger, *TANU Women*, xvi.

24. For definitions of personal narratives and life histories, see the Personal Narratives Group, *Interpreting Women's Lives: Feminist Theory and Personal Narratives* (Bloomington: Indiana University Press, 1989), 4–8. By way of example, see Geiger, *TANU Women*; Jean Davison with the women of Mutira, *Voices from Mutira: Lives of Rural Gikuyu Women* (Boulder, CO: Lynne Reinner, 1989); Sarah Mirza and Margaret Strobel, *Three Swahili Women: Life Histories from Mombasa, Kenya* (Bloomington: Indiana University Press, 1989); Belinda Bozzoli with Mmantho Nkotsoe, *Women of Phokeng: Consciousness, Life Strategy, and Migrancy in South Africa, 1900–1983* (Portsmouth, NH: Heinemann, 1991).

25. Ivor Wilks, *One Nation, Many Histories: Ghana Past and Present* (Accra: Anansesem Publications, 1996), 12. This work is the published text of the first of a series of lectures delivered by Wilks as the Aggrey-Fraser-Guggisberg Memorial Lectures, University of Ghana, 13–17 March 1995. The quotation is part of a passionate plea for recording reminiscences and life histories before it is too late: "This truly important work," Wilks stated, "should not only be sustained but intensified before yet another generation departs. . . . I suspect that scholars fifty years hence will be criticizing us for having failed to record more extensively the remembrances of those who are alive now. . . . It is not only that those who lived through events can often give us perspectives on them quite different from those in the written record. They can also give us access to perceptions of change that are not of the sort that are routinely documented, the stuff not of political but of social history" (12–13).

26. "The world of the departed"; "the world of the ancestors."

27. R. S. Rattray, *Ashanti Proverbs (The Primitive Ethics of a Savage People)* (Oxford: Clarendon Press, 1916), 190.

28. This comment was made in the 1990s to Takyiwaa Manuh, who shared it with members of a panel on gender and social change in Ghana for which she was discussant. African Studies Association Annual Meeting, Boston, 4 December 1993.

29. While Asante may have been the least hard hit of the regions, the death toll was still quite heavy. The pandemic swept Asante between September and November 1918, leaving over 9,000 dead by Patterson's conservative estimates. See K. David Patterson, "The Influenza Epidemic of 1918–19 in the Gold Coast," *JAH* 24:3 (1983), 485–502. For a discussion of the difficulty in assessing mortality figures for this period, see, especially, 495–97.

30. Tashjian: Ama Brago, Mamponten, 24 July 1990.

31. Tashjian: Kofi Owusu, Mamponten, 18 September 1990.

32. Audrey Smock, "Ghana: From Autonomy to Subordination," in J. A. Giele and A. Smock, eds., *Women, Roles and Status in Eight Countries* (New York: John Wiley and Sons, 1977), 191.

33. The title is taken from the saying "If I am divorced, I will not eat stone (*Me gyae aware a, menwe aboɔ*)," which is quoted in Aidoo, "Women," 24. While "not eating stone" refers in this context to women's specific ability to overcome any hardships that might result from divorce, it captured for us the broader resilience of the generation born in the tumultuous first decades of the twentieth century.

34. See Austin, "Between Abolition and *Jihad*."

35. See, for example, Margaret Jean Hay, "Luo Women and Economic Change during the Colonial Period," in N. Hafkin and E. Bay, eds., *Women in Africa: Studies in Social and Economic Change* (Stanford, CA: Stanford University Press, 1976), 87–109;

Elias Mandala, "Peasant Cotton Agriculture, Gender and Inter-Generational Relationships: The Lower Tchiri (Shire) Valley of Malawi, 1906–1940," *African Studies Review* [hereafter, *ASR*] 25:2/3 (1982), 27–44; Marcia Wright, "Technology, Marriage and Women's Work in the History of Maize-Growers in Mazabuka, Zambia: A Reconnaissance," *Journal of Southern African Studies* 10:1 (1983), 71–85; and, more recently (and with many new kinds of questions), Schmidt, *Peasants*; Jane Parpart, "'Where Is Your Mother?': Gender, Urban Marriage and Colonial Discourse on the Zambian Copperbelt," *IJAHS* 27:2 (1994), 241–71; Nancy Hunt, "Noise over Camouflaged Polygamy, Colonial Morality Taxation, and a Woman-Naming Crisis in Belgian Africa," *JAH* 32:3 (1991), 471–94; Carol Summers, "Intimate Colonialism: The Imperial Production of Reproduction in Uganda, 1907–1925," *Signs* 16:4 (1991), 787–807; Diana Jeater, *Marriage, Perversion and Power: The Construction of Moral Discourse in Southern Rhodesia, 1894–1930* (Oxford: Oxford University Press, 1993); Megan Vaughan, *Curing Their Ills: Colonial Power and African Illness* (Stanford, CA: Stanford University Press, 1991).

36. Margot Lovett, "Gender Relations, Class Formation and the Colonial State," in J. Parpart and K. Staudt, eds., *Women and the State in Africa* (Boulder, CO: Lynne Rienner, 1989), 24.

37. Ibid.

38. See, for example, Teresa Barnes, "The Fight for Control of Women's Mobility in Colonial Zimbabwe, 1900–1939," *Signs* 17:3 (1992), 586–608; Nancy Hunt, "'Le Bébé en Brousse': European Women, African Birth Spacing and Colonial Intervention in Breast Feeding in the Belgian Congo," *IJAHS* 21:3 (1988), 401–32; Jeater, *Marriage*; Susan Pedersen, "National Bodies, Unspeakable Acts: The Sexual Politics of Colonial Policy-making," *Journal of Modern History* 63 (1991), 647–80; Schmidt, *Peasants*; Summers, "Intimate Colonialism"; Vaughan, *Curing Their Ills*.

39. For an explanation of why European cocoa plantations failed in Ghana, see Gareth Austin, "Mode of Production or Mode of Cultivation: Explaining the Failure of European Cocoa Planters in Competition with African Farmers in Colonial Ghana," in W. Clarence-Smith, ed., *Cocoa Pioneer Fronts since 1800* (Basingstoke, England: Macmillan, 1996), 154–75.

40. Mahmood Mamdani, *Citizen and Subject: Contemporary Africa and the Legacy of Late Colonialism* (Princeton, NJ: Princeton University Press, 1996). Drawing from Ifi Amadiume's important work, Mamdani states briefly that colonial rule represented the "'world historic defeat of the female gender" (41). See Ifi Amadiume, "Gender, Political Systems and Social Movements: A West African Experience," in M. Mamdani and E. Wamba-dia-Wamba, eds., *African Studies in Social Movements* (Dakar: CODESRIA, 1995). Mamdani also provides a short synopsis of the implications of colonial constructions of customary law for gender relations (21).

41. Hunt, "Introduction," 330. As Hunt argues, a number of factors have worked against such comparison and synthesis. Africanist historians have long been "accustomed to approaching colonial studies through a single European power. . . . Language skills, national identities, funding sources, research itineraries, and perhaps even intellectual inquisitiveness have, thus far, worked against such approaches" (330).

42. Schmidt, *Peasants*, 4.

43. Parpart's recent article on the Zambian copperbelt, however, suggests that there were far more openings in southern Africa than earlier scholarship has recognized. See "'Where Is Your Mother?'" especially 241–42.

44. See Smock, "Ghana," 184–85.

45. Margaret Jean Hay and Marcia Wright, eds., *African Women and the Law: Historical Perspectives* (Boston: Boston University Papers on Africa VII, 1982). See also Martin Chanock, *Law, Custom, and Social Order: The Colonial Experience in Malawi and Zambia* (Cambridge: Cambridge University Press, 1985); Mann and Roberts, *Law in Colonial Africa*; Schmidt, *Peasants*; Parpart, "'Where Is Your Mother?'"

46. Martin Chanock, "Making Customary Law: Men, Women and Courts in Colonial Northern Rhodesia," in Hay and Wright, eds., *African Women and the Law*, 54.

47. Hay and Wright, eds., *African Women and the Law*, xiv.

48. Chanock "Making Customary Law," 60. Here Chanock emphasizes the colonial present in the making of customary law. In another passage, however, he recasts his approach as an effort to understand "the specific circumstances of the assertion of those forms of male power embodied in systems of customary law" (56).

49. See also Jean Allman, "Adultery and the State in Asante: Reflections on Gender, Class and Power from 1800 to 1950," in John Hunwick and Nancy Lawler, eds., *The Cloth of Many Colored Silks: Papers on History and Society, Ghanaian and Islamic, in Honor of Ivor Wilks* (Evanston, IL: Northwestern University Press, 1996), 27–65.

50. Sara Berry, *No Condition is Permanent: The Social Dynamics of Agrarian Change in Sub-Saharan Africa* (Madison: University of Wisconsin Press, 1993), especially 8–9.

51. Terence Ranger, "The Invention of Tradition in Colonial Africa," in E. Hobsbawm and T. Ranger, eds., *The Invention of Tradition* (Cambridge: Cambridge University Press, 1983), 251. A similar argument is presented in Mann and Roberts, "Introduction," 4.

52. See, for example, the list of "offensive acts" against native custom in J. N. Matson, *A Digest of the Minutes of the Ashanti Confederacy Council from 1935 to 1941 Inclusive and a Revised Edition of Warrington's "Notes on Ashanti Custom Prepared for the Use of District Commissioners"* (Cape Coast, Ghana: Prospect Printing Press, n.d., but ca. 1951), 42–43.

1

THE WORLD TO WHICH THEY WERE BORN: WOMEN'S LIFE STORIES AND THE PROBLEM OF COLONIAL CHRONOLOGIES

INTRODUCTION

The women whose life stories are at the core of this book were born after the British occupation of Asante in 1896 and the establishment of a protectorate in 1901.[1] By the prevailing historical chronologies, they are all "colonial women." Their lives begin with the dawning of British colonial rule in Asante, and they grow to maturity with the colonial state. We might expect, therefore, that their lives should tell us a colonial story. In many ways, they do not. The life experiences that were shared with us by Asante's first generation of colonized women resolutely defy facile chronological labels. Although they were born in the first two decades of the twentieth century, these women told stories that were as much about continuity with the lives of their mothers and their grandmothers as they were stories about change. Indeed, their myriad life experiences in their families, in their work, and in their communities seem embedded in other, alternative chronologies that defy the meta-timeline of Asante history–a timeline that is so often and so neatly fractured with the onset of colonial rule at the turn of the century.

As T. C. McCaskie lamented over a decade ago, "with very few exceptions there exists a rupture in African historiography; 1890, 1910, 1930?—the dates are not important, but the implications are. There clearly exists a curious intellectual 'deadzone' in time that effectively separates historical recon-

Photo 1.1   Village near Coomassie, ca. 1880s. (Copyright The Bodleian Library, Oxford, MS. Afr. s. 1956 [1], 16. Reprinted with permission.)

struction from contemporary analysis."[2] Yet the "intellectual 'deadzone'" lamented by McCaskie is not simply an unexplored gap in time, an unfortunate lacuna in a linear chronology. (If this were the case, the problem could easily be rectified by extending one's "starting point" a decade or two backward or forward in time!) Because the linear chronology and the meta-narratives accompanying it are based, for the most part, upon the lived experiences of elite males, the gap or intellectual deadzone is, more importantly, substantive and conceptual.

Through the lives of Asante's first generation of colonized women, we very quickly learned that words like "colonial" and "precolonial" lack explanatory power; that what historians have called "precolonial legacies" were part and parcel of a lived colonial world and that colonialism itself was experienced in uneven, episodic, and highly gendered ways. Through the prism of these life stories, we were reminded that "[c]ontinuity and change are," as McCaskie also wrote, ". . . seamless human experiences, ultimately resistant to the temporal carving knife of the historian and the social scientist."[3] Thus, the stories foregrounded in this book challenge us to cross the historiographical, chronological, and conceptual deadzone and to locate this generation of women within unfolding historical processes that neither began nor ended at the turn of the century.

CHRONOLOGIES OF CONJUGAL PRODUCTION AND EXCHANGE: A COCOA REVOLUTION?

A highlife song popular in the 1950s captured in lyrical ways what is probably the most salient presence in meta-narratives of twentieth-century Asante history—cocoa:

If you want to send your children to school, it is cocoa,
If you want to build your house, it is cocoa,
If you want to marry, it is cocoa,
If you want to buy cloth, it is cocoa,
If you want to buy a lorry, it is cocoa.
Whatever you want to do in this world,
It is with cocoa money that you do it.[4]

Indeed, few would dispute the contention that cocoa transformed the landscape of Asante, literally and figuratively. Cocoa spread throughout the region at an extremely rapid pace, first arriving in southern and eastern areas from the Gold Coast Colony around the turn of the century.[5] Following World War I, Asante cocoa farmers pushed the crop further west, first to available land around Tepa, Hwidem, and Goaso and then eventually south from Goaso to Sefwi and Wassaw in what is today Ghana's Western Region.[6] As its cultivation spread, cocoa quickly rose to prominence as the most important export of Asante and the Gold Coast Colony. First listed among official exports from the Gold Coast in 1885, it became the leading agricultural export by 1906 and the most valuable export of any category by 1910. As early as 1905, the governor of the Gold Coast Colony noted during his "Ashanti Tour of Inspection" that when the topic of cocoa arose with chiefs, he was "glad to hear that some of them have already commenced planting cocoa."[7] The Ashanti Report for 1910 indicated that Asantes had "devoted themselves more and more during the year to the culture of cocoa and rubber."[8] In fact, a note of alarm crept into the official record just a few years later with the 35 percent increase in cocoa for 1913: "The cultivation of cocoa is spreading, if anything too rapidly, with the result that farmers often possess more area under cultivation than they can properly care for."[9]

By and large, the growth of cocoa cultivation closely paralleled increases in its price. Though prices fell briefly in 1908 and also dropped during World War I, in both instances they recovered quickly and farmers continued to invest increasing time and resources in cocoa production. As one observer described the reaction: "Everyone went 'cocoa mad,' lawyers threw down their briefs, clerks gave up their berths and all devoted their time to buying and shipping cocoa."[10] Despite a generally sluggish market from the late 1920s

Photo 1.2   Cocoa tree on Peter Danso's farm, Oyoko, 1990. Photograph by Victoria Tashjian.

onward, the money that could be made in better years drew many Asantes into cocoa cultivation in the first three decades of the century and kept them there. It is not surprising, then, that the explosion of cocoa farming in Asante is so central to the reminiscences of women who came of age during these years. Once the price of cocoa increased, Akua Ababo of Mamponten recalled, "cocoa was the work of the day. Everybody took to it; it was profitable."[11] Afua Dufie of Oyoko, born around 1906, reminisced, "Cocoa came at my time. When I was a small girl my father went to the coast to buy cocoa seedlings, six of them, and gave them to my mother to plant. . . . I saw it come."[12] Adwowa Fodwo of Mamponten remembered how cocoa spread from south to north:

> So people increased cocoa cultivation when the price went up. It was during that time that the Akyem people increased cocoa production. So they

Photo 1.3 Cocoa drying, Oyoko, 1990. Photograph by Victoria Tashjian.

patronized it greatly . . . those Asantes who went there came back and took it to here. And the Bron people [to the northwest of Asante] too took it up. The land there was plentiful, so they did it on a higher scale. Later the price of cocoa was increased again, and people's interest was also increased.[13]

Historians and anthropologists who have focused specifically on cocoa, as well as those who have written more broadly on nineteenth- or twentieth-century Asante, have all argued that cocoa was transformative in giving a broad range of rural commoners access to cash and the cash economy—access that ushered in a host of related social as well as economic changes.[14] But in what ways was cocoa a revolutionary force (a force powerful enough to justify the 1900 rupture in Asante history's meta-timeline) and in what ways was it part and parcel of a much longer, gendered chronology of economic development? Reminiscences such as those of Adwowa Fodwo, as well as the dramatic statistics on cocoa's expansion, certainly suggest a twentieth-century, a colonial, chronology of revolutionary economic change. Yet there is much in the story of cocoa's rapid spread that extends well before the colonial period and into the lives of the mothers and grandmothers of those who planted Asante's first cocoa seedlings. As Kwame Arhin, Gareth Austin, Joseph LaTorre, Raymond Dumett, and several others[15] have argued, cocoa took root so firmly because it fit so well into preexisting patterns of production and exchange. Of particular importance is what Austin has described as the "widespread market-orientation" of farmers that resulted from Asante's long-standing involvement in production for the market and trade.[16] Arhin similarly points to the "capitalistic outlook and methods" and the "equipment and tools" utilized first in Asante's kola trade with the north and subsequently in the cocoa industry.[17] He also argues that cocoa relied heavily on the organizational patterns that dominated rubber production—renting land and sharecropping, migrating in order to maximize production and profits, and developing a professional trading class that "hired land, bought labour, and established broker connections."[18] But most importantly, like its predecessors—marketable commodities like gold, kola, and rubber—cocoa relied heavily upon conjugal labor. In short, even the twentieth-century cocoa "revolution" (so well captured in the verse "Whatever you want to do in this world, it is with cocoa money that you do it") was a "revolution" grounded in gendered patterns of labor long predating cocoa's arrival.[19] It is thus imperative that we briefly explore those patterns as they extend across the deadzone.

While Asantes were never significant consumers of kola nuts (just as they were not to be significant consumers of cocoa), a steady market for this product in the savannah regions to the north helped to drive a regular trade between the savannah and forest zones long before the emergence of the forest kingdom.[20] Recognizing its value, farmers in kola-producing regions spared kola trees when clearing plots of land for agricultural production and then at appropriate times of the year harvested, processed, and eventually sold the fruit. Both women and men were involved in kola's harvesting and preparation and, though kola producers could act individually, husbands and wives often worked together, with slaves and pawns forming an additional and significant sector of the kola labor force.[21] Kola thus helped pave the way for subsequent economic expansion not only because it was produced through conjugal labor but because, as Arhin has written, "kola trading was the basis of the accumulation of wealth in Asante in the nineteenth century"[22] and led to marketing and transportation networks later mirrored in brokerage systems for rubber and then cocoa.[23]

Photo 1.4   Women carrying cocoa to the coast, ca. 1900. (Copyright Basel Mission Archive, D-30.22.052. Reprinted with permission.)

And kola was not the only marketable good produced by conjugal labor before British colonial rule. Like kola, the extraction and trading of gold predated the founding of the Asante state; it was a seasonal activity engaged in by Asante commoners for whom farming remained the primary occupation.[24] Panning and mining for gold was concentrated in that period of the year when the demands of farming were at their lowest ebb, at the tail end of the dry season and into the first weeks of the rainy season.[25] The conjugal group remained the basic unit of production in gold-collecting activities. For the most part, women were concentrated in riverain panning for gold and in washing mined dirt for gold; men dug the shallow-pit, trench, and deep shaft mines that produced the auriferous soil subsequently washed by women. As Arhin succinctly states, the "organization of mining labour was done within the frame of domestic organization."[26] The labor of slaves and pawns might be added to the basic conjugal unit of production, but they constituted a source of labor decidedly secondary in importance to that of the conjugal unit in the production of gold.[27]

By the second half of the 1890s, rubber had become a significant Asante export, and the Gold Coast Colony was among the top five exporters of rubber in the world not long thereafter.[28] The organization of rubber production flowed logically and perhaps seamlessly from conjugal patterns of labor organization for kola and gold. However, some features in its production (and in the subsequent production of cocoa) began to diverge significantly from past practice. Though the conjugal family continued to be central to rubber tapping and transportation,[29] Arhin has documented the dramatic increase in slave labor that accompanied the development of the rubber industry: "the scale on which slaves featured in the rubber industry was impressive. . . . slaves were no longer used only to supplement family labour but had become the basis of a productive activity which was unrelated to the demands of the traditional domestic economy. . . . Rubber . . . demanded greater labour than could be supplied by family labour.[30] As Arhin has argued elsewhere, extra-household labor became a necessity for rubber production in a way it had never been for commoner production of gold or kola.[31] Indeed, the dramatic intensification in household labor and the increased reliance on extra-conjugal labor—both aimed at production for the market in rubber and, shortly thereafter, cocoa— marked real and substantive changes in domestic production.[32]

But what are the implications of these changes for constructing a chronology of conjugal production that not only crosses the historiographical deadzone but is able to capture and make sense of the lives of Asante's first generation of colonized women? A gendered chronology of continuity and change in domestic production, we suggest, would not put forth 1896 (the year of the Asantehene's arrest by British forces) or 1901 (the year Asante was annexed directly to the Crown) as significant points for the beginning or the ending of the story. Rooted in daily lived experience, the chronology needs to extend well back into the eighteenth century (if not earlier) in order to capture the ongoing ways in which free men and women jointly produced foodstuffs and, as time permitted, products like kola or gold for internal and external markets. It needs to explicitly link the lives of the first generation of colonized women with their mothers and their grandmothers. Yet at the same time, this alternative chronology must capture the changes in conjugal production that began to emerge in the closing decades of the nineteenth century and proceeded apace during the first decades of the twentieth century. Slowly and perhaps imperceptibly at first, increasing amounts of labor were devoted to production for the market. By the time cocoa was set to take off, the "traditional household economy," as Arhin termed it, may have looked on the surface very much as it did 50 years earlier, but the pressures upon it, particularly for labor, were without precedent. Yet these profound changes are not readily apparent if the historian's chronology does not reach back across the deadzone of scholarly inquiry or if the life stories of Asante's first generation of colonized women are not allowed to speak to a more deeply rooted past.

CHRONOLOGIES OF TRAVEL AND TRADE: THE FEMINIZATION OF THE MARKET

The lives of this generation were, of course, affected by economic and infrastructural changes reaching far beyond conjugal production and cocoa. One year after occupying Asante in 1896, the British government granted to E. Cade a concession to begin gold-mining operations in Obuasi; by 1898, the Ashanti Goldfields Corporation was up and running.[33] Together, the production of cocoa and gold for an external market fueled, and in many ways was fueled by, far-reaching developments both in the region's infrastructure and in other sectors of its expanding cash economy. Only a year after Asante's annexation to the British Crown (1901), the railway line from Sekondi in the Gold Coast Colony had reached Obuasi and the following year was "enthusiastically welcomed in Kumasi."[34] A line from Accra to Kumasi was begun in 1909, but, due to the war and the depression that followed, it was not completed until 1923.[35] Road construction followed a similar pattern. In the first years of colonial rule, progress was very slow.[36] After the war, however, as the money economy expanded, particularly in the southern areas where cocoa dominated, road expansion accelerated dramatically. By 1921, 500 miles of motorable roads streamed out of Kumasi. Only seven years later, that number had increased to over a thousand, and by 1934, there were 1,655 miles of roads in Asante.[37]

Motorable roads and rail lines were intended for and served the primary purpose of facilitating the export of Asante's cash-earning exports.[38] Yet export firms were not alone in seizing the opportunities presented by the expanding transport infrastructure. "As the roads pushed outwards from Kumasi," writes Kimble, "so did the motor lorries, which quickly came to represent one of the most lucrative forms of business in Ashanti; retail stores followed, and the large European firms opened branches in small towns that only a few years earlier had been considered far too remote."[39] For ordinary Asante women and men, however, roads and rail lines did not simply mean easier access to imported goods at local European shops. Trains, lorries, and motor cars came to be utilized on a daily basis by many farmers and traders who could now move, with their goods, far greater distances in far shorter amounts of time. "Business interests brought farmers from outlying districts into Kumasi," writes Tordoff,

> and took traders outside the borders of Ashanti. . . . In particular, the people moved away from their old homes as the network of communications im-

proved. They were alive to the economic advantage of establishing farms near newly-built roads, which provided quick link-up with the railhead at Kumasi. Old villages either declined in size or were totally abandoned, and a large number of new roadside villages sprang up. For others, the towns were a powerful magnet.[40]

The bottom line was that ordinary people became more mobile than they had ever been before. That mobility, coupled with the growth in rural income from cocoa farming, generated a dramatic increase in local and regional trade—an increase that could be measured both by the amounts of goods traded and the numbers of individuals involved.

Yet trade both within and outside Asante's borders had always been a vital part of the state's precolonial economy, so in many ways the expansion of markets in the first decades of the twentieth century, just like the dramatic growth in cocoa production discussed above, was firmly rooted in precolonial antecedents.[41] Even the road system set down by the colonial government constituted, in many ways, a regeneration of an earlier network, rather than a new development. We know, for example, that Asante's great precolonial roads, so well described by Wilks,[42] were plied, in the eighteenth and nineteenth centuries, by *batafoɔ* (state and, to a lesser degree, private traders) who brought a wealth of imported goods into Asante: for example, cotton cloth and threads, silks, gunpowder, slaves, guns, cushions, and tobacco. Retail traders (*adwadifoɔ*) then purchased commodities in bulk and, with the assistance of hawkers (*mpaafoɔ*), transported and sold them throughout the towns and villages of Asante's rural areas.[43] Although the great road system was destroyed by British, French, and German occupation of Greater Asante,[44] Wilks has argued convincingly that the colonial system of roads "follow[s] more or less closely the course of earlier great roads," and just as those were a major part of the "incorporative process" that brought precolonial Asante into being, so would they function in the creation of a colonial Asante.[45]

But it was not just in terms of state-sponsored roads and external trade that colonial economic expansion built on precolonial antecedents. As we have already seen in the context of conjugal production, ordinary men and women were actively engaged with markets throughout Asante's history. Still, as Austin has recently observed, historians have tended to accept Freeman's 1868 descriptions of a population that, "residing chiefly in farms and villages, [has] comparatively little occasion for extensive and well-arranged markets" and of a capital city that "possesses nothing deserving the name market."[46] Thus, historians have argued that external trade was virtually the exclusive domain of Asante state traders before 1831 and again from approximately 1840 to 1880, and that local markets were "conspicuous by their absence."[47] Although they have recognized the existence of markets in Kumasi, both for locally produced foodstuffs and imported items,[48] as well as the significance of Asante's major import-export entrepôts (like Salaga and Adubease), they largely contend it was not until the 1880s that local markets entered the picture in any significant way. It was only after the British sacking of Kumasi in 1874, they assert, and the subsequent breakdown in Asante state authority due to the secession of provinces, a civil war, and an interregnum that rural producers were able to actively engage with the market, and much of that engagement was shaped by the new, external demand for rubber.[49]

In his recent, pathbreaking work, Austin counters this prevailing view and thus opens the way for transcending the intellectual deadzone and complicating and enriching the chronologies of Asante's past. He argues that Asante's state traders did not hold a firm monopoly on external trade with the savannah and coast in the nineteenth century; there is ample evidence of private traders operating throughout the system. More importantly for our purposes, he also presents convincing evidence of local markets throughout the state, not only in Kumasi, where foodstuffs, forest products, and village crafts were sold. Slaves were also purchased in these local markets for "incorporation within the lineage framework" and for producing kola nuts and mining gold.[50] After the closure of the Atlantic slave trade at the beginning of the century, slaves who would have been exported were redeployed within Asante—a process that facilitated Asante's successful adaptation to "legitimate" commerce.[51] Moreover, "[t]hat the mass of commoner households could afford to buy slaves," Austin contends, "shows that they had acquired relatively substantial holdings of cash, while these purchases, in turn, would have increased their cash-earning capacity further."[52] Wealth for commoners in the nineteenth century was thus generated not with the simple intent of "'exchanging use values'" but with the purpose of "'transforming that wealth into more durable or productive forms.'"[53] Austin concludes that we must see the nineteenth-century Asante commoner, man or woman, as being continuously involved in a "process of production and trading of marketable goods in the time . . . left over from participation in food growing for the household's own consumption."[54]

The implications of Austin's arguments are profound. They suggest that ordinary men and women did not simply burst on to the scene in the twentieth century as producers and consumers of commodities, once the authority of the Asante state had been dismantled (as most early colonial sources indicate). The continuities between the precolonial and colonial past are indeed striking. While there was clearly a dramatic expansion in markets, especially with rubber and cocoa and the concomitant increase in rural incomes, it was a change of degree, not of kind. Thus, accounts of the early colonial market, which describe "the supplies brought daily into the market at Kumasi, large quantities of plantains, yams, cassava and maize,"[55] must not be read in contrast to, but in light of, nineteenth-century accounts by observers like Bowdich, who described Kumasi's larger market as containing some 60 stalls, where one could purchase everything from beef and mutton to forest products, yams, corn, sugar-cane, rice, and palm wine to pipes, beads, mirrors, silk, cotton, and sandals.[56]

To stress these striking continuities with the early nineteenth century, however, is not to discount the devastation of 1874 and the political instability that followed in its wake as British imperial interests pushed further and further north. Nor is it to diminish the degree of growth that occurred in markets and trade after the 1880s, and especially after British occupation in 1896 and Asante's annexation to the Crown in 1901. To the contrary, it is to further problematize chronologies of Asante history, which have tended to either begin or end roughly at the turn of the century and to suggest, for example, that the 1898 market in Kumasi, which attracted between 400 and 500 traders per day selling a range of locally produced and imported items,[57] could only be described as new and different in the specific context of two decades of instability and crisis. By looking over the longue durée, we can better appreciate that the market successes that would be claimed by British colonialism were largely rooted in the dynamism of a pre-1880 Asante economy. Just as importantly, they were "successes" only in the sense that they allowed for the partial reconstitution of what the British themselves had destroyed, both directly and indirectly, beginning in 1874.

Successes in this context, however, they were. From 1907 to 1913, for example, the trade in snails from Ahafo and Wam to Kumasi

> was valued at £50,000 a year. Fish came from the Colony in increasing quantities. Five hundred and nineteen tons were imported in 1910; two years later the import of fish was 989 tons. . . . From all of these various activities, from the sale of cocoa, kola, rubber, cattle, or hides, of foodstuffs or fish or snails, or European goods; from work on the road or farm or mine as skilled or unskilled labourers, from employment with trading firms as clerks or commercial middlemen, the people earned money, and bought more and more goods.[58]

Descriptions such as these certainly illustrate both continuity with the period before 1874 and expansion from the late nineteenth century through the first decades of colonial rule. But they also embody significant, though hidden, aspects of change. Just as the chronology of cocoa's expansion must not only reach back across the deadzone but be understood as a gendered process, so too must a chronology of markets and trade. The expansion of markets in the colonial period was profoundly gendered in ways that were strikingly discontinuous, especially with regard to women's participation. While we have fragmentary, rather inconclusive evidence that places women in the markets during the nineteenth century,[59] it is clear women did not hold the central role in market trading for which they would become so well known in the twentieth century. While they obviously participated in family production for the market, their role in retailing was probably limited.[60] Because women were responsible for childcare, food processing, cleaning, and other household chores, the gendered division of labor in the household, as Austin argues, "gave men a particularly large share of . . . 'extra-subsistence' time"[61] that could be devoted to gold, kola, and later rubber production and, presumably, to small-scale trading. Women had little such time.

By the 1930s, however, women were active as traders in the full range of imported goods available in Asante, and they monopolized the expanding local foodstuffs trade. By the 1940s, as Gracia Clark argues, "women had achieved their present commercial dominance of the markets . . . trading in more items and with more regions than ever before."[62] The change and the growth were dramatic, though not immediate. The first decade of colonial rule was one of confusion, with "rapid fluctuations in the ethnic and gender organization of trade as traders tested and negotiated changes in the regional balance of power."[63] By the second decade, however, cocoa production was expanding rapidly, there were numerous alternatives to subsistence agricultural production, especially for men, and the cash economy was entering nearly every facet of daily life. It was in this context that what Clark has called the "feminization" of Asante's markets began in earnest. Both Gracia Clark and Agnes Aidoo associate women's entry into the market with men's departures from it for more lucrative occupations in cocoa farming or waged work.[64] Women sold imported commodities like liquor and cloth in the markets, though some, according to Clark, also sold in stores. In addition, they began to trade "in some locally produced commodities, gradually taking over all of the larger market sections selling foodstuffs.[65] By the 1930s and '40s, having secured control of trade throughout the region, some Asante women ventured to the markets of the south and the north. According to Clark, "They moved into larger-scale intermediary trading positions, either formerly occupied by coastal women or newly created by the intensification of trade in some commodities. Asante women supplied cloth and other imports to traders and consumers in Asante and the North. . . . they also collected foodstuffs such as yams and beans from those regions to supply Accra traders."[66]

Whether they traveled to distant markets in Accra, Kintampo, or Bolgatanga, or simply transported surplus foodstuffs to the nearest larger regional market, Asante's first generation of colonized women were, in many ways, pioneers. Combining trade and travel, they forged places for themselves in the expanding cash economy. In reminiscences describing these pioneering years, Asante women use the word *-bata* ("to journey about with wares for sale, to travel on commercial business").[67] This was the same verb used in the nineteenth century to describe trading, but with the implicit connotation of state trade (thus, *batafoɔ*, "public traders," or *batahene*, "the official responsible for the organization of the trading parties"[68]). At present, a richly textured and not uncommon Ghanaian English translation of *-bata* is "to sojourney,"[69] a composite verb that combines the notion of travel (journey) with that of sojourn (to stay for a while). It is a verb that uniquely captures the activities of nineteenth-century men traders, as aptly as it captures those of women trading pioneers. For example, the descriptions of early trading and hawking by Afua Nyame of Mamponten sound remarkably similar to what we know of the activities of nineteenth century *mpaafoɔ*:

> I was selling cloth in Mamponten at the time of my first marriage. I got it from a relative in Kumasi. Once a month or so—I had to finish selling one batch before going back for another—I would go to Kumasi for cloth. . . . I took up the cloth and went around to sell [it]. I went to different villages, I always went when there was not a market day, so that I met people in their homes, at odd times when they would be at home. Because if you go on the actual market day, after the day is over you just came back. But if I went for a week, I could sell a lot.[70]

While some early women traders worked alone, others acted collectively in order to maximize their profits, particularly as they sought to take advantage of new and quicker forms of transportation. As Abena Afe of Mamponten recalled:

> I was cultivating cassava and was making brooms from branches and sending them to Kumasi to sell. I walked all the way to Kumasi from Mamponten. I got up at the crack of dawn. And we were many, about 20, all women, going to Kumasi. But when we were coming back home from Kumasi, we all gathered at one place and hired a car and it was about three shillings per person. We came back the same day. You may get, say, 20 shillings after everything.[71]

Though the cost of a ride home represented some 15 percent of the day's profits, avoiding the 15-kilometer walk home at the end of the day made the expense well worthwhile.

As traveling by motor vehicle along Asante's expanding roadways became more common, the distance women traders could cover and still return home each evening increased dramatically. Obaa Kro, a bead trader, remembers regularly making day trips from her home in Ashanti New Town, a neighborhood in Kumasi, to the towns of Nkawie, Bibiani, and Tekyiman, covering distances of up to 70 miles on a daily basis.[72] Ama Akyaa, who was based in Kumasi, also covered distances by car that would have been impossible on foot. She remembered her involvement in the fish trade:

> We bought [fish] in Kumasi when they were sent out from the coast, and some from Yeji. . . . I went in a car [from Nkawie to Kumasi] so I could go back in a day. Sometimes it took a week before I went back to Kumasi for more. When I got them from Kumasi I had to hawk them. I hawked it, walked around to nearby villages and sold it.[73]

This fish trade involved both medium-range trade to buy the fish in bulk at the regional market in Kumasi and then local hawking to retail it in small villages. Women's ability to travel far and still return home each evening was important, for if a woman was married, the daily domestic services that she was expected to provide for her husband often meant she needed to return home at night.

Motorized transport also meant that travel to even more distant places could require only an overnight stay, instead of a journey of many days, and these short trips might less seriously disrupt a woman's domestic routine. Theresa Anokye imported yams to Kumasi from areas some 75 miles to the north, where they were more commonly grown:

> I went to the interior . . . Ejura, Amanten. . . . They were always ready with the yams, so you could just go and buy them. I went in a passenger car. . . . I had no house to stay in up there. You just stay in the station [lorry park] because you may arrive in the night. So immediately you pay for your yams, you get in a car and start the journey back home. The yam sellers were right there in the station.[74]

But even with motorized transport, some early trading endeavors still required longer periods of time afield. Not surprisingly, these professions tended to remain male-dominated longest or to involve women working in conjunction with their husbands. Yaa Akom of Mamponten recalled how her involvement with palm wine tapping required extended travel with her husband: "After marrying . . . we went on sojourney to Tarkwa to tap wine. We bought the trees from the natives of Tarkwa and sold the wine itself and then made brooms out of the branches. . . . There were a lot of us. . . . It was a general sojourney, because of good palm wine."[75] In these reminiscences, as well as in colonial-era written accounts, we gather a picture of early women traders in perpetual motion. By their travels and their trade they surely wove together a colonial economy in much the same way that their male counterparts of the nineteenth century—*batafoɔ*, *adwadifoɔ*, and *mpaafoɔ*—wove rural Asante into the world market.

And at the center of that colonial economy stood Kumasi. It is a city that features prominently in the life stories of many Asante women; it is a city that underwent dramatic transformation during their lives. In many ways, Kumasi's role in the colonial regional economy mirrored its nineteenth-century significance. The place where all the great roads converged, Kumasi had been central to the planning and financing of precolonial trade, and its citizens, as state and palace functionaries, were the main consumers of both imported and locally produced goods. Yet in the nineteenth century, Kumasi's primary role was as a political and administrative center; it did not function as the major distributive point for the import and export trade. In the very first years of the twentieth century, however, that, too, began to change. In 1903, the acting chief commissioner foresaw Kumasi as the "headquarters of the kola and rubber trade,"[76] not just as the administrative center for British colonial rule in Asante. The arrival of the rail line at the end of that year and the fact that "merchants are shortly going to open stores here should give good impetus to trade," the commissioner wrote, "by giving Ashantis greater opportunity of spending money and a corresponding increase in their desire to earn it."[77] Over the next two decades, the commissioner's predictions were more than fulfilled as Kumasi became the main trading center for the entire region.[78]

The population statistics for the city provide ample evidence of its growth as an economic center. For much of the nineteenth century, its population ranged from 12,000 to 25,000,[79] while Asante's total population, up to the 1860s, was probably around 750,000.[80] From 1863 through the beginning of the twentieth century, both Kumasi and the region as a whole suffered a dramatic population decline. These years, as Wilks has written, "were ones of military campaigns against the British and against secessionist districts and provinces, of civil war, and of the British occupation and the final Anglo-Asante war of 1900." Indeed, Wilks reckons Asante's population in 1901 to have been only 250,000 and Kumasi's little over 3,000.[81] While the reliability of much of the colonial census data for the years 1901–1931 is questionable—given people's reluctance to be counted, the inefficiency of counting techniques, and the census committees' tendency to add and subtract population based on impressions—it is still clear that growth was rapid, with a dramatic increase for Kumasi occurring in the first decade of colonial rule.[82] In 1904, the commissioner reported that the population of Kumasi was now between 10,000 and 11,000, more than double what it had been the year before.[83] The official census for 1911 placed Kumasi's population at 18,853, a three-fold increase over the 1901 estimates.[84] A decade later, it had reached

23,624, and in 1931 it was reported to be 35,826. The first census regarded as fairly accurate, that of 1948, reported Kumasi's population as 81,870 and the region's overall population as 818,944.[85] As Alfred Kwasi Opoku has shown, much of this urban growth can be attributed to migration, as women and men flocked to Kumasi for jobs and trade.[86]

As an expanding economic center with a rapidly increasing population, Kumasi took on the look of a colonial city—bustling, chaotic, and full of contrasts. Yet unlike its counterparts in the colonial settler states of southern Africa, Kumasi's population did not feature a pronounced imbalance in the ratio of men to women. Although more men than women migrated to Kumasi in the early years of its colonial expansion, the differential between the numbers of men and women never approached the staggering figures of southern Africa (only one adult woman for every 157 adult men in 1934 Harare, for example)[87] and, in fact, lessened consistently from 1921, when there were 146.8 males for every 100 females, to a 1948 figure of 113.5 to 100.[88] A relatively balanced urban population meant a more or less permanent (as opposed to migratory) population. As early as 1905, the governor reported to the Colonial Office that many people were now putting up brick houses, with roofs of iron or wood shingles.[89] In 1925, a network of new streets fed into a "new central market that housed some 2,000 vendors, most of them women."[90] In the same year, the Kumasi Health Board was established to oversee the city's structural improvements, which included new roads and commercial buildings. This was not an easy task. "Though it could boast many imposing buildings and a number of tree-lined streets," writes Tordoff, "there was no electric lighting or pipe-borne water-supply. Other defects were more serious. Compounds were often insanitary—especially in Kumasi Old Town and the Zongo area; market accommodation was inadequate; there was no subsoil drainage system; and the water-supply was heavily polluted."[91] These chronic problems notwithstanding, the population continued to increase dramatically. By 1929, the Gold Coast governor reported in a speech that Kumasi had "changed more under British rule than any other town in West Africa."[92]

In many ways, the governor's characterization was appropriate; change was indeed dramatic in Kumasi, in terms of architecture, European trading firms, infrastructure, population growth, and ethnic diversity. It was most evident in the low-lying center of the city where the sprawling central market embodied some of the most profound changes of all: the feminization of trade and Kumasi's new role as an import-export center. But what the governor did not appreciate was the strong continuity with the precolonial past. While Asante's first generation of colonized women saw a city in 1929 that looked very different from the one their mothers gazed upon in 1901, the appellation by which Kumasi came to be known after the First World War—"Garden City of West Africa"—may well have suited the city their great-grandmothers knew in the early nineteenth century.[93]

CHRONOLOGIES OF COLONIAL
RULE, COURTS, AND "CUSTOM"

The alternative chronologies of production, travel, and trade we have explored thus far—chronologies embedded in the life stories of Asante's first generation of colonized women—have located women at the center of economic and material developments that cross the intellectual deadzone. As we turn to the politics of rule, to courts and to custom, we find that women shift quite dramatically to the margins. To be sure, the administrative and judicial structures that evolved during the colonial period were, like economic and infrastructural developments, a strange and often troubling combination of old and new. But while the British were intent on constructing a system of rule that built upon what they imagined to be the outlines of the precolonial political system (absent the centralizing power of Kumasi and the Asantehene), women were nowhere to be found in that imagined political landscape. When R. S. Rattray, the government anthropologist, queried old Asante men and women in the 1920s about this omission, they answered: "The white man never asked us this; you have dealings with and recognize only the men; we supposed the European considered women of no account, and we know you do not recognize them as we have always done."[94]

To argue that the British could not imagine a political landscape for Asante inclusive of women is not to suggest that they had a blueprint for rule when they occupied Asante in 1896, arrested the Asantehene, the Asantehemaa, important members of the royal family, and several powerful chiefs and sent them into exile as political prisoners. (The prisoners were first sent to Elmina, then to Sierra Leone, and finally in 1900 to the Seychelles Islands where they would remain until 1924.) Indeed, it would take the British nearly 40 years to articulate a judicial and administrative system for Asante that was in any way coherent. Yet in all of its incarnations over those 40 years and beyond, British political rule included two notable constants that marked a profound break with the precolonial past: the marginalization of women, particularly in their roles as queenmothers (*ahemaa*), and the suppression of institutions and channels through which commoners generally expressed their discontent with political authority.

Though the process began to unfold in January 1896, when the British government placed Asante under protectorate status, it was not until after the Yaa Asantewa Rising (1900) against British rule that Asante was annexed

Photo 1.5 Asantehene Agyeman-Prempeh and Asantehemaa Yaa Kyaa, Elmina, 1896. (From Paul Steiner, *Dark and Stormy Days in Kumassi*. London: S. W. Partridge, 1901.)

directly to the Crown and subsequently administered as a conquered territory.[95] Outside of Kumasi, in the outlying divisions, these first years of British occupation (1896–1901) had little impact on internal government. The British Resident was not to interfere in the daily administration of a division and the courts of the *amanhene* (territorial chiefs) were to proceed as usual, "except that in the cases of murder the chiefs were to sit with the Resident and another officer."[96] By contrast, however, confusion reigned in Kumasi. As Rattray wrote, "it lost not only a King but was deprived of its Ɔmanhene."[97] The governor sought to fill this void by appointing a Native Committee of Administration, a triumvirate that would support the British Resident and settle minor disputes among Asantes living in Kumasi.[98]

After the rising, the Order in Council of 26 September 1901 and the Ashanti Administration Ordinance in 1902 provided a structure for British rule in Asante, and the dense ambiguity of 1896–1901 gave way to a more defined, though still no more consistent, administrative and judicial system. Asante was initially divided into four districts, with a district commissioner assigned to each and the Central District, which included Kumasi, under the chief commissioner.[99] The internal organization of the various outlying *aman* (states) was not greatly affected by the initial intrusion of colonial law.[100] By contrast, Kumasi remained "seriously disorganized" and constituted an ongoing problem for the colonial administration.[101]

Still intent on keeping Asante fragmented, and therefore insistent that Kumasi not be allowed to assume its historic preeminence,[102] the government sought to administer the division through a council of "clan chiefs."[103] In 1905, at Chief Commissioner Fuller's instigation, the government formally recognized the Kumasi Council of Chiefs as the administrative apparatus for the division. The council was chaired by the chief commissioner and was meant to restore to Kumasi chiefs some of the power they had lost since 1896. Not one of the members of that council was an *ɔhemaa* (queenmother); thus Kumasi was the first division to experience the masculinization of its political realm. Moreover, many members of the council were men who had been directly appointed to stools by the British government in recompense for their loyalty during the rising. They had no legitimate claim to the positions they held and often utilized their offices to extort money and labor from their "subjects."[104] As W. R. Gosling, Kumasi's D.C. in 1927, reflected on the early council: its function was "to settle matters of importance relating to the town of Kumasi and the lands held by the members of the Council; it is clear, however, from the minutes that affairs affecting the whole of Ashanti were also considered and rules arbitrarily made which are still operative and have in practice come to be regarded as Native Custom."[105]

In the years up to the end of the First World War, many of these government-sponsored chiefs, as well as legitimate but unpopular chiefs, were challenged by their subjects in what seemed an endless series of destoolment efforts throughout the region. With few exceptions, the British faithfully backed the chiefs and in many instances punished those who led moves for destoolment.[106] By and large, the government considered such challenges to be the unfortunate byproduct of "Western Civilization and more liberal ideas."[107] As Chief Commissioner Fuller wrote in 1909, "In fact, a spirit of independence—not to say insubordination—has permeated throughout all classes of Ashantis with such rapidity of late years, that far from being able to oppress their subjects, it takes all the time of the chiefs to maintain their legitimate rights."[108] What the British did not appreciate, or perhaps preferred to ignore, was that the actions of commoners in the first decades of colonial rule had strong antecedents. Commoners (*nkwankwaa* or *mmerante*) in the precolonial period had access to mechanisms and processes through which to voice their grievances. (Indeed, the overthrow of Asantehene Mensa Bonsu in 1883 was largely engineered by a well-organized group of Kumasi *nkwankwaa*.)[109] At every level, from villages on up, commoners were organized and led by a spokesman, the Nkwankwaahene, who would present concerns to the elders. *Nkwankwaa* input into the political process extended to the election of chiefs. As K. A. Busia writes of the precolonial period, when the commoners were asked what they thought about the elders' decision regarding a particular candidate,

> the commoners would then approve or disapprove the decision of the elders. If the candidate was not accepted, the queen-mother was informed and the royals proceeded to make another nomination. If after three nominations the queen-mother's candidate was still unacceptable, the Divisional Council nominated a candidate from the royal family. It was for the queenmother to say whether or not the popular candidate had a kin-right to the stool. Both parties usually agreed on one of the eligible candidates.[110]

That a "royal does not install the chief" (*Ɔdehye nsi hene*), but rather those who serve him, was a fundamental political principle lost in the making of colonial Asante. The will of the people was replaced, for the most part, by the will of the British government.[111]

It is not mere coincidence that several of the destoolment efforts in the 1910s were waged by queenmothers in concert with the so-called "youngmen" or *nkwankwaa*. After all, they comprised the two groups most marginalized from formal political processes by British colonial rule. One of the most serious of these rebellions against British-recognized chiefs occurred in Agogo in 1917 and witnessed the *ɔhemaa*, Adjuah Jiawah, and a group of *nkwankwaa* "malcontents" calling for the ouster of the recently enstooled Kwabena Tandoh. The "malcontents" argued that Tandoh was not nominated by the queenmother, was not of the stool family, and had incurred serious debt. They also charged him with having "neglected a cocoa farm made for him by the people," having "discarded 10 stool wives after collecting head-money on them," and a host of other misdeeds, including administering "charms to the Elders to prevent them from telling the truth."[112] In the end, the chief commissioner found most of the charges unfounded, upheld Tandoh's possession of the stool, and deposed the queenmother. She and nine of the *nkwankwaa* were also forbidden to return to "Agogo territory." Much of the blame for the incident was placed squarely on the shoulders of the queenmother, who was described as being of a "relentless, revengeful and vicious disposition."[113] This was clearly not an isolated incident or a characterization specific to one woman, in one place and time. As the D.C. of Juaso lamented after similar difficulties in Kumawu: "There [*sic*] old ladies seem to have a blind malignity which must be very irritating to a chief."[114]

In addition to creating an administrative framework that marginalized royal women and commoners generally, the Ordinance of 1902 provided for the creation and recognition of structures that could implement and adjudicate "native custom" or "customary law." While it recognized a chief commissioner's court (replacing the Resident's court) and D.C.s' courts, all of which had civil and criminal jurisdiction, it also recognized native tribunals and empowered them to hear a variety of land and civil cases up to £100. The tribunals could enforce their own judgments, as long as those judgments were not "in any way repugnant to natural justice or to the principles of the law of England." Any decision by a native tribunal could be appealed to the chief commissioner or D.C.'s court.[115] Significantly, the ordinance did not recognize queenmothers' courts, though the evidence suggests that they continued to operate outside the purview of the colonial state. Despite early and rather elaborate attempts to systematize the customary judicial apparatus, the scheme looked better on paper than it worked in practice. As one colonial report bemoaned years later, the tribunals basically were left to function as they had done before the ordinance and were certainly not confined, as the ordinance required, to head chiefs recognized by the government.[116]

Most of the tribunals recognized by the government were not provided with clerks, and therefore we have little insight into their proceedings. The records for many of the government courts have survived, however, and provide a detailed picture of early British attempts to administer "customary law" and of Asante attempts to negotiate the terrain of colonial jurisprudence. Clearly those of subordinate status, including slaves and commoner women, viewed these early British courts as sites where they might challenge their subordination and receive a sympathetic hearing.[117] Women, in particular, seemed inclined to contest various forms of exploitation in the early British courts, either as complainants or defendants. Many early cases, in fact, centered on the legitimacy of an individual's dependent status, whether slave or pawn. Before 1908, the colonial government's policy on slavery and pawnage was ambivalent, to say the least, and in cases involving one's status as slave or pawn, that status was generally upheld by the court. Though the extension of the Gold Coast's criminal code into Asante in 1902 technically rendered slaving and pawning illegal, the government continued to recognize both statuses.[118] However, in 1908, slavery and pawnage were officially abolished, and shortly thereafter the floodgates opened, as case after case was brought before colonial officials in which a person's dependent status was contested.[119] For example, the chief of Senase appeared before the commissioner of the Western Province of Ashanti in 1913 to apply for adultery compensation. His female slave, mother of one of his children, had run away from him and refused to return. She was now living with a clerk in Sunyani with whom she had a child. The commissioner was unsure what to do, as "in all cases I have refused ever to put pressure on to a runaway slave to return to her master." Indeed, we can probably assume that this is precisely the context in which the woman had made her decision to flee. Yet the chief insisted that because the woman was a slave wife, she was not free to leave and therefore her subsequent actions warranted his compensation. The case was a difficult one for the commissioner, who was also concerned that "not now to allow damages for adultery on account of a slave woman would be to give slave women generally a free license to commit adultery." The commissioner finally decided to allow the adultery claim, heeding the chief commissioner's advice to "treat slave wives as legitimate wives for once you have done away with 'slavery' the status of wifehood must be one and the same. I make them or their paramount pay satisfaction on the same scale as regular wives."[120] Undoubtedly, the former slave and the Sunyani clerk hoped that, the status of slave no longer being recognized, the woman's right to leave her master would be upheld. But the commissioner could not allow such a transformation in the woman's social status without undermining the authority of Asante's chiefs. Thus, she was not transformed into a social adult, liberated from her obligations to her former master. Rather she was redefined as a legitimate wife, a dependent, who had committed adultery.[121]

In case after case, early colonial officials groped their way through thorny contests over dependent status, trying to meet two irreconcilable objectives: the abolition of slavery and the bolstering of chiefs' authority. Much of that authority, as they came to realize, rested on control over dependent persons, especially dependent women. Thus, the judgments in many of these early cases appear confused and, at times, contradictory. They are a real study in colonial ambiguity and ambivalence. A perfect illustration was the case brought before the chief commissioner in 1908 by Bantamahene Osei Mampon. (The Bantamahene also serves as Krontihene in the Kumasi Division.) Mampon was one of the more notorious loyalists who had been awarded a stool by the British after the rising, though as a Mampon royal, he had no legitimate claims to the Bantama/Kronti stools. He was a member of the early triumvirate set up by the British before the rising and also served on the Kumasi Council of Chiefs. In 1908, Osei Mampon complained that one of his "captive women" had been taken to Wassa without his knowledge. He reported that the late Asantehene, Nana Kofi Kakari, had "given the captive woman to a fetishman who sold her to his predecessor for £4." The woman was given to the predecessor's son to marry and they had five children. Her husband had since died and she had returned to Wassa. The Bantamahene claimed that

> If Adjua Badu's people, the Wassaw's, be allowed to take her and children away, it will instigate all other captives mostly forming the Ashanti towns, to leave for their native lands, and this place will be lessened in population. Should these claimants object . . . I will beseech your Honour, legal proceedings for the recovery of the amount of £4 and the children of the captive woman born in Ashanti.[122]

The woman in question, Adjua Badu, presented a seven-page letter to the commissioner in which she refuted Mampon's version of the case. She claimed that after the Wassa king was killed by Karikari, "we children were given to Chief Awoah of Bantumah." Once she came of age, she was given to Kofi Duo to marry. Although most of the Wassa people returned home after the British occupation, she remained with her husband in Kumasi because he had treated her well. After he died, she was brought before Osei Mampon and the issue of her status as slave or free contested. She concluded her letter with the following:

> I respectfully beg your honour to . . . allow me to go home with my children on the following grounds: (1) I was neither bought nor pledged by no one in Ashanti . . . (2) that during the time of Chief Aminamah and his eldest were killed we remain about 200 children and youths which the King of Ashanti handed us over to Chief Kobina Awuah of Bantumah to take charge of us temporary. . . . I respectfully beg that your humble petitioner may be allow to go home free with all her property and children as she came to Ashanti free.[123]

Adjua Badu's argument rested on her contention that she was a captive, had not been sold or pawned, and therefore was free.[124] Furthermore, implicit in that account was a refusal to recognize Mampon as Bantamahene Awuah's legitimate heir. In many ways, her case was compelling, but the commissioner could not accede to her request without undercutting the authority of one of the government's most cooperative and loyal chiefs. Thus, judgment went against her. She was required to pay "release money" of £4 to Osei Mampon. At the same time, and here is where the ambiguity enters the picture, she was allowed to return to Wassa, despite Osei Mampon's claims that such a decision would establish a precedent, which would result in the massive depopulation of much of Asante. [125]

That the authority of chiefs had to be upheld at all costs—even if other agendas were compromised in the process—would continue to inform post–World War I reworkings of the system of rule. Also reproduced in subsequent elaborations of the system was the marginalization of royal women and commoners. Despite the admonitions of Rattray, who argued vehemently that the position of queenmothers should be recognized and supported by the colonial state,[126] the first fully elaborated system for indirect rule in Asante, the 1924 Native Jurisdiction Ordinance, did not recognize the *ahemaa*. "Women," as Arhin has written, "were not recognized on the colonial chief-list, as members of the Native Authority coun-

cils and courts. They had no officially recognized shares in the stool trea-
suries."[127]

In other ways, however, the 1924 Ordinance cleared up much of the
ambiguity of the previous decades. As Tordoff has written, it "left no room
for doubt that Ashanti chiefs held office and exercised powers not by right
but by grace of the administration."[128] It also left little room for maneuver in terms of chiefs' tribunals: "No jurisdiction, civil or criminal, shall
be exercised by any native authority or tribunal whatsoever except as
provided by, and in accordance with the provision of this or some other
ordinance and any order or rules made hereunder."[129] Only chiefs listed
in the ordinance could exercise authority in their jurisdiction. The
ordinance's provisions would eventually be extended to the former
Asantehene, who, having been allowed to return to Kumasi in 1924 as a
private citizen, was recognized as "Kumasihene" in 1926 and ultimately
put in charge of the Kumasi division. The tribunals established under the
1924 Ordinance were empowered to hear both civil and criminal cases.[130]
After an initial period of confusion, made worse by practical problems
like finding enough qualified clerks to staff all of the tribunals, the system became fully operational by the late 1920s.[131]

By the early 1930s, the government had gained enough confidence in the
Asante version of indirect rule, particularly in the Kumasihene's ability to
rule over the troublesome Kumasi Division, that it could begin to imagine a
system of indirect rule that reinstated the Asantehene as traditional ruler over
a "restored Asante confederacy." Thus, in 1935, the Ashanti Confederacy
Council Ordinance created a fully elaborated system of indirect rule, with a
"restored" Confederacy Council and Asantehene Agyeman Prempeh II at the
helm.[132] Under the Native Courts (Ashanti) Ordinance of 1935, courts were
established for Asante in four grades—A, B, C, D—with civil and criminal
jurisdiction.[133] The Asante Confederacy Council itself served as a criminal
court for hearing major constitutional cases and, after 1936, was empowered
to make orders and rules on a number of topics, including so-called "native
custom."[134] As with the 1924 Ordinance, queenmothers were not listed, nor
were their courts recognized by the state.

The system of indirect rule that evolved, administratively and judi-
cially, from 1924 through the Second World War was clearly an odd con-
stellation of old and new, a "colonial hybrid,"[135] as McCaskie has termed
it. In superficial ways, the British could boast of the "restoration" of the
Asante state, but in meaningful and often subtle ways, such boasts ring
hollow. In terms of blocking channels for commoner dissent and
reconfiguring the rank and gendered boundaries of political participation,
the "restored" confederacy and its native courts were a mutation, a colo-

nial invention, having few, if any, parallels with the nineteenth century.[136] Certainly for Asante's first generation of colonized women they consti- tuted a lived chronology of political marginalization.

A COLONIAL CHRONOLOGY OF
MISSIONS, EDUCATION, AND CONVERSION

In contrast to colonial native courts and indirect rule, the stories of mis- sions and education easily cross the intellectual deadzone because mission- ary activity so often predated colonial conquest. Yet Asante, for the most part, kept missionaries at bay until the British occupation in 1896. The mis- sion stories embedded in the reminiscences of Asante's first generation of colonized women, therefore, are very much colonial stories not shared with mothers or grandmothers.[137] It was not until the British occupation of Asante in 1896 that the terrain for mission activity proved at all fertile. Members of the Basel Mission (led by Reverend F. A. Ramseyer), followed by the Wesleyans, were the first to establish a foothold in the region. Though they made some progress in those first years, there were few inroads with the Asante population. Most of the early converts were either migrants to Kumasi, particularly Fantes, or slaves who had been "liberated" by Ramseyer and settled at the mission station. The rising of 1900, moreover, soon destroyed virtually everything that had been built over the previous four years; the Basel station was burned to the ground. Indeed, at least one African catechist, J. A. Hanson, directly connected the Asante Rising to the presence of the mission and more specifically to Asantes' profound hatred of Ramseyer:

> The Ashantis did not like the Gospel which has been brought to them. So
> they intended to stop it, however they like school very well but not the
> Gospel; I say so, because during this rising, from all I heard and learned
> from the Ashantis and the Nkoranzas I saw it was their chief aim to get
> father Ramseyer in their power to do him what they like; they say he has
> been the cause of all the mischiefs done to their country and he has spoiled
> their country. . . . they say he has brought a curse to their country, so they
> all want him to be destroyed.[138]

Though Ramseyer survived the rising, his mission station did not, so in 1901 mission work in Asante was forced to begin anew, yet again.

After 1901, the early missions made slow but steady progress, though most of their schools and churches were primarily frequented by non-Asantes, much as they had been before 1900. Both the Basel and Wesleyan mission organi- zations viewed education as the primary mechanism for gaining converts, so much of their effort went into establishing schools. By 1905, the Basel Mis-

Photo 1.6 Temperance Society, Kumasi, with Rev. Ramseyer, 1908. (Copyright Basel Mission Archive, D-30.17.021. Reprinted with permission.)

sion had established ten schools, with 207 students in attendance, while the Wesleyans had seven schools, with an average overall attendance of 219.[139] The schools were at the infant or elementary level and constituted the only educational initiatives in Asante until the opening of the first government boys' school in January 1910.[140] Overall, the statistics on school attendance and conversion remained fairly stagnant during the first decade of colonial rule. In 1908, the total Christian population in Ashanti was estimated as "2,682, out of a population of half a million souls."[141] School attendance also remained low until the beginning of the First World War.

Why was the process of conversion and education such slow going in Asante during these early years? Certainly, it reflected some of the hostility toward Europeans, and missions specifically, that was described in Hanson's 1900 report. A common saying at this time, according to Hanson, was a stern warning to Asantes that "the white ants which will eat your flesh when dead, eat your clothes when alive."[142] Moreover, as Busia and others have suggested, the slow progress had much to do with the fact that chiefs, for the most part, refused to support or encourage mission efforts. As the 1905 "Report on Ashanti" concluded, "the chiefs are afraid to encourage a movement that experience tells them will, in course of time, undermine their power."[143] Indeed, writing from Bompata in 1901, African catechist Samuel Boateng reported that while some kings "are seeking after some teachers or scholars who will read and write their letters for them, they are . . . going after temporal but not spiritual helpers who would bring them to their Lord and savior."[144]

But the reasons for the limited progress made in these early years is, perhaps, more complicated than post-1900 hostility or lack of chiefly support. Conversion is often associated with moments of instability and uncertainty; the situation in Asante in those early years, it seems, could have easily led to mass conversion, but it did not. The reports of African catechists resident in Asante during these early years point to additional factors worthy of consideration. Catechist Martinson's biographer, for example, wrote that he found converts difficult to come by because Christianity was regarded "as the fetish of the white man." That Ramseyer's first converts and students were emancipated slaves also cast a pall over early initiatives: "people regarded schools as institutions purposely established for slaves."[145] It is also possible that cocoa, as it spread into Asante, worked against successful evangelization. That was certainly the conclusion drawn by the Basel Mission for the Gold Coast as a whole in 1902. Though admitting that it encouraged the spread of cocoa as "a more solid basis . . . for the moral progress of our congregations," the mission came to associate the "flourishing state of the Cocoa Industry" with the "lust of gain and self-indulgence . . . worked up by it to access. . . . A real hunger for money and pleasure has taken hold of the people."[146] That cocoa could be a strong competitor in the battle for hearts and souls in Asante was certainly predicted in catechists' reports from the south. Charles Martinson, then based in Apasare, reported a Sunday evening meeting in which someone asked, "How can we present our bodies a living sacrifice to the Lord?" An old man stood to answer: "Crucify the old man and then cocoa!" When asked why cocoa needed to be crucified, the old man explained, "Which of you can tell the number of times cocoa is mentioned in a day here. . . . I am sure most of you think more of your cocoa than you think of God. If God will have a full place in your hearts, the word cocoa will scarcely be mentioned."[147]

Cocoa, however, was not the only "belief system" competing for Asante adherents during these early years. As several Basel catechists reported, the anti-witchcraft cult, *Aberewa* ('old woman'), was widespread in Asante by 1907 and was far more successful at gaining adherents than were the Christian missions.[148] In his annual report from Kumasi, Nathan Asare wrote, "We were troubled and disheartened when the worship of *Aberewa* . . . prevailed in the country; all the people directed their special attention to that worship and none did care to become Christian."[149] McCaskie's more recent analysis of *Aberewa* provides ample insight into why the cult proved more popular than Christianity at this historical juncture of uncertainty:

> It is against . . . [a] background of ambiguity that the anti-witchcraft cults of colonial Asante must surely be set. When we come down to cases we can see that they flourished in a milieu of generalized anxiety. . . . they were quite consciously all things to all men. To those troubled by the aggravated tensions of kinship relations they offered protection against a teeming universe of threats—adultery, envy, theft, cursing, the bearing of false witness, poisoning, and barrenness. To those seeking enrichment in the cash economy they promised success, prosperity, and personal and economic protection against maleficence and even guarantees against bankruptcy. The extravagant range of their claim—itself a direct reflection of widespread popular concern—helped to ensure a broad constituency.[150]

Against such competition, the missions had little chance of success. In 1908, however, Asante's chief commissioner banned the worship of *Aberewa*, as a "political and social menace, which undermined chiefly power, unsettled the people, and drained the country of money."[151] And by all accounts, the cult virtually disappeared over the following year.[152] Though subsequent anti-witchcraft cults surfaced during the colonial period, none were considered by the missions as direct competitors with Christianity in the way *Aberewa* had been. Indeed, contemporary observers like Asare were certain that the abolition of *Aberewa* directly contributed to subsequent mission successes: "the Lord by his infinite power turned the matter quite otherwise. The celebrated worship of *Aberewa* which made the people even grow mad, was after all frustrated by the English government. . . . the door is [now] widely opened to the Gospel amongst the people."[153] More recent scholarship has shared this view by linking the abolition of *Aberewa* to an increase in conversions after 1908.[154]

And the conversion statistics for the period after 1908 do suggest dramatic growth. By 1912, the Christian population in Asante was estimated at over 6,000—an increase of nearly three-fold from 1908.[155] By 1926, the Wesleyan mission alone was claiming nearly 20,000 adherents.[156] The statistics for schools were equally impressive. By 1914, for example, the Basel Mission was operating 25 elementary schools with some 760 pupils; the Wesleyans had 11 day schools with 585 pupils; the Catholics had two schools with 222 pupils and the Anglicans (who began work in that year), had one school with 181 students. In the same year, the government opened its first girls' school in Kumasi. By the end of the year, it had enrolled 62 girls. Perhaps what was more indicative of change were the percentages of students who were actually Asante. Asantes made up 34 percent of the students at the Girls' Government School and nearly 53 percent at the Boys' School.[157] By 1927–28, there were over 1,000 children in the government primary schools and over 3,000 in the mission schools.[158] Though these statistics do not suggest widespread educational opportunities for Asante by the 1920s, given a population for the region of over 400,000,[159] they do suggest dramatic growth after 1910.

But if Christianity did, in fact, begin to take firmer root after 1908, the abolition of *Aberewa* could not take full credit. The figures charting the growing success of missions and schools must be understood in light of the rapid economic and social change described above. Catechists' reports from the period consistently lament the fact that the rapid growth in education and the concomitant process of conversion too often reflected the economic motives of aspirant women and men, rather than a desire for salvation. As early as 1907, Samuel Boateng was bemoaning the fact that "Xtians [Christians] became converts to free themselves from all the laws, not only slaves, but also free borns think so; because they believe Xtianity is a place of worldly gain, but not worldly loss." He and other catechists even found that when they tried to encourage their converts to pay taxes to the government or to the chiefs, the converts were astonished. "They do not understand why Xtians," wrote Boateng, "who had released themselves from all the legal authorities are to pay again such taxes; and if it be so, they rather wish to return to their old state. Those Xtians show plainly that they are nominal Xtians only."[160] Three years later, Martinson, reporting from Bompata, was similarly discouraged by people running "away to Christianity to shield themselves from the knives and tyranny of their chiefs and master or [to] protect their money; Christianity is a mere cloak for their lives and properties; their real god is money and they are therefore opposed to [the] Christian spirit of liberality."[161] The shallowness of conversion seemed to be a particular problem with regard to Kumasi, which was perceived as drawing adherents away from the Word. It was Boateng, again, who bemoaned the fact that Christian scholars, after returning from Kumasi, "have quite other minds." Rather than continue their course of study, they preferred to "become clerks, etc. as their mates in order to make money as quick as possible."[162]

That Asantes were turning to Christianity for "worldly gain" or to escape the power of their chiefs presented a real problem for mission leaders. Indeed, W.E.G. Waterworth of the Wesleyan Mission reported in 1915 that an entire congregation in one village left the church *en masse* because the mission did not "defend them when in trouble with their chiefs."[163] If the relationship between Christians and chiefs was a problem for mission leaders, it presented a peculiar quandary for British officials—not unlike the quandary they faced in attempting to abolish slavery and pawnage while still upholding the authority of chiefs. As the numbers of Christian Asantes began to grow after the first decade of colonial rule, the government was inundated with complaints from chiefs whose Christians were refusing to heed their summons or to provide service. In 1912, therefore, a meeting of mission heads, chiefs, and the governor was held in Kumasi in order to draw up a workable solution that would uphold chiefs' authority and at the same time further the work of the missions. The solution eventually agreed upon sought to distinguish secular duties owed to a chief from duties associated with "fetish rites." Thus, no Christian could be called upon to swear back an oath, but if an oath was sworn against him, "a Christian should be bound to accept it as a summons to attend the Court." If the Christian refused to attend the court, an official of the chiefs' court could be sent to apprehend him, the Christian thereby being responsible for paying "the cost of sending the messengers." The agreement further stated that "no Christian be called on to perform any fetish rite or service." However, "he shall be bound to render customary service to his Chief on ceremonial occasions in which no element of fetish worship is involved e.g. carrying an umbrella for a chief when proceeding to state to meet the Governor or any other senior official." The document concluded with a rather vague admonition that "an effort should be made to draw a distinctive [*sic*] between fetish and purely ceremonial service."[164] Overall, the agreement went some distance in clarifying the relationships between chiefs and Christian subjects, but enough ambiguity remained that Christians would continually find themselves in court throughout much of the colonial period accused of refusing to give service or to participate in "fetish rites."[165]

Asante women converts were certainly among those caught in the ambiguity. Though the bulk of mission conversion efforts, including educational initiatives, were aimed primarily at men until well into the 1920s, Asante women could be counted among the first converts, though it is unclear from the documentation what percentage they constituted. Their souls, by and large, were not won by the mission through schooling or catechism and, in this sense, their stories of conversion differ from those of many Asante male converts. Nor did they tend to flee to missions seeking refuge from forced marriages, abusive husbands and in-laws, or enslavement, as their counterparts did in many parts of southern Africa.[166] The Asante women who turned to Christianity in those early years, at least according to the catechists' accounts, tended to do so after a series of failed encounters with so-called fetish priests (*akɔmfo*). Often they were in search of fertility or a cure for an ailing child. One woman's first-person account of her conversion, included in Nathan Asare's 1908 report from Kumasi, was not atypical. Ama Seneapem, of Tanoso, was baptized on Christmas day and took the name Mina:

> I am a rigid heathen; I have worshipped several fetishes especially the celebrated Tanno. I have up till now spent all what I earned for the fetishes, I do this in order to be happy and prosper in my doings and to get a long life for myself, children and grand-children, but in the contrary my children used to die unexpectedly and untimely. Six months ago . . . my grand-daughter about 14 years of age who cares for me fell sick. I asked Tanno to save her; the fetish assured me that my sick grand-daughter would live, but I must bring one sheep and drinkable for a sacrifice; I immediately brought all to the fetish man and just on the following day, the sick girl expired. Now I have seen . . . by experience that fetishes are not real helpers, I worshipped and sacrificed many things to them for nothing, hence from this time forward, I want to put myself and the rest of my children under the protection of God alone.[167]

Stories such as Mina's are included in virtually every catechist's report. While they may tell us something of the motivation behind Asante women's conversions to Christianity, they do not provide the social historian with any sense of the numbers of women so moved. Indeed, with the exception of scattered statistics on mission education that are broken down according to sex, there is little quantifiable information in the colonial record that can help us to construct a full, gendered chronology of the missionary impact on Asante.

Yet in much the same way that gendered chronologies of markets or of cocoa demonstrate the ways in which women experienced historical change in profoundly different ways from men, surely a gendered chronology of missions and education in Asante would highlight the differential experiences of men and women with churches, missions, and schools. Despite the female conversion stories that provide so much color in early catechists' reports, most of the fragmentary evidence at hand, including the life stories we collected, suggests Asante women were little impacted by churches and schools (mission or government) before 1930. We do not have statistics that break down church attendance by sex, but we do know that girls' enrollment in mission schools lagged far behind that of boys. By 1928, there were only 347 girls in mission schools in Asante, compared to 2,743 boys.[168] On the qualitative side, the evidence is perhaps more compelling. There was virtually no official discussion in missionary circles in the first decades of colonial rule regarding the necessity of converting women. The first such calls date from the late 1920s when missions came to realize a pressing need for Christian wives to serve as partners for male catechists and teachers. As M. V. Hunter wrote in 1930, "Until this year there has been no girls' school in connection with the Ashanti Mission, a mass movement area, with the result that the two hundred and seventeen teachers and catechists have mostly been obliged to marry ignorant girls. How can a girl set an example of Christian homelife if she does not know what it is?"[169] By the late 1920s, the main mission organizations operating in Asante had begun to send out women missionaries to work closely with Asante women. In addition to serving as teachers in girls' schools and organizing fellowship and prayer groups, the women missionaries became involved in a variety of maternal and child welfare efforts.[170]

Certainly most of the women who are the focus of this book—those who made up Asante's first generation of colonized women—had only fleeting and fragmentary encounters with missions' education or maternal welfare initiatives until comparatively late in the colonial period. The overwhelming majority did not attend school; most did not begin attending church until the late 1930s or 1940s, some not until much later. Those who did were often brought into the church through women's fellowship groups organized by early women missionaries. Yet as subsequent chapters will show, in subtle and often indirect ways, the presence of missions and schools shaped the contours of women's daily lives much earlier. That many of their children, especially their sons, attended schools for at least a few years meant that the question of school fees featured prominently in conjugal negotiations. Indeed, reminiscences about this period suggest that school fees were a major source of contention within conjugal relationships as husbands and wives battled over who should pay the fees and what rights were conferred on the parent who did. In other ways, the missions had an impact upon women's lives by creating a broader public space in which new kinds of claims could be staked. For example, as the cash economy expanded and many wives found themselves providing labor to their husbands in cash-earning activities like cocoa farming, they would increasingly come to demand a share of the wealth produced, upon the death of their spouse. Such demands ran directly counter to the dictates of matrilineal inheritance in Asante but resonated closely with Christian mission policy on inheritance.[171] Though Asante wives undoubtedly would have challenged matrilineal inheritance regardless of the stance of Christian missions, the missions' quite public pronouncements on the rights of wives and children to inherit from their husbands certainly did their case no harm. In short, though Christian missions do not appear as salient features in life stories until after the 1930s, their presence profoundly shaped a range of life experiences—from school fees to cocoa farming to inheritance—and are thus intimately connected to alternative chronologies that cross the intellectual deadzone.

CONCLUSION

The chronologies of continuity and change explored in this chapter have been aimed at locating Asante's first generation of colonized women in unfolding historical processes that defy many of the prevailing meta-narratives of Asante historiography. These narratives, which either end or begin at the turn of the century, have, with few exceptions, conflated the lived experiences of men and women into one ungendered story. Alternative chronologies, when woven together, make evident the ways in which British colonialism in Asante was uneven and episodic, gendered and gendering. For example, the chronology of conjugal production and exchange, which reached far across the deadzone, demonstrates how women's labor changed steadily and continuously from at least the early nineteenth century, as ever-increasing proportions of a wife's labor were aimed at production for the market. By the time of the cocoa revolution, the process of incorporation into the market economy had accelerated exponentially. The market economy became a full-fledged cash economy, and monetization, as Arhin has demonstrated, reshaped nearly every aspect of social, religious, and political life.[172] But if the chronology of conjugal production and economic expansion was one that increasingly drew women in, the chronology of politics, of courts and custom, was one of marginalization, though even here, as we have seen, women experienced marginalization in uneven ways well into the 1930s. The chronology of missions and education—that most "colonial" of chronologies running through women's life stories—was the most attenuated of all we have explored. For most Asante women of the first colonized generation, missions and schools were first manifest as part of the chronology of conjugal production and reproduction, as husbands and wives struggled over responsibilities and obligations regarding school fees and inheritance. For most women, missions would not become part and parcel of a chronology of conversion until at least the 1930s.

While these alternative chronologies can help us cross the intellectual deadzone so lamented by McCaskie and can expose the gendered and episodic meanings of colonialism for Asante's first generation of colonized women, they are exceedingly difficult for the historian to handle. They are, as we have seen, complex and overlapping and present a fairly serious challenge to linear narration. Though they are woven "seamlessly" together, as McCaskie would say, in the life stories that were shared with us, weaving them into a historical narrative that is attentive to production and exchange *and* to the complex and contested ways women and men negotiated their daily lives requires some strategizing. As Jane Guyer has recently argued, "The history of exchange and the history of relationships must permeate one another, but to take on both phenomena at once, as they changed over time under separate influences and with interconnected dynamics, may demand strategic substantive entry points and new analytical tools that can reduce the complexity to manageability."[173] In many ways, the "strategic substantive entry points" that we utilize in the chapters that follow emerged from the life stories shared with us. In those stories, marriage and childrearing— conjugal production and reproduction—proved important entry points for understanding and rethinking the world in which this first colonized generation lived. Marrying (*-ware*) and parenting (*-tan*), therefore, are the lenses we utilize to bring into sharp relief the ways in which this extraordinary generation of women shaped and were shaped by the colonial world.[174]

NOTES

1. Although it was difficult to ascertain the precise ages of all the women we interviewed, there are probably two exceptions to this characterization. Afua Sekyiwaa of Effiduasi reported that four days after she was born, Prempeh was taken into exile (1896). Beatrice Nyarko, who was certainly over 100 when Allman spoke to her, claimed to remember, in detail, Prempeh's arrest. See Allman: Afua Sekyiwaa, Effiduasi, 24 August 1992; Beatrice Nyarko, Effiduasi, 30 June 1993.

2. McCaskie, "Accumulation II," 19.

3. Ibid.

4. Unpublished song quoted in Dennis Austin, *Politics in Ghana, 1946–1960* (London: Oxford University Press, 1964), 275. According to Austin, "the song was written in *twi* by Fred Sarpong, a journalist and trader and NLM member."

5. Earlier efforts to introduce cocoa made by the Basel Mission in the 1850s and 1860s were largely unsuccessful. See Polly Hill, *Migrant Cocoa-Farmers of Southern Ghana: A Study in Rural Capitalism* (Cambridge: Cambridge University Press, 1963), 170–72. The specifics of cocoa's arrival in the Gold Coast are disputed. One well-known account credits Tetteh Quashie, a Ga blacksmith, with bringing cocoa from plantations on Fernando Po to Akwapim in the Gold Coast Colony around 1878 and introducing its cultivation to area farmers. The other popular account centers upon Sir William Brandford Griffith, then governor of the Gold Coast Colony, who introduced cocoa from Sao Tome in the mid-1880s, set up nurseries for its cultivation at Aburi, and supplied the resulting seedlings to the local Akwapim farmers. See Arhin, "Monetization," 103; Austin, "Capitalist Relations," 65–66.

6. J. Adomako-Sarfoh, "Migrant Asante Cocoa Farmers and Their Families," in Christine Oppong, ed., *Legon Family Research Papers* 1 (Legon, Ghana: Institute of African Studies, University of Ghana, 1974), 130–34.

7. Public Record Office, London, Colonial Office [hereafter, PRO, CO] 96/433: Governor to Colonial Office, dated [hereafter dd.] Kintampo, 22 December, 1905, "Ashanti Tour of Inspection."

8. PRO, CO 98/18: Gold Coast, "Ashanti: Report for 1910" (London, 1911).

9. PRO, CO 98/24: Gold Coast, "Ashanti: Report for 1914" (Accra, 1915). The Ashanti Confederacy Council came to share this concern at a much later date. It ordered "a ban on deforestation for cocoa production" between 1938 and 1947 because of concerns that too little attention was being paid to food production. Arhin, "Monetization," 103. Also see K. A. Busia, *The Position of the Chief in the Modern Political System of Ashanti* (London: Frank Cass, 1968), 121.

10. Roger Southall, "Farmers, Traders and Brokers in the Gold Coast Cocoa Economy," *CJAS* 11:2 (1978), 196, citing Roberts Papers [University of Birmingham Library], Annual Dinner of the Cape Coast Chamber of Commerce, 21 May 1921.

11. Tashjian: Akua Ababo, Mamponten, 10 September 1990.

12. Tashjian: Afua Dufie, Oyoko, 31 October 1990.

13. Tashjian, Adwowa Fodwo, Mamponten, 1 October 1990.

14. See Austin, "Capitalist Relations"; Beverly Grier, "Pawns"; Mikell, *Cocoa and Chaos* and "The State," 225–44; Busia, *Position of the Chief*; David Kimble, *A Political History of Ghana: The Rise of Gold Coast Nationalism 1850–1928* (Oxford: Clarendon Press, 1963); Tordoff, *Ashanti*.

15. See, for example, Kwame Arhin, "The Ashanti Rubber Trade with the Gold Coast in the Eighteen-Nineties," *Africa* 42: 1 (1972), 33–43; Arhin, "Ashanti Northern Trade"; Arhin, "Economic and Social Significance of Rubber," especially 56–71; Arhin, "Trade, Accumulation and the State," 524–37; Austin, "Capitalist Relations"; Austin, "Capitalists and Chiefs"; Austin, "'No Elders Were Present'"; Raymond Dumett, "The Rubber Trade of the Gold Coast and Asante in the Nineteenth Century: African Innovation and Market Responsiveness," *JAH* 12:1 (1971), 79–101; Joseph LaTorre, "Wealth Surpasses Everything: An Economic History of Asante, 1750–1874" (Ph.D. dissertation, University of California, Berkeley, 1978).

16. Austin, "Capitalist Relations," 260. See also his "Capitalists and Chiefs," 66.

17. Arhin, "Ashanti Northern Trade," 370–72.

18. Arhin, "Ashanti Rubber Trade," 41; and Arhin, *The Expansion of Cocoa Production: The Working Conditions of Migrant Cocoa Farmers in the Central and Western Regions* (Legon, Ghana: Institute of African Studies, University of Ghana, 1985), vii–viii.

19. Austin, "'No Elders Were Present,'" 27. In this pathbreaking article, Austin dates that revolution to 1807 and the "closing of the Atlantic slave market," thereby undercutting arguments for a chronology that ruptures Asante economic history at the turn of the century. He also eschews later nineteenth-century events, like the British invasion of 1874 or the civil war of the 1880s, as significant moments of chronological rupture. Cf. Arhin, "Ashanti Rubber Trade," 33; Arhin, "Pressure of Cash," 455; Arhin, "Trade, Accumulation and the State," 528; McCaskie, "*Ahyiamu*," 175–76. Mikell argues for 1874 as the year from which to date "the modernization of Ashanti life." See her *Cocoa and Chaos*, 47 and 54.

20. Arhin, "Ashanti Northern Trade," 364; Arhin, "Pressure of Cash," 457; LaTorre, "Wealth Surpasses Everything," 67, 362–65; Austin, "Human Pawning," 134.

21. LaTorre, "Wealth Surpasses Everything," 66–69; Arhin, "Trade, Accumulation and the State," 528–29; Arhin, "Ashanti Northern Trade," 371; and Arhin, "Pressure of Cash," 354–55.

22. Kwame Arhin, "Savannah Contributions to the Asante Political Economy," in Enid Schildkrout, ed., *The Golden Stool: Studies of the Asante Centre and Periphery*

(New York: Anthropological Papers of the American Museum of Natural History, 1987), 57.

23. LaTorre, "Wealth Surpasses Everything," 361, 382; Arhin, "Trade, Accumulation and the State," 528–30; Arhin, "Savannah Contributions," 57; and Arhin, "Ashanti Northern Trade," 371.

24. For a discussion of mining under Asante royal or public control, see Ivor Wilks, "The Golden Stool and the Elephant Tail: Wealth in Asante," in his *Forests of Gold*,157; and Wilks, *Asante*, 435–36.

25. Wilks, "Golden Stool," 157; Raymond Dumett, "Precolonial Gold Mining and the State in the Akan Region: With a Critique of the Terray Hypothesis," *Research in Economic Anthropology* 2 (1979), 45; LaTorre, "Wealth Surpasses Everything," 60. In 1990, Adwowa Fodwo of Mamponten told Tashjian that "small boys who can see [well]" still gather gold dust when it rains. Tashjian: Adwowa Fodwo, Mamponten, 9 October 1990.

26 . Arhin, "Gold-mining," 92-93. On the conjugal and gendered production of gold, see also Arhin, "Succession and Gold Mining at Manso-Nkwanta," *Research Review* (Legon, Ghana: Institute of African Studies, University of Ghana) 6:3 (1970), 107; Dumett, "Precolonial Gold Mining," 44–48; LaTorre, "Wealth Surpasses Everything," 60–61; Wilks, "Golden Stool," 157.

27. Arhin, "Gold Mining," 93; Arhin, "Succession and Gold Mining," 107; Dumett, "Precolonial Gold Mining," 44–46. Slaves may well have served as a far more important source of labor in royal mines. On the use of slave labor to increase commoner gold mining productivity, see Austin, "'No Elders Were Present,'" 19.

28. Wilks argues that rubber collection in Asante reached significant proportions earlier than the late 1890s. See his *Asante*, 703. Arhin notes that an early attempt to introduce rubber, made by the Basel Mission in the 1860s, proved unsuccessful. Arhin, "Economic and Social Significance," 51; and Arhin, "Ashanti Rubber Trade," 34. The proportion of Colony rubber exports that came from Asante is not clear in the official export records, though historians generally assert that Asante rapidly came to contribute the lion's share of the Colony's rubber exports after 1896. Rubber dominated exports until the international disruptions of shipping occasioned by World War I; the region's rubber exports were subsequently supplanted by higher grade rubber obtained in the forests of southeast Asia. See K. B. Dickson, "Origins of Ghana's Cocoa Industry," *Ghana Notes and Queries* 5 (1963), 9; Dumett, "Rubber Trade," 79–100; Arhin "Economic and Social Significance of Rubber," 50–51.

29. Dumett, "Rubber Trade," 89; and Arhin, "Ashanti Rubber Trade," 38.

30. Arhin, "Economic and Social Significance of Rubber," 60–61.

31. Arhin, "Gold-mining," 93; and Arhin, "Ashanti Rubber Trade," 39.

32. Arhin, "Ashanti Rubber Trade," 41; and Arhin, "Economic and Social Significance of Rubber," 60.

33. Tordoff, *Ashanti*, 188.

34. Kimble, *Political History*, 30.

35. Ibid., 56–58.

36. In 1909 approximately 65 miles of district roads were completed, as Busia writes, largely by "unpaid or partly paid labour supplied by the chiefs." In 1911, similar labor arrangements produced 85 miles of roads. Busia, *Position of the Chief*, 119.

37. See Busia, *Position of the Chief*, 119; Kimble, *Political History*, 480. See also P. R. Gould, *The Development of the Transportation Pattern in Ghana* (Evanston, IL: Northwestern University Press, 1960).

38. That they could accomplish this, and at great savings for export firms, was obvious as early as 1904, when a head-load of 60 lbs. took eight days by foot, at a cost of 26s. to reach the coast, but by rail it could now be transported in three days at a cost of only 4s. per load. Kimble, *Political History*, 30.

39. Ibid., 480–81.

40. Tordoff, *Ashanti*, 191.

41. For related discussions of the ways in which women's history has challenged prevailing notions of continuity and change, see the roundtable "Theoretical Issues" section of the *Journal of Women's History* 9:3 (1997), 73–118. Contributors include Judith Bennett, Sandra Greene, Karen Offen, and Gerda Lerner. Africanists will be particularly interested in Greene's contribution, "A Perspective on African Women's History: Comment on 'Confronting Continuity'" (95–104).

42. Wilks, *Asante*, 1–79.

43. Wilks, "Golden Stool," 155.

44. For a definition of "Greater Asante," see Arhin, "Structure of Greater Ashanti." For a slightly different analysis, see Wilks, *Asante*, 43–47.

45. Wilks, *Asante*, 13 and 25.

46. Austin, "'No Elders Were Present,'" 11–12. Austin here is drawing from Wilks' citation of *The Western Echo*, 1:10 (14 February 1868), 8, which reports Freeman's views. See Wilks, "Golden Stool," 157. Cf. Arhin, "Trade, Accumulation and the State," 528–29; McCaskie, *State and Society*, 35.

47. Wilks, "Golden Stool," 157. For an overview of historiographical treatment of trade and markets, see Austin, "'No Elders Were Present,'" 11–16.

48. See, for example, Arhin, "Peasants," 472–75.

49. See, for example, Arhin, "Trade, Accumulation and the State," 528; Wilks, *Asante*, 699–705.

50. Austin, "'No Elders Were Present,'" 18–19.

51. Austin, "Between Abolition and *Jihad*," 107.

52. Austin, "'No Elders Were Present,'" 19.

53. Ibid., 19–20, quoting Elizabeth Eldredge, *A South African Kingdom: The Pursuit of Security in Nineteenth-Century Lesotho* (Cambridge: Cambridge University Press, 1993), 124.

54. Austin, "'No Elders Were Present,'" 20.

55. PRO, CO 96/433: Governor of the Gold Coast to Colonial Office, dd. Kintampo, 22 December 1905, "Ashanti Tour of Inspection."

56. T. Edward Bowdich, *Mission from Cape Coast Castle to Ashantee* (London: John Murray, 1819), 324.

57. Tordoff, *Ashanti*, 96, citing 1898 "Report on Ashanti."

58. Busia, *Position of the Chief*, 124.

59. LaTorre notes that few nineteenth-century sources mention women in wholesale or retail marketing. See his "Wealth Surpasses Everything," 146. An exception is Beecham, who describes women "transacting business in the market," but it is unclear from the account whether they were acting as buyers, or sellers, or both. John Beecham, *Ashantee and the Gold Coast* (London: John Mason, 1841), 129. W. J. Coppin, who was in Kumasi

during the interregnum, describes women and children moving from the market to the River Subin with baskets of earth on their head in order to pan for gold. (We know from Bowdich that before the breakdown in central authority it had been against the law to sweep up gold dust from the market. Anything dropped on the ground belonged to the state. See Bowdich, *Mission,* 76.) Coppin's description puts women in the market, but, again, it is unclear whether they were there to buy or sell or solely to gather earth in order to pan for gold. See Methodist Missionary Society [hereafter, MMS], London, Wesleyan Methodist Missionary Society [hereafter WMMS], Special Series/Biography: Reverend W. J. Coppin's Journal of Visit to Kumasi, 1885.

60. See LaTorre, "Wealth Surpasses Everything," 146–47.

61. Austin, "'No Elders Were Present,'" 20.

62. Gracia Clark, *Onions,* 318. Much of the argument that follows draws from Clark's important work. On the growth of the market in Asante, particularly in Kumasi, see, especially, 316–29.

63. Ibid., 316.

64. Ibid., 318; and Aidoo, "Women," 32.

65. Clark, *Onions,* 318.

66. Ibid., 321.

67. J. G. Christaller, *Dictionary of the Asante and Fante Language Called Tshi (Twi)* (Basel, Switzerland: Basel Evangelical Missionary Society, 1933), 10.

68. Wilks, *Asante,* 725. Wilks notes the generic meaning of *batani* was "trader" but argues it was "used especially to refer to the public or official traders." Cf. Christaller, *Dictionary,* 10.

69. See Tashjian, "It's Mine and It's Ours," 67–79.

70. Tashjian: Afua Nyame, Mamponten, 24 July 1990.

71. Tashjian: Abena Afe, Mamponten, 28 September 1990.

72. Tashjian: Obaa Kro, Mamponten, 7 August 1990. For a description of the bead trade and its history see Robertson, *Sharing the Same Bowl,* 103–6.

73. Tashjian: Ama Akyaa, Oyoko, 23 October 1990.

74. Tashjian: Theresa Anokye, Mamponten, 24 September 1990.

75. Tashjian: Yaa Akom, Mamponten, 11 October 1990.

76. PRO, CO 96/416: "Report on Ashanti for the Year 1903," by Lieutenant F. Henderson, Acting Chief Commissioner.

77. Ibid.

78. Busia, *Position of the Chief,* 123; Kwame Arhin, *The City of Kumasi: Past, Present and Future* (Legon, Ghana: Institute of African Studies, University of Ghana, 1992), 16.

79. Bowdich, *Mission,* 324; Wilks, *Asante,* 374; Kwame Arhin, "The Political Economy of a Princely City," paper presented at the Institute of African Studies Symposium on "The City of Kumasi: Past, Present and Future," 13–16 December 1990, 3. The numbers could fluctuate dramatically depending on times of war or peace. During festivals like *Adae* and *Odwira,* it could swell to 40,000 or more. Arhin, "Political Economy," 4.

80. Based on Wilks, *Asante,* 90. For a discussion of the method used to obtain these nineteenth-century population figures, see 87–93.

81. Ibid., 90–91; and Alfred Kwasi Opoku, "The Population of Kumasi: A Retrospect and Prospect," paper presented at the Institute of African Studies Symposium on "The City of Kumasi: Past, Present and Future," 13–16 December 1990, 4.

82. For a full critique of census-taking for this period, see E.V.T. Engman, *Population of Ghana, 1850–1960* (Accra: Ghana Universities Press, 1986), especially 34–47. See also Wilks, *Asante*, 90–93.

83. PRO, CO 98/14: Gold Coast, "Report on Ashanti for 1904."

84. Gold Coast, *Report on the Census of the Population, 1911* (Accra: Government Printer, n.d.).

85. Ibid., 5. See also Engman, *Population*, 77; and Gold Coast, *Census of the Population, 1948* (Accra: Government Printer, 1950).

86. Opoku found that 26.3 percent of population growth between 1921 and 1931 and 26.5 percent between 1931 and 1948 was due to migration. Opoku, "Population of Kumasi," 5.

87. Teresa Barnes, *"We Women Worked So Hard": Social Reproduction in Colonial Harare, Zimbabwe, 1930–1956* (Portsmouth, NH: Heinemann, 1999).

88. Opoku, "Population of Kumasi," 11. It is important to note that this trend continued through the independence period to such an extent that by 1984 there were 94.3 males to 100 females.

89. PRO, CO 96/433: Governor of the Gold Coast to Colonial Office, dd. Kintampo, 22 December 1905, "Ashanti Tour of Inspection."

90. Tordoff, *Ashanti*, 193. By 1957 the market covered 25 acres and had almost 8,000 traders (193 n. 3). Here Tordoff cites P. C. Garlick, "African Traders in Kumasi," African Business Series, no. 1, Economics Research Division, University College of Ghana (Legon: mimeographed, 1959).

91. Tordoff, *Ashanti*, 194.

92. Tordoff, *Ashanti*, 194 n. 2, citing the speech as quoted in K.A.J. Nyarko, "The Development of Kumasi," *Bulletin of the Ghana Geographical Association* 4:1 (Legon, Ghana, January 1959), 6.

93. See, for example, Bowdich, *Mission*, 322. Wilks also cites "Huydecoper's Journal," entry for 26 May 1816, which contains the following description: "the streets are very clean and straight, and the houses excellently built, the latter being fairly tall but for the most part of only one storey." Wilks, *Asante*, 375.

94. Rattray, *Ashanti*, 84.

95. Tordoff, *Ashanti*, 67–109. Tordoff's account remains one of the most thorough treatments of the imposition of colonial rule in Asante.

96. Tordoff, *Ashanti*, 79–80; 82–83.

97. Rattray, *Ashanti Law*, 105–6.

98. Tordoff, *Ashanti*, 83. For examples of cases referred to the Native Committee, see National Archives of Ghana—Kumasi [hereafter, NAGK], SCT/204: Magistrates Court, Civil Record Book 1, 1897–1898. Please note: all reference numbers to files in the National Archives in Kumasi reflect the listing system in use prior to 1997. In 1997–1998, the archive underwent a massive reorganization and new classes and listings have been created. Most files, however, will be easily identifiable under the new improved system.

99. See Busia, *Position of the Chief*, 102–4. In the years before 1924, there were numerous changes in administrative structure. In 1907, the divisions were renamed "provinces." In 1913, the provinces were subdivided into districts. See R. B. Bening, "Evolution of Administrative Boundaries of Ashanti, 1896–1951," *JAS* 5:2 (1978), 123–50; and Tordoff, *Ashanti*, 119–21.

100. Tordoff, *Ashanti*, 165.

101. Ibid.

102. McCaskie, "*Ahyiamu*," 185.

103. Tordoff, *Ashanti*, 151.

104. See, for example, McCaskie's fascinating discussion of the careers of Kwame Tua and Kwame Frimpon in "Accumulation II," 11–13.

105. PRO, CO 96/675: Ashanti Native Jurisdiction Ordinance, "Some Notes on 'The Kumasi Council of Chiefs'" by W. R. Gosling, District Commissioner, Kumasi, 1927.

106. Busia provides a number of such cases in *Position of the Chief*, 105–7.

107. PRO, CO 98/17: "Report on Ashanti, 1908."

108. PRO, CO 96/493: Chief Commissioner to Acting Colonial Secretary, dd. Coomassie, 24 December 1909.

109. For a full account, see Wilks, *Asante*, 535–38. Wilks describes the overthrow as a "coup." Austin's recent revisionist account, which builds from his argument that commoners were broadly involved in trade, characterizes the overthrow as a "rising of the commoners." Austin, "'No Elders Were Present,'" 24.

110. Busia, *Position of the Chief*, 11.

111. Ibid., 106 and 11.

112. See National Archives of Ghana—Accra [hereafter, NAGA], ADM 11/1/1318: Agogo Native Affairs, 1920, for correspondence relating to this case.

113. Ibid., "Enquiry Held at Bompata," 8 May 1917.

114. NAGA, ADM 50/5/18: "District Commissioner's Diary," Juaso, entry for 20 February 1917.

115. Gold Coast, Ashanti Administration Ordinance, No. 1 of 1902. For a summary of the provisions and tribunal jurisdictions, see PRO, CO 554/653: Gold Coast, *Report of Commission on Native Courts* (Accra: Government Printer, 1951).

116. Ibid., 31. See Victoria Tashjian, "The Diaries of A. C. Duncan-Johnstone: A Preliminary Analysis of British Involvement in the 'Native Courts' of Colonial Asante," *Ghana Studies* 1 (1998), 137–53, for an overview of the ways in which D.C.s were legally empowered to meddle in the tribunals' functionings before 1924. The relatively few recognized tribunals may actually have been affected by these regulations since D.C.s held considerable power over tribunals between 1902 and 1924, at least in theory, and, as this article argues, sometimes in practice.

117. See, for example, NAGK, SCT/204: Kumasi Magistrate's Court, Civil Record Books, 1897–1924; SCT/24: Record Books of the Chief Commissioner's Court, 1897–1924; ADM 175/1–10: Kumasi District Commissioner's Court, Civil Record Books, 1907–35. On the proliferation of legal venues in the colonial period and the recourse subordinates made to those new venues when they judged them more likely to be sympathetic than indigenous courts, see Sally Engle Merry, "The Articulation of Legal Spheres," in Hay and Wright, eds., *African Women and the Law*, 68–89.

118. For a rich collection of correspondence on slavery and pawnage for this period, see NAGK, Ashanti Regional Administration [hereafter ARA]/234: "Domestic Slavery in Ashanti."

119. Though pawnage was technically abolished, it continued to exist in a variety of forms. See Austin, "Human Pawning," especially 134–44 and chapters 2 and 3.

120. NAGK, ARA/238: Commissioner, Western Province Ashanti, to Chief Commissioner, Coomassie, dd. Sunyani, 5 September 1913; Chief Commissioner, Coomassie, to Commissioner, Western Province Ashanti, dd. Coomassie, 10 November 1913.

121. Cf. Claire Robertson, "Post-Proclamation Slavery in Accra: A Female Affair," in Claire Robertson and Martin Klein, *Women and Slavery in Africa* (Madison: University of Wisconsin Press, 1983), 220–45, especially 238–42.

122. NAGK, ARA/905: "Chief Osei Mampong complaining of his captive woman, etc." and Head Chief Osei Mampong to High Commissioner, Supreme Court, dd. Coomassie, 20 June 1908.

123. Ibid.

124. Here she is drawing a rather interesting distinction between slaves and captives that, to our knowledge, has not been explored in the literature on slavery in Asante.

125. It is unclear from the file whether her children were allowed to accompany her or not.

126. Rattray, *Ashanti*, 83–85.

127. Arhin, "Political and Military Roles," 97. See also Rattray, *Ashanti*, 81–85, especially 84.

128. Tordoff, *Ashanti*, 248.

129. Gold Coast, Native Jurisdiction Ordinance, No. 4 of 1924, Part VI, Sec. 43.

130. Gold Coast, Native Jurisdiction Ordinance, No. 4 of 1924. See Part VI, Sec. 29–52 for civil and criminal jurisdiction courts.

131. See Tordoff, *Ashanti*, 248–64, on difficulties encountered in implementing the ordinance.

132. Prempeh I died in 1931. Nana Agyeman Prempeh II succeeded him.

133. Gold Coast, Native Courts (Ashanti) Ordinance, No. 2 of 1935. For a summary of the structure of Asante's post-restoration native court system, see W. M. Hailey, *Native Administration in the British African Territories, Part III* (London: HMSO, 1951), 244–45.

134. See Matson, *Digest*, 32.

135. Thomas C. McCaskie, "Inventing Asante," in P. F. de Moraes Farias and K. Barber, eds., *Self Assertion and Brokerage: Early Cultural Nationalism in West Africa* (Birmingham, England: Centre of West African Studies, 1990), 61–62.

136. McCaskie does a fascinating job of interrogating the question of continuities in "Inventing Asante," and in "Accumulation II." See also Jean Allman, "Be(com)ing Asante, Be(com)ing Akan: Thoughts on Gender, Identity and the Colonial Encounter," in C. Lentz and P. Nugent, eds., *Ethnicity in Ghana* (London: Macmillan, forthcoming).

137. This is not to suggest that no missionaries ever visited Asante. Reverend A. Riis was in Kumasi in 1839, but " 'came back,' " as Reverend Ramseyer reported, " 'with the impression that we had to wait for better hints from the Lord.' " Quoted in Kimble, *Political History*, 152, from PRO, CO 96/122: Ramseyer to Freeling, dd. 18 December 1877. Later that same year, the Wesleyan Missionary Society posted Reverend T. B. Freeman to Asante, though as Kimble writes, "despite the elaborate and courteous exchanges between the Rev. T. B. Freeman and the Asantehene from 1839 onwards, the Wesleyans had little success." As tension mounted between the British and Asante from 1862 onward, any mission efforts were doomed to failure. As the Wesleyans were told in 1876

when they sought permission to reestablish work in the area, "'We will never embrace your religion.'" Kimble, *Political History*, 153, citing G. G. Findlay and W. W. Holdsworth, *The History of the Wesleyan Methodist Missionary Society, Vol. IV* (London: Epworth, 1922), 175.

138. Basel Mission Archive, Basel, Switzerland [hereafter, BMA], D-1, 73: J. A. Hanson, "Short Report about Our Mission to Nkoranza in the Present Rising, Sept., 1900."

139. PRO, CO 96/441: "Annual Report on Ashanti, 1905."

140. PRO, CO 98/18: "Annual Report on Ashanti, 1910."

141. PRO, CO 98/17: "Annual Report on Ashanti, 1908."

142. BMA, D-1/73: J. A. Hanson, "Short Report about Our Mission to Nkoranza in the Present Rising, Sept., 1900."

143. PRO, CO 96/441: "Annual Report on Ashanti, 1905."

144. BMA, D-1/73: "Report to the Committee of the Evangelical Mission-Society in Basel, Switzerland, by Samuel Boateng in Bompata," dd. Bompata, 15 February 1901.

145. A.P.A. Martinson, *Reverend Benjamin A. Martinson, 1870–1929* (Accra: Presbyterian Press, 1965), 12.

146. BMA, D-1/75: Basel Mission Society on the Gold Coast, West Africa, "General Review of the Year 1902."

147. BMA, D-1/75: "Annual Report," by Charles Martinson, dd. Apasare, 10 January 1902.

148. See Tordoff, *Ashanti*, 196–97 on *Aberewa*.

149. BMA D-1/90: Nathan Asare, "Annual Report of Kumase Congregation, 1908," dd. Kumase, 22 February 1909. See also Martinson, *Martinson*.

150. McCaskie, "Anti-Witchcraft Cults," 137.

151. Tordoff, *Ashanti*, 196.

152. McCaskie, "Anti-Witchcraft Cults," 141.

153. BMA D-1/90: Nathan Asare, "Annual Report of Kumase Congregation, 1908," dd. Kumase, 22 February 1909.

154. See, for example, Tordoff, *Ashanti*, 195–96.

155. Tordoff, *Ashanti*, 196, citing "Annual Report on Ashanti, 1912."

156. Ibid.

157. PRO, CO 98/24: "Annual Report on Ashanti, 1914."

158. PRO, CO 98/50: "Annual Report on Ashanti for 1927–1928."

159. PRO, CO 98/53: "Annual Report on Ashanti for 1928–1929."

160. BMA D-1/86: "Report of Samuel Boateng," dd. Bompata, 23 January 1907.

161. BMA D-1/93: "Report of E. Martinson," dd. Bompata, 4 February 1910.

162. BMA D-1/86: "Report of Samuel Boateng," Bompata, no date, but probably 1905.

163. MMS, WMMS, Correspondence, Gold Coast: W.E.G. Waterworth to Rev. Wm. Goudie, dd. Coomassie, 22 November 1915.

164. NAGA, ADM52/5/3: Mampong District Record Book, 1931–1946: "Missions and Relations between Christian and Heathen," dd. Coomassie, 1912. [Although the document is dated 1912, the full text appears in these later Mampong records.]

165. That the difficulties were not solved in 1912 is further evidenced by the memorandum presented to Prempeh II in 1942 by representatives of the Christian churches in

Asante and aimed at resolving the "cleavage between Christians and non-Christians in the country." The memorandum is reproduced in Busia, *Position of the Chief*, appendix 3, 220–22.

166. Secondary accounts are extensive, but see, for example, Edward Alpers, "The Story of Swema: Female Vulnerability in Nineteenth Century East Africa," in Robertson and Klein, eds., *Women and Slavery*, 185–99; Schmidt, *Peasants,* especially 92–97; Deborah Gaitskell, "Devout Domesticity? A Century of African Women's Christianity in South Africa," in Cherryl Walker, ed., *Women and Gender in Southern Africa to 1945* (Cape Town: David Philip, 1990), 251–72; Heather Hughes, "'A Lighthouse for African Womanhood': Inanda Seminary, 1869–1911," in Walker, ed., *Women and Gender*, 197–220; Paul Landau, *Realm of the Word: Language, Gender, and Christianity in a Southern African Kingdom* (Portsmouth, NH: Heinemann, 1995).

167. BMA D-1/90: Nathan Asare, "Annual Report of Kumase Congregation, 1908," dd. Kumase, 22 February 1909.

168. PRO, CO 98/50: "Annual Report on Ashanti for 1927–1928."

169. MMS, WW, M. V. Hunter, "The Gold Coast and Its Women," *Woman's Work* (October 1930), 86. The magazine was the official mouthpiece of the Women's Work Section of the Wesleyan Methodist Mission Society. Mmofraturo Girls' School opened in Kumasi in 1930. The school is discussed at some length in chapter 5.

170. It was also at this time that the government began to focus on maternal and child welfare. The first government-sponsored center devoted to maternity and child welfare was opened in Kumasi, in temporary quarters, in 1928. See Jean Allman, "Making Mothers: Missionaries, Medical Officers and Women's Work in Colonial Asante, 1924–1945," *History Workshop Journal* 38 (1994), 23–48; and chapter 5 of this book.

171. The issue of inheritance will be taken up in subsequent chapters, especially chapters 2 and 3. For excellent discussions of the impact of missionaries on notions of inheritance in areas to the south of Asante, see Roger Gocking, "Competing Systems of Inheritance before the British Courts of the Gold Coast Colony," *IJAHS* 23: 4 (1990), 601–18; and Stephan Miescher, "Of Documents and Litigants: Disputes on Inheritance in Abetifi, a Town of Colonial Ghana," *Journal of Legal Pluralism and Unofficial Law* 39 (1997), 81–119.

172. See, especially, Arhin, "Monetization"; and Arhin, "Pressure of Cash."

173. Jane Guyer, "Wealth in People, Wealth in Things: Introduction," *JAH* 36:1 (1995), 87.

174. Although parenting is not her primary focus, Barbara Cooper's recent work shares much with ours in approach and methodology. Like Cooper, we found that "[f]ocusing on marriage has made it possible . . . to bring together political economy and cultural analysis, for marriage is both a fundamental principle organizing productive and reproductive arrangements and a key element of . . . cultural and social life. . . . [I]t serves well as a point of entry into a consideration of how gender shapes and is shaped by broader processes." Cooper, *Marriage in Maradi*, xvii.

2

"It's Mine" and "It's Ours" Are Not the Same Thing: Marrying and Marriage on a Shifting Colonial Terrain

I will not use my money when he can provide. What would be the sense of marrying?[1]

INTRODUCTION

One of the first western scholars to attempt to make sense of marrying in Asante was R. S. Rattray, a British government anthropologist who researched and wrote in the 1910s and 1920s. Rattray was clearly confounded by conjugal relations in this matrilineal society, particularly by what he saw as the ambiguous position of "wife":

the wife retains her own clan identity and name and transmits both to her offspring. . . . At first sight, when we consider all that this means, and the possible results socially, the innovation seems in the nature of a revolution. . . . Her position (apart from the contract she has entered) appears to be one of almost complete isolation and independence, among strangers, for the very children she may bear will not belong to her new lord. . . . To her husband she does not appear to be bound by any tie that—in Ashanti—really counts. . . . Such appears to be the status of a wife in Ashanti in relation to her husband.[2]

In this chapter, we argue that, at the very moment Rattray drew these puzzled conclusions and pondered their "revolutionary" implications, Asante women were becoming more closely bound to their husbands by new kinds of ties that increasingly counted. As a result of the expansion of cocoa, the monetization of the economy, and the "customary" interventions of indirect rule, the meanings and makings of conjugal relations in Asante were being substantially rewritten. If "independence" could aptly describe the conjugal positionings of the free mothers and grandmothers of Asante's first colonized generation, it proved more and more elusive for those born after 1900. We must begin, therefore, by addressing the question so stridently posed in the opening quotation: "What was the sense of marrying at all?"

WHY WOMEN MARRIED

Of the more than 150 women we interviewed in the course of our work, we encountered not one among this first colonized generation who had not been married at least once in her life. Marriage for Asante women was, and still for the most part is, a ubiquitous given. For the first colonized generation, we found considerable diversity in how women married, when they married, how long they remained married, and how many times they married, but for all of them, being married was a shared experience. Why they married may seem self-evident, but it warrants some initial interrogation. As we shall see, despite increased demands upon their labor as wives and shifts in the meanings and making of marriage that worked to undermine their economic security and autonomy, women, by and large, still married during their childbearing years. Why? What were the reasons for marriage beyond the demands of conjugal production?

Not unlike their mothers and grandmothers, women of Asante's first colonized generation explained their motivation to marry in terms, first and foremost, of their desire to bear children. Because Asante lineage affiliation is traced maternally, and since marriage is exogamous, lineages can only be reproduced through female members of the matrilineage. Continuing one's matrilineage was (and remains) of the greatest importance for both practical and cultural reasons. For much of its history, Asante consistently faced shortages of labor power relative to the other major productive variable, land, and thus increasing the size of the lineage was of paramount practical importance. The connections between the ancestors, the living, and those yet born also provided a strong impetus for childbearing: if there were no female descendents, the connection was broken and the lineage ended. As the oft-quoted proverb explains, *Wo na awu a, wo abusua asa*, "When your mother dies, you have no kindred left." Indeed, the importance of increasing the size of one's matrilineal family (*abusua*) usually outweighed any concerns and undercut any stigma regarding childbearing outside of marriage. As Kyei argued, "it was an unheard-of-thing in Asante in the past for parents to claim 'damages' from a man who made a woman pregnant before she was lawfully married to him."[3]

But women who shared their reminiscences with us recalled that childbearing in marriage was held in yet higher esteem, and they therefore sought to bear children through marriage. Their families, in turn, would do everything in their power to facilitate childbearing, including providing money so that women could visit husbands away on "sojourney." As Akua Foku pointed out, "when you don't deliver, it is bad for the family."[4] Ama Akyaa, who was born around 1924 and was thus one of the younger members of Asante's first colonized generation, made the connection between marriage and children most explicit: "If . . . you don't beget . . . then it means the marriage was not useful."[5]

Because of the strong link between marriage and childbearing, a marriage that produced no children typically ended in divorce. Though women and men both desired children, the social stigma and personal costs of childlessness were remembered as being attached more firmly to women than to men. A woman without children had to endure being referred to as "a useless person" and faced ridicule and scorn.[6] If the pinnacle of male achievement lay in accumulating wealth, for women it lay in bearing children. Adwowa Fodwo, who was perhaps exquisitely attuned to the value of children, given her personal history as the only one of her mother's eight children to survive childhood, explained:

> Maybe the woman may not even be having a brother or a sister, so once she got children, she considered them as very valuable. People are more valuable than anything. If you have, say, trunks of cloth and you fall sick, the clothing and the trunks will not make you well, but if a woman is ill, she could send for her grandchild to get her medicine or something. So if even a man gives you a single person, he has given you more than you can expect.[7]

Because children were seen as a woman's insurance for the future, women typically terminated marriages that did not result in offspring. Infertility was considered a good reason for divorce, as was the death of most or all of the children from a particular marriage. If a husband stayed away on "sojourney" for too long a period of time, making conception an impossibility, he too might be divorced. Akua Foku explained that in such a situation, "I will approach the [husband's] family head and tell him that I can't stay while I am prepared to conceive and deliver."[8] As Ama Akyaa recalled, "Even if you send her things, send her money all the time, the money can't make her conceive. That was important."[9] Indeed, some women remembered being encouraged to divorce if they only bore sons, since those sons could not continue the lineage into succeeding generations.

Because of the social premium placed upon childbearing, women who failed to bear and raise children in one marriage but succeeded in a subsequent marriage often felt considerably beholden to the man with whom they eventually bore children. Marital obligations and expectations, in these cases, were often recast. As Akua Kyere recalled,

> Kwaku didn't give me anything. He never gave me a piece of cloth. Because of the children, I never bothered about Kwaku not giving me money, and cloth, and things like that. Kwaku said because I was not giving birth to children, and since I started giving birth to children when I got married to him, that is why he didn't give me money. And I wasn't disturbed by that. Because of the children I had become happy.[10]

It is not altogether surprising that women were willing to forgo some of the expected benefits of marriage from a husband with whom they conceived, since childlessness was the worst of all possible female fates. The premium placed on reproduction meant that women were willing to compromise their economic interests in marriage for their reproductive interests. Such a compromise was not difficult to make, given the long-term social and economic security children represented to their mothers. It was a security well understood by fathers. As Yaw Dankwa of Mamponten explained: "I have begotten children with her. That means I have given her many properties [*agyapadeε*]. . . . since our inheritance is matrilineally inclined, the children were hers and not mine. . . . I don't believe that when the children get valuable things in their treks and come back with them, that they will bring them to my house." In short, for a woman to have children "is a profit itself."[11]

While childbearing was clearly a paramount reason for women of this generation to marry, it was not the only one. As was clear in the reminiscences we heard, women viewed marriage as a means of broadly safeguarding themselves and their interests. Through sexual activity in marriage, a woman gained the protection of her husband's spirit and derived numerous benefits. First and foremost was a general state of protectedness, since a husband's spirit "shadowed" and "guided" a wife and made all of her endeavors successful. A man's spirit also protected against gossip, unwanted sexual attention, ill health, and even death.[12] Only sexual activity in marriage conferred the protective shadow of a man's spirit, and the lack of such protection, women remembered, could lead to grave consequences.[13] A husband's spirit protected not only his wife but their children too; the belief that children were endowed with a spiritual identity, called *ntoro*, by fathers underlay men's capacity to "shadow" their children.[14] The spiritual protection of self and children motivated women to marry and to regard the overall well-being of their marriages as a priority quite apart from their strictly economic interests.

The strength of a husband's spirit is perhaps best evidenced in women's vivid accounts of what could happen if a wife crossed her husband's spirit and that spirit, in turn, sought vengeance. The most common way to hurt a husband's spirit was adultery. As Adwowa Fodwo remembered:

> Some men will divorce their wives when they go to other men because they may by that destroy their spirit. When the woman goes to another man and then comes to sleep with her real husband . . . it kills his spirit. . . . when couples stay together and the man looks after the wife very well and she bypasses him to go to another man, and the man finds it out, he will become hurt, and it will be this which will not make anything that the woman does successful.[15]

An adulterous woman thus ran the risk of losing the protection of her husband's spirit, and with it the likelihood of having all go well in life. And adultery was not the only action that might incite a man's spirit to seek retribution. Any sort of perceived disrespect or misbehavior on a wife's part could result in punishment meted out to her either directly or through her children. "There was a woman here that my father married," recalled Adwowa Fodwo. "They had nine children. The spirit of the father killed six of them. When she does the man wrong like that, say, insults my father, or when my father engages in concubinage with other women, the woman will just go and slap him, and within two days a child will die."[16] The power of the husband/father's spirit, recalled by Adwowa Fodwo and so many others, was clearly not of recent origin. In his interviews with Asantes whose memories reached well back into the nineteenth century, Rattray found that following a divorce, mothers often hesitated to contest their children's residence with their father, "lest the father's *nton* (totemic spirit) should kill them, and she should thus lose them altogether."[17] Clearly, the omnipresent threat of retribution could and did serve as a powerful means of discouraging women from challenging their husbands, though as we shall see in subsequent chapters, it was not always successful.

For Asante's first colonized generation, then, just as for their mothers and grandmothers, marriage remained a central feature of life, particularly during their childbearing years. It was through marriage that a woman expected to bear children; it was through marriage that she hoped to increase the numbers in her own family and insure her security and well-being in old age; it was through marriage that she sought spiritual and economic protection for both herself and her children. Inducements to marry were at once practical, material, and spiritual. But if the inducements to marry seemed constant and clear, the meanings and makings of marriage for this generation, as we shall see, were anything but.

DEFINING ASANTE MARRIAGE: ANTHROPOLOGICAL PERSPECTIVES

Unfortunately, much of the literature on marriage that might help us make sense of women's lived experiences of marrying in the colonial period is not particularly attuned to change, even though it was based on research undertaken during years of social, political, and economic transformation in Asante (1910s–1940s) and even though the researchers themselves were well aware of the changes occurring around them. Rattray, the author of three classic ethnographies in the 1920s, conceived of his mission as recording "before it was too late a record of Ashanti customs and beliefs." He was convinced that had his work been delayed at all, "it is doubtful whether much information would have been obtained."[18] Though aware of the magnitude of change, Rattray and his successors, most notably Meyer Fortes who led the Ashanti Social Survey in the 1940s, were more concerned with capturing and categorizing an increasingly illusive past than with exploring the nature and magnitude of the social change occurring around them. Thus, for Rattray, marriage in Asante neatly fell into six discrete categories: marriage between a free man and a free woman (*adehye awadie*); concubinage or, as he termed it, "the mating of lovers" (*mpena awadie*); marriage between a free man and a pawn (*awowa awadie*); marriage between a free man and a slave (*afona awadie*); levirate marriage (*kuna awadie*); and sororate marriage (*ayete awadie*).[19] Because his perspective was clearly androcentric, marriages between free or royal women and men of a lower standing or of a different ethnicity were missing from the list.[20]

The vast majority of women who shared their stories with us had experienced marriages that fell roughly within the first three categories described by Rattray, so it is upon those that we will focus here. Marriage between a free man and a free woman, according to Rattray, was a union formalized by the "giving and acceptance of *aseda* [thanksgiving] by the contracting parties," thereby forming a "strictly legal marriage."[21] Such a marriage conferred certain rights and imposed certain responsibilities on the spouses, the most important of which Rattray understood to be the husband's right to claim adultery fees (*ayefare sika*) or monetary damages from any man with whom his wife had a sexual relationship. (This right derived from a wife's obligation to provide exclusive sexual access to her husband.) In the less formal *mpena awadie* (concubinage), *aseda* had not been presented to formalize the union, but the couple lived in a relationship that was "based on mutual voluntary consent, intended to be permanent, and carried out openly." Once again Rattray focused upon the question of sexual rights and obligations; it was his understanding that the most significant distinction between full marriage and concubinage lay in the fact that concubinage did not give men the right to collect adultery fees. Rattray added that the absence of *aseda*, "while rendering a union in a sense irregular, did not . . . brand a couple who lived together openly as man and wife with . . . [any] stigma." Consequently, he wrote, "I have included it among regular marriage formalities because I think that in olden times it constituted a more or less recognized form of union," which had been considered a "strictly regular" relationship.[22]

The third type of conjugal union discussed by Rattray, marriage between a free man and a pawned woman (*awowa awadie*), occurred when a man took as his pawn a woman whom he had already married, or when a man married a woman already held in pawn by him.[23] Rattray suggested that pawn marriages were most likely to occur when a free wife became her husband's pawn, since a married woman was the family member most likely to be pawned by a family in need of cash.[24] When a family decided to pawn a married woman to raise money, they first offered her in pawnship to her husband, and it was considered very bad form for her husband to refuse what was essentially a firm request for a loan from his in-laws. Though a husband who took his wife as a pawn lost the use of the money he loaned to his in-laws, he also gained substantially in this arrangement since his marital rights increased dramatically. Among other things, he gained far greater control over the use of his now pawn wife's labor. Overall, Rattray's writings leave us with a highly structured, if not schematic, understanding of what marrying meant for the first colonized generation of women. Either they were in a formalized or nonformalized marriage with a free man, the primary difference being the right of the husband to collect adultery compensation, or they were in a marriage in which they were both wife and pawn and were subject to greater control by their husbands.

Rattray's structuralist account of marriage in Asante was challenged to some degree by the work of Meyer Fortes in the 1940s[25] but more effectively in the work of T. E. Kyei, which only recently appeared in print. In many ways, Kyei bridged the gap between academic ethnographies of Asante and the reminiscences of Asantes born in the first quarter of this century. Born in Asante in 1908, Kyei's own life experiences clearly informed his work. At the same time, he collaborated closely with Fortes in the 1945 Social Survey and many of Fortes' own conclusions regarding marriage in Asante were based on Kyei's careful work. Though Kyei's *Marriage and Divorce among the Asante: A Study Undertaken in the Course of the Ashanti Social Survey (1945)* is largely ahistorical in its approach, his position as an insider allowed him to uncover far more of the complexity, and at times fluidity, of Asante marriage during the first decades of this century. Like Rattray, his perspective remains male-centered (thus the chapter "Acquisition of a Wife" leaves women's experiences to be inferred); however, his work captures, in ways that Rattray's does not, the lengthy dialogical process that embodied marrying for many of his generation. For example, the routes to finding a spouse identified by Kyei included courting and wooing (*mpena twee*), early childhood betrothal (*asiwaa*), an offer from a relative or friend (*dɔ yere*), the "obligatory" wife (*kuna yere* and, in the case of chiefs, *aye-tɛ*), and, finally, the wife as pledge or pawn (*awowa yere*). In courting and wooing, as the name implies, a man and a woman met on their own, fell in love, decided to marry, and then sought their families' and fathers' approval for their marriage. The second possibility, early childhood betrothal, resulted from the fact that parents could promise a young or a yet-unborn daughter in marriage. The parents could initiate such a betrothal, or the man who wished to marry a daughter of the couple could initiate the arrangement. In either case, the marriage could not occur before the girl reached puberty and went through her nubility rites. In the case of what he calls an "offered wife," Kyei noted that parents or maternal uncles offering a woman in marriage to a particular man might be motivated to take this action because of their affection for him or because of their perception that he would make a desirable father for the woman's children. (According to Kyei, family members inquired closely into the personal and family reputation of potential husbands for the express purpose of weeding out anyone whose family was tainted by association with undesirable traits such as inherited disease, thievery, mental illness, alcoholism, and the like.) Kyei's fourth category, the "obligatory" wife, referred to levirate and sororate marriage, and his final category, marriage to a pledge, described men who married women they held in pawn.

Once potential spouses found one another by any of the means outlined above, their conjugal relationship had to be solemnified. Kyei gives a far more detailed description of the actions involved in formalizing a full marriage than can be found in any of Rattray's writings. The process always involved numerous steps and stages, which might occur over a lengthy span of time. Initially, the husband-to-be gave small presents, called "seeing things" (*ahudeɛ*) or "doorknocking things" (*aboboɔm-bɔ-deɛ*) to the woman's family and father. Presentation of these gifts gave formal notice of the couple's desire to marry, while acceptance of them indicated that the woman's family approved of the proposed marriage. The presentation of knocking gifts also gave the couple the right to an open sexual relationship or, as Kyei put it, the right to "live as . . . concubines."[26] In the second stage of marrying, the husband-to-be presented marriage gifts to the woman, her family, and her father.

The man's family became involved in the third stage of marrying, when the man's senior relatives formally asked the woman's family for permission for the marriage to take place. This step was followed by the central act that, according to Kyei, indisputably formalized the marriage, the presentation of *tiri nsa* (literally "head drinks"; the term for *aseda* given at marriage) to the woman's family and father.[27] Next, the newly married woman prepared an elaborate meal for her husband in order to showcase her domestic skills. Finally came the payment of *anyame-dwan* (literally "god sheep"). This final step recognized that the spiritual protection a daughter had received from her father from conception until puberty would now come from her husband. Kyei identified one additional stage, which occurred only in some marriages. If, at some time following a marriage, a woman's family found itself in financial difficulty and in need of a loan, her relatives might turn to her husband as a potential creditor. They could ask him to loan them the sum they needed, with the understanding that his wife would then become his pledge or pawn. If her husband agreed to her family's request, he made them the loan, the sum of which was known as *tiri sika* (literally "head money"), and with that the woman became his pawn as well as his wife.[28]

In describing the processes of marrying, Kyei recognized a crucial point that Rattray had missed: marriage occurred in stages, and moreover in stages that could be spread over a period of years. In fact, frequently, couples and their families never completed all of them. For example, once the first step of presenting the knocking things had been taken, Kyei wrote,

> the couple can live together as husband and wife for as long as they wished. It depends also upon the complaisant attitude of the woman's parents to the noncompletion or the long postponement of the performance of the remaining formalities which make a customary marriage lawful. A saying that bears this out is *"woase pe woasem a, na oma wogye adwaman-yefare"* (If your parents-in-law have grown fond of you they may collude in a claim of adultery compensation during concubinage).[29]

In other words, families defined marital relationships in large part as they wished, ceremonies and formalities aside. After a man undertook only the first step toward marrying, a family that wanted to could define the union as a full marriage, with all of its formal rights and obligations.[30] This fluid, family-centered picture of marriage stands in stark contrast to Rattray's rigid categorizations, which separated marriage and concubinage into mutually exclusive categories, distinguished by the presentation (or not) of *aseda* and separated by the ability (or not) of men to claim adultery fees.

In recognizing a fundamental fluidity in Asante marriage, Kyei provides an incomparably more nuanced description of marriage than Rattray—a description that provides richer insight into the lived experiences of Asante's first generation of colonized women. Still, Kyei, like Rattray and Fortes, was primarily concerned with describing normative "customs and beliefs" and not with documenting how the meanings and makings of marriage might have changed or been contested over the life span of his own generation. It is to the reminiscences and life stories of that generation that we now turn in order to understand, as lived experience, the fluidity and complexity of marrying in colonial Asante.

MEANINGS AND MAKINGS OF MARRYING: PERSPECTIVES FROM ASANTE'S FIRST COLONIZED GENERATION

For women of Asante's first colonized generation, marriage was clearly not a state of being but a series of multiple, often overlapping, processes— processes that do not fit easily into Rattray's rigid typology. Most people to whom we spoke described conjugal relationships along a continuum of what can best be described as "degrees of knowing." Thus, at the fully formalized end of the continuum, marrying (*awareε*) was signified by the payment of *tiri aseda* in the form of drinks and/or money by the husband and his family to the family of his wife. The husband was fully known to and recognized by the wife's family as her husband and she, likewise, as his wife. Because *tiri aseda* was usually accompanied by a large number of gifts that could make effecting a marriage quite costly for a man and his family, there were other ways of initiating the marrying process, while postponing, as it were, the payment of *tiri aseda*. Less formal or less "known," therefore, might be a relationship based on *ahudee* or *aboboɔm-bɔ-deε* ("seeing" or "knocking" things, which often meant drinks). In these cases, a man was known to his wife's family, though how "known," as we shall see, was open to debate. The process of marrying was recognized as being underway, with the expectation that *tiri aseda* would formalize the relationship in the future. Other conjugal relationships along the continuum fell within the range of what has been loosely and unfortunately translated as concubinage.[31] In these relationships, the man and woman were lovers (*mpena*). The lovers might be known to both families, but the woman's family would not have been formally approached; typically, only the woman's mother was informed of the relationship, and this knowledge was transmitted by either her daughter or her daughter's lover. In some cases, however, lovers kept their relationship private and families remained ignorant of the connection. With the exception of these more furtive relationships, the crucial factor differentiating conjugal relationships one from another was the degree of knowing: the level of formality with which the couple's families had been made aware of the union.

In some ways, women's and men's recollections of marrying are in accord with Rattray's understanding that a clear distinction could be drawn
between a fully formalized marriage and other types of conjugal relationships, all of which reputedly involved lesser rights and obligations between
partners than did a fully regularized marriage. At the same time, however,
their lived experiences suggest that formalities distinguishing marriages, door-
knocking relationships, and known "concubinages" often made little or no
difference in actual practice. Frequently, women's families extended the status of husband to men in door-knocking relationships or to a known lover
(*mpena*). People's understanding and definitions of what constituted marriage was, as Kyei recognized, very much a situational family affair, open to
the interpretations of the parties involved at a particular moment in time.
Indeed, many to whom we spoke viewed door-knocking (*aboboɔm-bɔ-deɛ*)
relationships as legitimate marriages precisely because the families had formal knowledge of them. Consequently, many people said of a man who had
presented only the knocking fee, "He is called a husband. He has gone to the
house," and, "It is taken into account that you are a husband. They have seen
you."[32]

Known concubinages or love affairs, while not sharing the official stamp
of drinks that defined door-knocking relationships, could also be sanctioned as legitimate marriages. As Kofi Anto explained: "It is the concubinage which leads to marriage. . . . when it is clear to the family that the
man will sometime come to do the actual rites, it is considered fine. . . .
they ask you whether that man will marry you or what. And when he says
so, they will know that you are heading toward marriage."[33] Kwame Dapaa,
who never entered into a formal marriage, said, "the idea behind doing
the [*awareɛ*] rites was to let the parents of the wife be aware that you are
with her."[34] As long as this occurred, according to Dapaa and many others, as long as you were known, the particular mechanism by which you
became known was not especially important, except in cases of adultery.
In a union not fully formalized by the presentation of *tiri aseda*, the
woman's family retained authority over defining the relationship and could
interpret it as either a marriage or a nonmarriage. Consequently, backing
a man's adultery claim by naming the relationship a true marriage remained a strictly discretionary course of action for families of women in
door-knocking or *mpena* relationships. As Kwabena Manu explained:

> once you propose love to a woman, though you may not have done the
> actual marriage rites she will be cooking for you and you will be giving
> her chop money. You can sleep together. . . . But if she goes to another
> man and has an affair with him, if her family permits, you can claim adul-
> tery fees, but if they don't, you can't. If the family loves you, they will

Photo 2.1   Kwabena Manu, Mamponten, 1990. Photograph by Victoria Tashjian.

support you to claim the adultery fees, though you may not have done the actual rites. As I said, if the family loves you, they can support you to claim it, but if not, they will not stand by you to claim the adultery fees.[35]

Choosing whether or not to back a man in a less known or formalized relationship typically depended upon the degree to which the woman's family viewed him as a good husband and father and a responsible son-in-law to their family. As Peter Danso added,

When her family accepted you, and something of this nature arises whereby you intend claiming adultery fees, you can inform her family and they will help you claim it. In Asante, the wise old men have something that if even the man has not done anything pertaining to marriage to enhance his standing as a husband, and there happens to be a case whereby they will need to support him, they would support the man when they like him. There is a saying that "if your father-in-law loves you, he helps you to get adultery fees."[36]

Clearly Danso and others of his generation understood formalizing a marriage with the presentation of *aseda* as merely "enhancing" the status of husband, not as singularly defining or signifying "husband" (*kunu*). Panin Anthony Kofi Boakye remembered that being recognized as a husband was not solely dependent upon entering into a formal marriage, though that was the only guaranteed route to such status:

The adultery fees depend on the woman's family. . . . They could help the man claim the adultery fees even when they have not done the actual rites. They just declare that the man has done the rites to them. They back him . . . . it is the family who have the final say to declare whether she has been married or not. Whatever they say will be upheld. . . . They only tell such a lie when the family loves the man, because if the family doesn't want the man to get married to the woman they will not say that.[37]

For this generation of Asantes, therefore, marriage—its meanings, its makings, its very definition—remained very much an ongoing family affair. Families retained the power to define the status of any known conjugal relationship, at any point in time, as they saw fit. If families considered a door-knocking relationship or a relationship between two lovers as marriage, marriage it was.[38]

For husbands, there was certainly a lack of security vis-à-vis one's in-laws in conjugal relationships not based on *tiri aseda*, since the right to define the relationship remained squarely with a wife's family. For this reason, a fully formalized marriage represented a social ideal for men. It also served as an important way for them to acquire prestige, since being able to perform all of the rites in lavish style demonstrated that one had reached the status of an *ɔbarima paaaa*, that is, a financially successful "big man."[39] But for many men, this was not an easily attainable goal, and many families forwent full marriages because men simply did not have the money to conduct the marriage rites. In the late 1940s, for example, when the sum involved in *tiri aseda* might be the equivalent of two bottles of gin, this was more than some men could afford.[40] The pressure to indicate one's status by giving gifts in excess of the bare-bones requirements for marrying also left many men unwilling to perform the rites in what could be seen as a highly unimpressive manner. For example, Kwabena Manu of Mamponten was involved in four door-knocking relationships and pointed to a lack of money to explain his state of affairs: "If even I had done the [marriage] rites, it would have been a useless thing."[41] Kwabena Boahene, who had entered into full marriages, described them by saying: "You may love the girl so much . . . that to show your greatest affection for her, you may like to make it extravagantly grand. . . . [Marriage] has no fixed price; it depends on the individual. An individual may like to enhance his dignity by making it grand. It all depends on the man."[42] If a man were not able to embellish the *tiri aseda* sufficiently, he sometimes considered it preferable to enter into a less known or less formalized relationship than to perform the rites in what might appear to be a miserly or lackluster fashion. If a woman's family liked the man, it still accepted the relationship as a valid marriage.[43]

Though there were clearly benefits on both sides to entering into more fully formalized marriages, door-knocking relationships and recognized love affairs were extremely common, and their widespread acceptability as legitimate conjugal relationships illuminates not only this first colonized generation's elastic or fluid definitions of marriage but also their understanding of marriage as a process rather than as an event occurring at a single point in time. Thus, families sanctioned or recognized "concubinage" or love affairs because they were understood as steps along the road to *awaree*. As a common saying put it, "It is concubinage that leads to marriage." Admittedly, in the lived experience of many, fully formalized marriage through presentation of *tiri aseda* never occurred at all, but the universal fiction of one step always leading to the next allowed families to forgo a high-status, formal marriage while retaining the illusion that eventually it would be performed. Thus, all the steps along the way, from being lovers through the presentation of "knocking" drinks, were explained in terms of partners testing their compatibility. As Yaw Dankwa of Mamponten observed of door-knocking relationships:

> We do the knocking aspect merely to wait and find out about the true character of the woman. She could be a thief or she could be a prostitute. When you perform the knocking rite like that, it guarantees you the right to come to the house. And it also affords you the opportunity to study the girl and know her true character. Yes, the girl too studies the man. And the man too studies her.[44]

Families themselves advocated the wisdom of this course of action, since such conjugal relationships were seen as a way to avoid—or at least tip the balance toward avoiding—marriages doomed to failure. As Afua Fosuwa remembered, "when the man was prepared to go and do the actual rites, the family head could tell you to suspend it for a while and do the knocking rites to study yourselves before you come to do the actual rites . . . because he couldn't stand receiving another marriage rite and then later [the husband] comes to divorce her."[45] The desire to choose a marriage partner wisely led many in this generation to conclude that marrying without first "testing" life with an intended spouse was foolish, indeed. Both "concubinages" and door-knocking relationships were seen as trial runs that would lead to more formally recognized marriages if the relationships proved mutually satisfactory; a range of unions were understood as the logical precursors to full marriage since engaging in them helped a couple ascertain the odds of their marriage succeeding.

Though marrying-as-process was remembered as a means of avoiding divorce, most people with whom we spoke believed a marriage was not likely to last a lifetime, even though long-lasting conjugal relationships remained something of an ideal. The acceptability of divorce was reflected in the ease with which people could divorce: men and women alike were free to end a marriage at any time, for any or no reason, even against the wishes of their spouse, and the process of divorcing was relatively simple and inexpensive. There did not have to be some cataclysmic event to justify divorce (though not surprisingly some specific dissatisfaction typically sparked it); simply tiring of the marriage provided sufficient cause. As Kofi Dware said, "The woman divorced me. That was that, we didn't sit to go into it. . . . The woman said she could no more marry. When you marry, and each of you becomes fed up, and decides to end it, that is that."[46] Maintaining a marriage for life, then, was not the overriding goal; the vast majority believed it made sense to divorce in the face of marital discontent.[47] In spite of the fact that divorce was broadly accepted and widely practiced, many expressed ambivalent feelings about it, since marriages that remained successful over the long term were held in high regard.[48] But longevity in marriage proved difficult for many in execution. As Clark has written, "Asantes prefer long-lasting marriages, but not long, bad marriages."[49] Thus, many of the women with whom we spoke, though married for most of their childbearing years, did not necessarily remain married to the same man. What was of supreme importance was not the type or the length of the relationship but the fact that it entailed a commitment to that particular conjugal relationship for so long as it lasted, though this was understood to be "for some time," rather than for all time. As Aduwa Yaa Ama of Oyoko explained:

What I don't like is going to different men at the same time, but [it is good] when you are engaged with one man who genuinely will marry you, and the family are aware that you are with him and you want to get married for some time.[50]

SHIFTING RIGHTS AND OBLIGATIONS IN
CONJUGAL RELATIONSHIPS

Although men and women of Asante's first colonized generation remembered marrying processes that probably differed little from those of earlier generations, in that they were fluid and dialogical, their stories of the rights and obligations in conjugal relationships reveal seismic shifts in the makings of marriage. While Rattray emphasized as the most significant rights and obligations of a formal marriage a wife's duty to provide her husband with exclusive sexual access and a husband's right to collect adultery compensation, those who shared their memories with us spoke far more broadly of a wife's responsibility to work for her husband and of a husband's responsibility to provide care. Their reminiscences also provide incomparable insight into the ways in which obligations to labor and provide care were gradually transformed with the increased monetization of the Asante economy. At the center of these processes of transformation was the very meaning of conjugal labor.

Although descent in Asante was (and still, for the most part, is) determined through the matriline, basic production was organized around and through conjugal relationships—a point already introduced in chapter 1's discussion of the collection of gold, kola, and rubber. A reliance on conjugal labor also characterized agricultural production in Asante. For example, while large exogamous matriclans served to incorporate and organize production for labor-intensive tasks like the felling of trees or the clearing of land, planting, weeding, and harvesting were largely accomplished by groups composed of a husband, wife, and any dependent children, slaves, or pawns. This organization of labor long predated the formation of the Asante state at the end of the seventeenth century and, as Wilks has persuasively argued, effectively coincided with the transition in the Akan forest from hunting and gathering to subsistence agriculture.[51] It was a system of conjugal production distinguished by a high degree of reciprocity—a salient feature of marriage in Asante. For example, Asante men had the right to call on the labor of their wives and expected them to provide a broad range of domestic services, including fetching water, cooking, cleaning, and looking after children. In turn, women expected to receive from their husbands care or maintenance, in the form of meat, clothing, and food crops. Kyei defined a husband's primary duty as *ɔbɔ no akɔnhama*, "he maintains her with food."[52] Additional reciprocal obligations linked husbands to the families of their wives and wives to the families of their husbands, in a series of ongoing transactions and inter-actions. If either partner failed to meet any of the myriad reciprocal re-sponsibilities fundamental to Asante marriage, divorce could be initiated quite easily by either spouse. That marriage was centered on ongoing reciprocal obligations and responsibilities meant that it was an institution continually renegotiated and reaffirmed between families, rather than a state of being entered or exited by two individuals at single points in time.[53]

As a central and ongoing feature of the marrying process, in the eigh-teenth and nineteenth centuries partners provided mutual assistance in cul-tivating their farms. In most marriages between free commoners, men and women both had access to plots of family land on which they grew the staple root crops, plantains, and vegetables that formed the basis of the Asante diet. Women typically had food farms located on their family prop-erty, men had theirs on their own family's property, and spouses helped each other farm. Joint labor was mutually beneficial, and producing crops together helped ensure a steady supply of food for the couple and any dependents. Although spouses jointly produced a reliable source of food-stuffs, joint labor did not give rise, over time, to jointly held property. Instead, as is the case in most matrilineal societies, property was owned by one spouse or the other instead of being jointly owned by both—a circumstance that accounts for the very high value Asante women have historically placed on economic independence. Consequently, if divorce came, as it frequently did, division of conjugal property was virtually a non-issue, since both spouses had benefitted equally from conjugal labor, and since each retained access to the farms located on his or her *abusua* (matrilineal family) land. Moreover, any food farms the spouses had cre-ated together were of limited value. First, the crops were produced pri-marily for consumption rather than for sale, and so they did not possess a significant monetary value.[54] Second, the farms were of value over a limited period of time only, since the nature of tropical forest agriculture, with shifting plot cultivation, meant any particular farm was productive for a period of only one to three years before being fallowed.

As we saw in chapter 1, in addition to jointly producing foodstuffs, hus-bands and wives engaged in market-oriented production. European observ-ers of the eighteenth- and nineteenth-century Asante economy regularly com-mented on rural commoners being engaged during the agricultural off-sea-son in panning and mining for gold and in the collection and sale of first kola and later rubber. Once again the primary source of labor was the conjugal family unit, which was supplemented by any pawns or slaves. Though the majority of Asantes worked primarily in subsistence agriculture during the eighteenth and nineteenth centuries,[55] market-oriented roles were, as Joseph

LaTorre recognized in his masterful dissertation, "roles temporarily played by ordinary farmers" on a regular, indeed annual, basis.[56]

With the rapid spread of cocoa cultivation in the early twentieth century, however, conjugal labor aimed at production for the market was no longer a temporary state of affairs. Increasingly, it was the central focus of conjugal production, and the implications for the meaning of marriage were profound. While the spread of cocoa farming in Asante is well documented,[57] only recently have scholars like Austin and Grier been concerned with gender and the exploitation of unpaid labor in the initial years of cocoa's expansion. Their writings provide material for a gendered periodization of the development of the cocoa economy that brings the chronologies outlined in chapter 1 into the twentieth century and provides a context for understanding the profound transformations in marriage experienced by Asante's first colonized generation. As Austin has shown, the labor necessary for the rapid spread of cocoa came "very largely from established, non-capitalist sources."[58] Initially, these sources included the "farmowners themselves, their families, their slaves and pawns, cooperative groups of neighbors and, in the case of chiefs, corvée labor provided by their subjects."[59] However, with the abolition of slavery and the prohibition of pawning in Asante in 1908, wives' labor became, for most men, absolutely essential, particularly to the initial establishment of the farm. Few had the means to pay for hired labor.[60] Wives' provision of labor in the initial creation of cocoa farms flowed logically, as it were, from the pre-cocoa productive obligations between spouses already discussed. Wives commonly grew food crops on land cleared by their husbands—crops that both fed the family and provided a surplus that wives were entitled to sell. When cocoa farms were first established, the pattern differed little. In the first three to four years of their existence, the only returns from cocoa farms were the food crops—particularly crops like plantain or cocoyam—which were planted to shade the young trees during their first years. After that point, however, food crops, which were the wife's only material and guaranteed return on her labor investment in the farm, diminished. The main product of the farm now became the cocoa beans, all of which belonged to the husband.[61] Any labor invested by a wife after a cocoa farm became mature was directly compensated "only in the continued obligation of her husband," as Roberts writes, "to provide part of her subsistence from his own earnings."[62]

Cocoa rapidly set a model replicated in other kinds of conjugal labor aimed at the newly expanding market economy, as husbands attempted to divert much of their wives' labor to their own income-generating activities in the expanding cash economy. This is illustrated by the case of Aduwa Yaa Ama of Oyoko, whose husband was a tailor, for he relied on her to help sell the clothing he produced. Before she married him, she had been making clay pots, the income from which was her own, but after their marriage, she said, "He didn't allow me to make pots. [Instead], when he sewed uniforms, I took them around selling them. I went round the villages." As with cocoa farming, the money realized from the sale of the uniforms remained his: "I gave him the money, all of it."[63]

Rattray's elderly informants, reflecting on the rights and obligations in late nineteenth-century marriages, painted a very different picture for the anthropologist. While a husband did gain a legal right to "profit by the fruits of . . . [a wife's] labor and later that of her children," Rattray later wrote, "Such a right does not by any means entitle the husband to order about either wife or children like slaves, and in reality amounts only to the mutual assistance that persons living together and sharing a common menage would naturally accord to each other."[64] By 1922, however, as he reflected on the duties of wives, J. B. Danquah argued that wives had to "do all domestic and some of the farm work."[65] The picture had changed even more dramatically two decades later when, in the 1940s, Kyei described a radically different state of affairs: "On the farm a wife must assist her husband by doing any work that she feels her strength would permit. In particular she is expected to plant food crops, to clear weeds growing in a new farm, and to lend a hand in cocoa harvesting operations."[66]

In the reminiscences that were shared with us, it is clear that during the childbearing years of the first colonized generation, husbands began to assert an increasingly unfettered right to draw on the labor of their wives. And the ramifications of this profound shift in obligations shook the domestic economy of conjugal production to its foundations. Men's ability to assert increased rights to their wives' labor was facilitated by the particular circumstances of cocoa's expansion. Because all of the suitable lands in central Asante rapidly came under cultivation, men traveled to new areas in order to obtain land on which cocoa could be grown. With travel, both the balance and the significance of conjugal labor shifted dramatically. Spouses no longer resided in a village where both held rights to family land, land on which they produced foodstuffs to which each alone held indisputable claim. Instead, the couple often traveled to vacant land far afield and, once there, in the vast majority of instances, only the husband obtained rights to land. In theory, both husband and wife could gain access to separate plots of individually owned land, a right effected by paying an annual fee to the local ruler, and thus reproduce village property-holding patterns. In practice, however, this was not done, and overwhelmingly the husband was the only one who acquired use-rights to land. This resulted in farms that belonged to him alone, but on which both he and his wife labored.

In this setting, where both spouses did not retain use-rights to land, husbands' rights to wives' labor took on entirely new meanings. The balance of conjugal labor described above—mutual assistance on each other's farms—did not exist on the cocoa frontier and was replaced by a unidirectional flow of labor from wives to their husbands' farms. Travel thus eroded the reciprocal nature of conjugal agricultural labor and disrupted a woman's independent agricultural production. Since a wife usually did not gain the right to farmland herself, and as she was often too far from family land in her home village to make use of it, she no longer had her own farms, and with them the indisputable right to their crops. Travel to a husband's distant cocoa farms also meant that it was difficult for a wife to continue any income-generating activities of her own, for cocoa cultivation is highly labor-intensive in its early stages and allows little time for other activities—like soap making, pot making, or petty trading. Furthermore, the sheer quantity of time women spent on agricultural labor rose dramatically with cocoa farming because the labor requirements of food farms remained constant alongside the new labor demands of cash cropping. All of the work of cocoa farming was simply added to preexisting agricultural responsibilities, with the result that women worked markedly longer hours in farming than had previously been the case, and thus they had less time to engage in income-producing pursuits of their own.

The profound shifts in conjugal production and the pervasive burdens borne by women on the cocoa frontier are brought into stark relief by the life stories of women like Akosua Mansah. Born in the first decade of the twentieth century, Akosua married shortly after her nubility rites and traveled with her husband to Ahafo. Initially she focused her attention on selling kenkey, while her husband "went for a piece of land to farm on." After the farm was acquired, they settled near it, outside Boma, and Akosua devoted all of her labor to assisting her husband on his farm. Over the course of the years, she gave birth to thirteen children. Because they were located far out on the cocoa frontier, Akosua did not have access to a midwife or any other female birth attendant, so her husband helped her deliver the children. "No one was around," she remembered, "We were the first people at the place." When she and her husband went to work on the farm, they brought their young children with them. "We would put down plantain leaves and they would lie on them and I would work." Akosua's husband passed away in the 1980s. Although he had given her part of the farm they had jointly worked, she recalled with great bitterness that "his family members got it away from me because I did not pour drinks to . . . signify the gift."[67]

Clearly, the effects of this new pattern of conjugal farming were numerous, profound, and enduring. Because many wives traveled with their husbands in order to farm cocoa, they were distanced from their families, from family land that might provide alternative economic security, and from female kin who could share childcare responsibilities. In marked contrast to conjugally produced food farms, moreover, cocoa farms created through a couple's joint labor were not entities from which both necessarily derived benefits, since only the owner of a property had a right to its fruits. Thus, a woman had no incontrovertible right to any portion of her husband's cocoa farm or its profits, as Akosua Mansah and many others discovered. Most significantly, cocoa farms were valuable in ways that food farms simply were not: cocoa was a cash crop with noteworthy monetary value, produced for the global market, in marked contrast to foodstuffs grown primarily for personal use. That cocoa farms were productive for many years more than food farms were created a long-term financial interest in these conjugally produced properties that simply had not been at stake with food farms. These multiple factors, as we shall see in chapter 4, led to obvious problems in cases of divorce: leaving a husband now meant a woman was walking away from properties of considerably greater value, and also properties of value over a substantially longer period of time, than had been the case with food farms. Besides, a woman who accompanied her husband to his distant cocoa farms often no longer had access to food farms of her own to turn to in the case of divorce, increasing even more the costs of leaving her husband. In short, conjugal labor in the production of cocoa severely undermined the reciprocity that had previously been a defining element of Asante marriage. The long-standing right of Asante husbands to the labor of their wives did not create gross inequalities in a primarily subsistence economy, so far as can be determined. But it created increasingly unequal and inequitable financial rewards for husbands and wives in the more fully monetized economy of the twentieth century.[68]

Cocoa and the expansion of the cash economy, with their reliance on conjugal labor aimed at production for the market, not only had profound repercussions for the fluid, dialogical underpinnings of conjugal relations but also for husbands' obligations to provide care for wives. As men's participation in the cash economy expanded and as urbanization intensified, even the produce that men had historically contributed to the conjugal pot came, increasingly, not from their own cultivations but in the form of "chop money" (*adidi sika*)—that is, money given to a wife to purchase food with which to prepare a husband's meal. Little information exists on amounts and uses of chop money before the 1920s, but one can assume that the routine provision of chop money rather than goods-in-kind represented a significant departure from earlier years, when most food items would not have been purchased on a regular basis.

Though chop money mattered on the most pragmatic level—it helped put food in men's stomachs—it also embodied the very essence of conjugal relationships. The Asante verb *di*, which means "to eat," has multiple meanings, including "to have sexual intercourse." Consequently, giving chop money to a wife and cooking for a husband were the reciprocal acts at the very heart of thriving conjugal relationships. The monetization of this cooking-sex nexus had profound implications. Generally, husbands distributed chop money to wives on a weekly or monthly basis in rural areas, while in the city of Kumasi, where people depended much more heavily on purchased food, they gave it every day. Though chop money meant that husbands routinely gave cash to wives, the money did not represent a significant economic windfall for women. In many cases, it was given expressly to purchase food so that the husband, not his wife or children, could eat.[69] Furthermore, as many women remembered, the chop money frequently did not fully cover even this limited expense. When a husband's duty to provide food entailed bringing produce he had cultivated or hunted himself, it was clear when what he brought was not sufficient. Chop money placed the burden of making it sufficient upon the wife and her resourcefulness. Moreover, the symbolic significance of chop money made it difficult for a woman to ask for more, to tell her spouse that what he gave her was not adequate to purchase his food.[70] Consequently, women frequently supplemented the chop money given by husbands with their own money so that they could still prepare attractive meals.[71] In short, the acceptance of chop money, rather than improving or supplementing a wife's economic resources, constituted for many people something of an economic liability.

The monetization of marriage also played out more broadly in men's general obligation to care for wives, since increasingly this care had to be met through the cash economy. From the perspective of men of Asante's first colonized generation, this development led to onerous new costs that they often resented. For example, husbands had long given certain material objects, known as *aware deε*, or "marriage things," to wives during the course of a marriage. As Kyei has written, the term covered "all goods and chattels given by a husband to a wife during the effective period of their marriage . . . cloths, handkerchiefs, beads, ear-rings and other personal property."[72] Before the broad monetization of the economy, the return of *aware-deε* was, as Kyei explains, largely symbolic. Thus, a "prudent wife would securely keep small pieces of old worn-out cloths and other *aware-deε*" in the event that she divorced her husband and was required to return the marriage things.[73] With the development of the cash economy, however, *aware-deε* increasingly assumed a cash value, and marriage "things" were increasingly spoken of as marriage "expenses."[74] As a result, the refund of these expenses at the termination of a marriage became a hotly debated topic through most of the colonial period.[75]

In fact, tracing claims for *aware-deε* through the colonial court system demonstrates not only that marriage "things" became marriage "expenses" but also that those expenses escalated over the course of the colonial period. In the early years of the twentieth century, colonial courts recognized only small sums as legitimate marriage expenses, but over the decades, especially as these claims were heard in native courts after 1924, the amounts claimed as expenses rose and men showed themselves increasingly willing to effect their claims. In 1907, for example, an assistant district commissioner, Captain H. A. Kortright, recorded a case in his "Palaver Book" in which a man named Kwami Pong attempted to claim marriage expenses of £39.2.0 from his divorced wife, Affuah Chiawa.[76] Pong came to the new British legal forum after receiving an unfavorable ruling from the Agonahene, who had arbitrated the couple's divorce settlement. Kortright solicited testimony from the Agonahene's *ɔkyeame* (spokesman), and upon ascertaining that Kwami Pong's marriage expenses were unfairly inflated, essentially found in Affuah Chiawa's favor by awarding Kwami Pong only £4.10.0. While this case is not necessarily an unadulterated reflection of Asante "custom" near the turn of the century, it does suggest a cap on reclaimable marriage expenses as seen in the Agonahene's original ruling, which allowed Kwami Pong even less than he received in the settlement negotiated by Kortright.

Unfortunately, there is a gap in the record for the years between the time covered by this "Palaver Book" and the restoration of the courts beginning in 1924. Once the native court system was established, however, judicial views on the recovery of marriage expenses can be picked up once again. The case of *Adjuah Nsiah v. Kojo Krampah*, which came before the Kumasihene's court on 17 August 1931, also indicated both the low value of typical marriage expenses and men's willingness to forgo their recovery. Adjuah Nsiah's son, Akwasi Adae, and Kojo Krampah's daughter, Abba Kurapina, married around 1927. The couple had gone to Obuasi to work, but while they were there Akwasi Adae had broken Abba Kurapina's arm, and so Kojo Krampah had insisted that they divorce. The case reveals that even when it might result in a financial loss, a man could choose not to demand repayment of his marriage expenses. During the divorce arbitration, Akwasi Adae took a fairly common step when he "said that if he had presented anything to his wife, he dashed it to her," that is, he gave it to her and did not demand the return of his marriage expenses. His decision, however, is particularly striking because Akwasi owed his wife's family £1.19.0, an amount that he repaid as part of the divorce negotiation, and that he could have offset with a claim for reimbursement of his marriage expenses.[77]

By the 1950s, however, more and more cases showed men resorting to inflated claims for marriage expenses to recoup their investment in a marriage or as a tool for gaining some desired end. In *Kwasi Baffuor v. Adjua Adai*, for example, adjudicated in 1953 before the Kumasi Division Native Court C, both recently divorced spouses claimed a certain farm that they had created together on Kwasi's land while they were married. Kwasi Baffuor brought suit because, though he claimed the land as his, Adjua Adai kept trespassing on it. The farm did belong to Kwasi, although at the time of the divorce settlement, Adjua's family had sought a share of the farm for her. Kwasi countered with a weighty claim for marriage expenses to the tune of £197, the value of the monies and goods he claimed to have given Adjua during the course of their marriage. Faced with such an exorbitant bill, Adjua's uncle quickly came around to Kwasi's point of view, and he agreed to forgo the claim for one-third of the farm in return for Kwasi's promise not to enforce his right to be reimbursed for his marriage expenses. [78]

In an attempt to resolve contests over marriage expenses, the Asante Confederacy Council had earlier assembled a committee to examine the question of divorce accounts. The council accepted the committee's recommendations at its third meeting (1938):

> If under any circumstances, the husband divorces a wife, the Council declared, "no claim to any article of dress, nor money given for maintenance or funeral expenses should be claimed: save, if he likes, valuable trinkets in the woman's possession or debt. . . . If the woman divorces the husband, only articles of dress, valuable trinkets not damaged or loan given should be claimed and not damaged or worn out dress or moneys given for maintenance fees."[79]

After the order was published, however, the council continued to debate what it actually meant when it said that "'properties given' are claimable but 'should not include gift.'" It finally ruled that "'gifts such as a house, a cocoa farm or money' . . . can be covered unless the transfer is validated by the payment of *aseda*."[80] Obviously, much ambiguity over reclaimable marriage expenses remained long after 1938. Thus, it is no surprise that, as late as 1953, Adjua Adai's family considered Kwasi Baffuor's threat a real one. Men continued to rely upon hefty claims for marriage expenses, sometimes reaching hundreds of pounds, to offset women's claims for a share of jointly produced farms. Though in this case the court did not comment on the legitimacy of Kwasi Baffuor's claims, since he prevailed on the simpler grounds of an already agreed upon divorce arbitration that gave him possession of the farm, the case clearly illustrates the use of marriage expense claims to ward off the property claims of disgruntled wives.

Marriage expenses and chop money were not the only manifestations of monetized conjugal relationships. Many men recalled altogether new obligations as a result of the monetized economy. They reported giving or loaning their wives seed money so that they could enter petty trading, an occupation of increasing importance with the commoditization of a broadened range of consumer goods in rural Asante, and paying their children's school fees.[81] These were remembered as heightened obligations that required men to bear more than their fair share of the burden. As one man rather dourly observed, "Normally how much would a wife give to a husband? It is men who are stupid [and] who give their money to the wives."[82] Over and over, men of the first colonized generation articulated their belief that husbands provided all-encompassing care for wives, which involved the expenditure of significant and burdensome amounts of money. As Kofi Dware put it in an entirely representative statement, "I was giving her everything, chop money, clothing, and everything."[83]

Indeed, the conventional wisdom among this generation of men was that the significant expenditures husbands made on wives' maintenance represented more than adequate compensation for the conjugal and domestic labor wives had to provide. As men saw it, they retained control of the profits of conjugal labor but women, in return, received all-inclusive and highly valuable care.[84] The actual value of the care a husband routinely provided must be considered critically, however, in light of the reminiscences of women from this same generation. While at a minimum, care was supposed to comprise the provision of chop money, cloths, and support of any children, even these basic items were not necessarily forthcoming, or, as in the case of chop money, they might be transformed into a money-making proposition for the husband. For example, if a husband subsidized his wife's production of agricultural goods intended for the market by providing land or labor, he might maintain that this assistance replaced the direct provision of chop money. Likewise, if a husband helped to finance a wife's trading by providing seed capital, he could press her to siphon off a portion of her profits as chop money. In short, a husband could reap very real, ongoing financial benefits from meeting chop money obligations in these indirect ways. And, in a surprising number of instances, men provided no chop money at all.

Women recall that these new financial obligations in marriage were met in a variety of ways. Some did remember all-encompassing husbandly care. As in the case of Akosua Addae of Tafo, their husbands "provided all the finances . . . and when I wasn't there he could even bathe [the children]."[85] For others, the new financial burdens were shared equally with their husbands. As Grace Boakye of Kumasi remembered, "We both helped. We both contributed to school fees, food, clothing, everything."[86] Yet others shouldered these expenses temporarily when a husband could not, for whatever reasons, meet his obligations.[87] For countless others, however, the new expenses were a burden shouldered alone, or, if one were lucky, with the assistance of matrikin. Victoria Adjaye of Effiduasi was a trader and farmer. Her husband, as she remembers, "didn't give me anything—not a *pesewa*! He didn't . . . help. He knew that I could take care of the children, so he didn't help." Because Victoria's mother was also a successful trader, she used some of her money to help Victoria meet her expenses.[88] These stories and the many like them belie most men's claims that husbands gave "everything" their wives needed. In fact, women could and did support themselves in the expanding cash economy. Yet the perception of universal husbandly care mattered, for it was one of the arguments used to justify men's broad-based access to married women's labor.

THE CHANGING CONTENT AND
MEANING OF MARRIAGE PAYMENTS

Men's increased access to and control over the labor of their wives, as well as the general monetization of marriage, were articulated in the changing content and meaning of marriage rituals. Money, even in small amounts, became central to the rituals between a man and a woman's family to such a degree that the line between *tiri aseda* and *tiri sika* (a husband's loan to his wife's family, in return for which the wife stood as a pledge or pawn for the debt) grew increasingly blurred. The result was the gradual conflation, or collapsing, of the distinctions between a free and a pawn wife. As we have seen, the giving and receiving of *aseda* (thanksgiving) was the one event that indisputably created a fully regularized marriage. Before the heightened monetization of the rural Asante economy that occurred in the early decades of the twentieth century, *aseda* in marriage took the form of drinks, known as *tiri aseda*, "thanks for the head," or more commonly *tiri nsa*, "head drinks." People with fewer assets presented palm wine, a relatively inexpensive drink tapped and sold locally, while people who could afford it might purchase more costly and thus more prestigious imported alcohol, generally schnapps or gin. Formalizing a marriage, then, required only the presentation of drinks, which were shared among both matrilineal families and with fathers in order to make them all legal witnesses to the fact that a marriage had indeed occurred.

In the first half of the twentieth century, the composition of *tiri nsa* underwent significant changes. As Asante became progressively more monetized, so did *tiri nsa*. Rattray made no mention in *Ashanti Law and Constitution*, in his legal discussion of marrying, of the presentation of anything other than drinks.[89] However, in a passage in an earlier book, which also addressed marrying, he noted a schedule of fees to be paid at the time of marriage, ranging from nine shillings for a slave, to 10/6 for a commoner, to £8 for royals. He also suggested that such payments had previously been unnecessary, drinks alone or even the simple consent of the families and parents being sufficient to effect a marriage.[90] In his research several decades later, in the 1940s, Kyei found that while drinks alone might still be accepted in some localities, increasing numbers of families now required cash (*sika*) along with drinks. He found that the amounts of money presented ranged from £1. 3.0 to £2. 7.0.[91] According to Takyiwaa Manuh, who provides a very useful overview of *tiri aseda* in the town of Kona for the entire first half of the twentieth century, the *tiri nsa* intrinsic to marrying involved a cash payment, either in addition to or in lieu of drinks, by the 1920s. The amount presented rose from ten shillings in the 1920s, to as much as £3 by the 1940s, to more than £8 in the 1950s.[92] Manuh connects the large jump in *aseda* in the 1950s to an increase in cocoa prices, which caused an "increased demand for wives" (and their labor) among men who wished to grow cocoa.[93] Arhin has also concluded that during the twentieth century, money became an important part of the *aseda* presented in marrying.[94] Those who shared their recollections with us recalled that while drinks alone had sufficed to formalize marriage in their childhoods, by the time they themselves married, money had become a common component of the marriage *aseda* required by most, if not all, families. Although cash came to replace or accompany drinks in the formalization of marriage, it retained the name *tiri nsa*. It was not generally referred to as *tiri sika*, or "head money," the term used for the loans made by men when they took a pawn wife. Yet the monetization of *tiri nsa* would gradually work to obscure earlier distinctions between the two types of marriage payments.

That *tiri sika* continued as a marriage payment, even though pawnage was abolished in 1908, only served to render those distinctions all the more blurred. And as one marriage payment faded, in substance and meaning, into the other, the differences that marked the status, rights, and obligations of a free versus a pawn wife grew increasingly blurred. Marrying and pawning thus became overlapping systems of exchange, and the implications were substantial. As female pawnage was subsumed within the colonial category of "wife," it disappeared from the colonial gaze,[95] and, as both Austin and Grier have argued, wives-as-pawns were absolutely crucial to the expansion of the cocoa economy both before and after 1908. Indeed, Austin writes of the "feminization of pawning" and Grier of a "coercive and exploitative precapitalist relationship [becoming] relegitimised and harnessed to . . . accumulation."[96] Yet the blurred distinctions between free and pawn wife had profound implications not only for pawnage—allowing it to persist, gendered female, long after abolition—but for marriage generally. As female pawnage was collapsed into the now singular category of "wife," women's rights and obligations in marriage, across the board, shifted dramatically.[97]

Let us look first at some of the statistics on the relative incidence of free and pawn wives over the course of the first five decades of the twentieth century. Clearly, there was a relatively high occurrence of wives-as-pawns during the first two decades of the cocoa boom, 1900–1920—the period during which men relied heavily upon unfree conjugal labor, among other forms of labor, to work their emerging cocoa farms. Both Fortes and Kyei, working from the same data collected during the Ashanti Social Survey of the 1940s, found that in the "haphazard sample" of 608 marriages, 227 "involved the payment of *tiri sika*."[98] Kyei concluded that pawn wives constituted close to 50 percent of the women who, given their age, were highly likely to have been married during the initial establishment of the Asante cocoa industry. Among women born between 1890 and 1909, a group that would have begun marrying between 1905 and 1924, on average 45 percent were pawn wives. Kyei's findings then indicate a gradual decline in the incidence of wives-as-pawns among women born between 1910 and 1919, who would have begun marrying around 1925 to 1934; 28 percent of this cohort were pawn wives. The decline continued for women born between 1920 and 1929, who would have begun marrying around 1935 to 1944: members of this group became pawn wives only 14 percent of the time.[99]

Austin has posited that the decline in *tiri sika*, and thus in female pawnage, can be connected to women's increased economic autonomy after the 1920s, as women moved to become cocoa farmers in their own right or to enter the cash economy through trade or production of foodstuffs for the market. In this changing context, "*tiri sika* was less worth paying because the wife felt less obliged to her *abusua* to respect the marriage on the terms that her elders had accepted on her behalf."[100] This argument, while compelling in many ways, needs to be set against the evidence presented in the previous section—gleaned both from life histories and from the observations of scholars like Rattray, Danquah, and Kyei—that demonstrates a trend toward husbands demanding and obtaining increased labor from their wives. The "mutual assistance" obliged in the free marriages described by Rattray for the 1910s had clearly given way by the 1930s to a set of obligations that eerily mirror Rattray's description of late nineteenth-century and early twentieth-century pawn marriage (*awowa awadie*):

> Half of any treasure trove found by the pawn was to belong to the husband; . . . the husband [was] to have authority to take the wife on trading expeditions without consulting any of her abusua; the wife henceforth [was] to have no alternative but to reside in her husband's home; the wife was now under a definite obligation "to rise up when called upon and accom-

pany the husband to his farm, to cook for him and to perform the house-hold duties." Hitherto she would ordinarily have carried out these tasks, but she was apparently under no legal obligation to do so; a man's mother often cooked for him.[101]

Rattray's description clearly captures the life experiences of many women in Asante's first colonized generation who, as free wives, found themselves more obligated to and under more extensive control of their husbands than their free mothers had ever been. It is because the clear distinction between pawn and free wives had collapsed, beginning in the 1930s, that *tiri sika* began to disappear, and it is not simply coincidence that as *tiri sika* disappeared, *tiri aseda* (or *tiri nsa*) carried a growing monetary component. The conflation of pawn wife and free wife simply rendered the separate payment of *tiri sika* meaningless. Since free wives had to labor for their husbands as fully as did pawn wives, men lacked any incentive to incur the additional expense that gaining a pawn wife entailed. It is thus not surprising that in 1945 Kyei found that "*tiri-sika* is not paid in many marriages these days."[102] In some instances it may not have been worth paying because "a wife felt less obliged to her *abusua*." In others, however, it may not have been worth paying because a wife, with the simple payment of *tiri nsa*, was already fully obliged to her husband.

"WHAT WOULD BE THE SENSE OF MARRYING"?
WOMEN'S REACTIONS TO A SHIFTING CONJUGAL TERRAIN

While we explore in subsequent chapters the multiple strategies women employed in the face of these profound shifts in the meanings and makings of marriage, this chapter would not be complete without briefly introducing women's immediate responses to the increased demands on their labor and to the monetization of marriage. In the first decades of the twentieth century, women of Asante's first colonized generation were, initially as children and then as young wives, drawn into the cash economy on terms that were largely not of their own making. Obviously, for wives, the investment of labor in a husband's cocoa farm or any other cash-generating enterprise had very different implications from investing labor in a food farm. It might mean benefits in the short term but almost always serious liabilities in the long run. It certainly did not provide for future economic autonomy or security. For this reason, as Christine Okali observed, "wives working on new and young farms were always aware that they were not working on joint economic enterprises. They expected eventually to establish their own separate economic concerns."[103] And the evidence suggests that this is precisely what many did, after the initial establishment of cocoa in an area. As Austin has recently argued, women's ownership of cocoa farms in Asante during the first two decades of the twentieth century was exceedingly rare. After that point, it became far more common and was directly correlated to the length of time cocoa had been cultivated in a given area.[104] Thus, by the third decade of the century, women in Asante began to establish their own cocoa farms—an option that provided far more long-term economic security than laboring on a husband's mature farm did. And the independent establishing of a cocoa farm was only one in a series of options that opened to women in areas where the cocoa economy was fully in place. "The growth of male cocoa income," according to Austin's recent account, "created economic opportunities for women in local markets, both as producers (for example, of food crops and cooked food) and as traders."[105]

It was thus during the 1920s, with cocoa well established in many parts of Asante, that women's role in the cash economy was both changing and diversifying. Many wives were making the move from being the most common form of exploitable labor during the initial introduction of cocoa to themselves exploiting the new openings for economic autonomy and security presented by the established, though still rapidly expanding, cocoa economy. Adwoa Addae of Effiduasi recalled this period as a time in which women asserted a great deal of autonomy and independence, much of it linked to the establishment of cocoa farms or to engagement in foodstuffs trade. "In those days," she recalled, "women were hard working, so we could live without men. . . . we were independent. We could work without the assistance of men."[106]

The chronology embedded in the life stories of women of this first colonized generation points to the 1920s and early 1930s as a period of increased economic opportunity for them. As we shall see in subsequent chapters, women's efforts to seize these opportunities are evident not just in the statistics documenting the increasing number of women cocoa farmowners or in descriptions of the growing market in foodstuffs, particularly in towns like Kumasi and Obuasi, but in the crisis in conjugal production, in marriage itself, which is so well documented in customary court cases and in life histories. In this critical transition period, many women appeared quite prepared to divorce husbands who refused to set up farms for them. Others routinely divorced men who did not provide them with at least the basics of chop money, clothing, and support of the children. Drawing on his research in the 1910s and 1920s, Rattray argued that the "[r]efusal to house, clothe, or feed her properly" were common grounds for divorce.[107] And many did divorce. As Afua Fosuwa explained: "[care] is why we marry."[108] And if proper care was not forthcoming, then divorce was the solution. "I will not use my money when he can provide," said Yaa Akom of Mamponten. "What would be the sense of marrying?"[109]

And as some women increasingly turned to divorce, others turned to customary courts to challenge matrilineal inheritance, demanding portions of a divorced or deceased husband's cocoa farm in recognition of labor invested.[110] Still others sought to avoid marriage altogether or, at the very least, to insist, as their mothers and grandmothers had, on its fluidity and the mutuality of conjugal obligations.[111] These conjugal struggles, which engulfed Asante between the two world wars, were about control over women's productive and reproductive labor and about the very definition of conjugal obligations at the moment when women were negotiating their own spaces within the colonial economy. The changes unleashed by the movement of women into the cash economy, not as wives but as producers in their own right, combined with a host of other factors—urbanization, western education, Christianity, and British colonial courts[112]—to produce nothing short of widespread gender chaos throughout the interwar years. It was chaos engendered by cash and cocoa, by trade and transformation.

YOU EITHER ARE OR YOU'RE NOT: DEFINING WHO IS MARRIED IN THE COLONIAL COURTS

Asante's first colonized generation viewed marrying as a fluid, dialogical process, largely defined, as we have seen, by the families involved. But the conjugal chaos set in motion by cash and cocoa did not and could not remain a family affair. The presence of native courts, particularly after 1924, meant that defining marriage was also an affair of the colonial state, as mediated by the evolving structures of indirect rule. With the monetization of the economy and with the financial stakes in conjugal relationships dramatically higher, there was little room for ambiguity or for recognition of process. Either you were married or you were not. Thus, in case after case from the late 1920s onward, Asante's native courts struggled to assert a singular definition of marriage by focusing on *tiri aseda* as the defining component of marriage. Only unions in which *tiri aseda* had been presented were considered true marriages, and all other conjugal relationships were consigned to the category of "mere" concubinages.[113] As the defining of marriage moved from the family to the native court, therefore, marrying was quickly transformed from fluid process to state of being.

Not atypical was the case of *Kojo Amankwa v. Yaw Buo*, which came before the Native Tribunal of the Kumasihene on 26 April 1927.[114] Kojo Amankwa sued Yaw Buo, the brother of his former wife, Abina Nsia, in an effort to recover his marriage expenses (that is, all gifts of clothing, household goods, and small sums of money other than chop money given to the wife by the husband during the marriage) from his wife, who had left him. In his testimony, Kojo Amankwa described his relationship with Abina Nsia as a marriage, and he referred to her as his wife. He testified that after they agreed to end their relationship, Abina Nsia's family told him "I should go and claim my expenses . . . so that they might pay me my costs."[115] The testimony of Yaw Buo upheld Kojo Amankwa's version of events, confirming that Abina Nsia's relatives had asked him to reckon his marriage expenses and even referring to Abina Nsia as Kojo's wife on several occasions. The court, however, having ascertained that no money had been paid as *aseda*, labeled the "marriage" as concubinage and ruled that the plaintiff did not have the right to recover marriage expenses.

The litigants in *Kofi Pipra v. Ama Agyin* also found their fluid definitions of marrying in conflict with the static definitions of the colonial native court. Heard on 18 July 1927 in the Native Tribunal of the Kumasihene, the case involved a dispute between the couple, who had separated some time previously.[116] When they first decided to marry, and in recognition of this intention, Kofi Pipra presented gin to Ama Agyin's parents as a door-knocking drink. Everyone who testified agreed that he presented nothing else in recognition of the marriage, and that he never followed up the door-knocking drinks with *tiri aseda*. Nonetheless, all of the witnesses, as well as Kofi and Ama themselves, considered the couple fully married. Kofi Pipra's description of their relationship reads: "I saw defendant we agreed to marry. I went with two bottles of gin to see defendant's parents. . . . They agreed, drank the gin and defendant and I lived together as wife and husband awaiting to pay dowry or headrum.[117] Ama Agyin described the nature of their relationship in greater detail: "Plaintiff is my husband still and he can claim satisfaction [that is, an adultery fee] should anyone have carnal connection with me."[118] The testimony in the case indicates that although the couple never formalized their marriage with the presentation of *tiri aseda*, they and their families considered the relationship to be a marriage. The native court, however, once again perceived the relationship as a concubinage, not as the marriage described by the litigants and their families.

The recollections of rural Asantes, as well as the testimony of many of the individuals who came before the courts as litigants or witnesses in court cases, demonstrate that the strict definition of marriage adhered to by the courts continued to diverge significantly from the views of the majority of Asantes who lived their lives and settled most of their conflicts outside of the court system. Many couples (and their families) never bothered to formalize a marriage with the presentation of *tiri aseda*, yet all involved still considered it a true marriage. Their fluidity of interpretation stands in stark contrast to the courts' far more rigid view of monies and drinks serving a fixed and unchangeable purpose. The point is not that ordinary Asante believed conjugal relationships defined as marriages and conjugal relationships defined as "mere concubinages" were one and the same. As we have seen, they acknowledged openly that a conjugal relationship accepted as a valid marriage did differ from a conjugal relationship understood as concubinage. However, they parted company with the courts in their continued willingness, for a variety of reasons and under a variety of circumstances, to extend conjugal status to many relationships that the courts recognized only as concubinages.

The marked divergence between the courts' theory of marriage and the practice or process of marrying, as defined particularly by those who could not afford the growing costs of *tiri aseda*, finally led the Ashanti Confederacy Council to intervene in 1942. After lengthy discussion, the council decided that spouses married according to "native law and custom" should register their marriages, so as to streamline the courts' ability to differentiate actual marriages (as the courts understood them) from more informal conjugal relationships:

> It was suggested . . . that marriages should be registered, "to enable the Native Courts to decide without any waste of time as to whether the union between the man and the woman is strictly in accord with native law and custom, when another man is accused of adultery with the woman," and the husband claims the adultery fee. The Council resolved that "registration of native marriages be adopted," and a fee of 5/- be charged in each case, (reduced to 2/6 the next year).[119]

While native court and council definitions of marriage did not immediately or uniformly affect those outside of the court system, they constituted a state-generated definition, a counter-discourse on marriage, that would increasingly shape definitions and processes of marriage in general. A husband who had not paid *tiri aseda* in years past, though in a less secure position than a husband who had, could still count on his wife's family to recognize his status, if he met his obligations to his wife and their children. His wife, moreover, could expect and demand full husbandly care. But as affairs of the family became affairs of the state, transactional marrying processes like this one were legally characterized as concubinages, and no conjugal rights, claims, or obligations were recognized; more importantly, they could not be enforced. Because virtually every conjugal contest that made its way to the native courts in the colonial period—divorce, inheritance, child or spouse maintenance, adultery—hinged directly or indirectly on verifying the legality or nonlegality of the conjugal relationship, the transformation of marrying processes into a single act of marriage, as we shall see, broadly reshaped the terrain of social reproduction in Asante.

CONCLUSION

Women and men from Asante's first colonized generation witnessed profound transformations in the meanings and makings of commoner marriage as they moved from childhood to adulthood. As children, they came to understand the marriages of their parents and grandparents as largely family affairs—fluid, processual, reciprocal, and dialogic. They carried that understanding into their own adult lives, but it was an understanding that would prove to be at odds with the harsh realities of an increasingly monetized world. With the expansion of the cash economy—an expansion shaped profoundly by the organization of labor in cocoa production—seismic shifts remapped the conjugal terrain. By the time this generation married, a free wife was obliged to provide far more labor to her husband than her mother or grandmother had. She quickly discovered, moreover, that the value of her conjugal labor in a monetized economy was mediated through and realized solely by her husband. As the changing content and meaning of marrying rituals like *tiri aseda* and *tiri sika* evidenced, a free wife, despite her free status and despite the abolition of pawnage, was subordinated to her husband much as a pawn wife had been.

Faced with the realities of a shifting conjugal terrain, many women from this first generation sought economic security and autonomy, beginning in the 1920s, by entering the cash economy on their own terms—as cocoa farmers, produce farmers, or traders—and in their own right. Their movement challenged that shifting terrain of conjugality in Asante and marked the beginning of nearly two decades of conjugal chaos. In response, Asante's native courts sought immediately to impose "conjugal order" by asserting a singular definition of marriage that hinged on the payment of *tiri aseda*. Their narrow, jural definition, as we shall see in chapter 3, worked to further undermine the reciprocity that had so long been a hallmark of social reproduction in Asante. It was a definition that upheld the rights of a husband/father to the labor of his wife and children, while detaching those rights from any reciprocal responsibility to provide adequate care.

NOTES

1. Tashjian: Yaa Akom, Mamponten, 11 October 1990.
2. Rattray, *Ashanti Law*, 22.
3. Kyei, *Marriage*, 53. Historically, it was only *kyiribaa*, pregnancy before a young woman went through her nubility rites, that was strictly forbidden.
4. Tashjian: Akua Foku, Oyoko, 7 November 1990.
5. Tashjian: Ama Akyaa, Oyoko, 27 November 1990.
6. Tashjian: Afua Nyame, Mamponten, 24 July 1990.

7. Tashjian: Adwowa Fodwo, Mamponten, 1 October 1990.

8. Tashjian: Akua Foku, Oyoko, 27 November 1990. A husband's lengthy absence led to divorce in the early nineteenth century, too. See Bowdich, *Mission*, 260.

9. Tashjian: Ama Akyaa, Oyoko, 20 November 1990.

10. Tashjian: Akua Kyere, Mamponten, 8 August 1990.

11. Tashjian: Yaw Dankwa, Mamponten, 27 September 1990; and Adwowa Fodwo, Mamponten, 14 September 1990. *Agyapadeε* has been variously defined as "family property" and "heirlooms" by Rattray, *Ashanti*, 51 and 227, and as "heritage," "inheritance," and "treasures" by Christaller, *Dictionary*, 154.

12. See Tashjian: Ama Akyaa, Oyoko, 23 October 1990, and 27 November 1990.

13. See Tashjian: Ama Akyaa, Oyoko, 23 October 1990, 20 November 1990, and 27 November 1990. For a parallel discussion of spiritual protection in marriage among Akan peoples south of Asante, see A. B. Ellis, *The Tshi-Speaking Peoples of the Gold Coast of West Africa* (London: Chapman and Hall, 1887), 18, 94, 104, 149, 235.

14. For further discussion of *ntoro*, see chapter 3.

15. Tashjian: Adwowa Fodwo, Mamponten, 23 November 1990.

16. Tashjian: Adwowa Fodwo, Mamponten, 23 November 1990.

17. Rattray, *Ashanti Law*, 10. Many authors, including Rattray and Kyei, use the terms *nton* and *ntoro* interchangeably to describe the spirit that is transmitted through fathers.

18. Rattray, *Ashanti*, 6.

19. Rattray, *Ashanti Law*, 22–32. *Awadie* is Rattray's spelling of what is more commonly rendered *awareε*.

20. For example, queen mothers could marry servants, craftsmen, or slaves. See Vellenga, "Who is a Wife?" 145.

21. Rattray, *Ashanti Law*, 24–25. *Aseda*, or "thanksgiving," played an important role in formalizing any transaction in Asante. Historically, *aseda* was presented in the form of an alcoholic beverage (*nsa*). Giving *aseda* on the one hand, and receiving it on the other, meant that both parties agreed to a transaction and that the transaction had become legally binding on each. Everyone who witnessed the giving of *aseda* received a share of the drinks and upon accepting them became legal witnesses to the transaction, obligated to testify to its occurrence should any dispute arise.

22. Ibid., 22–32.

23. Marriage could also occur between a pawned woman and a man other than the individual who held her in pawn. Pawning was a common arrangement in precolonial Asante whereby, in lieu of cash interest on a loan, a creditor received the use of a pawned person's labor for the duration of the loan. For a thorough investigation of the history of pawning in Asante, see Austin, "Human Pawning."

24. Rattray, *Ashanti Law*, 49.

25. See, for example, Fortes, "Ashanti Social Survey"; Fortes, "Demographic Field Study"; Fortes, "Kinship and Marriage."

26. Kyei, *Marriage*, 27.

27. Very frequently, men worked on their in-laws' farms, in addition to providing *tiri nsa*. See Arhin, "Monetization," 101; and Arhin, "Pressure of Cash," 460.

28. Kyei, *Marriage*, 26–39. For another description of the stages of marrying, which adds much interesting detail to the outline sketched above, see Manuh, "Changes in Marriage," 190–92.

29. Kyei, *Marriage*, 27.

30. Vellenga has shown that among the Akwapim, another Akan people, concubinages could likewise be recognized as marriages so long as there was "some indication of family recognition and approval of the relationship." Dorothy Dee Vellenga, "Who Is a Wife? Legal Expressions of Heterosexual Conflicts in Ghana," in Oppong, ed., *Female and Male*, 147.

31. The translation of *mpena* as "concubine" is unfortunate because, in English usage, "concubine" is clearly gendered female and describes a woman who cohabits with a man outside of marriage. In Asante, *mpena* is used to describe both men and women. Moreover, it carries no pejorative connotation as it tends to in the western context.

32. Tashjian: Adwowa Fodwo, Mamponten, 9 October 1990; and Peter Danso, Oyoko, 25 October 1990.

33. Tashjian: Kofi Anto, Oyoko, 6 November 1990.

34. Tashjian: Kwame Dapaa, Oyoko, 8 November 1990.

35. Tashjian: Kwabena Manu, Mamponten, 21 September 1990.

36. Tashjian: Peter Danso, Oyoko, 25 October 1990.

37. Tashjian: Panin Anthony Kofi Boakye, Oyoko, 22 October 1990. The absence of any elaborate, public marriage ceremony meant that outsiders would not have witnessed the event and thus would not necessarily know whether a formal marriage had occurred. As Oppong notes of the Akan generally, "customary marriage is almost devoid of public ritual or display." See Christine Oppong, "Notes on Cultural Aspects of Menstruation in Ghana," *Research Review* 9:2 (1973), 33–38.

38. The concept of "widow" could also be contingent upon "degrees of knowing" or familial recognition. Vellenga argues that "widow" can refer to any woman recognized as a wife by a deceased man's family, even if no formal marriage had occurred. Dorothy Dee Vellenga, "The Widow among the Matrilineal Akan," in Betty Potash, ed., *Widows in African Societies* (Stanford, CA: Stanford University Press, 1986), 224–25.

39. On the pressures to give lavishly, see Manuh, "Changes in Marriage," 196; and Katharine Abu, "The Separateness of Spouses: Conjugal Resources in an Asante Town," in Oppong, ed., *Female and Male*, 157.

40. Lack of resources did not completely prevent men from marrying, however. If the family allowed it, services to in-laws like labor could take the place of some of the money or drink. See Arhin, "Monetization," 107 n. 6.

41. Tashjian: Kwabena Manu, Mamponten, 21 September 1990.

42. Tashjian: Kwabena Boahene, Mamponten, 11 September 1990.

43. The description of Asante marrying captured here fits well with the approach outlined by John and Jean Comaroff for Tshidi marriage, which treats "marriage as a problem in the strategic construction and management of social reality." See John Comaroff, "Preface"; and John and Jean Comaroff, "The Management of Marriage in a Tswana Chiefdom," in E. Krige and J. Comaroff, eds., *Essays on African Marriage in Southern Africa* (Cape Town: Juta and Company, 1981), xvi and 29–49.

44. Tashjian: Yaw Dankwa, Mamponten, 27 September 1990. When rural Asantes of this generation speak of prostitution, they are generally referring to perceived promiscuity rather than to the exchange of sex for money. For further discussion of how to define prostitution for the colonial period, see chapter 4.

45. Tashjian: Afua Fosuwa, Oyoko, 28 November 1990.

46. Tashjian: Kofi Dware, Mamponten, 14 September 1990.

47. For a fuller discussion of divorce, see chapters 3 and 4.

48. On the pressures families exerted on couples to mediate problems and salvage marriages, see Kyei, *Marriage*, 64–67.

49. See Gracia Clark, "The Position of Asante Women Traders in Kumasi Central Market, Ghana" (Ph.d. Dissertation, Cambridge University, 1986), 239–42. Clark argues that women who did not receive the "personal satisfaction" they expected from marriage were more likely to divorce, while marriages that met their expectations might persist into old age.

50. Tashjian: Aduwa Yaa Ama, Oyoko, 5 November 1990.

51. Wilks locates this transition in the sixteenth century. For a fuller discussion, see Wilks, "Land, Labor, Gold," 41–90. See also McCaskie, "State and Society," 483–85; and McCaskie, *State and Society*, 25–26.

52. Kyei, *Marriage*, 40.

53. See Manuh, "Changes in Marriage," 188; and Vellenga, "Who is a Wife?" 145.

54. LaTorre, "Wealth Surpasses Everything," 31 and 357. See also Wilks, *Asante*, 668; Ray A. Kea, *Settlements, Trade and Polities in the Seventeenth Century Gold Coast* (Baltimore: Johns Hopkins University Press, 1982), 196–97; Arhin, "Trade, Accumulation and the State," 525–56.

55. Exceptions included people engaged in craft production, hunting, and fishing, as well as large-scale and long-distance traders. See LaTorre, "Wealth Surpasses Everything," 20–56; and Austin, "'No Elders Were Present,'" 8–10.

56. LaTorre, "Wealth Surpasses Everything," 68. LaTorre identifies hunting and snail collecting as other seasonal activities (24). Because commoner participation in the extra-subsistence economy was "discontinuous," Austin prefers to characterize nineteenth-century commoners as "supplier[s]" rather than "trader[s]" or "producer[s]." Austin, "'No Elders Were Present,'" 20.

57. Among the most easily accessible sources are the following: Austin, "Capitalist Relations"; John Dunn and A. F. Robertson, *Dependence and Opportunity: Political Change in Ahafo* (Cambridge: Cambridge University Press, 1973); Grier, "Pawns"; Hill, *Migrant Cocoa-Farmers;* Christine Okali, "Kinship and Cocoa Farming in Ghana," in Oppong, ed., *Female and Male*, 169–78; Dorothy Dee Vellenga, "Matriliny, Patriliny, and Class Formation in Two Rural Areas of Ghana," in Claire Robertson and Iris Berger, eds., *Women and Class in Africa* (New York: Africana Publishing Company, 1986), 62–77.

58. Austin, "Capitalist Relations," 260–62.

59. See Austin, "Human Pawning," 140.

60. Austin's earlier work ties the abolition of slavery and pawnage to the use of hired labor on cocoa farms but not to changes in gender relations within the household. His recent work, however, demonstrates quite convincingly that pawnage was not simply abolished but declined in uneven, ambiguous, and very gendered ways that had a profound impact upon conjugal relationships. See Austin, "Capitalist Relations," 264–65; and Austin, "Human Pawning," 137–44.

61. Roberts, "The State," 54.

62. Ibid.

63. Tashjian: Aduwa Yaa Ama, Oyoko, 5 November 1990.

64. Rattray, *Ashanti Law*, 25.

65. J. B. Danquah, *Gold Coast: Akan Laws and Customs* (London: Routledge, 1928), 153. Also cited in Kyei, *Marriage*, 41.

66. Kyei, *Marriage*, 41.

67. Allman: Akosua Mansah, Kumasi, 3 June 1992.

68. See, especially, Grier, "Pawns"; and Vellenga, "Matriliny, Patriliny." For a description of how the "exchange economy" affected "traditional Ashanti pattern of resource allocation," see Katharine Abu, "The Separateness of Spouses: Conjugal Resources in an Ashanti Town," in Oppong, ed., *Female and Male*," especially 167–68.

69. As Kwabena Boahene said, "I have given you chop money to cook for *me*." Tashjian: Kwabena Boahene, Mamponten, 11 September 1990. Clark notes that when men took additional wives, they did not necessarily increase the amount of chop money to reflect the increase in the size of the household. Clark, "Position of Asante Women Traders," 243.

70. Abu, "Separateness of Spouses," 161.

71. Christine Oppong, *Middle Class African Marriage: A Family Study of Ghanaian Civil Servants* (London: George Allen and Unwin, 1981), 87 and 95.

72. See Kyei, *Marriage*, 67.

73. Ibid.

74. The first steps in marrying underwent a similar monetization. While Kyei wrote of the presentation of "seeing *things*" and "door knocking *things*," by 1990 Tashjian's informants widely used the phrase "knocking *fees*" in reference to this first stage of marrying. For a fascinating discussion of transformations in the content and meaning of marriage gifts in a very different context, see Barbara Cooper, "Women's Worth and Wedding Gift Exchange in Maradi, Niger, 1907–1989," *JAH* 36:1 (1995), 121–40. Here Cooper concludes that "while the outward form of the wedding ceremonies gives the appearance of continuity with the past, the changing contents of the gifts exchanged embody new understandings of wealth, prosperity and worth as well as new aspirations among those taking part in the ceremonies" (140).

75. The disposition of marriage things/marriage expenses at divorce is taken up in chapters 3 and 4.

76. MRO: Palaver Book, *Kwami Pong v. Affuah Chiawa*, dd. Kumasi, 3 June 1907.

77. MRO: Native Tribunal of Kumasihene, Civil Record Book 9A, *Adjuah Nsiah v. Kojo Krampah*, dd. Kumasi, 17 August 1931, 53–60.

78. Melville Herskovits Library of African Studies, Northwestern University Library, Evanston, Ivor Wilks Papers, typed transcript: Kumasi Division Native Court C, Nana Kwasi Baffuor per *Kojo Kakari v. Adjua Adai*, dd. Kumasi, 17 November 1953.

79. MRO: Ashanti Confederacy Council, Minutes of the Third Session, 7–23 March 1938; and Matson, *Digest*, 24–25.

80. Matson, *Digest*, 24–25.

81. A full discussion of changing parental roles is provided in chapter 3.

82. Tashjian: Barima Tawia, Mamponten, 16 October 1990.

83. Tashjian: Kofi Dware, Mamponten, 14 September 1990.

84. See Tashjian: Ama Atta, Mamponten, 25 September 1990; Kwasi Amankwa, Mamponten, 8 October 1990; and Ama Bra, Mamponten, 10 October 1990.

85. Allman: Akosua Addae, Tafo, 22 June 1992.

86. Allman: Grace Boakye, Kumasi, 27 May 1992.

87. Allman: Ama Nyarko, Kumasi, 8 June 1992.

88. Allman: Victoria Adjaye, Effiduasi, 25 August 1992. See also Tashjian: Ama Akyaa, Mamponten, 10 October 1990; and Yaa Akom, Mamponten, 11 October 1990.

89. Rattray, *Ashanti Law*, 24.

90. Rattray, *Religion and Art*, 81, 82, 84.

91. Kyei, *Marriage*, 29–30. In Tashjian's research, the specific cash amounts people mentioned accorded closely with those recorded by Kyei; £2.10.0 was the amount most frequently named.

92. Manuh, "Changes in Marriage," 189, 193.

93. Ibid., 194. Manuh also gives data showing the amount of money that changed hands in marriages contracted in Kona, a rural town outside Kumasi, between 1900 and 1955.

94. See Arhin, "Pressure of Cash," 460; and Arhin, "Monetization," 98, 101. Along with *tiri nsa*, other transactions, which had formerly not involved cash, became monetized at this time. For example, the *aseda* that formalized *abusa* sharecropping contracts was increasingly rendered as drinks or money. See Vellenga, "Matriliny, Patriliny," 68. The *nto* or tribute paid by strangers in return for use-rights to land, which had been paid in meat or foodstuffs, has more recently become a cash payment. Arhin, "Pressure of Cash," 455.

95. Austin, "Human Pawning," 139.

96. Austin, "Human Pawning," 137; Grier, "Pawns," 182.

97. Barbara Cooper's work on Maradi suggests a parallel process in Niger. "The abolition of slavery," she writes, "set in train a series of redefinitions of marriage as slave-owning families attempted to recast master/slave relations onto the intra-household hierarchies of women." See Cooper, *Marriage in Maradi*, xliv–xlv and 1–16.

98. Cited in Austin, "Human Pawning," 157 n. 150. See also African Studies Centre, Cambridge, England, Meyer Fortes Papers, "Ashanti Marriage Statistics" [no date].

99. Kyei, *Marriage*, 99.

100. Austin, "Human Pawning," 143.

101. Rattray, *Ashanti Law*, 49.

102. Kyei, *Marriage*, 99.

103. Okali, "Kinship and Cocoa Farming," 170.

104. Austin, "Human Pawning," 141. Okali has also argued that women began to withdraw their labor from the cocoa farm once it matured. See her "Kinship and Cocoa Farming," 172. This pattern makes sense in light of the Nowell Commission's finding that by 1938 a reliance upon migrant labor had begun to replace the previous reliance upon conjugal labor on male-owned cocoa farms. See Arhin, "Monetization," 103.

105. Austin, "Human Pawning," 142–43.

106. Allman: Adwoa Addae, Effiduasi, 30 June 1993.

107. Rattray, *Religion and Art*, 97–98.

108. Tashjian: Afua Fosuwa, Oyoko, 28 November 1990. That being cared for was one of the significant ways women conceptualized marriage is also indicated by Akosua

Nyantakyiwa's statement about widowhood: "You get married to the children the dead husband begot you. I didn't marry anyone when the children can take care of me." Tashjian: Akosua Nyantakyiwa, Oyoko, 24 October 1990.

109. Tashjian: Yaa Akom, Mamponten, 11 October 1990.

110. Countless numbers of such cases can be found in the record books stored at Manhyia Record Office. See, particularly, the records of the Kumasihene's Native Tribunal, 1926–1935; the Asantehene's Divisional Native Court B, 1935–1960; and the Kumasi Divisional ("Clan") Courts, 1928–1945 (Kyidom, Kronti, Gyasi, Ankobia, Oyoko, Benkum, Akwamu, and Adonten).

111. Roberts noted a similar pattern in Sefwi Wiawso. See her "State and Marriage," 54–55.

112. For an important discussion of the ways in which women to the south of Asante used the British judicial system during this period, see Roger Gocking, "British Justice and the Native Tribunals of the Southern Gold Coast Colony," *JAH* 34:1 (1993), 93–113, especially 108–10.

113. Cf. John and Jean Comaroff, "Management of Marriage," 44–45. In contrast to Asante courts, whose singular definition of marriage diverged markedly from popular commoner definitions of marrying as process, Tshidi courts continued to recognize the "pervasive reality–that all Tshidi may engage in the strategic management of affinity."

114. MRO: Native Tribunal of Kumasihene, Civil Record Book 2, *Kojo Amankwa v. Yaw* Buo, dd. Kumasi on 26 April 1927, 48–50.

115. Ibid.

116. MRO: Native Tribunal of Kumasihene, Civil Record Book 2, *Kofi Pipra v. Ama Agyin*, dd. Kumasi, 18 July 1927, 593–94 and 598–601.

117. Ibid.

118. Ibid.

119. Matson, *Digest*, 23.

3

SIKA YƐ MOGYA/ "MONEY IS BLOOD"?: TRANSFORMATIONS IN THE DOMESTIC ECONOMY OF CHILDREARING

Cocoa sɛe abusua, paepae mogya mu.
(Cocoa destroys kinship and divides blood.)[1]

INTRODUCTION

In chapter 2, we focused on the ways in which the economic changes of the nineteenth and twentieth centuries reshaped conjugal relations between men and women, and we saw that previously negotiated and fluid marrying processes gave way to a more rigid, singular definition of marriage in which husbands had greatly increased authority over their wives. In this chapter, we turn to our "second strategic substantive entry point" for understanding the world in which Asante's first generation of colonized women lived—childrearing and the changing rights and obligations of mothers and fathers vis-à-vis their children. Just as the expanding cash economy profoundly challenged the meanings of marriage in Asante, so too did it recast the terrain of parenting (*-tan*). Fluid relationships based on reciprocity and exchange gave way to essentialized, "natural" categories within which were conflated a range of relationships of subordination. For Asante's first generation of colonized women, as we have seen, being a free wife increasingly entailed obligations that, for a previous generation, were only incumbent upon pawn wives. For the children of this generation, male and female, a very similar process unfolded as fathers came to assert rights in their free children that, in previous times, they only claimed if they held their child in pawnage. Yet, as we shall see, the emergence of the "natural father," with inalienable rights in his children, could cut in a number of ways. If it implied, on the one hand, that a father had increased authority over his children, it also opened the door for those same children (and their mother) to stake a claim to any wealth a father produced and to challenge the very foundations of matrilineal inheritance in Asante.

THE CHANGING DYNAMICS OF CHILDREARING

Much of the early anthropological literature that addressed parenting in the colonial period tended to treat the raising of children as an unchanging set of clear-cut, gender-specific responsibilities that began at conception. As Rattray wrote in the 1920s, "it is the *ntoro* of the man, mingling with the *mogya* of the woman that . . . forms the child . . . thus each man and woman have in them two distinct elements–*mogya* (blood) and *ntoro* (spirit); the former inherited from the mother and transmitted by her alone, and the latter received from the father and transmitted by him to his offspring." While the mother's blood determined the lineage of the child, that is, his or her *abusua*, the father's *ntoro* provided "that spiritual element . . . upon which depend health, wealth, worldly power, success in any venture, in fact everything that makes life at all worth living." [2] After a child was born, according to the early anthropological accounts, the rights and responsibilities remained clear cut. A mother was responsible for the daily care of the child, for feeding and bathing. The father, though "he has no legal authority over his children," was duty-bound to "feed, clothe, and educate them, and, later, to set them up in life." [3] Yet the bottom line, according to Fortes, was "the bond between mother and child [which was] the keystone to all social relations," for your "'mother is your family, your father is not.'" [4]

While it was expected that children, especially sons, would live with their father once they passed infancy, [5] a father by no means owned his children. According to Rattray, he could not pawn them, and they could be removed from his care by their maternal uncle, should the father be "too poor to bring up the child properly." [6] One informant explained to Rattray, "A father has no real (legal?) power over his grown-up children. If they wish to go to their *abusua* (blood), he cannot prevent them." [7] While a man passed his *ntoro* (spirit) to his children, was responsible for naming them, [8] and, at the other end of the life cycle, his children were responsible for providing a coffin upon his death, obligations and rights during the intervening years were not rooted in notions of absolute ownership or final authority.[9] In short, a father was expected to raise his children, to discipline them, and to train them; in turn, he could expect to be served by them, but under no circumstances did he own them.

Though the accounts of childrearing by scholars like Rattray and Fortes are cast in a normative present, they were based on the reminiscences of informants who provide an important window on to the last half of the nineteenth century and the first decades of the twentieth. Indeed much of Rattray's presentation on the "status and position of the Ashanti father" consists of quotations from "fathers and mothers and uncles themselves."[10] From them we are introduced to a system of childrearing governed by notions of reciprocity (duty and obligation in exchange for rights of use), which brought a husband/father and his wife/children's *abusua* into an ongoing process of exchange. We can see, for example, that a father's rights of access to his children were initiated with his completion of the rites of naming. As a result of naming his child, the father accepted the responsibility for training the child. He now had certain legitimate duties toward and claims upon that child. If the child had come to an age when he/she should be serving the father but did not, the father could demand compensation because he had met his obligations but was being denied his rights of use. Alternatively, if the father failed to meet his obligations toward his children, he could be denied access to them by their *abusua*. A father's rights in his children, therefore, were rights of use only, despite the fact that a child, particularly a male child, might spend his entire life in his father's house. As an Asante proverb unambiguously explains, *Gyadua si abontene ne hi wo fie*—"the *gyadua* (tree) stands in the street, but its roots are in the house."[11]

The accounts by Rattray's and Fortes' informants certainly echo those of many of the women whose childhood reminiscences we recorded. Maternal uncles tended to figure prominently in those recollections. "Concerning the children," Yaa Akyaa of Tafo explained, "if the uncle is there, he will be responsible for everything. . . . It was the uncle, always the uncle."[12] The rights and responsibilities of mothers and fathers were remembered in an equally clear-cut way. As Kwame Nkansah of Agogo recalled, "The father brings the meat. The mother cooks it to eat. He disciplines the children. The wife cooks, does the washing."[13] Yet any authority the father wielded over his children, any rights he had to their labor or service, were contingent upon his looking after the children well. As Adwoa Brefi of Kumasi explained, "if you took care of the children well, you had authority."[14] If you did not, "you can't say anything."[15]

The transactional process of childrearing captured in Adwoa Brefi's remarks—that is, rights dependent upon fulfilled duties—is clearly evidenced in the fluidity of children's living arrangements. Many recalled that, when mothers and fathers lived separately, it was common for children, especially sons, to live with their fathers. Children might go to a father's house any time after the earliest years of infancy. Ama Akyaa of Mamponten described a typical pattern when parents resided in neighboring villages: "If they are in separate places like . . . Oyoko and Abuontem, the children could go to visit the father and come back. They could go for, say, a week. . . . [They] could go and give a helping hand."[16] Afua Dufie remembered a similar pattern: "I was staying with my mother. The father was in Ahenkro and we were here in Oyoko, so when I missed him, I went to him in Ahenkro."[17] Such fluid living arrangements were interrupted only if there were evidence that a father was not caring properly for his children. In those cases, the children's *abusua* would refuse to allow them to go to the father.[18] Generally, however, an *abusua* would have no objection to children living with their fathers for, as Afua Fosuwa explained, "even if [the mother] gives them to the man, the children will invariably come back to her."[19]

As many also recalled, however, the fluidity in childrearing and living arrangements was gendered in quite specific ways. Sons were more likely to reside with a father than daughters were, because of the training a father was supposed to provide for his son.[20] Kwabena Boahene, born around 1907, remembered that his father provided him with seed money so that he could begin tapping palm wine. When he was in his early twenties, his father helped him a second time: "My father took me to a place to learn shoemaking. . . . I learned all the shoemaking in Nsawam. When I came out of my apprenticeship I came to Kumasi . . . it was common for a father to help."[21] A father could apprentice a son in his own craft or pay to apprentice him to someone else. Providing a son with an apprenticeship that resulted in a durable skill was remembered as being equivalent to providing capital. As Barima Tawia explained, "In this sense he would not need to give you money to start a business or something like that. It is the work you are learning that will give you everything."[22]

Writing in the 1940s, Fortes sought to explain the tendency of fathers to provide for their children, especially their sons, via apprenticeships. Paternal assistance was most commonly given in this form, he argued, because it was viewed as not in conflict with competing claims for resources from the father's own *abusua*. Historically, children have not been able to inherit their fathers' estates, he wrote, "[b]ut what a father is quite free to do is to equip his children with non-material, non-heritable assets. That was why, formerly, craftsmen tried to teach their skills to their sons."[23] Fortes' reasoning certainly makes sense of the childhood recollections of many people with whom we spoke. However, it appears far less apposite as we follow that first colonized generation into adulthood and encounter their own recollections of parenting.

Just as caring for a wife increasingly involved larger outlays of cash as chop money and start-up capital for petty trading grew in importance in marriages, so too did the costs of caring properly for a child. The equation was no longer the simple one outlined by Fortes or Rattray, for fatherly care increasingly involved a cash component that was material, arguably inheritable, and clearly in competition with the claims of that father's *abusua*. When Akua Addae reflected on the gendered division of parenting in her childrearing years, she recalled, "I bathed the children when they got up, and then they went to their father for money, and then they went to school. . . . [My husband] paid the school fees and all other financial matters."[24] Akua Addae's recollections were echoed by countless others who remembered that they bathed, cooked, and fed the children, while their husbands were responsible "for all their debts, all their clothes, and their school fees."[25] As Ama Akyaa of Oyoko said, in language strikingly reminiscent of men's conceptions of wifely care, fathers now gave children "almost everything they need."[26] Admittedly, in many of these reminiscences, adding cash to the parenting equation did not appear to undermine the historically fluid, reciprocal relations between a father and his wife/children's *abusua*. When Sarah Obeng of Asokore was asked about the repercussions for a father who did not care properly for his children, she replied, "Then he has no say. If he doesn't look after them, he can say nothing."[27] Moreover, most women recalled that they, too, provided money toward the care of their children. Like Adwoa Agyewaa, who was a cloth dyer in Kumasi, they used the money they earned from trading, farming, or craft production to "look after the children properly."[28]

But a mother's cash contribution to a child's upkeep simply did not and could not have the same long-term implications as a father's. A mother's monetary contributions were seen as self-interested in ways a father's never were, since a woman's children belonged to her *abusua* and any material investment in their future was a material investment in her own. Thus, as many women remembered, it was not simply a question of cash or finances being added to a fluid parenting equation and all other variables remaining the same. As their reminiscences underscore, a father's authority over and rights in his children could be completely transformed by the monetization of fatherly care. "It is what the father says that is taken seriously, that has weight. . . . Yes, they [the children] are mine, but he was responsible for the school fees and did everything in terms of finance."[29] As Abena Sikafo bluntly explained, "Authority resides in the one who takes care of the child."[30] In the accounts of others, the transformation in the paternal role appears even more profound. As Akosua Addae of Tafo explained: "Whatever the man says is it. I only delivered them, but the *man's blood is in them. His blood flows through the children.* . . . Yes, they are in my maternal family, but they belong to the father."[31] Peter Danso of Oyoko echoed similar sentiments. "Your child is your blood," he explained, "and therefore you can't look after your maternal family at the expense of them. . . . That is my mind."[32]

When Fortes encountered statements similar to Danso's and Addae's, he attributed no particular significance to them: "Even among the more sophisticated (but not necessarily literate) men and women, who maintain that a child has its father's blood (*bogya*) as well as its mother's, the belief that there is a closer physiological bond with the mother than with the father prevails."[33] But these statements are clearly positing a very different meaning here—one that captures in simple, metaphorical language the profound transformations in parenting experienced by many of Danso's and Addae's generation. In a society in which lineage/blood had been understood, historically, as passing through the mother, both Addae and Danso utilized blood—that most potent symbol of natural connections—to articulate the connections between fathers and children. Their choice of language should not be dismissed as mere rhetorical flourish. It should force us to consider if cash, as a father's now material and inheritable investment in his children's upbringing, was capable not just of undermining the "natural" connections articulated through blood but of replacing them altogether. Was money fast becoming the "blood," and thereby the embodiment, of new "natural" connections in the expanding cash economy?[34]

CASH, CARE, AND INALIENABLE PATERNAL AUTHORITY

In order to make sense of the complex matrix of cash, care, and paternal authority, we need to look at one of the primary cash expenditures in childrearing for the first generation of colonized Asantes: education. While most of the women with whom we spoke did not attend school, by the time they had become parents themselves, the value of formal education in colonial Ghana was widely recognized. Literacy was the route to employment as a clerk, teacher, shopkeeper, or cocoa broker, all relatively high-status and high-paying occupations.[35] Writing in the 1940s, however, Fortes attributed no particular significance to the fact that a father's contribution to his child's training was increasingly monetized, particularly through the payment of school fees. In fact, he considered it as an almost seamless continuation of a father's historic duty to train his children. "Nowadays," he wrote, "one of the most valuable non-material assets with which a child can be equipped for the future is school education. As one Ashanti father put it 'education is something that you put in your child's head and nobody can ever take it away from him.'"[36] Yet the life stories we have heard suggest that the transition from a father's nonmaterial training of his children to the payment of school fees was anything but smooth. Indeed, nearly every older Asante with whom we have spoken over the past years has mentioned school fees—for boys and for girls—as a never-ending source of conflict between mothers and fathers.[37] School fees reached into the web of criss-crossing obligations and rights within the conjugal family and cut right to the heart of daily negotiations over childrearing. A focus on this particular expenditure, therefore, provides important insight into transformations in the domestic economy of childrearing, especially into the changing rights and obligations of fathers.

As paying for education became part of the definition of good fathering, the cash outlay required of attentive fathers increased substantially, since school fees, supplies, and uniforms were costly. When Akua Foku of Oyoko was asked to define a father's responsibilities toward his children, she replied quite simply, "Taking care of the children means taking him or her to school, and then spending on him or her."[38] Indeed, education became so central a part of expected paternal care during the childrearing years of the first colonized generation that many came to equate paternal care with paying for schooling. While it is not surprising that, when schools entered the picture, most understood the fees to be the responsibility of the father, a father's cash expenditure on education did not simply replace a father teaching a son, for example, to farm or to hunt. It brought with it, as we shall see, an assumption of greater rights of use in, and even paternal ownership of, children. In other words, cash investment in a child's education transformed a father's role within his conjugal family.

We can catch glimpses of this process in a case heard in 1936 before the Asantehene's Divisional Court B. Kwasi Quansah filed suit against R. A. Mensah for £100 in damages. He claimed that his daughter, Mary Quansah, while engaged to another man, was impregnated by Mr. Mensah, a teacher at his daughter's school in Kumasi. The future husband subsequently refused to marry Quansah's daughter. The £100, according to the plaintiff, represented the expenses he had incurred as a result of supporting his daughter through her pregnancy and after the birth. It also reflected the fact that the defendant had "spoiled my daughter's school time," thus adversely affecting her future economic well-being.[39] In many ways the facts of this case are telling. Mr. Quansah filed the suit alone; no representatives of Mary's matrikin were present. None, apparently, assisted her during her pregnancy. Moreover, unlike the typical daughter in early anthropological accounts, who was trained in her father's house, served him, and then went off to marry,

Quansah's daughter went to school. Quansah invested heavily in her education and appeared to exercise full rights of ownership over her. As a result of
the pregnancy, his cash investment in her future was jeopardized, so he sought
legal recourse.

Kwasi Quansah's case was not unique. The testimony recorded in a
host of colonial-era cases provides invaluable insight into the transformations in childrearing that played out during the lives of Asante's first
colonized generation. The judgments in child custody/child maintenance
cases, moreover, suggest a gradual movement away from insisting on the
transactional nature of the father's rights (that is, rights dependent upon
fulfilled duties) and toward the recognition of paternal rights independent of the fulfillment of any obligations toward a mother and her children. The very earliest recorded cases (before 1910) were heard before
colonial officials who seemed to be utterly confused about how to proceed. They understood that children "belonged to the mother's family"
but were in complete disagreement among themselves over what this meant
in terms of a father's rights. An incident in 1906–1907 in which the Adansi
ɔmanhene claimed the child of a deceased Adansi woman on behalf of
her family demonstrates the depths of misunderstanding and discord
among British officials. The woman had been married to an Assin man,
and the man refused to give up the child. The Adansihene demanded the
child's return. For months, colonial officials forwarded reports and traded
minutes on Asante "customary law" regarding ownership of children. Virtually no one agreed with anyone else.[40] Unfortunately, the case disappeared from the historical record before a judgment was rendered.

In the period after 1924, when native tribunals were established throughout the region, we encounter a wide range of customary court documentation
that allows us to chart more closely changes in so-called "customary law."
Many of the judgments in child custody/child maintenance cases from the
late 1920s and early 1930s seem to echo what we know of rights in and
obligations toward children in the precolonial period. In these cases, reciprocity–the transactional or dialogical process of child-rearing–was upheld.
For example, in the 1929 case of *Kwadjo Safo v. Kwame Antwi et al.*, the
plaintiff claimed £100 in damages from his wife's family because, as he testified, "they had deprived me of my children." When subsequent testimony
proved that the father had not supported his children over the years, judgment was entered against the plaintiff and he was made to pay costs since
"his action is inconsistent with Native Customary Law."[41]

As time went on, however, judgments were less likely to enforce reciprocity and more likely to uphold paternal rights independent of paternal
duties. *Ama Manu v. Kwasi Buo* (1940) is a case in point. Here, Ama
Manu claimed £8.5.0 in maintenance and subsistence from her ex-hus-

band. She testified that she had been married to the defendant's brother, but that the brother had become quite sick and was unable to support her and their children. She asked for a divorce, but her husband's family asked that she wait. After her husband died, his brother agreed to take her as his wife. "Nine months passed," Ama testified, "and nobody subsisted me and so some man had sexual connection with me." Kwasi Buo then demanded that she name the offender so he (Kwasi) could collect an adultery payment. In his defense, Kwasi argued that he was "not liable to pay any subsistence or maintenance fee to her, especially as her husband was sick and she was misconducting herself with other men." The court ruled against the plaintiff, finding that her "behaviour toward her sick husband" meant she was "customarily not entitled to any subsistence by the defendant."[42] The judgment in this case is particularly telling because the reciprocity we noted in earlier cases is simply not enforced here or, from another perspective, is enforced, but in one direction only. Ama's and her children's rights to subsistence were made dependent upon Ama's fidelity. Paternal rights, however, stood alone. They did not rest on the ability or the willingness of either her first husband or his brother (her second husband) to provide subsistence to Ama and her children.

Changes in paternal rights were not just evident in child maintenance or custody cases in the courts. They were also manifest in more subtle ways— in the rites associated with the marriage of a man's children (especially his daughters), in his increased access to his children's labor, and in contests over who was responsible for a child's debt. Asante fathers had always played an important role in the marriages of their sons. Rattray learned from his elderly informants, for example, that a father had to "find a wife for his son, and to pay 'head-money' for him even if his son has money."[43] However, a father's role in his daughter's marriage was far less prominent for the obvious reason that members of an *abusua* had a much greater stake in the marriage of a female family member; her children belonged to the *abusua*, while the children of a male relative belonged to their mother's family. Writing of the early nineteenth century, Bowdich found that fathers could nominate husbands for their daughters and could also apply pressure to have their choice accepted.[44] But at least from the turn of the century, if not earlier, a father's authority over a daughter's marriage seemed to increase as her *abusua*'s authority decreased. Rattray was told by his elderly informants in the early 1920s that the ability of a woman's maternal uncle to force cross-cousin marriages with his own sons had declined.[45] By 1945, Fortes found that the maternal uncle's power in arranging marriages for female family members had further decreased.[46] Reminiscences from the period reinforce these perceptions. Speaking of his own marriage sometime between 1924 and 1931, Kwasi Anane of Mamponten explained that mothers, fathers, and maternal kin could all be involved in choosing a potential husband and in judging such an individual's acceptability. However, both parents had greater authority in the matter than the maternal uncle, because "they have given birth to her . . . [but] the father was more powerful than the mother, in the sense that if he asked the girl to marry a certain man, she had no say. . . . It is even there up to now."[47]

But even beyond a father's growing influence over the choice of a daughter's husband came the question of his share of the *aseda*, the thanksgiving drinks and/or money presented at the time of a daughter's marriage. It is here that the most far-reaching change in men's involvement in their children's marriages can be found. According to Rattray, only fathers who held their daughters as pawns received the largest portion of the marriage *aseda*; in the case of free children, that share went to members of the marrying woman's *abusua*.[48] By the time many of the people we interviewed were marrying, however, it had become quite unexceptional for fathers of free children to get the larger share of the *aseda*. For example, Kofi Ntim said of his marriage: "I saw her father. I used £2 and a bottle of schnapps. I gave it to her father. I gave her mother 13/-. It was he who gave life to the girl, he had the power. He has to get a larger share than the mother, because the father was more powerful than the mother. That was common with all men in Asante. They get a larger share."[49] Panin Anthony Kofi Boakye remembered that the woman's father even controlled the distribution of the *aseda*: "It is given to the father. And he gives what is supposed to be given to the maternal side, to them."[50] Enhanced paternal control over *aseda* was clearly contested. Many remembered that mothers and fathers received equal shares or that the matrikin had to be given their *aseda* directly rather than through the father.[51] Nevertheless, the fact that some fathers were beginning to receive the largest share of marriage *aseda* is striking. It certainly suggests a trend toward paternal authority superseding that of the matrilineage. And because that authority so resembled that of the nineteenth-century pawnholder, it hints at the ways in which older forms of subordination, like pawnage, could be subsumed within post-abolition familial relationships.

As fathers assumed far more prominent roles in the marriages of their children, especially their daughters, they also began to assert more direct control over their children's service or labor, again in ways that mirror the power of a paternal pawn-holder. Rattray, whose informants' memories reached back into the nineteenth century, found that children might work with their fathers during their childhood and adolescence, but "'when they grow older will begin to take more interest in their uncle's property, for they will know it may one day be theirs, while all the father possesses will go to his *abusua*' (blood relations)."[52] Many with whom we spoke remembered that as children they similarly served their fathers. Some worked on a father's cocoa farms, others tapped palm wine with their fathers. Occasionally, daughters helped fathers weave *kente* cloth and provided domestic services. However, the experiences of this generation and especially those of their children began to diverge from earlier patterns in one key aspect: they and their *abusua* had increasingly less say in the matter, as fathers began to claim an incontestable right to their children's labor. Yaa Akom explained that this paternal right transcended even that of the child's matrikin:

> Though the children belong to the mother's side, it is the father who has authority over the children. He can instruct them to do whatever he likes for him. They could do any type of work the father so wishes, say, farm for him, and the uncle cannot take the children to do some work, farm on his farm, without consulting the father. It is true that we are maternally inclined to the uncle, but the uncle cannot . . . use you anyhow without the sanction of the father.[53]

Clearly, Yaa Akom's explanation differed markedly from Rattray's understanding that only a father who held his child as a pawn had "a legal right to the child's services."[54]

Judgments in cases brought before native tribunals after 1930 increasingly reinforced this changing perception of paternal control. For example, in 1932, Kwame Adu brought suit against the father of his nephews and nieces, Kwaku Yipay, for "seducing" them from him. According to Adu's testimony, Yipay had refused to allow his daughter (Adu's maternal niece) to take part in "communal work" that involved clearing debris from two roads. According to the uncle, Yipay said "his daughter had no 'master' in the village of Boaman and therefore . . . he would not allow her to take part in the road work." In his testimony, the father replied that since the mother of his six children had died four years earlier, he had "been nursing them." On one occasion, he reported, the uncle's brother "said to me that I was 'kwasie'[55] who boasted over his children, adding that the children did not form part of my family. I replied to him that even he who had only two children prided himself in them, how much more I who had six children living. A quarrel ensued between us. I swore the Great Oath that I would not allow my daughter to be responsible for the two roads." When the case was brought first to the Boamanhene, he decided that the girl should clear only one road. Apparently not satisfied with this decision, her uncle swore the Great Oath that her father had "seduced" the children from him. In its judgment, the Kumasihene's Tribunal found that the uncle had not proven his case of seduction, since it is evident that "the Defendant has not prevented his children from visiting the Plaintiff who is their uncle."[56] In many ways, this judgment completely reversed earlier formulations of the respective rights and obligations of fathers and maternal uncles. Here, the father's rights of control were inalienable, while those of the maternal uncle were rights of use only. While Rattray found that only a father who held his child as a pawn could exercise such authority over his child's services,[57] many courts after 1930 began to issue judgments that defined a similar authority for the fathers of children not held as pawns.

A third and final manifestation of the transforming role of fathers can be found in contests over a child's debt. According to Rattray, a father was not liable for the debts of his free child (*adehyɛ wo*). In fact, "Should a father pay a debt for his son," he wrote, "the latter becomes his pawn, unless he makes it clearly understood that the payment of the debt was in the nature of a gift."[58] A father who held his child as a pawn was obliged to pay half of his debts, while the child's matrikin assumed responsibility for the other half. Yet long after the abolition of pawnage in 1908, we begin to see customary courts rendering judgments that upheld, in quite specific and explicit ways, the sorts of rights and duties that were associated with fathers and pawn-children, although all children, at least in the eyes of the law, were freeborn. For example, in the 1929 case between Akosua Adae and Kwaku Ahindwa, the plaintiff complained that her ex-husband was not paying the debts incurred by their children. The court ultimately ruled that Ahindwa could have no "right of commanding his children" until he paid one-half of the debts they had incurred. While the judgment in this case upheld some sort of reciprocity, it was the reciprocity of a father/pawn-child relationship, not that of a father and freeborn child.[59] Moreover, as some remembered, that reciprocity could be easily undermined by a father simply refusing to pay a debt. As Ama Akyaa recalled, "if the father can't [pay] and the mother has [money] . . . she pays . . . because the mother can't stand for her child to be taken away."[60] Thus were enhanced paternal rights severed from paternal duties.

In the cases discussed here—of marriage, of service, and of debt—we catch glimpses of an evolving relationship between a father, a child, and a child's *abusua* that bears more than a faint resemblance to the relationship that prevailed in precolonial and early colonial times when a father held his child as a pawn, a practice technically outlawed by the British in 1908.[61] The fact that pawnage, rather than disappearing, became hidden within a changing family economy had implications that were profound and enduring. As the status of pawn was collapsed into the categories of son and daughter, rights, duties, and obligations in Asante were broadly recast. The rights of the colonial father (and husband, as we saw in chapter 2) became the rights of the nineteenth-century pawn-holder. And those rights, in turn, became increasingly detached from reciprocal obligations and duties. This transformation occurred at a time, moreover, when the economic costs of rearing children rose dramatically, particularly as a result of school fees. These new costs would not be integrated into an ongoing system of exchange between a father and his children's mother and their *abusua*. A father would not be obliged to meet them in order to retain his rights of use in his children. Indeed, there were fewer and fewer ways to encourage or force a father to view these costs as his obligation because none of his actions or inactions could threaten his now inalienable rights in his children. Fathering was no longer something men did, something they negotiated and transacted through extended processes of exchange involving rights, duties, and service. Fatherhood was a status, a position endowed with inalienable rights.

FADING RITUALS OF RECIPROCITY

The transformations in childrearing, care, and paternal authority discussed so far are perhaps best evidenced by the virtual disappearance in the twentieth century of two notions central to the definition of fathering for previous generations—*ntamoba* and *ntoro*. Knowledge of *ntamoba* had already declined precipitously by the early years of the twentieth century,[62] while familiarity with *ntoro* began to lessen somewhere between the time of Rattray's research in the second decade of the century and Fortes' fieldwork in the 1940s. Many Asantes are familiar with neither term today. It is our contention that both of these concepts—the first mediating a father's interactions with his children's *abusua*, and the second articulating the spiritual connection that bound fathers to their children—sank into obsolescence as fathering was transformed from a transactional relationship to a status imbued with inalienable rights.

Of the two, the concept of *ntamoba* is the more difficult to track, since, by the early twentieth century, there were already only vestigial traces to show that it had ever existed. The first evidence that we encountered was buried in a 1921 court case. Only four or five volumes in the rich collection at Manhyia Record Office predate the Native Jurisdiction Ordinance of 1924, and it was in one of those rare early volumes that Allman came across *Kojo Asamoah v. Kojo Kyere*—a rather puzzling case between a matrilineal uncle, acting as head of family, and his niece's husband—heard before the Native Tribunal of Bompata, Ashanti-Akyem, on 18 February 1921.[63] This was an oath case[64] in which the plaintiff, Asamoah, charged the defendant, Kyere, with having "falsely accused Plaintiff of depriving [him, the defendant, of] his two children." According to Asamoah, his niece, Abena Esein, was married to the defendant and had two children with him. One day, the niece complained that the defendant was not treating the children properly. The next morning, one of the children came with a message from the father that he was claiming *ntamoba* fee. The uncle replied he was not claiming the children, and the husband swore that he was.

In his opening statement, the husband, as defendant, testified that his wife complained that he was depriving her of the children and that he had replied, "they are my children and the only work I am getting from them is my water for my bath." A few days later, according to Kyere, the uncle came to his house and asked if he were claiming *ntamoba*. If he were, the uncle agreed "to pay including any other expenses." Kyere decided to make a claim but testified that he did "not receive any amount. Plaintiff swore that he was not claiming the children and I swore that he is claiming them." The defendant's son, Kojo, supported his father's testimony by stating that his uncle, the plaintiff, "claimed back the children and Abena Esien to his people and he is the head. Plaintiff afterwards swore that he is not claiming the children, and my father the Defendant swore that he is claiming them." Unfortunately, the court reporter did not record the details of the tribunal's deliberations, nor the reasons justifying its finding. The case abruptly concludes with the tribunal having "entered judgement for Defendant with costs hereunder assessed for depriving Defendant of his children."

What is striking about this case is the word *ntamoba* which was obviously central to the claims being put forth. It appears that if the matrikin were claiming back their own, then the father had the right to demand *ntamoba*, a sort of compensation for the loss of his children and their services. Not only did *ntamoba* seem to mediate the criss-crossing web of obligations, responsibilities, and rights that bound a matrilineal family (*abusua*) to the husbands/fathers of its members, but it appears singularly important in defining and circumscribing a father's responsibilities toward and rights in his children vis-à-vis the matrikin. Yet if *ntamoba* were so crucial in mediating these primary social relations, how could it have left so few traces in the historical record? Indeed, only a decade later, in the case of *Kwame Adu v. Kwaku Yipay* discussed above, there is no mention of *ntamoba*, although the facts of the two cases are strikingly similar.

Fortunately, among our few written sources, we can glean a few insights into the historical meaning of *ntamoba* that are relevant to the Bompata case. Christaller's 1875 *Dictionary of the Asante and Fante Language* defines *tammoba* as "indemnification to parents for a child that refuses to stay with them and runs away to the relations, to be paid by the latter."[65] This definition obviously works in the Bompata case, although the father in that case was the only parent being "indemnified." Danquah's *Akan Laws and Customs* (1928) provides a more elaborate but similar definition, which warrants fuller quotation:

A father has right of use over his children, but the true ownership is vested in their maternal family. The tie between mother and child can scarcely be broken; but the relationship between father and child can be destroyed by a customary process. This is the process involved in "Tamboba." It is not infrequently happens that a father has to part with his "right of use" over his children in favour of their maternal relations. This demand is generally made by the wife's family. . . . For the father to part with his life interest in the children our customary law provides that a sum of money fixed by law and called Tamboba should be paid to him in respect of each child so taken away by its maternal relations.[66]

Danquah's explanation of *ntamoba*, though derived from his experiences in the neighboring Akan state of Akyem-Abuakwa, obviously resonates strongly with the details of the Bompata case in suggesting that a father's rights in his children could be terminated by the payment of compensation known as "Tamboba" by the maternal family.

Yet, of the many elder Asantes with whom we have spoken over the past years, most had never heard of *ntamoba* and could provide no definition at all. Those who could offered many and contradictory meanings, only a handful of which seemed applicable at all to the Bompata case. Many who spoke with any confidence remembered *ntamoba* as a marriage payment—either to the matrilineal family, or, more commonly, to the father of the wife-to-be. As Akosua Mansah of Kumasi remembered: "If a man wants to marry a woman, he goes to see the mother and the mother says he should go and see the father. The father will ask that you pay the *ntamoba*. . . . It is the father who receives *ntamoba*. That is to let him know that he has a daughter who is married to someone."[67] The recollections of Nana Kyeame Owusu Banahene, also of Kumasi, provide additional detail:

The one who begets the woman is called *ɔbanintan* [father; parent]. Now this man, whether he begets a girl or a boy, will be nursing the baby while the woman is cooking. Sometimes, that child will be urinating on him. When the child grows up, and someone wants to marry her . . . that pain that he endured . . . means the man was really *ɔbanintan paa* [a good parent]. The money, you call *boba*. So when the man is now coming to take the daughter, he has to pay for the pain. That is called *ntamoba*. It is for the girl's father . . . [and] if anything happens in the family, he [the father] will know that the man has really married his daughter.[68]

Other older Asantes, particularly outside of Kumasi, connected *ntamoba* not with rites of marriage but with rites of birth. Yaa Dufie of Effiduasi explained that "when you give birth to a child and you are going to name the child, the things that the father brings to the child after the naming are called *ntamoba*.[69]

Photo 3.1 Kwame Nkansah, Agogo, 1995. Photograph by Jean Allman.

Efua Tebiaa of Agogo provided a similar definition, along with some etymological detail. She suggested that the term comes from the phrase ɔtan a ɔwo ba (the father who has given birth to a child), and that in order for a man to be recognized as ɔtan a ɔwo ba, he must meet certain financial obligations: "if the father gives birth to a child and he doesn't look after the child, and the child grows and he wants to go for the child, he will be asked to pay all of the expenses that the woman incurred in looking after the child."[70]

We encountered only one elderly Asante whose recollections of *ntamoba* made sense of the 1921 case. In 1995, Allman came across a man in Agogo, Kwame Nkansah, whose definition not only paralleled the meaning implicit in the Bompata case but derived from personal experience. Nkansah, who was over 90 years old when he and Allman spoke, explained: "You have given birth to a son. You have raised him up and then he says he will not serve you, then you have to get *ntamoba*. You will get it from his family." He then recalled that he was told as a child that *ntamoba* was demanded from his family. His grandmother had given birth to his mother and an uncle. Instead of serving their father, the two went to stay with their uncle in Akyem. "When they came back," he recalled, "the father said no, he would not respond and they asked why. He said now they know where they come from and he will demand *ntamoba*. He demanded [from the family] three pounds for each of them."[71]

Although *ntamoba* appears to have survived into the twentieth century as a collection of disparate, seemingly contradictory shards, we should recognize that the multiple definitions emerging in both oral and written sources are not entirely unconnected. They all share an underlying concern for a husband/father's reciprocal obligations and rights vis-à-vis his wife's and/or his children's *abusua*. Nkansah's definition is not the only one that situates *ntamoba* as a mechanism through which an *abusua*'s relationship with the husbands/fathers of its members is mediated. Indeed, all of the definitions and explanations we encountered seem to boil down into one transactional meaning, to articulate the kind of exchange in marriage and parenting whereby a husband/father and an *abusua* entered into an ongoing process of transacting duties for rights of use.

We can posit, for example, that a father's rights of access to his children were initiated with his completion of the rites of naming. (This coincides with the few extant definitions of *ntamoba* as a rite of birth and naming.) As a result of naming his child, the father accepted responsibility for training her/him and, in turn, had claims upon the child that the child's mother and her *abusua* were bound to recognize. If the child did not serve the father, the father could demand *ntamoba* in compensation because he had met his obligations but was being denied his rights of use, either by the child's actions or by a decision of the *abusua*. Paternal obligations and rights, therefore—the father's connection with his child's *abusua*—could be terminated by the father demanding and receiving *ntamoba* or by the mother's family offering and the father accepting *ntamoba* as indemnification. (Evidence of this manifestation of *ntamoba* is present in the Bompata case and in Kwame Nkansah's narrative.) *Ntamoba* next appears to have mediated the relationship between a father and the man his daughter intended to marry. The father, as *ɔbanintan a ɔwo ba*, as the one who parented this girl-child, was compensated by the husband-to-be and, in turn, was now released from any obligations toward his daughter. The primary reciprocal relationships (obligations in exchange for rights of use) involving this daughter were now between her *abusua* and her new husband (who in some senses replaced her father). Of course, what is particularly interesting about *ntamoba* at this stage of the life cycle is its gender specificity. There was nothing similar to mark a transformation in the father's responsibilities toward and rights of use in his grown son. Indeed, much of the evidence we have suggests that a father's reciprocal relationship with his son and his son's family was far more enduring than that with his daughter.[72] A father's active reciprocal relationship with his son/son's *abusua* was maintained throughout the father's lifetime.[73] The relationship with his daughter/daughter's *abusua* virtually ended with the daughter's marriage, the only remaining service due being the daughter's obligation to help pay for her father's coffin.

The multiple manifestations of *ntamoba* posited here all have in common a recognition that ultimate power over or ownership of children rested firmly with their *abusua*. A father's rights in his children were rights of use only and were contingent upon the father successfully fulfilling his paternal duties. Over the course of a life cycle, a father's rights of use in and duties and obligations toward his children changed according to the children's age and gender, and thus *ntamoba* may have been transacted in many forms. Still, its basic role as definer and mediator of paternal obligations and rights of use appears consistent, from naming to marrying. But by the beginning of the twentieth century, and probably much earlier, *ntamoba* began to fracture into multiple, seemingly unrelated meanings and then to rapidly vanish. Rattray, who wrote extensively about the respective roles of mothers and fathers, makes no mention of the term in any of his works. The reason for *ntamoba*'s disappearance, we argue, is that, by Rattray's time, it no longer made sense; it no longer articulated a lived social reality. As Kwame Nkansah himself explained, "Now, the parents take good care of their children. They send them to school, feed them, do everything for them. . . . there is no need for the father to demand *ntamoba* from the children's relatives."[74] As we have already seen, a commoner father's rights in his children were increasingly viewed as inalienable. His relationship to his offspring was no longer envisioned as part of a complex process of exchange with their *abusua*. It stood alone as "natural" fact; it no longer worked as process. In this new configuration, how could a father be compensated for the loss of use-rights in his children when those rights had been transformed into rights of ownership that were, at once, inalienable? Although *ntamoba* survived in Asante as a marriage payment from son-in-law to father-in-law, its persistence in that muted form in no way worked against the trend toward inalienable paternal rights of ownership. As a marriage expense, *ntamoba* represented only a one-time, one-way payment from son-in-law to father-in-law in recognition of all the father had endured in raising the child. It marked the moment when (certainly not the *process* whereby) a father passed control of his daughter to her new husband and she, in turn, moved from a status that looked very much like daughter/pawn to one that resembled all too closely that of a nineteenth-century wife/pawn.[75]

If *ntamoba* embodied the material, transactional relationships between a husband/father and the family of his wife and children, *ntoro* captured the spiritual relationships. And perhaps because it seemed to explain the importance of fathering in a matrilineal system, anthropologists have historically devoted a great deal of attention to its meanings and the rituals associated with it. Through their works over the first half of the twentieth century, we not only gain a rich description of *ntoro* but can trace its gradual disappearance as the spiritual connection between a father and his children. Translated as everything from "patri-spirit," to "male transmitted spirit," "patrilineal exogamous division," or simply "patrilineal group,"[76] *ntoro* was understood as articulating the spiritual connection between fathers and their children. Although the number of *ntoro* groups was widely debated among anthropologists, most argued that there were nine. *Ntoro* was believed to be transmitted only through men, and thus every Asante child received his or her *ntoro* from the father. It was, moreover, considered to be a key determinant of personality since a father transmitted his personality to his children via his *ntoro*.

There were numerous rituals associated with this paternally inherited spirit. In order to keep one's *ntoro* "pure, neat, clean and spruce," one day of the week was set aside for the "washing" of the spirit.[77] Each *ntoro* was associated with certain taboo foods, which were to be avoided lest they cause illness or even death. A married woman was supposed to honor her husband's *ntoro* taboos until menopause, since failure to do so could impede conception, harm the *ntoro* of any child she was carrying, or cause severe difficulties in childbirth, all because of injury or insult to the father's and the child's spirit. Finally, *ntoro* was considered to play a significant role after a person's death, when the deceased's *ntoro* helped to assure the well-being of surviving relatives with whom the deceased shared *ntoro* membership.[78]

Clearly, there was a critical distinction between membership in a family or *abusua* and membership in an *ntoro*. Historically, the former articulated natural rights in children, as well as legal rights over them, while the latter did not. However, the dialogical bond created by *ntoro* was of great significance; it underlay the importance men attached to fathering children and more particularly to fathering the sons who alone would continue to transmit *ntoro* to succeeding generations. It also accounted for the reciprocal responsibility many adult children felt for aging or needy fathers.

In contrast to *ntamoba*, *ntoro* appears in the early written record with some regularity. In 1923, in the first anthropological study of Asante, Rattray chose to devote the second chapter of his book to *ntoro*, and he revisited the topic in subsequent works. Melville Herskovits wrote a short piece on *ntoro* in 1937, and Meyer Fortes took up the topic in the 1940s. Indeed, *ntoro* continued to appear in more recent works like those of A. C. Denteh in the 1960s and Peter Sarpong in the 1970s, though it was accorded far less significance. Yet the early emphasis on *ntoro* in anthropological writing may tell us more about the interests or priorities of anthropologists than about the lasting significance of the term in the early part of the twentieth century. Rattray, for example, devoted an entire chapter to *ntoro* before he discussed the *abusua* and matrilineal descent,[79] and it is clear in his text that he had a difficult time getting past his own notions of the "natural" father and the "natural" affinity between fathers and their children. For him, matrilineal affiliations were "man-made" while a father's role was original, essential. "*Patria potestas* in Ashanti," he wrote, "dwindles to rather vague unsubstantiated claims based on the natural, no less than the supernatural, forces at work in his favour, but opposed by all the man-made customary laws of the tribe."[80] It is impossible to say at this late date whether *ntoro* was simply a more enduring concept in Asante than *ntamoba* or whether it only appears as such because it captured the imaginations of early anthropological writers, who struggled with the puzzle of fatherhood in a matrilineal society and who therefore preserved the concept in their writings. What is clear, however, is that there was already confusion over the meaning of *ntoro* by the early 1930s, when several of Herskovits' informants reported that it referred to the *abusua*.[81] By the mid-1940s, both Fortes and Kyei found that the majority of Asantes whom they interviewed either had not heard of *ntoro* or believed it to refer to the family or *abusua*.[82] "[I]t is only the old generation and only a very few of the young," wrote Kyei, "who have some knowledge or awareness of it."[83] Moreover, the "ritual beliefs and practices associated with the *ntoro* concept," according to Fortes, "are becoming obsolete. To most young people the term is a vaguely understood archaic word for kinship, hence they equate it with terms for the kinship groups which rule their life."[84] By the time Denteh conducted his research in the 1960s, knowledge of *ntoro* was sketchy at best, and by 1990 Tashjian found that the few people who recognized the term generally believed it to refer to the *abusua*.[85]

The fading of *ntoro*, like the disappearance of *ntamoba*, was rooted in the changing dynamics of childrearing, particularly in the transformation of a father's rights in his children. That *ntoro* seemed to endure somewhat longer than *ntamoba*, we suggest, may very well be the result of anthropological intervention, rather than a reflection of inherent differences in the tenacity of spiritual versus material reciprocity. If *ntamoba* and *ntoro* were central to defining childrearing in the years before cash became a key factor in the childrearing equation, by the time the women of Asante's first colonized generation had come of age, neither of the concepts resonated with lived experience. The strictly limited paternal authority over children, which had been rooted in the spiritual significance of shared *ntoro* membership, was being replaced by an uncontestable paternal authority based on ownership. The rights of use in children that had been mediated and transacted through *ntamoba*, through a father's successful fulfilling of his duties, were being replaced by inalienable rights, detached from reciprocal obligations. Rituals of reciprocity, in other words, were fast disappearing.

INHERITING FROM THE "NATURAL" FATHER?

Transformations in the domestic economy of childrearing, as we have seen, eroded the transactional, reciprocal relationship between a father and his wife/children's *abusua* and gave rise to notions of a "natural" father—at times articulated in terms of blood—whose ultimate authority and inalienable rights mirrored those of a nineteenth century pawn-holder. But the processes at work cut both ways, for if a father's connection to his children was increasingly viewed as inalienable, then those same children could, in turn, claim a right to the wealth that father produced, based on their "natural" connections to him. And this is precisely what began to unfold as women and men of Asante's first colonized generation, acting as mothers and fathers, challenged the laws of matrilineal inheritance, which decreed that an individual's estate be left to a member of the matrilineage, most commonly of the same sex as the deceased.[86]

Some have explained the challenge to matrilineal inheritance by pointing to new ideological forces, namely the presence of Christian missionaries whose increased activity in the 1920s and 1930s more or less coincided with a growing debate, public and private, on inheritance.[87] Although we are only beginning to understand the complex and conflicting ways in which missionary activity affected Asante life (and Asantes, in turn, shaped mission efforts[88]), few would deny that most missionaries came with clear ideas about the importance of the conjugal unit and of the centrality of the father to that unit. All mission groups active in Asante in the early twentieth century encouraged their members to marry under the government ordinance,[89] which limited a husband to one wife, made divorce much more difficult, and entitled a wife to one-third of her husband's estate and children to one-third of their father's estate. (The matrikin were left with one-third.) Most missionaries seem to have shared the views of Reverend K. Horn, who wrote in 1931:

> Some . . . feel that . . . Christians . . . have no quarrel with the matriarchal system. They would maintain that the father-mother-children group is Eu-

ropean rather than specifically Christian, and urge that it has as many dis-
advantages as the matriarchal system. I feel myself that the guardianship
of children belongs inherently in Christian marriage to their parents, and
the inclination of thoughtful Ashantis seems to be definitely in this direction. In other words, on almost every count the Ashanti and Christian ideals of marriage and the family are opposed.[90]

The Wesleyan Methodist Missionary Society, one of the more active in
the region, reported in 1931 that all of its African ministers were married
under the ordinance, as well as all of its trained catechists and most of its
teachers and circuit agents.[91] Yet to encourage ordinary members of the church
to marry under the ordinance remained a difficult task, and much of the Methodist Mission effort in the early 1930s seems to have been devoted to facilitating this process.[92] C. Eddy, who taught at Kumasi's Wesley College, made
a plea to mission headquarters in the late 1930s for permission to bring his
wife and young twins to Kumasi. He argued that their presence would serve
as an example "that we hope to set to our staff and students of Christian
family life" and that it would provide a place where students from the neighboring girls' school (Mmofraturo) could receive training.[93]

Eddy's remarks highlight the importance of education in the missionaries' ideological battle against matrilineality and customary marriage.
The success or failure of that battle remains an open question, although
the evidence we have encountered suggests that, at least for Asante's first
generation of colonized women and their children, the missions were not
particularly effective.[94] The challenge to matrilineality may have been
buttressed by Christian missions, but it did not spring from them. The
challenge to matrilineal inheritance, we argue, emerged directly from the
cocoa farm. As we saw in chapter 2, cocoa and the broad-based exchange
economy that followed in its wake upset the "old order of economic relations between wife and husband," as Katharine Abu has written.[95] After
the abolition of slavery and pawning in 1908, wives' and children's labor
became increasingly important, particularly for the establishment of farms
on the cocoa frontier. By the end of World War I, with little land available for cocoa cultivation around Kumasi or to its south and east, the
industry spread westward,[96] and in these frontier areas, particularly when
farmers had little access to cash, a heavy reliance on the labor of wives
and children remained.[97] In the process, the conjugal family economy was
fundamentally transformed as joint labor produced a cash crop for sale
and not just food for consumption. The family's successful reproduction
was now based on production *and* exchange, and the husband/father was
the central, mediating figure through whom the value of wives' and
children's labor was realized.[98]

Quite early, therefore, the reliance upon conjugal labor on the cocoa frontier pitted mothers and children against the father's matrikin. Throughout the first decades of the twentieth century, mothers, children, and at times even fathers challenged matrilineal inheritance on the grounds that because a mother's and child's labor investment in a cocoa farm contributed to the husband/father's wealth, they should have the right to inherit at least a portion of the estate. That many cocoa farms were established on self-acquired rather than family/*abusua* property, moreover, lent weight to their claims. Historically, family property was vested in the entire lineage and could not be alienated without its approval. Thus, if a man gained the right to cultivate a cocoa farm on family land, he could never dispose of the use-rights to that land without the family's approval. Those rights belonged to the family, and the individual family member had only temporary custodianship of the land. Self-acquired property, on the other hand, was under the control of its owner. If a man grew cocoa on nonfamily land, without financial assistance from his matrikin, the resulting farm was his alone, and it could technically be disposed of in whatever manner he saw fit.

Asante fathers, therefore, had for a long time had the right to give some portion of their self-acquired property to their children. Bowdich included an account from his early nineteenth-century travels of a father giving some of his movable property (in the form of gold dust) to his child.[99] More commonly, men made deathbed bequests of personal items to children, typically sons, a practice well documented from at least the early nineteenth century. Rattray described this type of bequest as *samansie*, "that which is left or set aside by the ghost," and stated that a father generally granted such a bequest if he had been well served by the child.[100] He added that families discouraged men from giving property to their children in this (or any other) manner by reminding them of the family's responsibility for any debts the man owed at the time of his death.[101] The bequest, if granted, had to be formalized by the son's presentation of *aseda* and by the family's approval of the proposed property transfer, or else it was not binding.[102] But despite the long-standing right to freely dispose of self-acquired property, the value of personal items generally transferred in this manner remained relatively small, and the deceased's family typically expected to inherit the bulk of his or her self-acquired, as well as family, property.

By the 1920s and 1930s, however, the value of a deceased man's self-acquired property might greatly exceed that of any family property he had worked. It was no longer just small personal items that were the object of competing claims by a man's matrikin and his children but also cash-generating properties that were often conjugally developed. At times, fathers willed cocoa farms to their children and the mothers of their children, to prevent their matrikin from inheriting the property and in acknowledgment of the labor invested by their conjugal family. Though men of the first colonized generation did not themselves inherit much from their fathers, many of them spoke freely to us about their desire to leave property to their own children. For example, Panin Anthony Kofi Boakye, who was born around 1918, explained that his own father had left him nothing: "Those minds were different from now. . . . The majority of them did not leave anything to their children . . . [but] to the family alone. I accompanied my father to cultivate farms at Abesua, but my father gave them to his family." Boakye, however, felt a strong sense of responsibility to his own children and had given them a gift of some of his cocoa farms, formally witnessed, because, "Once I have brought forth children, I have to see to their welfare . . . so I thought it proper to leave them something for when I am no longer here." Because of matrilineal inheritance, he added, "normally the man goes to a different place to farm, and gives it to the children. . . . I can't leave [family property] to my wife and children. That is why I decided to cultivate some in a different place for them."[103]

Boakye's recollections are extremely significant because they demonstrate that the only foolproof way for a father to ensure that his children and/or their mother inherited anything from him was to develop self-acquired properties and then see to it that they were distributed before his death and in the presence of witnesses. Anthony Kofi Boakye of Oyoko, himself the head of his family, made the importance of gifting property before his death very clear: "I have to do that because of my family. . . . Death can come unannounced. . . . If I don't give her some before I die, nobody will give her some when I am dead."[104] When a man did bequeath his property before his death, the transfer of ownership had to be formalized to ensure that his *abusua* acknowledged and honored the gift. Mothers and their children accomplished this by presenting a formal *aseda* (thanksgiving drinks or money) that made both their own *abusua* and that of their husband/father formal witnesses to the transaction. As Obaa Kro remembered:

> He gave me some [cocoa farms] before his death. . . . Even if his family was disturbed by this, they couldn't say anything, because I had given drinks to accept the gift. My family was there, it was my *abusuafoɔ* [family members] who presented drinks to thank Owusu and to accept the gift. They gave the drinks to Owusu and he called his family and informed them about it.[105]

By giving property to his wife, a man was in essence giving it to his children, too, as they were likely to be the eventual inheritors of their mothers' estates.[106] As Abena Kwa of Oyoko explained, "he may give you some when you have children with him, with the intention of giving it to the children. . . . He can also choose to give you some and ask you to share it with your children."[107] Panin Anthony Kofi Boakye concurred: "When you give to your wife, it becomes your children's."[108] And those property transfers were irrevocable so long as any of the gifts of property were properly witnessed by members of both families.

But as many people whom we interviewed had learned, there were countless ways by which a man's family could try and prevent the passing of his self-acquired property to his children and their mother. In the absence of *aseda*, for example, a man's *abusua* was under no obligation to recognize valuable gifts presented to his wife. In such cases, as Abena Kwa said, "after his death they may express ignorance of his gift,"[109] and the woman had no way to prove her husband's action or intent. Afua Fosuwa's husband told her that he was giving her a certain share of his cocoa farms, but before the gift could be witnessed, he fell ill and died. His intent was not enough to enable her to enforce the property transfer, and as she explained:

> He had said it, but I had not been given [the farms]. I would only pour drinks to it when I have been given. . . . He fell sick and stayed in the room for almost three years, so he couldn't go there to declare what should be given to me. He said it, and I asked that I be taken to that place to see it for myself. So I went and saw it, and surprisingly what they [his family] gave me was about the size of this house, so I refused, since it was not what my husband had said. So I refused to pour drinks to that. . . . It was after his death that they took me to the place and what they gave me, I thought, was not what the husband had initially said. It happens most often, and it is a cheat.[110]

In spite of the fact that a man could best guarantee that his wife or children gained a share of his property by giving it before he died, many who intended to pass on their property still hesitated. Sometimes they postponed the finalizing of intended transfers of property because completing the transaction decreased their own property holdings and income. Many more balked because they knew that giving even self-acquired property to children or a wife could bring the wrath of the family down upon their heads. As Adwowa Fodwo observed: "Some men fear their family members, so they may not like to give their wives gifts while alive because the family may feel offended by him. . . . They fear the family members. . . . [If] he is even sick in bed they will be insulting him all the time. . . . They will insult him for bequeathing his property to the wife when he was with the family."[111] For similar reasons, wives and children often neglected to pay the *aseda*, even though it was vitally important to establishing their claim to gifted property. It alerted a man's family to his intention to distribute property away from the family and gave them an opportunity to convince him to do otherwise.[112] In order to avoid these conflicts, many men waited until they were on their deathbeds to make gifts to wives or children. Not infrequently, these men died before their wives or children had time to present *aseda* to formalize the gift.

Because there were so many disincentives to gifting properties before death, many men chose to leave all of their self-acquired property to their families and merely indicate their wish that the family then give some portion of their estate to their wives and children.[113] This did not, however, guarantee the interests of the mother and her children, for the family could honor or dishonor the request as they wished. Some families acceded to the man's request, but more commonly, as we shall see in the next section, families ignored the deceased's wishes and left their widows and children entirely uncompensated for the labor they had expended on a husband/father's farms.

And if mothers and children had a difficult time inheriting the property of a deceased husband/father when it was the intent of the deceased that they do so, all the more difficult were the circumstances of the many whose husbands/fathers had no such desire. Indeed, countless others from the first colonized generation faced much more dire predicaments. Like Akua Addae of Tafo, who, with her two daughters, assisted on her husband's cocoa farms for many years, they faced a situation in which the father of their children refused to give them a share of his property or make any provision in his will.[114] In Akua's case, the solution was divorce. "I would not continue to marry him," she recalled. Yet others began to turn to the courts, and they were joined by those whose husbands/fathers had made provision for them to inherit, but the man's *abusua* had refused. As Ama Akyaa recalled, "widows took relatives to court when they had helped [husbands] cultivate farms and the family took everything over."[115] It is to those cases—to mothers, daughters, and sons challenging matrilineal inheritance in the courts of colonial Asante—that this chapter now turns.

CONTESTING KIN:
INHERITANCE IN THE COLONIAL COURTS

Most widows and children who litigated ownership of a man's self-acquired property in Asante's colonial courts did not claim full rights of inheritance. Rather, they sought a share of self-acquired farms or other properties, either on the basis of equity—because of their labor and/or monetary inputs— or on the grounds that the deceased man had made a gift of the disputed property to them before he died. As we saw in the earlier part of this chapter, mothers and children were increasingly unsuccessful in child custody/maintenance cases in which they tried to insist on a father's rights of use in his children being reciprocally tied to the fulfillment of his duties and obligations. In stark contrast, however, those same courts, over the same period, showed an ever-increasing willingness to back the claims of widows and children to a share of the self-acquired portions of their husbands' and fathers' estates. Through the official record, we can trace the gradual shift in court reasoning, from the 1930s through the 1950s, which rendered the claims of widows and children more easily successful.[116]

A typical case involving a widow's claim to a share of her deceased husband's cocoa farms came before the Ankobia Clan Native Court on 1 August 1936.[117] In *Adjua Agyako v. Yaw Puni and Yaw Donkor,* both the plaintiff and the co-defendants argued their right to ownership of a contested portion of the estate of Kwaku Yamoa, the late husband of the plaintiff and a relative of the defendants. Adjua Agyako brought suit against her deceased husband's family to try to force them to give her a share of the many cocoa farms she had helped her husband make. Adjua Agyako's testimony made it clear that on numerous occasions, both she and her children had provided significant assistance to her husband, including allowing him to use his daughter as security on a loan: "when the deceased husband was owing any debt, I was responsible with my children. . . . My deceased husband asked the nephews to accompany him to go to find some loan, but they refused to go. . . . My deceased husband appealed to me to allow my daughter Effua Fofie to go and secure for him [that is, stand as security for a debt] . . . and I permitted him."[118] Adjua's case is particularly revealing because it clearly demonstrates how the emergence of the "natural father" could cut both ways. Adjua's husband, Kwaku Yamoa, had no control over his nephews' labor, he drew heavily on the labor of his wife and children, and, even though, historically, a father did not have the right to pawn his child, he had pawned his own daughter, albeit with his wife's consent. The word "pawn" never appears in the court record, since pawnage had long been illegal, but we see the ways in which it was subsumed by and survived within domestic relations. These very same facts, however, rendered Adjua's case against her husband's *abusua* extremely compelling.

The court concluded, in most uncompromising language, that Adjua's husband's family had been notably remiss in contributing either labor or capital to the development of the farms and that Kwaku Yamoa's relatives had "more or less deserted him."[119] In the end, the sympathies of the court members clearly lay with Adjua Agyako, and they granted her six of the contested farms. The court outlined very clearly its reasons for supporting her claim:

> The Court had to consider the 42 years period of marriage. . . . The hard
> labour performed by the Plaintiff during the 42 years stay with the hus-

band till time of death . . . the great assistance given by the Plaintiff to the Deceased together with the help of the children to cultivate the 29 farms as alleged . . . The old age of the Plaintiff . . . The quantity of children Plaintiff had with the Deceased which children most of them gave assistance to the father in cultivating his farms and securing his debts whilst his relatives failed to give him support.[120]

The court members believed that these combined factors gave Adjua Agyako and her children a legitimate stake in Kwaku Yamoa's properties.

Although the courts did not always support the widow and her children in these earliest cases, court members always took a keen interest in the manner in which the widow framed her right to a share of her husband's property. For instance, the Ankobia Clan Native Court noted with approval that Adjua Agyako had not tried to claim outright ownership of any of the farms and had not claimed to be a legitimate successor to her husband:

> The first point in this case is that Plaintiff did not bring Defendants here [claiming] that she is a . . . successor to the Deceased and so she should get share of the Deceased properties. But her point of bringing them here is that she has married the deceased husband for a long time and has assisted the deceased husband in many ways and has . . . become an old lady and therefore should have [a] share in his farms. This is the Claim before this court.[121]

Clearly, had Adjua made what would have been perceived as a spurious claim to outright ownership of any portion of her husband's property, the court would have thrown out her case. In 1936, the native courts of Asante were not ready to automatically recognize a "natural" connection between fathers and children and thereby undermine the basic tenets of matrilineal inheritance. They were, however, increasingly persuaded by the compelling facts surrounding such cases. Thus, Adjua Agyako brought suit not as a legitimate successor or as the mother of legitimate successors, but as a good, hardworking woman, who had been married to her husband for 42 years, had borne him numerous children, and, with those children, had provided a wealth of assistance to her husband.

That the court believed Kwaku's rightful successors had an obligation to his conjugal family based on their long and faithful service was made abundantly clear. The court noted disapprovingly that before it "started the case, the Court willingly asked the Defendants whether it would not be advisable for Defendants to give Plaintiff little share of the Deceased properties to live on as she has become an old lady. Defendants were asked to go and think of the question."[122] In the court's eyes, Kwaku's successors should have taken care of Adjua of their own volition. This was the right thing to do. While there is ample historical evidence that successors did have some customary obligation to provide for the widow of the deceased man (among other things by allowing her to continue to harvest foodstuffs from his food farms[123]), it is clear from the oral testimony we have gathered for this period that families did not feel obligated to assist elderly widows in these ways. And as we have seen in the previous section, men's growing tendency to leave some share of self-acquired property to a wife or child and women's and children's growing tendency to assert their material interests in properties to which they had contributed money or labor often clashed with families' inheritance expectations. From the time widows began bringing their cases to court in the mid-1930s, the courts neither blindly upheld nor explicitly undermined matrilineal inheritance. Rather, they focused on the facts of each case and argued for the rights of widows and children to share in the estates of husbands and fathers, if (and generally only if) the deceased had benefited substantially from their labor.

Adjua's case typifies the general approach of native courts to the question of widows and children inheriting from their husband/father in these early years. It is notable, however, for the lack of attention paid to the matter of *aseda*, no doubt because Adjua did not base her claim on a putative gift from her husband. As we have seen, *aseda* was used to formalize any large gift, including gifts of farms men made to wives and children. In the absence of *aseda*, a man's family could successfully challenge the legality of any gift he made to non-family members. In many of the court cases disputing men's estates, families pointed to widows' or children's nonpayment of *aseda* to bolster their claims to full ownership of the contested properties. In a majority of the cases from the 1930s and 1940s in which widows or children contested ownership of property with the relatives of a man, the payment or nonpayment of *aseda* became the pivotal issue upon which the cases turned.

In the earliest of those cases, the importance of presenting *aseda* remained unchallenged by the courts. For example, the case of *Kwasi Agyei v. Kwame Basoah*, heard in the Native Court of Kumawu on 18 October 1935, demonstrated both the courts' recognition of the legitimacy of men giving a share of their self-acquired cocoa farms to their children, and the necessity of paying *aseda* to finalize such gifts.[124] In this case, the plaintiff sued his brother, the defendant, because the defendant had given a cocoa farm to his sons. The plaintiff argued that he should inherit the farm in the event of his brother's death and therefore brought suit to prevent his brother from giving the farm to his sons. Here, the Kumawu court affirmed the right of men to alienate self-acquired property to their children. They found, however, that because the defendant, Kwame Basoah, had neglected to tell his matrikin that he was giving the farm to his sons, the conflict between the two brothers was inevitable. They thus ordered the litigants to regularize the gift by conducting "the necessary customary rites,"[125] that is, the presentation and acceptance of *aseda*. Kwame complied by presenting one bottle of rum and one sheep to his kin as an apology for not informing them of his intention to give the farm to his children.

In addition to demonstrating the continued importance assigned to presenting *aseda*, the Kumawu case typifies the concern of courts, during this period, with the facts or the merits of a case. It was not a question of privileging or undermining matrilineal inheritance; it was a question of equity and moral obligation. As the Kumawu court explained in its final judgment:

> Defendant is not a bad man in the family. He has made four large cocoa farms with the assistance of his wife and children and out of which he intends presenting one to his children and the family after his death can take possession of the other three farms is a fair play. . . . the Defendant after having settled the misunderstandings between the family and himself is entitled to present the farm to his children.[126]

Clearly, a man who intended to leave the bulk of his property to his matrikin met with no censure in the court for choosing to leave a smaller portion to his children. The court also listed its reasons for finding Kwame Basoah justified in giving a farm to his children. They pointed out that he retained full control of self-acquired property during his lifetime, and this included the right to give it to non-family members. As in the Ankobia case, the court noted the assistance the husband/father received from his wife and children in making all four cocoa farms, and contrasted their input with his matrikin's minimal involvement in the disputed farm. Because Kwame Basoah had not yet died, the court was able to order that his gift to his children be ratified by the presentation of the usual *aseda*.

Yet even among early cases, we see the beginnings of a major evolution in the courts' thinking about *aseda*. For example, *Kojo Mama v. Yaw Mensah* came before the Asantehene's B Court in December 1938 and was then heard on appeal in the Asantehene's A Court in January 1939.[127] The plaintiff brought suit claiming ownership of a cocoa farm that, he claimed, his father Boadi had given to him before dying. The defendant, the brother of Boadi, testified he had told Boadi that he objected to the proposed gift. In deference to his brother's objections, Boadi agreed not to give the farm to his son and, in fact, refused to accept any *aseda* from his son, thereby voiding the proposed gift. Three days later, Boadi died. Consequently, Boadi's brother refused to allow Boadi's son to take ownership of the disputed farm. The son brought suit.

This case is particularly revealing because it points to the growing lack of consensus within the courts themselves on the importance of *aseda* and thus on the legitimacy of many widows' and children's claims. In the lower court, the plaintiff, the aggrieved son, conceded that his father had refused to accept his *aseda*. The court asked him, "Since the 'ASIDA' was not accepted, are you entitled under the custom to call the farm your own?" The plaintiff had to acknowledge the truth: "Of course I am not." He nonetheless persisted in his claim, adding, "but my father said he had given it to me."[128] The members of the lower court found this argument entirely uncompelling and in their judgment said:

> The customary law, connected with presentation of a thing or property of importance is as stubborn as the truth is, and in a case where an "ASEDA," which is the stamp or seal to transaction of business or settlement of a dispute has not been accepted the transaction or the settlement of a dispute or even a presentation of a property, whether landed property or otherwise, is said to be incomplete and could be vetoed by any recognized member of the family of the parties concerned.[129]

The lower court not only asserted the necessity of presenting *aseda* to finalize a gift; it also fully supported the defendant's decision to encourage his brother not to make the gift:

> because Boadi was not free from debt . . . and since his liabilities would be incumbent upon his brother . . . the Defendant and the other relatives of Boadi objected to what Boadi proposed to do. There is a proverb that, he who kills the leper wears his sandals. Kojo Boadi then understood the objection raised by the Defendant and did not accept the "ASEDA" offered by the Plaintiff.[130]

Based on the facts of this case, which included no information on the amount of labor or capital invested by Boadi's son in the farm but conclusive evidence that Boadi had left a substantial debt for his family to cover, the court found in Yaw Mensah's favor. In support of its decision, the court referred to recent (1938) deliberations of the Ashanti Confederacy Council. "At a meeting of the last Confederacy Council," the court stated,

> it was decided that where a father who was assisted by his wife or wives and children in cultivating farms died, one-third or at least a portion of his farms should be possessed by his said wife or wives and children, if the

deceased died free of debt. This decision of the highest Tribunal of Ashanti
is entirely applicable to this case. The deplorable position of one's children in this country, as far as a father's belongings are concerned is well
known but where customary law does not permit, it will appear ultra vires
to do otherwise than to abide by the custom at the present. The Defendant
stated that it was because of the debt he had been made to embrace hence
he raised the objection and Boadi saw the point with him. . . . This is not
unjust and the Plaintiff ought rather to have sympathized with the Defendant for the unpleasant position in which he had been placed.[131]

While finding children's lack of inheritance rights "deplorable," the court
found even more compelling the issue of debt, debt to be borne not by the
son but by the deceased's brother.

Given the forcefulness with which the lower court stated its decision, it is
noteworthy that a mere six weeks later, the appeals court to which the son
next took his case reached a radically different conclusion. The new judgment read in part:

The facts of the case are very simple and clear. The Plaintiff who is a boy
of about 18 or 19 years of age was given a cocoa farm . . . by his father in
grateful appreciation of his filial services toward him . . . for no just and
reasonable cause he (deft) objected to half of the said farm being given to
the plf. . . . Owing to this interference on the part of the Deft., the plf's
father did not take the customary aseda and three days later he died. . . .
the gift is valid whether an "Aseda" was accepted or not since it was made
in recognition of services rendered.[132]

In reaching the decision that *aseda* did not have to be presented to finalize a
gift, the appeals court not only diverged from the ruling of the lower court of
this case and other courts hearing parallel cases around this time. In fact, in
overturning the lower court's ruling and in awarding the disputed property to
Boadi's son, the appeals court went where the deceased himself had refused
to go—recognizing the claims of a son over those of the family that would
be saddled with the outstanding debt.

Kojo Mama v. Yaw Mensah illustrates the extent of divided opinion on the
issue of mothers and children inheriting from a deceased husband/father. While
the courts attempted to provide leadership on this pressing social question, it
is clear that, even within a single court, members had trouble reaching any
sort of consensus. At the same time, the case also marks the beginning of a
dramatic shift in native court thinking about the necessity of presenting *aseda*
to regularize a gift. The appeals court initiated a bold reform when it dis-
pensed with the necessity of presenting *aseda* in order to legitimize widows'

and children's property rights. In the coming years, Asante's native courts were more and more likely to reach similar judgments, which disaffirmed the importance of *aseda* and thereby privileged the claims of widows and children.

The decisions on inheritance being reached by individual native courts were also echoed in the deliberations of the Ashanti Confederacy Council (ACC). After debating at length the issue of fathers leaving property to their children, and despite severe internal dissension, the council ruled in 1942 to validate gifts of self-acquired property made by fathers to children even in the face of family disapproval. "When a person makes a gift," the ruling read, "of his own personal or self-acquired property to his children or to any other person in the presence of accredited witnesses, whether the relatives of the donor approve of it or not, it becomes valid."[133] By allowing others to serve as "accredited witnesses," the ACC removed the family's ability to withhold acceptance of *aseda*, thus effectively undermining the direct familial authority that had previously enabled families to control men's disposal of self-acquired property.[134]

In subsequent years, there continued to be a growing recognition in the native courts of a man's right to leave or give property to his children and wives, much of it hinging upon extended timeframes for the payment and acceptance of *aseda*. *M. P. Mensah v. Kojo Fordwuo*, which came before the Asantehene's A1 Court on 13 September 1950, is a case in point.[135] The defendant, Kojo Fordwuo, claimed that his father, Kwame Wee, gave him a cocoa farm some eight years before dying. Fordwuo acknowledged that he did not pay the requisite *aseda* during the years between the time of his father's gift and the time of his father's death. However, some years after his father's death, he testified, he did present *aseda* to his father's family in order to formalize the transfer of property. The plaintiff, M. P. Mensah, the brother of Kwame Wee, argued that the late payment of *aseda* nullified the putative gift and that he had only accepted it under duress, as he was pressed to do so by a local officeholder. In its judgment, the court argued for a great deal of flexibility in the timing of *aseda*: "It may however be recalled here that the accepted native customary usage allows that should a beneficiary fail under any circumstance to validate a dying declaration before the death of the benefactor the beneficiary has the right to perform the customary rite of validation of the declaration to the lawful successor or the family as a whole of the deceased."[136] The court's assertion that presenting *aseda* after a donor's death represented long-standing custom was simply unfounded. That "custom" with regard to *aseda* was continuing to evolve is amply demonstrated by a comparison of this judgment with the court rulings from the 1938 and 1943 cases discussed above. In the 1938 case, the court ruled that the necessity of presenting *aseda* was "as stubborn as the truth is"; the 1943 case deemed *aseda's* presentation "elementary." It is likely that the Ashanti Confederacy Council ruling of 1942, which allowed children to inherit property "whether the relatives of the donor approve of it or not," helped to bolster this court's broad interpretation of when *aseda* could be presented.

In addition to loosening the protocol for presenting *aseda*, many courts, particularly by the late 1940s, began to dispense with debates over *aseda* altogether and to render judgments based solely on the perceived merits of a case. If a widow and her children worked on a husband/father's farms, for example, they deserved to receive a share of the man's self-acquired properties. *Afua Kosia et. al. v. Kwadjo Nimo*, which came before the courts in 1949–1950, typified this new approach.[137] Here, the plaintiff brought suit against the successor of her late husband, Yaw Bio, who had died in 1947. The plaintiff sought ownership of a portion of the cocoa farms that she had helped her husband cultivate. In his defense, the defendant claimed that the plaintiff had no right to the property, since "custom demands only nephews are entitled to inherit the properties of their deceased uncles." The lower court that first heard the case found in favor of the plaintiff, primarily on the grounds that she had given considerable material assistance to her husband in creating and maintaining the disputed farms. The appeals court concurred, arguing that simple equity demanded that a wife and children who provided substantial material assistance should receive a share of their husband/father's farms. "I am of opinion," the Oyokohene explained, "that the Defendant-Appellant should have applied the law of equity in deciding this matter. . . . the Plaintiff-Respondent [Afua Kosia] should not be left to the mercy of other people while the Defendant-Appellant [Kwadjo Nimo] enjoys the fruits of her labour." A second court member, the Akwamuhene, concurred: "The Plaintiff-Respondent assisted the late Yaw Bio because she naturally expected something from him. . . . it should be remembered that we Ashantis have our own unwritten laws. The labourer is worthy of his [*sic*] hire. . . . I think in equity the Plaintiff is entitled to a share of the 2 farms."[138] The claims of the *amanhene* of Oyoko and Akwamu notwithstanding, the "law of equity" was not an "unwritten law" that had always informed decisions regarding the property claims of widows and children. Indeed, the references to equity that appear in this case (and in others dating from the same period) were of very recent origin. They reflect, in general terms, a growing recognition of the rights of mothers and children—recognition won after years of wives, mothers, sons, and daughters pressing their claims both inside and outside the courts. But they also reflect, in specific terms, the deliberations and decisions of the most powerful political body in the post-1935 era, the Ashanti Confederacy Council.

That inheritance was of immediate and pressing concern is evidenced by the fact that the council took it up only three years after the council was constituted as the paramount native authority in Asante. And the deliberations of the council, from 1938 to 1948, do more than hint at the divisive nature of the debate. According to Warrington, a British official who prepared a synopsis of the minutes of council meetings, the Asantehene had a particular interest in promoting this agenda, and it was he who encouraged the council to consider inheritance practices initially in 1938. Though Warrington says that "general opinion" on the council at this time backed giving one-third of a man's estate to his wife and children, some members showed strong opposition to the idea. The Drobohene, for one, said, "I think you will all agree with me that the women of these days have no character. . . . they even go so far as to take away the lives of their husbands by means of noxious juju; this is very common in Ashanti and I tell you that a wife can easily poison her husband since she is responsible for his meals."[139] In the face of such entrenched opposition, the council decided not to make a formal ruling on the inheritance rights of widows or children at the 1938 meeting.

In 1941, the issue was brought before the council again, and the rights of widows and children to a portion of a deceased man's self-acquired property were given lengthy support by the Asantehene:

> One fact with us Ashantis is that we appear to be too conservative. We always like to stick to custom even though it may have outlived its day. I do not deprecate the idea of brothers and nephews succeeding their deceased brothers or uncles, neither do I propose that the custom should be abolished, but I want you to understand that our children are blood of our blood and bone of our bone for whom we are accountable to God for bringing them into this world. God and our country expect us to make provision for the children we bring into this world. They and their mothers help us in our farm and domestic work. Sometimes you find that all your nephews and nieces do not come near you at all. It is only your children who care for you. Is it not fair then that we should make provisions for them and their mothers who look after our interest and welfare, so that they may not become useless and wretched after our death?[140]

Here, the Asantehene presented an argument based not just on equity, which was the case in so many native court rulings, but on the connections—the "natural" connections—between a father and his children. "Our children," he argued, "are blood of our blood and bone of our bone," and thus they had a right to inherit from their fathers. Despite the passion of his plea, however, and the fact that his remarks seemed to articulate an increasingly common conviction that children were connected to their fathers by blood, the

Asantehene did not win the day. Many members of the council remained unconvinced and spoke against a specified share of a man's property going to his children and wife. As Warrington explained, in the intervening three years opposition to the proposal had, if anything, hardened.[141] The only ruling the council could agree upon, before 1948, was the 1942 decision, discussed above, which allowed a father to gift his self-acquired property to his children without the consent of his *abusua*, as long as there was some formal witness to the exchange.

In subsequent years, the colonial government pressured the Asantehene and the council to issue a ruling that would automatically entitle a man's wife and children to one-fourth of his property.[142] In fact, between July 1947 and the time the council finally ruled on the matter in February 1948, the chief commissioner of Ashanti sent a series of five letters to the Asantehene asking him to consider modifying customary law so as to grant a share of a deceased man's estate to his wife or wives and children.[143] It is possible that the Asantehene pushed the matter with his council because of government pressure. He did indicate in his 1941 plea that "God and our country expect us" to do so. Christian ideals, moreover, may have also played a role, as the Asantehene was a staunch member of the Anglican Church. But whatever the underlying factors, the contentious issue of inheritance came before the council again in 1947–1948 and the following ruling was approved: "The Council finally ruled for operation in Ashanti that when a father dies intestate, a third of his personal and self-acquired property should go to his wife and children. This third share would be equally divided amongst wives and children in the case of a polygamist."[144] The council's ruling never gained formal legislative approval from the British colonial government and thus never became official law. However, reference to the ruling was frequently made in subsequent court judgments, and it is clear that it profoundly shaped post-1948 judgments, which, in theory anyway, could rule in favor of widows and children without reference to *aseda* or to any unwritten laws of equity.

Indeed, the case of *Afua Kosia vs. Kwadjo Nimo* discussed above evidenced the importance of the ruling for Asante's native courts. The lower court members who first found in favor of Afua Kosia actually read the 1948 ruling into the court record. The defendant Kwadjo Nimo, obviously dissatisfied with the ruling, appealed the case. In his Grounds of Appeal, he argued that for the 1948 council ruling to be legally enforceable under British colonial law, the ruling had to be given force of law by the governor or chief commissioner, and that neither individual had ever validated it. Though from a strictly legal standpoint he was correct, his argument did not sway the appeals court members, as we have already seen. They upheld the lower court ruling in favor of Afua Kosia. The case, however, was not over yet. Still convinced he was in the right, Kwadjo Nimo appealed the ruling once again, this time to the Supreme Court of the Gold Coast. Here the case came before a British judge, who took a more narrowly legalistic approach to the case than had the Asante court members. He pointed out that under the Native Law and Custom Ordinance of 30 March 1940, the Ashanti Confederacy Council had the right to "submit . . . any recommendation for the modification of native law and custom which it may consider expedient for the good government and welfare of the Confederacy," but that the 1948 "recommendation" (as he termed it) "has at no time received the sanction of the Governor in Council and is of no effect." Why this was the case is not clear since members of the colonial government had pushed hard for the council to agree on such a ruling. In any event, taking a decidedly ahistorical approach all too common among colonial officials, the judge added, "The Native Customary Law as to inheritance stands as it did upon the foundation of ancient custom." As such, he argued, it should not be meddled with under any circumstances. Both the lower and appeals court had erred in this case, he argued:

> It is the duty of all Judges whether of the inferior or of the superior Courts to administer the law as they find it, and not in the manner that they might individually wish it to be. The Asantehene's Court has invoked the aid of Equity to overcome what their members believe to be a difficulty and an injustice. It must be clearly understood that justice implies the fair and impartial administration of the law. . . . the maxim of equity applicable in the circumstances shown in their action is that "equity follows the law". . . . Quite clearly the Native Court of Juaben were wrong when they held that the "ruling" of the Ashanti Confederacy Council had the effect of modifying native law and custom, and the Asantehene's Appeal Court was equally wrong when it held that equity could be invoked to do something which custom forbade, namely to inherit outside of the blood group. For these reasons I do allow the appeal and do set aside the judgment of the Native Courts below and do enter judgement for the defendant.[145]

At last, Kwadjo Nimo was vindicated—his victory predicated upon colonial notions of a static, unchanging African "tradition," which, with no small irony, overrode Confederacy Council efforts to modify property rights along lines advocated by both missions and local colonial officials!

For mothers and children, increasingly favorable native court judgments on inheritance, as well as the 1948 council ruling, constituted the small but important victories that were won out of the volatile mix of cash, kin, and childrearing. Yet those small victories have to be measured within a broader social context; they should not be allowed to obscure the high price paid and the burdens that continued to be borne by mothers in the development of

Asante's cash/cocoa economy.[146] By the 1950s, the native courts of Asante may have considered unremarkable the pronouncement that "[t]he Plaintiff-Respondents [a widow and her children] assisted the late Yaw Bio because they naturally expected something from him."[147] Yet recognition of a woman's claim still depended heavily on court definitions of a "good" mother and wife. Thus, widows benefited from changes in court formulations of customary law, but women who divorced, as we shall see in chapter 4, found it exceedingly difficult, both inside the courts and outside, to recoup what they had invested in their husbands' farms. And if children were increasingly seen as legitimate successors to their fathers, just as widows were viewed as deserving of a portion of the properties they jointly worked with their husbands, it was because of fundamental shifts within the domestic, conjugal economy. These were shifts that eroded the autonomy and security of the mother/wife, as they marginalized the mother and child's *abusua* in daily conjugal negotiations over childrearing. The husband/father was now the central, mediating figure through whom the value of a wife and her children's labor was realized. In an increasingly monetized world, where cash connections between fathers and children were increasingly articulated as "blood connections," a child might have a right to a part of his father's estate, but that father could now exercise control over his child and demand services (without the consent of the child's *abusua*) in ways that recalled relationships of pawnage in an earlier day. And as pawnage was subsumed in the relationship between a father and his free child, mothers and children found it increasingly difficult to insist on a father's rights in his children being dependent on his fulfillment of paternal responsibilities. Thus, at the very same time that courts were supporting the inheritance claims of mothers and children, they were dismissing claims for child maintenance and supporting the inalienable rights of fathers to the service of their children even when those fathers failed to maintain their children.

CONCLUSION: MATRILINY, PATRILINY, AND WHAT GETS LOST IN BETWEEN

Cash and cocoa, mission schools and school fees transformed the domestic economy in Asante and profoundly altered the terrain of childrearing for Asante's first generation of colonized women. Previously fluid, processual relationships between a man and his wife/children's *abusua* were ossified. As a result, the process of fathering became the status of fatherhood, a position endowed with inalienable rights, largely detached from reciprocal responsibilities. The implications of these changes, for wives and for mothers, were profound, as they recast the very core of social reproduction in Asante. In the early part of this century, one of Rattray's elderly male informants explained to him that even if his wife "bears me ten children, they are not mine but her and her *abusua* (clan's)."[148] If this was the perception of the grandparents of the first generation to be born under colonial rule, it was still echoed by many parents of that generation. As an elderly informant told Kyei in the 1940s, "Fathers do not beget children and own them. This child belongs to me."[149] But the childrearing terrain negotiated by Asante's first colonized generation in the 1920s to 1940s was a very different one indeed. "If honestly the Akans will accept it," pondered one elderly woman in 1990, "the child belongs to the father, the mother just looks after the baby."[150]

The ossification of fluid domestic relationships and the advent of a "natural" or essentialized father also had striking implications for the ways in which wealth was passed on. By the 1930s, men were increasingly distributing shares of their property to children and wives. Most people with whom we spoke remembered this transition quite clearly. As Adwowa Fodwo of Mamponten, born around 1914, recalled:

> These days . . . [men] don't even give much to their family. They give most to their wives and children at the expense of their kin. [In the time of my parents] it was matrilineal inheritance, so husbands were not looking after their children. But these days, they will tell you when they go to farm their nieces and nephews don't send them anything; it is their children who look after them, so they bequeath their children everything.[151]

The pressure to do so, as Afua Fosuwa remembered, was increasingly strong. If a father "gives his nephews and nieces some of the cocoa farms and doesn't give some to his children, it will . . . bring trouble."[152] Given these profound changes in inheritance—changes clearly fueled by the rapid development of the cocoa industry—it is not surprising that many from this generation repeated some version of the axiom "Cocoa destroys families,"[153] as they sought to explain the transformations they had witnessed in their lives. The small bequests of personal items men had made to their sons before the cocoa boom did not threaten their families' economic interests in any significant way. Property of an entirely different magnitude, however, could now pass out of family hands and into the possession of wives and children. As a farmer near Mampong told Busia 50 years before we began our work, "*Cocoa see abusua, paepae mogya mu.*"[154]

That "cocoa destroys kinship and divides blood" was seen as a crucial development by colonial-era anthropologists, who tended to frame their analysis of the problem in terms of an inevitable, ongoing battle between matrilineal and patrilineal tendencies in Asante society. Rattray ruminated on the *ntoro* (spirit) inherited from one's father versus the *mogya* (blood) one inherited from the mother. Fortes described a "submerged descent line" and cast the matri- versus patri- battle in terms of continued efforts to "adjust the jural and moral claims and bonds arising out of marriage and fatherhood to those imposed by matrilineal kinship."[155] "Left to itself," Field even predicted for neighboring Akyem in 1938, matrilineality would "die a natural death."[156] What these early analyses have in common was a tendency to view social forces or social power as part of a zero-sum game, with patrilineal forces of the twentieth century counterbalancing matrilineal success.[157] In other words, if matrilineality and avuncular power eroded or diminished, then patrilineality and the power of the father must have increased by precisely the amount by which the other had decreased. This equation, we argue, does not get us very far and obscures much that was going on. The evidence we have presented here in fact suggests that a society like Asante could be tenaciously matrilineal and *at the same time* experience an increasing degree of patriarchal power, and we use "patriarchal" here in its most literal sense as "rule by the father." Indeed, a quarter century later, Mary Douglas's argument that matriliny is not necessarily doomed by increasing wealth still holds water. "Matriliny would be capable of flourishing in market economies," she wrote, "whenever the demand for men is higher than the demand for things. Because of the scope it gives for personal unascribed achievement of leadership, matrilineal kinship could have advantages in an expanding market economy. On my view the enemy of matriliny is not the cow as such, not wealth as such, not economic development as such, but economic restriction."[158] But the flexibility or adaptability highlighted by Douglas and others requires historicizing. We must not mistake the durability of matriliny in Asante for immutability. Over the course of their life cycle, Asante's first generation of colonized women lived through fundamental transformations in the power of husbands/fathers vis-à-vis their wives/children, even while the basic structures of matrilineal kinship remained intact.

But what were the real, lived consequences for them of these broader processes, of an empowered patriarchy tightly woven into a tenaciously matrilineal social fabric? For Asante women, as mothers, they were clearly immense. While some women were fortunate in that the father of their children assumed responsibilities for the school fees of these children, provided funds for clothing and feeding them, cared for them in their mother's absence, and provided for them after his death, many others were not so lucky. Elizabeth Adjaye of Kumasi spoke for many when she remembered, "By the grace of God, I traded. The firstborn daughter died. She didn't go to school. The second two went to school. I paid their school fees. I fed them, bought their clothes, everything. . . . I raised them on my own."[159] Yet for women whose husbands did not contribute to the children's subsistence, much less to school fees, what recourse was there? What pressure could be brought to bear? With the children's *abusua* marginalized from the domestic economy of childrearing, with the children's father endowed with inalienable rights in his children that were detached from any reciprocal duties, the obligation to parent (-*tan*) and to provide subsistence for children was now, in the final instance, a woman's alone. Though by appearances, Asante mothers of this generation were doing much of what their own mothers had done—feeding, bathing, and clothing their children—they were doing it in a world in which there were far fewer safety nets for them or for their children. It was a world in which so much more was expected, but so much less was obliged. As eighty-year-old Efua Sewaa of Tafo lamented, "You conceived the child. You delivered that child. It is the duty of the mother, whether she likes it or not, to look after the child. An uncle, or aunt, or father, or anyone else, they just look after a child when they feel like it."[160] The burden of social reproduction, in other words—a burden once shared via a complex web of fluid social relationships between matrilineal kin and conjugal units—fell squarely on the shoulders of Asante's colonial mothers.

NOTES

1. The title of this chapter is inspired by Pat Thomas's 1991 hit song. Pat Thomas, *Sika Yε Mogya* (Fire Records, 1991). The opening quotation is from Busia, *Position of the Chief*, 127.

2. Rattray, *Ashanti*, 36 and 46. *Bogya* is an alternate rendering of *mogya*.

3. Fortes, "Kinship and Marriage," 268.

4. Ibid., 263 and 265. The primacy of the connection between a mother and child is also captured in the proverb *Wo na awu, wo abusua a*sa, "When your mother dies you have no kindred left." Rattray, *Ashanti Proverbs*, 129.

5. That children were to be raised in the father's house is evidenced in the oft-cited proverb *Wo yere nkɔ mma mmra* (Your wife may go, but your children come). Rattray, *Ashanti Law*, 11.

6. Rattray, *Ashanti Law*, 8–10.

7. Ibid., 10.

8. On *ntoro*, see, especially, Rattray, *Ashanti*, 44–76. On naming, see also Fortes, "Kinship and Marriage," 266.

9. Kyei, *Marriage*, 52; and Fortes, "Kinship and Marriage," 268–69.

10. Rattray, *Ashanti Law*, especially 1–17.

11. Rattray, *Ashanti Law*, 19. *Fie* (house) is also used colloquially to refer to *abusua* or family.

12. Allman: Yaa Akyaa, Tafo, 24 June 1992.

13. Allman: Kwame Nkansah, Agogo, 25 August 1995.

14. Allman: Adwoa Brefi, Kumasi, 2 June 1992.

15. Allman: Eponuahemaa Efua Fom, Asokore, 1 September 1992.

16. Tashjian: Ama Akyaa, Oyoko, 27 November 1990.

17. Tashjian: Afua Dufie, Oyoko, 31 October 1990.

18. Tashjian: Ama Akyaa, Oyoko, 29 November 1990; and Abena Sikafo, Mamponten, 15 October 1990; Rattray, *Ashanti Law*, 10.

19. Tashjian: Afua Fosuwa, Oyoko, 28 November 1990.

20. Rattray makes this case for the early twentieth century. Austin argues it is also applicable to the nineteenth. Rattray, *Ashanti Law*, 9–10; Austin, "'No Elders Were Present,'" 21.

21. Tashjian: Kwabena Boahene, Mamponten, 11 September 1990. Many men served apprenticeships in Nsawam. It was also a popular place to tap palm wine.

22. Tashjian: Barima Tawia, Mamponten, 15 October 1990.

23. Meyer Fortes, "The Submerged Descent Line in Ashanti," in I. Schapera, ed., *Studies in Kinship and Marriage* [Occasional Papers of the Royal Anthropological Institute] (London: Royal Anthropological Institute, 1963), 64.

24. Allman: Akua Addai, Kumasi, 3 June 1992.

25. Allman: Akua Kusiwaa, Kumasi, 27 May 1992.

26. Tashjian: Ama Akyaa, Oyoko, 27 November 1990.

27. Allman: Sarah Obeng, Asokore, 26 August 1992.

28. Allman: Adwoa Agyewaa, Kumasi, 9 June 1992; Jean Asare, Effiduasi, 24 August 1992.

29. Allman: Akosua Mansah, Kumasi, 3 June 1992.

30. Tashjian: Abena Sikafo, Mamponten, 15 October 1990.

31. Allman: Akosua Addae, Tafo, 22 June 1992. Emphasis ours.

32. Tashjian: Peter Danso, Oyoko, 25 October 1990.

33. Fortes, "Kinship and Marriage," 264.

34. Akyeampong and Obeng's recent article (which focuses primarily on power and the political realm) suggests that blood, *mogya*, has often been at the center of major shifts of power in Asante. "Spirituality," 481–99. See also Akyeampong, *Drink*, 10–12.

35. Busia, *Position of the Chief*, 132.

36. Fortes, "Submerged Descent Line," 64. See also his "Kinship and Marriage," 268.

37. Mikell encountered similar concerns in her work. See Mikell, *Cocoa and Chaos*, 119.

38. Tashjian: Akua Foku, Oyoko, 7 November 1990.

39. MRO: Asantehene's Divisional Court B, Civil Record Book 4, *Kwasi Quansah v. R.A. Mensah*, dd. Kumasi, 13 March 1936, 90.

40. Most of the correspondence can be found NAGA, ADM 11/1/1299: "Ashanti—Native Laws and Customs." Some additional material is located in NAGK, ARA/1408: "King of Adansi Requesting Inkwantabissa's Child to Return to Her Family," and ARA/2462: "Complaint from Omanhin of Adansi Requesting Return of a Child of an Adansi Woman Who Died at Akyinase in Assin."

41. MRO: Native Tribunal of Kumasihene, Civil Record Book 7, *Kwadjo Safo v. Kwame Antwi et. al.*, dd. Kumasi, 10 September, 1929.

42. MRO: Asantehene's Divisional Court B, Civil Record Book 20, *Ama Manu v. Kwasi Buo*, dd. Kumasi, 25 September 1940.

43. Rattray, *Ashanti Law*, 9.

44. Bowdich, *Mission*, 303.

45. Rattray, *Religion and Art*, 320. Also see Kyei, *Marriage*, 94.

46. Fortes, "Kinship and Marriage," 282. More recently, Manuh has discussed fathers' heightened roles in the marriages of their daughters. "Changes in Marriage," 196.

47. Tashjian: Kwasi Anane, Mamponten, 5 October 1990.

48. Rattray, *Ashanti Law*, 51.

49. Tashjian: Kofi Ntim, Mamponten, 3 October 1990. See Kyei, *Marriage*, 26–39.

50. Tashjian: Panin Anthony Kofi Boakye, Oyoko, 22 September 1990.

51. See, for example, Tashjian: Yaw Dankwa, Mamponten, 27 September 1990; and Panin Anthony Kofi Boakye, Oyoko, 22 October 1990.

52. Rattray, *Ashanti Law*, 10 and 17.

53. Tashjian: Yaa Akom, Mamponten, 11 October 1990.

54. Rattray, *Ashanti Law*, 51.

55. An extremely derogatory term, meaning "fool."

56. MRO: Native Tribunal of Kumasihene, Civil Record Book 14, *Kwame Adu v. Kwaku Yipay*, dd. Kumasi, 16 January 1932.

57. Rattray, *Ashanti Law*, 51.

58. Ibid., 14–15.

59. See MRO: Native Tribunal of Kumasihene, Civil Record Book 4, *Akosua Adai v. Kwaku Ahindwa*, dd. Kumasi, 23 February 1929, 374.

60. Tashjian: Ama Akyaa, Oyoko, 20 November 1990.

61. Austin provides a fascinating discussion of the ways in which pawnage continued long after abolition. "Human Pawning," especially 137–45.

62. For more detailed reflections on *ntamoba*, see Jean Allman, "Fathering, Mothering and Making Sense of *Ntamoba*: Reflections on the Economy of Child-Rearing in Colonial Asante," *Africa* 67:2 (1997), 296–321.

63. MRO: Native Tribunal of Bompata, Ashanti-Akim, Record Book, *Kojo Asamoah v. Kojo Kyere*, dd. Bompata, 18 February 1921.

64. For a discussion of the origins and uses of oaths in bringing about court cases, see Rattray, *Ashanti Law*, 128, 379–80, and 388–89.

65. Christaller, *Dictionary*, 493.

66. Danquah, *Gold Coast*, 189. In a footnote, Danquah provides a brief etymology of the term. He states that it is derived from " '*tam*'—uterus, '*boba*'—small stone. Hence a small weight of money payable when emancipating an offspring of marriage." This definition was included in E. L. Rapp's 1933 additions to Christaller's dictionary. See appendix F, Christaller, *Dictionary*, 604. Differences in spelling reflect the Akan tendency in speech to render the *mb* or *nb* consonant combination as *mm*.

67. Allman: Akosua Mansah, Kumasi, 9 June 1992. See also Allman: Adwoa Amoam, Effiduasi, 21 August 1992; K.A.M. Gyimah, Kumasi, 26 August 1995; Bafuor Akoto, Kumasi, 29 August 1995.

68. Allman: Okyeame Owusu Banahene, Kumasi, 22 August 1995. M. J. Field, an anthropologist hired by the Gold Coast government in 1938 to investigate the "native state" of Akim-Kotoku, one of Asante's Akan neighbors, found a similar meaning for *ntamoba*. Her informant reported, "'When the praising-money is sent you also send the girl's father *tamoba* money because his daughter often soiled his cloth when she was a baby and sat on his knee.'" See M. J. Field, *Akim-Kotoku: An Oman of the Gold Coast* (Accra: Crown Agents, 1948), 107.

69. Allman: Yaa Dufie, Kumasi, 25 August 1992.

70. Allman: Agogohemaa Abena Sewaa, with Efua Tebiaa, Agogo, 10 August 1995.

71. Allman: Kwame Nkansah, Agogo, 25 August 1995.

72. Rattray attributes the longevity of the father/son bond to the fact that certain offices in Asante "descended from father to son, e.g. executioners, swordbearers, and so

on." In an accompanying footnote, he also points to the bond created by *ntoro*. Presumably what he is referring to here is the fact that a son will pass on the same *ntoro* that his father passed to him. In contrast, his daughter's children will inherit not his *ntoro* but that of their *own* father. See Rattray, *Religion*, 102. See also Mikell, *Cocoa and Chaos*, 68.

73. Cross-cousin marriage, a fairly common practice in the precolonial period, may also go some distance toward explaining the longevity of a father's relationship with his son. When a son married his father's sister's daughter (his niece), the offspring of that union were, of course, members of the man's *abusua*. The next generation insured the longevity, as it were, of the father/son bond, as the son became the father of his own father's nieces and nephews. In contrast, no matter to whom the father's daughter was married, the grandchildren could not be members of his matrilineal family. The father's reciprocal relationship with his daughter and/or her *abusua*, therefore, could not be extended by marriage or by the birth of the next generation. For a discussion of cross-cousin marriage and the disappearance of *ntoro*, see Mikell, *Cocoa and Chaos*, 123.

74. Allman: Kwame Nkansah, Agogo, 25 August 1995.

75. *Ntamoba* as static marriage payment rather than ongoing exchange recalls a similar process in southern Africa with the transformation of *lobola* from continuing exchange between two families to the payment of a single "bride-price" in the late nineteenth century. See, for example, Cherryl Walker, "Gender and the Development of the Migrant Labour System c. 1850–1930: An Overview," in Cherryl Walker, ed., *Women and Gender in Southern Africa to 1945* (Cape Town: David Philip, 1990), 184–85.

76. Kyei, *Marriage*, 115; Rattray, *Ashanti Law*, 32; Rattray, *Ashanti*, 22; Peter Sarpong, *Ghana in Retrospect: Some Aspects of Ghanaian Culture* (Tema, Ghana: Ghana Publishing Corporation, 1974), 60. Herskovits stands alone (and on the basis of very limited research) in claiming that *ntoro* refers to the *abusua*, a claim for which Fortes took him gently to task in "Kinship and Marriage," 265 n. 4. On the question of nomenclature, see A. C. Denteh, *"Ntoro* and *Nton," Research Review* 3:3 (1967), 91–96; Fortes, "Kinship and Marriage"; Melville Herskovits, "The Ashanti *Ntoro*: A Re-Examination," *Journal of the Royal Anthropological Institute* 67 (1937), 287–96.

77. Kyei, *Marriage*, 117. Fortes refers to this washing as "ritual purification" in "Kinship and Marriage," 267.

78. This description draws from Denteh, *"Ntoro"*; Denteh, "Birth Rites of the Akans," *Research Review* 3,1 (1966), 78–81; Fortes, "Submerged Descent Line"; Fortes, "Kinship and Marriage"; Herskovits, "The Ashanti *Ntoro*"; Kyei, *Marriage*; Rattray, *Ashanti*; Rattray, *Ashanti Law*; Sarpong, *Ghana*.

79. Rattray, *Ashanti*, chapters 2 and 3.

80. Rattray, *Ashanti Law*, 16.

81. Herskovits, "The Ashanti *Ntoro*," 291.

82. Fortes, "Kinship and Marriage," 265; Kyei, *Marriage*, 115.

83. Kyei, *Marriage*, 115.

84. Fortes, "Kinship and Marriage," 265 n. 4.

85. Denteh, *"Ntoro"*; Tashjian: Kofi Owusu, Mamponten, 18 September 1990, and Kofi Ntim, Mamponten, 3 October 1990. Tashjian found in 1990 that, although use of

the term *ntoro* had died out, recognition of patrilineally derived food taboos remained. See Tashjian: Kofi Ntim, Mamponten, 3 October 1990.

86. In the early years of the twentieth century, the ideal inheritor of a man was a full brother or maternal half brother or, in the absence of brothers, a maternal nephew. Women were succeeded by full sisters or maternal half sisters or, in their absence, daughters. When no suitable candidate existed, the same-sex preference could be ignored, and brothers and sisters, for example, could inherit from each other.

87. See, for example, Fortes, "Ashanti Social Survey," 15; and Danquah, *Gold Coast,* 184.

88. See Allman, "Making Mothers," 23–47. See also the rich collection of essays brought together by Karen Tranberg Hansen (ed.) in *African Encounters with Domesticity* (New Brunswick, NJ: Rutgers University Press, 1992).

89. The 1884 Gold Coast Colonial Marriage Ordinance was extended to Ashanti with the implementation of the Ashanti Administration Ordinance, No. 6 of 1919.

90. MMS, WMMS, Correspondence, West Africa, Miscellaneous: Rev. K. Horn, "Native Marriage Custom: Marriage Custom in Ashanti," typescript, 1931.

91. MMS, WMMS, Correspondence, West Africa, Miscellaneous: A. H. Mildren, "The Present State of Our Church (Gold Coast)," typescript, 1931.

92. A conference on marriage in West Africa was held at the Methodist Mission headquarters in London in 1931. There was significant participation by Gold Coast missionaries. See documents collected in MMS, WMMS, Correspondence, West Africa, Miscellaneous. Eventually the mission instituted a process by which individuals could marry according to custom but then have their union blessed by the church. This method was far cheaper and provided far more flexibility than marrying under the ordinance. J. C. DeGraft-Johnson argued for such an alternative in "Christian Marriage and Gold Coast Social Life," typescript, Accra, 1928.

93. MMS, WMMS, Correspondence, Gold Coast: Eddy to G. Ayre, dd. Kumasi, 27 January 1938. For Danquah's thoughts on the influence of Christian missions on the family, see *Gold Coast*, 184. For a discussion of the mission house as a site for training in domesticity in the Belgian Congo, see Nancy Hunt, "Colonial Fairy Tales and the Knife and Fork Doctrine in the Heart of Africa," in Hansen, ed., *African Encounters*, 143–71.

94. See chapter 5.

95. Abu, "Separateness of Spouses," 60.

96. Adomako-Sarfoh, "Migrant Asante Cocoa Farmers," 130–31.

97. Okali, "Kinship and Cocoa Farming," 170.

98. As we saw in chapter 1, changes in domestic economy occurred in some areas of Asante long before the advent of cocoa. The rubber trade of the last quarter of the nineteenth century or even the kola trade of earlier decades had already begun to transform domestic relations of production and exchange. On the ways in which pawning (including pawning of wives and children) was affected by the expansion of the kola and rubber trades. See Austin, "Human Pawning," 134 and n. 110, 155. See also Arhin, "Ashanti Rubber Trade," 32–43; Arhin, "Market Settlements in Northwest Ashanti: Kintampo," *Research Review, Ashanti and the North-west Supplement* (1965), 135–55; Dumett, "The Rubber Trade," 79–101.

99. Bowdich, *Mission*, 254. Writing about the Gold Coast generally, at the end of the seventeenth century, Bosman argued that "paternal love" encouraged fathers to

give property to their sons, even though their estates were supposed to go to their families. William Bosman, *A New and Accurate Description of the Coast of Guinea, Divided into the Gold, the Slave, and the Ivory Coasts* (London: J. Knapton, 1705), 203.

100. Rattray, *Ashanti Law*, 15. Christaller translates *samansew* as "the last will of a dying person." Christaller, *Dictionary*, 424. Wilks writes that "*samansee* . . . has the ominous sense of 'the curse of the ancestor,'" since in precolonial Asante, bequests by fathers to sons were often made to evade death duties. The belief, therefore, was that "nothing but grief was likely to come to the living recipients of the bequest." Wilks, "Golden Stool," 149–50.

101. Rattray, *Ashanti Law*, 338–39.

102. Rattray, *Ashanti*, 238–39.

103. Tashjian: Panin Anthony Kofi Boakye, Oyoko, 22 October 1990. Looking at Akwapim, to Asante's south, in the 1960s, Vellenga found strong evidence of transfers of property from fathers to daughters as well as to sons. Ten percent of women who owned cocoa farms in the area of her research had acquired them from their fathers. "Matriliny, Patriliny," 72–74.

104. Tashjian: Panin Anthony Kofi Boakye, Oyoko, 22 October 1990.

105. Tashjian: Obaa Kro, Mamponten, 7 August 1990.

106. This method of passing self-acquired property from fathers to children succeeded only because of changes in succession that have appeared in the twentieth century wherein women's children, rather than siblings, and sons as well as daughters most frequently inherit women's estates. The growing desire to pass property from father to child may well be behind these changes in inheritance patterns within the matrilineal family. However, in interviews, some women and men voiced the concern that allowing sons to inherit from mothers will have the long-term effect of bleeding wealth from the matrilineage, since these sons may, as fathers, give their property to their own children.

107. Tashjian: Abena Kwa, Oyoko, 12 November 1990.

108. Tashjian: Panin Anthony Kofi Boakye, Oyoko, 22 October 1990.

109. Tashjian: Abena Kwa, Oyoko, 12 November 1990. On the necessity of presenting *aseda*, see also Kyei, *Marriage*, 30 and 85.

110. Tashjian: Afua Fosuwa, Oyoko, 1 November 1990.

111. Tashjian: Adwowa Fodwo, Mamponten, 23 November 1990.

112. Bosman found that a similar caution existed on the seventeenth-century Gold Coast, where fathers liked to give property to their children "privately" lest the relatives claim it back. Bosman, *Description of the Coast*, 203.

113. A man might also request that a share of the profits be given to his children. Tashjian: Afua Fosuwa, Oyoko, 28 November 1990.

114. Allman: Akua Addae, Tafo, 23 June 1992.

115. Tashjian: Ama Akyaa, Oyoko, 23 October 1990. Writing of the Akan generally, but drawing many of her conclusions from research in Brong Ahafo, Mikell found that as recently as the 1980s, people deemed "audacious" those women who asserted their right to inherit a share of a deceased husband's property. Mikell also discusses a 1990 inheritance case in which a man sued his father's family on behalf of himself, his siblings, and his mother, claiming that the family had inherited valuable properties from their father/husband. Mikell argues that the plaintiff hesitated

to mention his mother's labor contributions to the creation and acquisition of these properties because "most Asante hesitate to publicly recognize . . . that a wife's labor helped create valuable property." See Mikell, "The State," 234–35. Interestingly, the women with whom we have spoken over the past years did not hesitate to state their contributions.

116. Cf. Mikell, who argues that "traditional authorities" in Asante and other Akan areas "have been unwilling to address" modifications in customary law that would reward women for their conjugal labor. Mikell, "The State," 233, 241.

117. Ivor Wilks Papers, typed transcript: Native Court of Ankobia Clan, *Adjuah Agyako v. Yaw Puni and Yaw Donkor*, dd. Kumasi, 1 August 1936.

118. Ibid., 7–8.

119. Ibid., 24.

120. Ibid., 27–28.

121. Ibid., 10.

122. Ibid., 11.

123. The levirate, in its various forms and obligations, provides further evidence for some responsibility to the widow and children on the part of a man's successor. See Tashjian, "It's Mine and It's Ours," chapter 13.

124. MRO: Native Court of Kumawu, *Kwasi Agyei v. Kwame Basoah*, dd. Kumawu, 18 October 1935 [typed transcript].

125. Ibid., 11.

126. Ibid., 11–12.

127. MRO: Asantehene's Divisional Court B, *Kojo Mama v. Yaw Mensah*, dd. Kumasi, 3 December 1938 and heard on appeal in the Asantehene's A Court, dd. Kumasi, 19 January 1939 [typed transcript].

128. Ibid., 11–12.

129. Ibid., 23.

130. Ibid., 23–24.

131. Ibid., 24–25.

132. Ibid., 35–37.

133. Matson, *Digest*, 26.

134. According to Busia, when a man gave a cocoa farm to a non-family member, "the consent of his matrilineal lineage is required to validate it. This consent has often been refused." Busia, *Position of the Chief,* 125.

135. Ivor Wilks Papers, typed transcript: Asantehene's A1 Court, *M. P. Mensah v. Kojo Fordwuo*, dd. Kumasi, 13 September 1950.

136. Ibid., 5.

137. MRO: Native Court B of Juaben, *Afua Kosia et al v. Kwadjo Nimo*, Juaben, 26 July 1949; heard on appeal in the Asantehene's Court A1, dd. Kumasi, 24 January 1950; heard on appeal in the Supreme Court of the Gold Coast, Ashanti, at a land court, dd. Kumasi, 12 June 1950 [typed transcript].

138. Ibid., 37.

139. Matson, *Digest*, 26.

140. Busia, *Position of the Chief*, 125–26.

141. Matson, *Digest*, 26.

142. Ibid. See also MRO: "Akan Laws of Succession," 5 July 1947–16 December 1954.

143. MRO: "Akan Laws of Succession."

144. Matson, *Digest*, 27.

145. The quotations from this Supreme Court decision are all contained in a transcript (pages unnumbered) of the hearing, which is appended to the case of *Afua Kosia v. Kwadjo Nimo*, cited above.

146. Indeed, wives and children have continued to struggle for a share of a deceased husband/father's cocoa farm right down to the present. Akosua Mansah of Kumasi lamented in 1992 that years ago her husband had given her a share of his farm, but it had been taken away by his family because she had not paid *aseda*. After her husband passed away, that portion of the farm was inherited by the husband's brother. Akosua's daughter took the case before the chief of Boma, and "he ruled that the child was entitled to that land because he saw that child always working on the farm with the father." Akosua's husband's family appealed the decision, and in 1992, she and her children were still awaiting a ruling from the Sunyani High Court. See Allman: Akosua Mansah, Kumasi, 3 June 1992.

147. MRO: Native Court B of Juaben, *Afua Kosia et al v. Kwadjo Nimo*, Juaben, 26 July 1949; heard on appeal in the Asantehene's Court A1, dd. Kumasi, 24 January 1950; heard on appeal in the Supreme Court of the Gold Coast, Ashanti, at a land court, dd. Kumasi, 12 June 1950 [typed transcript].

148. Rattray, *Religion and Art*, 83.

149. Kyei, *Marriage*, 61.

150. Tashjian: Nana Ama Kwandu, Mamponten, 23 July 1990.

151. Tashjian: Adwowa Fodwo, Mamponten, 1 October 1990.

152. Tashjian: Afua Fosuwa, Oyoko, 28 November 1990.

153. Tashjian: Juabenhene Nana Otuo Serebour II, Juaben, 29 May 1990. Vellenga cites a study from 1960 showing that protection shrines in Ghana "have grown in number parallel to the growing cocoa output. . . . most rural envy and strife concerns cocoa-profits and the inheritance of cocoa-farms and cocoa-wealth." Dorothy Dee Vellenga, "Changing Sex Roles and Social Tensions in Ghana: The Law as Measure and Mediator of Family Conflicts" (Ph.D. Dissertation, Columbia University, 1975), 127.

154. Busia, *Position of the Chief*, 127.

155. For example, Fortes, "The Submerged Descent Line," 58–67; and Fortes, "Kinship and Marriage," especially 283. For Kyei's thoughts on the future of matriliny, see *Marriage*, 57.

156. Field, *Akim-Kotoku*, 118.

157. This is a paraphrasing of Fortes, "Ashanti Social Survey," 15. For an alternative critique of this approach, see Mikell, *Cocoa and Chaos*, 112–23.

158. Mary Douglas, "Is Matriliny Doomed in Africa?" in M. Douglas and P. M. Kaberry, eds., *Man in Africa* (Garden City, NY: Anchor Books, 1971, orig. 1969), 123–37, especially 133.

159. Allman: Elizabeth Adjaye, Kumasi, 8 June 1992.

160. Allman: Efua Sewaa, Tafo, 25 June 1992.

4

"SERVING A MAN IS WASTED LABOR": WOMEN'S CONJUGAL STRATEGIES IN A WORLD OF CASH AND COCOA

If you fear divorce, you never sleep on a good bed.
—Asante proverb[1]

INTRODUCTION

We have seen how the accelerated growth of the cash economy, particularly with the spread of cocoa in the first two decades of the twentieth century, challenged the meanings and makings of marriage and childrearing in Asante. Conjugal expectations, obligations, and responsibilities became sites of ongoing contestation as women and men sought to reshape marriage and parenting to the demands of the expanding cocoa economy. For Asante wives the burdens were particularly heavy, as the growth of the cocoa industry was predicated largely upon the exploitation of unpaid, often conjugal, labor. By the 1920s, however, many wives were making the move from being the most common form of exploitable labor during the initial introduction of cocoa to themselves exploiting the new opportunities for autonomy and security afforded by an expanding cash economy. Included among them were many from that first colonized generation who shared their reminiscences with us. In order to safeguard their precarious positions, wives of this generation began to formulate new conjugal strategies in the interwar years and to redeploy older ones in struggles that were, more than anything, about control over their productive and reproductive labor. It is to those strategies that this chapter turns.

OLD STRATEGIES/NEW CONTEXTS: SEDUCTION AND DIVORCE IN A CASH ECONOMY

For much of Asante's history, as we have seen, marriage between free commoners was a fluid process of transaction and reciprocity. The husband provided meat and other foodstuffs, as well as clothes, and the wife, in exchange, provided farm produce, prepared food, performed other domestic services, and allowed her husband exclusive sexual access to her. That a husband's care was absolutely central to the transactions of being married meant that the ending of marriage (*gyae aware*) was often tied to claims of improper care. Divorce, which had long been relatively easy to undertake for both men and women, thus continued to be one of the primary conjugal strategies utilized by Asante women in the tumultuous interwar years. Just as women in the nineteenth century utilized divorce to end marriages in which they did not receive proper care, women in the colonial period, as care increasingly assumed cash value, opted for divorce as a strategy to gain and/or defend economic security.[2]

The divorce rates in the generation of women upon whom this study is based provide some indication of the prevalence of divorce.[3] In Oyoko and Mamponten, Tashjian found that approximately two-thirds of the informants asked about divorce had had at least one marriage—and up to five—finish in divorce, while just over one-half of all marriages specifically mentioned by informants resulted in divorce.[4] Allman found a similarly high rate of over 50 percent of marriages ending in divorce in the towns of Effiduasi and Asokore, though she found the reported divorce rate to be somewhat lower in the urban areas of Tafo and Kumasi.[5] The Ashanti Social Survey of 1945 produced results similar to ours for rural areas. Fortes reported that "more than half of all men over 40 and about the same proportion of all women over 35" had been divorced at least once and that a "high divorce rate has been characteristic of the Ashanti for the past twenty to thirty years."[6] That divorce had long been a readily accepted outcome of marriage meant it was a relatively easy strategy for women to employ in the colonial period. Women, as well as men, could initiate divorce proceedings. As Adwowa Fodwo of Mamponten explained, "I decided to end that marriage. I said I would not marry him, and once a woman says that, she meant it, so Kwaku didn't try to get me back."[7] Kwadwo Paul Adum seemed to sum up the prevailing attitude toward divorce at that time when he said, "If somebody is in your grasp and he or she wants to free himself or herself, just let her go."[8]

The reminiscences shared with us suggest that once divorce was decided upon, the process was simple and straightforward.[9] The first step involved meeting with mediators (*badwafoɔ*) to find the reason (if any) for the divorce and to attempt reconciliation. If the spouse seeking divorce resisted the mediators' pleas to reconcile, the families of the wife and husband then discussed whether any property settlements were required. Once these were agreed upon, drinks were poured to signal that the marriage was irrevocably ended, and that the woman was free to remarry. Kwabena Boahene of Mamponten explained that the drinks poured at the divorce nullified the marriage drinks:[10]

> [B]efore you get married to somebody, you have to go and pour drinks before the relatives of the woman to show that their child is with you. If you now come to divorce, they have to bring drinks to show that you are no more together. If you took say four bottles of schnapps to perform the marriage rites, and there is divorce, they may just bring one bottle to show that their child is no more with you. It is not that they are bringing you back your drinks, but just to show that she is also no more with you. Just like you had brought drinks to show the child was with you . . . So the drink is acting more or less like a witness.[11]

Because divorce brought an end to the husband's exclusive sexual rights in his wife, the rites associated with it were intended to make a woman's unattached status clear. Ama Akyaa of Oyoko explained: "The drink she pours when there is divorce means that when the woman gets married, the man has nothing to do with it."[12] The drinks also served as a potent and final symbol that the marriage was over, and that all parties agreed to the property settlements which had been negotiated. Once drinks were poured, neither party could demand a further adjustment in property holdings, and the former husband no longer bore responsibility for the woman's well-being.

As in earlier times, divorce in the colonial period was undertaken for a range of reasons,[13] and even for no apparent reason at all, though in a vast majority of the cases initiated by Asante's first generation of colonized women, improper care seems to have been at the heart of the proceedings. Pragmatic reasons for seeking divorce for both women and men continued to include problems with childbearing. But most commonly women now blamed divorce upon a husband who did not care adequately for them and their children.[14] As Aduwa Yaa Ama of Oyoko stated, "when you marry and he was taking care of you, you continued to stay with him, but if not, you divorced him."[15] This was necessary, explained Abena Kwa, even if ending a marriage required some exertion: "If you are energetic and the man is not taking care of you, definitely you will divorce him and find another one."[16]

It is important to note that not all women of this generation directly associated a decline in levels of care with the demands of the expanding cash economy. Many remembered that care declined simply because a marriage lasted a long time, or because a husband took another wife. In both of these instances, divorce was considered a viable option. "When you get married to somebody," Ama Sewaa Akoto remarked, "in the initial stage he will be treating you fine, but if later it turns sour, you just have to divorce him. . . . when you become exceedingly annoyed, you just end it."[17] As a result of his work on the Ashanti Social Survey in the 1940s, Kyei concluded that one of the major causes of divorce in Asante was a husband taking a second wife and the senior wife's perception that she experienced a concomitant decline in care. He supported his observation by citing a "favourite song" of senior wives:

> *Mmarima nyɛ o-o-o!*
> *Mmarima nyɛ.*
> *Mmarima, moyɛ boniayɛ.*
> *Wahunu ɔfoforɔ ato daa atwene*
> *Mmarima, moyɛ boniayɛ!*

> (Men are no damn good!
> Men, are no damn good!
> Men, you are ungrateful.
> He has got a new one and discarded the old.
> Men, you are ungrateful.)[18]

The idea that women would and should actively look for good care was not of recent invention. It was central to the long-recognized art of seduction or *bɔ asɔn*[19] (a man's active wooing of a married woman in an attempt to persuade her to divorce her husband and marry him). Though nineteenth-century visitors to Asante were not acutely observant when it came to the domestic affairs of commoners, two references in Bowdich's travel account provide some indication of the art of seduction in the precolonial period. In the first, Bowdich describes the case of Quancum, one of the Asantehene's linguists, who was caught intriguing with the wife of "a captain of great consequence." In punishment for his wrong-doing, Quancum was "despoiled of all of his property" including his "favourite wife." Bowdich reports that the captain was "much smitten with her and assured her of an indulgence and preference, even greater than that she had enjoyed with Quancum." In this particular case, the woman had no interest in being seduced, and she "intreated to be sold." Although this seduction case is complicated by the act of adultery, compensation for adultery, and the status of the wife as "amongst the spoil," the parallels with our twentieth-century evidence are still striking.[20]

Equally intriguing are the lyrics of a popular song recorded by Bowdich during the same mission. In performing the song, men and women sat opposite each other as stanzas alternated between them in a playful debate over the meanings and implications of love and seduction:

1st Woman:	My husband likes me too much,
	He is good to me,
	But I cannot like him,
	So I must listen to my lover.
1st Man:	My wife does not please me,
	I tire of her now:
	So I will please myself with another,
	Who is very handsome.
2nd Woman:	My lover tempts me with sweet words,
	But my husband always does me good,
	So I must like him well,
	And I must be true to him.
2nd Man:	Girl you pass my wife handsome,
	But I cannot call you wife;
	A wife pleases her husband only,
	But when I leave you, you go to others.[21]

While love and physical attraction have their place in this lyrical debate, of equal importance are promises "with sweet words" and husbands who extend proper care. Similarly, in the colonial period, to be seduced was almost always connected to the notion of care, for a man so courting a married woman inevitably based his appeals, as did the captain in Quancum's case, on promises of care superior to what she was receiving in her current marriage. Obviously, a woman dissatisfied with her husband's care might be receptive to such inducements. Since *bɔ asɔn* was predicated upon improving the financial state of the woman involved, the man who persuaded her to leave her husband also assumed responsibility for paying off any debts she owed her husband at the time of their divorce. Given the often economic appeals of *bɔ asɔn*, this only made sense, for if the woman had to repay the debts herself, the cost of leaving her former husband might make divorcing and remarrying an unappealing course of action. As Aduwa Yaa Ama of Oyoko explained, "Some women were not bothered about the things the man would reclaim [at divorce]. . . . It could be another man who will pay for that and marry her."[22]

Seduction is significant for the overt connection between marriage and economic interests, particularly expectations of care, that it continued to embody in the colonial period. It was not simply a matter of a woman's extramarital sexual affairs. Rather, seduction remained a process through which a woman could attain a state of material well-being superior to that afforded by her current marriage. Indeed, if a woman discovered that the promises of her seducer were inflated, she considered it grounds for complaint. Abena Kwa of Oyoko, who remembered that such complaints were "not uncommon," explained: "You sue him for wooing you and failing to honor what he promised. . . . [If] you promise someone who is properly married . . . and you fail to honor that promise, that is serious."[23] The existence of seduction as an identifiable, if not always condoned, means of gaining a wife and the recognition of a woman's right to sue for losses incurred via seduction underscore the financial expectations Asante women have had of marriage. Those expectations are perhaps best expressed in the common proverb "If you fear divorce, you never sleep on a good bed."[24] It simply made sense for a woman to marry the husband who could care for her best. This was not a purely mercenary urge to "marry up." As Abena Kwa explained, it reflected a need for self-protection: "if the man doesn't take care of her well, she will divorce to find someone who will take good care of her."[25]

In being seduced by promises of better care or in opting for divorce on the grounds of improper care, Asante women in the first decades of the twentieth century were utilizing conjugal strategies not unlike those of their mothers or grandmothers before them. But they were utilizing those strategies to protect far more and at a far greater price than their mothers could have imagined. Women increasingly connected the notion of improper care to their unrewarded labor on a husband's cocoa farm, and such uncompensated investments became a major reason for divorce from the 1920s onward. Likewise, the disposition of conjugally worked cocoa farms at the time of divorce became a significant and ongoing source of contention, and it remained so throughout the colonial period.

Whether or to what extent women should be compensated for diverting their labor to their husbands' farms was an area of immense social and customary ambiguity. Though women remembered having expectations that they should be given a share of conjugally developed farms, they also understood that husbands were under no absolute, enforceable obligation to share them out. Many recalled that whether a husband did so or not was entirely discre-

Photo 4.1   Abena Kwa, Oyoko, 1990. Photograph by Victoria Tashjian.

tionary: "They were doing whatever they pleased then. They were not compelled. It was dependent on the goodwill of the man."[26] As one man remembered, "in our time you gave the wife according to how you felt."[27] Faced with this ambiguous reality, women who had agreed to work on their husbands' cocoa farms increasingly opted for divorce when it seemed likely they were not going to be adequately compensated for their labor. Divorce was a strategy that allowed women to withdraw their labor and invest it in their own enterprises, most commonly a farm of their own or small-scale trading.

While this strategy did not result in any compensation for the time and effort a woman had already put into a husband's cocoa farm, it did allow her to cut her losses. Thus, a wife's power—like that of her mother and grandmother— lay in her ability to easily remove herself and her labor power from her husband's control. However, in so doing, she accepted a loss for the years she had labored without recompense.[28]

Life histories for this period echo with the uncertainty women faced as they weighed their options, often after protracted periods of learning from experience. Abena Kwa, who had worked with her husband on his farms but realized almost nothing in return, balked when asked by her second husband to go with him to his farms. "I declined to accompany him," she recalled,

> . . . I didn't want to go because of what I had experienced with the first man. If someone had cheated me before the first husband, I would not have gone with the first husband, but it was because the first one cheated me, that was why I was reluctant to go with the second one. Once I have been cheated by an earlier marriage and divorced, if I happen to marry again and the husband wants to make farms with me, I will enquire, and if I sense cheating that will come from the man, I won't go; I would rather divorce.[29]

Others, like Awo Afua A., only came to the realization that they had invested their labor unwisely when they reached old age and had few remaining options. Awo Afua had been married for 30 years and had given birth to nine children when she told Kyei in the 1940s:

> Because I used up all my energy in helping my husband I have nothing of my own on which I can fall back. But if he does not give me part of his farm while he is still alive—and I have no hope that he will—I shall be left in this world, in spite of all my hard work to help Yaw, with only Providence to look to. *Wosom ɔbarima a, wobrɛ gu kwa* (Serving a man is wasted labour). A woman must feel secure, but if she depends on an Asante man, she will live to regret it in her old age, in the same way I am regretting it today.
>
> From my experience, I personally do not blame the modern woman. She is wiser in her trying to acquire her own property and to safeguard her future when she is still young. If she feels that one man cannot help her, why should she not try another?[30]

For women of Abena and Awo's generation, the terrain was difficult, and it was largely new. While their mothers or grandmothers may have been involved in limited conjugal production for the market of items like kola, gold,

Photo 4.2   Ama Akyaa, Oyoko, 1990. Photograph by Victoria Tashjian.

or rubber, by and large their labor was primarily aimed at jointly producing food crops for consumption. For Abena, Awo, and others of their generation, however, cash cropping was a significant part of daily life, and they came to know the new terrain only through bitter experience. They then struggled to protect themselves by refusing either to commit to conjugal labor directed at a husband's cash crop or to marry a man who expected it. As Adwoa Addae of Effiduasi remembered, "I was marrying my husband and I told my husband that he should go and cultivate a cocoa farm for me, but he refused, so I divorced him."[31]

But if divorce were a viable strategy for withdrawing labor—one of the few that women could exercise in these uncertain times—the price for exercising that option could be quite high. Indeed, some men seemed to exploit the fact that, if their wives divorced them, even the tenuous expectation that they should give out some portion of a jointly produced farm would evaporate. Consequently, at the time when he might otherwise give a share of the farm to his wife, a husband might behave in ways likely to encourage a wife to leave him. "Maybe the time has come for you to give her some," Adwowa Fodwo explained. "Intentionally you decide to go for another woman so that it will anger her to leave. Some people will think of that and not leave. It is very frustrating and some women grow lean out of their brooding."[32] The differences between this bleak situation and the descriptions of divorce in the days before widespread cash cropping are striking. As Akosua Nyantakyiwa of Oyoko recalled of divorce when couples only jointly worked each other's food farms: "when we decided to cultivate on our family lots, both of them, and there happened to be a divorce, none could be a loser. . . . when you have yours and there is divorce you won't be worried."[33] With cash cropping, divorce was no longer a circumstance in which "you won't be worried." Instead, it resulted in women who, with no means of recovering the labor invested in a spouse's cocoa farm, grew "lean out of their brooding." Given the frequency of divorce in Asante, this was far from an insignificant transformation. Indeed, like many of her generation, Ama Akyaa recalled in detail cocoa's profound impact on the financial consequences of divorce:

> Before cocoa, [people] were farming, cultivating cassava, plantain and others, so they were helping their husbands still. They did it on a subsistence basis. Nobody would buy it if you decided to sell. . . . In those days when they cultivated foodstuffs and they ate the fruits of it, and the man decided to divorce her, each went his or her way. But when she helps him to cultivate cocoa farms, and she doesn't get anything out of it, then it means she has done a useless job.[34]

Once a woman came to the realization that she had done "a useless job," however, the decision to divorce was still not an easy one. While she could certainly minimize her losses by divorcing, it was effectively impossible to force a husband to share jointly worked cocoa farms once drinks had been poured and the marriage ended. The reasonings of Kwasi Anane were probably not atypical: "I didn't give her a portion of the Kotokrom farm. . . . I would not give her. . . . She divorced me. . . . that was why I didn't give her a share. I would have given her some if I had divorced her, but not when she had divorced me and made me angry."[35] Though in some cases men shared conjugally produced farms with wives when a marriage stayed intact, if the sharing had not occurred by the time divorce threatened, it was unlikely to occur at all. As Afua Dufie of Oyoko recalled, "if you help him cultivate cocoa farms and he even divorces you before they ripen, you will just take it like that. What will you do? We didn't know suing."[36] In short, for many Asante women, particularly

in the early years of cocoa's expansion, the questions had no easy answers. Should a woman divorce and cut her losses? Should she stay married and hope for the best? From all perspectives, it appeared to be a no-
win situation.

But as women came to appreciate the nature of their predicament, many
found ways to protect themselves from the hazards of "wasted labour" and
from the inequitable distribution of conjugally produced wealth at or after
divorce. Many discovered, particularly after 1920, that the surest safeguard
was to invest their labor in their own enterprises, whether farming or trading.
As Adwowa Fodwo remarked, "If a woman gets money to cultivate her own
farm . . . the man cannot get it from her. . . . So if the man chose to go for
other girls, she will not mind, because she has money and other things."[37]
Akosua Nyantakyiwa echoed these sentiments. Women should farm by themselves, she argued, in order to protect their economic status in the event of a
divorce. As long as a woman was financially independent, she explained, she
could leave an unsatisfactory marriage: "If he is careless about you, you divorce him."[38] Indeed, as women began to secure their own places within the
expanding cash economy, they felt less constrained by the possibility of re-
alizing nothing from previously invested conjugal labor and chose divorce
as a preferable course of action, even if it did mean they incurred a financial
penalty with this choice.

WOMEN, DIVORCE, AND COLONIAL COURTS

Initiating divorce proceedings or redirecting labor power were two strategies employed by Asante's first generation of colonized women that were
consonant with tactics employed by their mothers or grandmothers. Other
strategies were new, however, shaped by the specific context of British
colonial rule. Quite early on, for example, some women turned to the
courts—first to the courts of colonial officials and later to the native courts
that were established after 1924. The first women to test this strategy
tended to have some connection with Asante's first missions, either the
Basel or the Wesleyan. The missions had long argued against what they
perceived to be the injustices of matrilineal inheritance and advocated
that wives and children each be given one-third of a man's property upon
his death. Thus, women who were members of Asante's first Christian
congregations, even if they were not married in the church, were also the
first to challenge the inequitable distribution of conjugally worked properties in cases of divorce and inheritance. Perhaps one of the very first of
these cases was heard before the district commissioner of Juaso in 1915.
Emilia Boakruwa claimed £48 from her husband, Emmanuel Frimpong,
as her share of the cocoa farms they had jointly developed and tended.

Emilia stated that Frimpong was her husband but had divorced her. Together they had made ten farms—seven in cocoa and three in plantain. "When he divorced me," she reported, "he refused to give me any money for the farms. I have had five children, two are dead and three alive, one male, two females. As he has divorced me, I came and sued him for half of the farm so that I can look after myself and my children. . . . I kept the children." Frimpon responded that the claim was groundless: "When you marry a woman she ought to help you make a farm, but it does not mean she should take a share in it." For added measure, in case the court did consider that labor invested warranted a share of the property, Frimpong added, "When I married her I hired men with my own money to make the farm. . . . She never cleared and planted cocoa. When she was leaving she said the only thing she wanted was that the children go to school. As she said she did not want anything, I gave her nothing." Two witnesses then testified that Frimpong had a lover in town and that his wife had found out and therefore wanted a divorce. The Rev. C. E. Martinson of the Basel Mission was then called to testify, and he reported that the case had been brought before him and the church elders and they had urged the man to apologize. By that point, however, Frimpong had decided he wanted the divorce. Martinson reported that he had written to mission headquarters for advice, but they could offer none because "it was the first case in the district . . . [so] they cannot give me any definite instructions." In the end, Martinson advised Emilia and her family to bring the case before the district commissioner. After hearing the testimony, Commissioner G. H. Sumner Wilson ordered that the value of the farms be divided, with one-third going to Emilia, one-third to her children, and one-third to Frimpong. "As the woman is keeping the children," he concluded, "the woman will get one-third plus one-third and the man one-third."[39]

Emilia's case was one of a handful of very early cases in which women sought to claim their right to properties jointly developed with their husbands in the courts of British officials. That Emilia was so successful in her claim, however, was not a harbinger of things to come. Partly, it was a matter of timing. In terms of the gendered chronology of cocoa's expansion, Emilia's appreciation of her predicament came relatively early; she and her husband were surely among the earliest pioneers of cocoa production in Asante. Her challenge, moreover, was bolstered by mission support at a time when the Christian population in Asante was slim and scattered. For the majority of Asante women, the full burden of cocoa's expansion would not be felt for several more years, and, by that time, the venues for appealing to colonial officialdom for redress were far fewer in number. With the Native Jurisdiction Ordinance of 1924, the government created the infrastructure for a native court system, and cases like Emilia's were meant to be heard in "native tribunals," rather than in the courts of colonial officials. That so few cases appear in the record books of those tribunals during the interwar years may very well be indicative of women's perception that the chiefs' courts would be hostile to their claims.

Not until the 1940s did many women begin to bring to Asante's native courts their divorce claims for portions of farms they had helped their husbands create, and the reasons behind the shift remain uncertain. Perhaps women were moved by the Asante Confederacy Council's discussions of inheritance in 1938—discussions in which many members argued in favor of wives being allowed to inherit one-third of a husband's property. The fact that in some inheritance cases women were beginning to win claims for portions of a deceased husband's estate probably provided an additional impetus.[40] For whatever reasons, the numbers of cases brought by women to the court increased dramatically in the 1940s, though only on rare occasions in that decade did the chiefs recognize a divorced woman's claims. One of these exceptional cases, *Affua Kraah v. Kojo Tanoah*, was heard in the Asantehene's "A" Court on 1 April 1947.[41] When Affua and Kojo divorced, Kojo offered his wife, as part of the formal divorce settlement, one of three farms they had produced together. Later, however, he reneged on this offer, so she brought suit against him to enforce the settlement. The court found in Affua Kraah's favor and, in a nod to equity, wrote, "It is most unbelievable that the Appellant who had lived with the Respondent as man and wife for about 30 years and have had 7 issues by . . . [him] did not assist him in the making of the three cocoa farms one of which he offered to her at the request of the arbitration called by himself after the dissolution of the marriage."[42] Yet the tensions that could attend the practice of alienating self-acquired property to non-family members were readily apparent. The court emphasized that Kojo Tanoah chose not to honor the divorce settlement after a family member, his sister, encouraged him to rescind his offer so that the family would not lose the farm. Though Affua Kraah prevailed, in a majority of the cases divorced women brought in the 1940s they were not successful. Many failed because they involved divorces that had been finalized many years previously with settlements that did not grant the women any share of conjugally produced properties, and the courts consistently refused to reopen divorce settlements when both parties had formally agreed to a settlement's terms.[43]

Not until the 1950s did women's claims in divorce cases stand a greater chance of success,[44] though the wide disparities in the disposition of cases from even this decade point to the utter lack of a consensus over how divorced women's complaints should be treated. The case of *Yaa Agyiwah*

v. Kofi Asante, heard in the Kumawu Native Court "B" on 17 January 1955, clearly illustrates the growing sympathy many courts now demonstrated toward divorced women's claims. The plaintiff, Yaa Agyiwah, brought suit in order to enforce upon the family of her deceased husband, Osei Kodjo, the family's promise to give her a cocoa farm that she had made with him. During their marriage the couple had made some farms together, including the one being contested in this case. After creating the farms, Osei divorced Yaa. Subsequently, he became seriously ill, and his family begged Yaa to remarry him and care for him in his sickness. At first she refused, but upon their promise that she would be given some of the jointly worked cocoa farms (which she had clearly not received in their divorce settlement), she agreed to remarry him. The defendant, the successor to Osei Kodjo, testified that, following Osei's death, he had been willing to honor the pact the family made with Yaa, but that the rest of the family refused to allow it. Consequently, the disagreement ended up in the courts. In the end, the court found in Yaa Agyiwah's favor. It is noteworthy that, in explaining its decision, the court did not focus upon the broken contract but instead reached further back in time, into the history of the couple's first marriage: "Defendant's witness Adwoa Forsuah admitted the fact that plaintiff assisted in the cultivation of the farm at Adeimbra. It is customarily legal that when a wife assisted a husband in the cultivation of a farm, the husband has to give a share to the wife."[45] The Kumawu court's rendition of the "customarily legal" as mandating that a husband share conjugally produced properties with a wife constituted a radically new interpretation of Asante custom. Indeed, the bold statement of this 1955 Kumawu court notwithstanding, numerous cases in the 1950s provide ample evidence that far from all Asante courts adhered to this new "custom."[46]

One particularly notable case illustrating the continued reluctance of many courts to recognize divorced women's claims was *Nana Kwasi Baffuor v. Adjua Adai*, which we first introduced in our discussion of marriage expenses in chapter 2.[47] Heard before Kumasi Division Native Court "C" in 1953, the case involved a recently divorced couple who both claimed a certain farm, which they had created together on the husband's land while they were married. Kwasi Baffuor brought suit because, though he claimed the farm as his, Adjua Adai kept trespassing on it. While the case revealed court members' sympathy with a woman's right to possess a share of conjugally produced properties in the early 1950s, theirs was sympathy only in theory, not in practice. That Adjua's family had agreed to give Kwasi uncontested ownership of the farm at the time of the divorce settlement ten months earlier, in February 1953, undermined Adjua's claim from the outset, given the continued inviolability through the 1950s of the basic principle that divorce agreements could not be retroactively overturned. As the court stated:

> It is on record that during the final stage of the dissolution of the marriage the plaintiff claimed ownership of the farm in dispute . . . and no word came out of the mouth of the defendant in defiance. . . . It is evident that she was present, heard plaintiff and her non-challenge of plaintiff's words is a vital piece of evidence of fact the ownership of the farm is in plaintiff and not defendant.

Still, the court expressed sympathy for Adjua's plight and asserted that if she had aggressively pursued her claim either at the right time, during the divorce arbitration, or on more suitable grounds she might well have effected a claim to a share of the disputed property:

> It would have been a wise attempt for defendant to adopt by asking the favour of plaintiff to consider in her valuable services rendered to pltff. during the life time of the marriage and to favour her with a reasonable remuneration or compensation. . . . we consider if defendant had brought her action in the appropriate way she should have [been] considered in that, but not in an action where defendant argued about absolute title or ownership to property.[48]

The court's opinion made it abundantly clear that women had no legal right to demand a share of conjugally produced properties. A woman could appeal to her husband's sense of fair play, but if he chose to ignore her request, she had no legal remedies. Limited to appeals of fairness, women were severely constrained in their ability to enforce through the native courts a more equitable distribution of conjugally produced farms at the time of divorce. Indeed, throughout the 1950s, if a woman did not successfully negotiate for ownership of a share of conjugally produced properties in the process of finalizing her divorce, she was left with no legal recourse.

Though the native courts of the post-restoration era came to acknowledge in principle the legitimacy of divorced women's equity claims to a portion of any jointly produced cocoa farms, in fact, more often than not, they turned down divorced women's claims on procedural grounds. If the divorce was already finalized, women lost their suits. Of course, in the vast majority of these cases, the divorce arbitration had already occurred, for it was precisely because they were unable to force husbands to share properties with them in arbitration that women turned to the courts. Granted, some men did voluntarily share conjugally produced properties with their wives before divorce, recognizing this practice as only fair, and some women were able to gain a portion of conjugally produced farms by begging for it during divorce arbitrations or by pressing their claims before a sympathetic native court. But with no legal bases for their claims, divorced or divorcing women of this generation found that they would continue to have no legally enforceable mechanism to guarantee a return on the labor they had expended on their husbands' farms.[49]

OPTING OUT OF MARRIAGE? *BAASIFOƆ*, SPINSTERS, AND MORAL CRISIS IN THE INTERWAR YEARS

Exercising their right to divorce or attempting to press their claims in the colonial courts were multifaceted strategies utilized by Asante women to assert control over their productive laboring during the colonial period. Yet as the stakes grew higher with the increasing monetization of the economy, the odds were not particularly favorable in either scenario. For some women in the first colonized generation, another strategy would involve avoiding marriage altogether, at least for periods in their life cycle—an option that was shared by other African women in different colonial contexts. Indeed, the recent works of Teresa Barnes, Jane Parpart, Elizabeth Schmidt, Cherryl Walker, Luise White, and others[50] provide striking evidence of women migrating to cities to avoid marriage and subsequently entering the cash economy through prostitution, beer-brewing, or petty trading. In these cases, however, which come largely from colonial settler states with large male migrant labor populations, opting out of marriage meant migration to colonial urban centers and, at times, the severing of ties with kin. But opting out of marriage for Asante women was, for the most part, a very different process from those described, for example, by White.[51] There was during this period no mass migration of single Asante male laborers to Kumasi, nor was there a colonial state bent on controlling the movement of Asante labor in or out of the region.[52] Moreover, the relatively easy nature and frequency of divorce in this matrilineal society made it possible for Asante women to opt out of marriage, without having to opt out of their communities or challenge the harsh labor influx control laws of a colonial state.

That said, we do have limited evidence for the colonial period of some women in Asante (it is unclear whether or not they were Asante women) seeking economic autonomy and security through prostitution, like the early women migrants to Nairobi of whom White has written. A rather strange petition from Atta Baasi, "head-woman of the *Baasi* Community"[53] in Kumasi, to the chief commissioner in 1943 asks for recognition of the *Baasi* community, an organization of prostitutes, by the colonial state and for the implementation of licensing and medical supervision "like European prostitutes." The petition, which was rejected, is extraordinary both because of the historical insight it provides into the *Baasi* community in colonial Asante and for the description it provides of newer forms of prostitution, which involved "Corner-Side" women who had taken up the profession, presumably during the war.[54] The petition warrants quotation at some length:

Your Most Obedient Maid Servant has the honour most respectfully to [submit] this humble petition for myself and on behalf of about thirty other women. . . . That, your humble Petitioners are the Baasi Community in Kumasi, that we have formed our unity . . . under the title commonly known and called Baasi; that our unity is specialised from that of the other women who . . . practice contrary to ours in the City of Kumasi . . . who are called the "Corner-Side Women." . . . The Unity of the Baasi-Women Community [was] . . . established in Kumasi, Ashanti over 25 to 30 years ago. We have our . . . residency in the City of Kumasi which is known as Odum Street. . . . After the Ashanti Confederacy, we did not hide ourselves. We appeared before Nana Asantehemaa and Otumfuo, Osaagyefuo, Asantehene, Kumasi and introduced ourselves to him and explain to him our unity with our aim to substantiate to him Otumfuo, Asantehene, that our acts and doings . . . are not of the scale as that of the corner-side women. Otumfuo, Asantehene having accepted us, handed over to one of his chief called Oheneba Bempah-Worakosehene of Kumasi. Oheneba Bempah has since then become our Chief Patron. . . . We have from time immemorial [been] dealing with our natives (African) and have our wartime moderate rates. . . . We deny having friendly connection with any White-man (European). We always deal with our natives. We deny that for over 25 to 30 years since our establishment no man had ever contracted disease through the cause of sexual connection with a member of our Unity. The question of our personal cleanliness is the major part of our byelaws and regulation. . . . We have good and excellent discipline in all of our dealing and how we treat our men friends in joyful hospitalities and liberty to satisfy their wish before we are awarded. . . . Our Unity . . . is of a great use to the male population of the City of Kumasi-Ashanti. We are of good and helpful to old and young bachelors whom according to their Employment, Income and their world crises cannot afford to maintain partners (wife) during their term for services in the time of their bachelorship. . . . The corner-side women mentioned in Paragraph 1 . . . Your Honour, the gang of women who are no members of our Unity, thinking shameful to be in our Company, as our title of "Baasifuo" is filthy name to be carried by them, have now become abundant throughout the City . . . moving here and there as if they are women of husbands and going about . . . doing mischievous acts extorting old and young men, giving them diseases and shortening promising young men's lives. These corner-side women are the gang of women that goes about to Europeans in the meantime having African friends. . . . We are clear in our dealing, but the Corner-Side women are underminers who used to ruin both Europeans and African bachelors. . . . We [submit that] . . . "Baasifuo" are harmless women. Our system of dealing with our own African friends are always delicious charming and faithful. . . .We regret we are not under the Medical Supervision and unlicensed [and ask to] be under the supervision of Medical Authorities with or without the payment of fees.[55]

Clearly the evidence in Atta Baasi's petition suggests that early on in the colonial period some women in Asante opted out of marriage and secured a niche in the expanding cash economy, much like their counterparts in Nairobi, through prostitution, especially in Kumasi or in mining towns like Obuasi, which drew substantial numbers of male migrants. It also suggests that a second wave of women made similar decisions during the course of the Second World War. But if the motivations of *Baasifɔɔ* and "Corner-Side Women" to attain and secure economic autonomy were not atypical, their activities, for the most part, were. They were not representative of the process by which most Asante women entered the cash economy. For the vast and overwhelming majority, opting out of marriage did not mean prostitution. The spaces most women sought to secure in Asante's colonial economy entailed farming and trading, although, as we shall see, economic autonomy often drew charges, especially from chiefs, of widespread prostitution and female uncontrollability.

And the strategy of opting out of marriage was not entirely new. For example, it was not uncommon, historically, for postmenopausal Asante women to choose to be unmarried. Tashjian found that in Mamponten and Oyoko, the vast majority (90 percent) of postmenopausal women were, in fact, single. After menopause, the main reasons for marrying—to bear children and to gain spiritual and economic protection—were no longer compelling, and many older women, after a divorce or a husband's death, simply did not remarry and instead devoted their energies entirely to their own economic activities.[56] But in the 1920s and 1930s, some Asante women were avoiding marriage even though they were still very much in their productive and reproductive prime, and they were opting instead for what Fortes termed "illicit and casual unions."[57] The evidence we have for this "opting out" is slim and scattered, but it is certainly sufficient to challenge normative descriptions of unmarried women in Asante as "an anomaly."[58]

For example, in March of 1933, the district officer's "Quarterly Report" for the Mampong District in Asante contained a rather strange entry for the town of Effiduasi. "Becoming alarmed at the amount of venereal disease spread in the town by unattached spinsters," the officer wrote,

> the *Ohene* [chief] published an edict commanding that all unmarried maidens should forthwith provide themselves with husbands. This shook the Wesleyan Mission somewhat but only one complaint was received. In fact, the husband hunt seems to have been rather enjoyed by the girls than otherwise. The *Ohene*, however, was warned against the futility of publishing unenforceable orders and against advertising the frailties of his maidens.[59]

Although the district officer portrayed this so-called "husband hunt" as a minor, isolated incident in the town of Effiduasi, there is enough written evidence and ample oral testimony to suggest that it was anything but minor and certainly not isolated. Between 1929 and 1933, in a number of villages and towns throughout Asante, chiefs were ordering the arrest of all women who were over the age of 15 and not married.[60] As one of those who was arrested recently recalled:

> We were arrested and just dumped into a room—all of the women of Effiduasi who were not married. . . . The *ahemfie* [palace] police [did the arresting]. The women were flirting around and so they became an embarrassment to the King. So, he decided that they should get married. . . . they announced it that on such a day all women should be able to show a husband. . . . When we were sent there, we were put into a room. . . . When you mentioned a man's name, it meant that was the man you wanted to marry, so they would release you. . . . You would go home with the man and the man would see your relatives and say, "I am getting married to this woman."[61]

The pattern, it seems, was similar in each town. A gong-gong was generally beaten to announce the arrest of unmarried women (*asigyafoɔ*).[62] A woman was detained, usually at the chief's court, until she spoke the name of a man whom she would agree to marry. That man was then summoned to the court, where he would affirm his desire to marry the woman and then pay a "release fee" of 5/-. If the man refused to marry the woman, he was fined. In some cases, the fine was 5/-, in others it was as high as £5. After the woman's release, the man was expected to pay a marriage fee of 7/- and one bottle of gin to the woman's family.[63]

We have found no references to anything that even remotely resembles the rounding up of younger, unmarried women in eighteenth- and nineteenth-century sources. For the colonial period, the primary written sources on the subject are scanty at best, limited to a small collection of colonial correspondence, a quarterly report entry, and a few customary court cases.[64] Meyer Fortes made brief mention in his field notes from the Ashanti Social Survey of the fact that

> periodically the political authority stepped in and decreed that all unmarried women must get married; in some cases they were placed in a cell and told to name their choice; theoretically the men could refuse, but in practice it appears to have been difficult for them to refuse. In order to facilitate marriages in this situation, marriage by registration was introduced, so that only a small fee (usually 5/-) [was paid]; the *tiri nsa* was also paid, often such small amounts as 6d of palm wine being cited.[65]

In the more recent, published literature, there are only two brief references to the detention of unmarried women in Ghana's colonial period—and those in sources not pertaining specifically to Asante. In a 1983 article, Vellenga made general reference to chiefs' concerns about the number of women not properly married. "Some even went to the extreme measure," she wrote, "of locking up such women until their lovers would pay a fee to release them, thus legitimising the relationship."[66] Roberts discovered similar, but more detailed, information on the arrest of unmarried women in Sefwi Wiawso—an area to the southwest of Asante that was incorporated into the empire in the early eighteenth century as a tributary state.[67] She found evidence of a 1929 "Free Women's Marriage Proclamation," which ordered that "such women . . . be arrested, locked up in the outer courtyards of the *ɔmanhene*'s palace in Wiawso and held there until they were claimed by a husband or by any other man who would take charge of them. The male claimant was required to pay a fine of 5/- to release the woman."[68]

British government officers in Asante first expressed concern about the detention of unmarried women in 1932. In July of that year, the chief commissioner wrote a brief memorandum to his assistant requesting that enquiries be made and a report furnished. "I am informed," he wrote, "that there is a custom in Ashanti that young girls of 15 years of age upwards are ordered to marry. It is even alleged that any who refuse are placed in prison."[69] Shortly thereafter, the assistant commissioner, having sought information in Bekwai and Mansu Nkwanta, filed his response, which included letters from the chiefs of both towns and from the district officer resident in Bekwai. The officer wrote that the Roman Catholic priest first informed him of the practice and that "no complaint was made . . . by any Ashanti or for that matter any african [*sic*], one or two africans [*sic*] rather took it as a joke." He added that he had heard of similar actions being taken in Adansi, Edweso, and even Kumasi a few years earlier, although he understood "the Kumasihene is not in favour of it."[70]

The chiefs confirmed the detentions of unmarried women and justified their actions by arguing that venereal diseases and prostitution were prevalent in their divisions.[71] The Bekwaihene and his councillors and elders submitted a three-page letter defending their actions in terms of a desire "to prevent prostitution which we have notice[d] to bring sterility and incurable venereal diseases." The solution was, they argued, to "encourage conjugal marriages among our womenfolk." If the chiefs were prepared to offer a concrete solution to the problem of unmarried women, they were far more equivocal in explaining why the problem of women not marrying existed in the first place.[72] On the one hand, they argued that "the tendency . . . is attributable to the prevalent financial depression which renders the men incapable to conform with . . . the expenses of our native customary laws concerning marriage." On the other hand, the chiefs betrayed much concern about women's growing uncontrollability, fondly recalling "the good old days of our ancestors . . . [when] no girl or woman dared to resist when given away in marriage to a suitor by her parents and relatives as is the case now."[73] Yet in their letter to colonial officials, the customary rulers of Bekwai were less intent on explaining the marriage crisis than on exposing its dreadful symptoms—immorality, prostitution, and disease. They assured British officials that their intentions were "clean" and that they would continue the practice of detaining unmarried women "unless there is any justifiable reason to encourage prostitution and its attendant prevalence of sterility and venereal diseases."[74] As for the district officer, he was not fully convinced by the chiefs' arguments. The idea of stopping "the spread of venereal disease is a good cloak," he wrote, "behind which to hide a money making proposition." The Bekwaihene collected a release fee of 5/- on every woman caught, the officer noted, and a fine of £5 on every man whose name was called but who refused to pay the fee and marry.[75]

How women viewed these arrests in the late 1920s and early 30s is far more difficult to reconstruct than the views of chiefs or colonial officers because so few sources recorded women's voices. But at least one woman's experience of being arrested has been preserved in a 1929 customary court case from Asokore. In *Kwaku Afram v. Afuah Buo*, the plaintiff sought judicial relief, asking the defendant to explain her reasons for refusing to marry him after 5/- had been paid on her behalf "during the capture of spinsters in Asokore." The plaintiff claimed that he saw a "certain young man from Seneajah connecting with the girl. . . [and] upon the strength of that . . . found out that the defendant did not like to marry" him. Afuah Buo's defense was brief and direct:

I live at Asokore. I am a farmer. Some years ago, a gong-gong was beaten that spinsters are to be caught. I was among (and previous [to] that I was told by Plaintiff that I must mention his name and he will clear me out). I did and he came and paid 5/- and discharged me. . . . About two weeks after Plaintiff does not care for me, nor subsist me. I informed one Attah Biom of the treatment and Plaintiff said because he was ill hence he did not do it. What I have to say is that because Plaintiff did not care for me, nor subsist me, hence I connected with someone, to get my daily living. That's all I know.[76]

In the end, the Asokore Native Tribunal ruled against Afuah Buo, fining her £5.9.0—£3.4.0 of which went to the plaintiff as costs and compensation.

Although brief, Afuah Buo's testimony raises a number of important issues concerning unmarried women and their arrests. First and most obviously, that Afuah's case was brought before the court in 1929 and that the "capture" of spinsters in Asokore had occurred "some years" prior to that time suggests that the problem of unmarried women was not simply a symptom of high marriage costs during a time of "financial depression." Secondly, Afuah Buo's testimony points to the serious social contest, discussed in chapter 2, over the very meaning of marriage in the late 1920s and to the strategies women employed in this contest. It demonstrates that the crisis was not simply about marriage and nonmarriage, as the chiefs' arguments suggest, but about what constitutes a marriage and what responsibilities are incumbent upon each partner. For the plaintiff and, indeed, for the court, the payment of the release fee constituted "marriage" and entitled Afram to exclusive sexual rights in his wife. The marriage was a fact, a state of being, recognized by the court as nonnegotiable. It either was or it was not; there could be no modifying factors. For Afuah Buo, the exclusive sexual rights were contingent upon and tied directly to a man's ongoing provision of minimal subsistence or "chop money." In her view, marriage was, as Vellenga has written, "a process . . . tenuous and fluid in nature."[77] Buo's definition of the marrying process allowed her to move in and out and between the categories of wife and concubine—a strategy easily branded as prostitution by Asante's colonial chiefs.

In recalling the capture of those who were unmarried, Asante women do not speak with one voice.[78] Their recollections reveal a host of sentiments and reasonings—some echoing the perspective of Afuah Buo, others that of Asante's chiefs. Still others speak from a singular and personal perspective that defies simple categorization. Yet these multiple truths help us to appreciate the complexities of the colonial experience for Asante women. They bring the personal to bear on the structural relationship between economic and social change and, for the purposes of this chap-

Photo 4.3 Beatrice Nyarko, Effiduasi, 1992. Photograph by Jean Allman.

ter, are essential for disentangling charges of prostitution and concerns about morality from women's assertions of autonomy in a rapidly changing cash economy. Interestingly, none of the women with whom we have spoken in recent years point to the economic depression or to men's inability to afford marriage payments as a reason for women's nonmarriage. Akosua Atta saw the root of the problem as men not proposing marriage to women, but she could point to no economic reasons for this. "I don't know why," she recently pondered. "Things were not expensive then as they are now."[79] Others, like Mary Oduro and Rosina Boama, both of Effiduasi, saw the problem as a straightforward one of numbers. Women were not marrying because "the women outnumbered the men." It was feared, Boama explained, "that they [the women] would contract some venereal disease."[80] From the perspectives of Oduro, Boama, Atta, and a few others, nonmarriage was not a choice that women made, it was something that happened through no fault of their own. Because of men's refusal to propose or simply because of the demography of the times, some women were left unmarried.[81]

Most reminiscences of the period, however, go further in underscoring women's agency in the process of nonmarriage by characterizing the decision not to marry as a choice, though there is little agreement on how to portray that agency. Even Rosina Boama, who was sure that the main reason women did not marry was that there were not enough men, allowed that some women might have chosen not to marry. "I can't say," she recalled. "They were just roaming about. Whether they were not having [husbands] or were not getting [husbands], I can't say."[82] Other women were not so torn in their reasoning and echoed quite clearly the sentiments expressed by chiefs in the early 1930s as they pointed to women's uncontrollability. "During that time," recalled Beatrice Nyarko, who was nearly 40 years old during the capture of unmarried women at Effiduasi, "young girls were misbehaving." Jean Asare, who was a child at the time, remembered that "women were just roaming about, attending dances, sleeping everywhere. Some even went as far as Kumasi to sleep with boyfriends, so . . . it was a disgrace to the town and to the people here in the town."[83] As Yaa Dufie explained, it was "because of the fear of contracting that disease [babaso, or venereal disease]. That's why they locked them up."[84] Indeed, several women did not hesitate to call those who had been captured "prostitutes." When asked if she were sure these women were prostitutes (atutufoɔ) and not concubines of one sort or another (mpenafoɔ), Beatrice Nyarko responded, "It was proper prostitution. If they see you as a waiting man, they will come to you and say the price, but it wasn't a bargaining thing. If she sees you, you can give her money and she will come to you. The next time, she may see another man, too, who can give her money, [and] she can go to him."[85]

Many women, however, had more difficulty leaping to the assumption that those who had not married were prostitutes. As Akosua So remembered:

AS: Some girls don't want to marry. It's a personal thing. Some don't like it. Some don't want to lead good lives.

JA: Were they prostitutes or concubines or . . . ?

AS: They can't openly declare themselves as prostitutes, but the ones who weren't married, people assumed they were prostitutes.[86]

Perhaps some were; probably most were not. Eponuahemaa Afua Fom reported that both unmarried women and prostitutes were arrested. When asked why some women had chosen not to marry, she replied, "Each person had

Photo 4.4   Adwoa Addae, Effiduasi, 1993. Photograph by Jean Allman.

their own reason. Some were lazy. They didn't like to go to farm and to cook for the husband, so they wouldn't marry. . . . The men wanted to marry, but the women didn't want to marry and it's even worse now."[87] In a subsequent conversation, Afua Fom would reveal that she was among the 60 spinsters caught in Effiduasi in the early 1930s.[88]

According to Afua Fom and her sister, Adwoa Addae, both of whom are now in their mid-eighties, women were choosing *sigyawdi* (being unmarried or the state of nonmarriage) for reasons that had far more to do with the economics of conjugal obligations than with laxity in morals. Adwoa Addae has always lived with her sister in the family house (*abusua fie*). She had four husbands but never any children, and she helped her sister raise her eight children. The first time Allman spoke to Addae, she explained the events behind the capture of unmarried women in this way:

Men were not buying! That is why the women were saying that they would not marry. The men were not taking care of them. . . . The men were not serving us well. You would serve him, go to the farm with him, cook for him and yet he would not give you anything. . . . The man and woman may farm together, but the woman would do the greater part of it. . . . [The men] prefer to sit and do nothing.[89]

Although Adwoa was not captured, she recalled those days as ones in which women asserted a great deal of autonomy and independence—much of it linked to the establishment of cocoa farms or to engagement in food-stuffs trade. Adwoa herself divorced at least one of her husbands because he refused to cultivate a cocoa farm for her. "I got married to my husband," she explained, "because I had wanted some benefits from [him] . . . so that maybe, in the future, I would not suffer. . . . If the cocoa is there, the proceeds—I will enjoy them. But my husband was not prepared to think that far, so I decided to divorce [him]."[90] Adwoa Addae did not consider her actions or attitudes to be personal or nonrepresentative and her reminiscences, though lengthy, warrant extensive quotation. "In those days," she recalled,

women were hard working, so we could live without men. The only thing we did not get were children, so we were forced to go in for these men. Apart from that, we were independent. We could work without the assistance of men. I don't know, but that might have accounted for what the chiefs did. . . . Those days are better than these days. In those days women could work hard and get a lot of things they wanted. But today it is not like that. Even if you try to assert some form of independence, you will see that it doesn't work as it used to work. In those days, even though women wanted to be independent, they still got married to men, but it was because they wanted to. . . . In those days, if you had a wife and you did not look after her well, she would just go. If you looked after her well, she would stay.[91]

If Adwoa Addae remembered her years as a young woman as years of autonomy, she also remembered them as ones of broader disorder. It was as though the gendered world of Asante was turned upside down, if only for a few fleeting moments. Not only were women not marrying and un-married women being arrested, she recalled, but women who were mar-ried were instructed by the chief to "buy cloths for our husbands, which we did, and even in some cases sandals and other things. . . . We really did not understand why the chief was saying that, but we had to do it."[92] As we have seen, one of the main liabilities that a husband incurred upon marriage was responsibility for his wife's maintenance. Providing cloth was considered an important aspect of maintenance, and dowries in the precolonial and early colonial periods often included provision of large pieces of cloth.[93] The order by the Effiduasihene that men need no longer provide cloths for their wives and that wives should provide cloths for their husbands—an order recalled in detail by Afua Fom, as well—undercut one of the fundamental obligations of marriage, that a husband must maintain his wife.[94] Afua Fom remembered the order only as a "temporary measure that the king took. . . . It was not customary, so it did not last long." She viewed the order more as a ritual—something the king was advised by a diviner to do in order to ward off some imminent danger. When asked if she thought it was related to the capture of unmarried women, she replied, "We could not ask because, customarily, when the chief says something you cannot ask a question."[95]

Although Afua Fom did not draw a direct correlation between the capture and the order concerning cloth, her recollections point to a series of attempts to assert control over women's productive and reproductive labor during the years of gender chaos. Not only were there the arrests of "spinsters" and the recasting, however temporary, of marital obligations, there was an attempt, according to Fom, to register girls upon passage of their first menses:

> The King was also using another means [to determine who was unmarried, but eligible for marriage]. When the woman was old enough, when she starts passing the menses, you will go to a registrar who will register that this woman is old enough to marry. . . . [Women registered] at the court . . . so that they'll have a rough idea which people are not marrying but are eligible to marry. There are puberty rites, too. Because of the puberty rites . . . people got to know which girls are eligible for marriage. . . . By this they got to know who was married and who was not.[96]

We have not come across any written documentation that provides details on the registration of girls at puberty. Nonetheless, it does not appear to be outside of the realm of possibility in a world in which, for the moment, anyway, confusion reigned.

CONCLUSION

So how can one make sense of the charges and counter-charges—of prostitution, venereal disease, immorality, and "bad girls," of captured "spinsters," wives clothing husbands, and chiefs registering girls at menarche? In short, how does one sort through the chaos that seemed to engulf the gendered world of colonial Asante in the late 1920s and early 1930s? Certainly, it is not a question of figuring out who was telling the "truth" and who was "lying," or of simply ascertaining the precise number of prostitutes in a town like Effiduasi in 1929 (whose population was estimated as 3,778 in 1931)[97] in order to evaluate the veracity of the chiefs' charges. The reminiscences of women like Afua Fom and her sister, Adwoa Addae, we argue, point us in the right direction. Their repeated references to women's quest for and, at times, realization of autonomy and independence during this period—whether through complaints that men were "lazy" or through matter-of-fact statements like "in those days, the women were able to get money faster than the men"—highlight the importance of economic and social contexts in framing critical questions about marriage and divorce in the colonial period. Why were women perceived as being prostitutes, as being out of control in this period, and why was that "uncontrollability" consistently articulated in terms of a moral crisis?

These questions are certainly not unique to Asante. In recent years they have been posed quite dramatically in the growing body of comparative literature on gender and colonialism.[98] As Nancy Hunt recently reflected: "where women most often appear in the colonial record is where moral panic surfaced, settled and festered. Prostitution, polygamy, adultery, concubinage and infertility are the loci of such angst throughout the historical record."[99] Hunt and a number of other historians concerned with gender issues, particularly in areas with sizable white settler populations, have devoted much energy to exploring why this has been the case. Most have come to conclusions similar to Megan Vaughan, who has argued that

> "the problem of women" was shorthand for a number of related problems including changes in property rights, in rights in labour and relations between generations. . . . The real issue, of course, was that with far-reaching changes taking place in economic relations, so enormous strains were placed on both gender and generational relations. . . . these complex changes were described in terms of degeneration, of uncontrolled sexuality and of disease.[100]

Asante, we argue, provides no exception—except that in the Asante equation there were no white settlers and cocoa was absolutely key. Women who withdrew their labor from conjugally developed cocoa farms, who divorced their husbands and demanded portions of farms, or who made the decision not to marry and to invest their labor in their own enterprises were engaging in struggles to defend their economic autonomy.

That those struggles would be captured, articulated, and debated in a public discourse about "bad girls," prostitutes, and "uncontrollable women" should come as no surprise. As Penelope Roberts so succinctly put it, women's economic alternatives were easily represented "as the removal of constraints upon their sexuality."[101] But how could constraints be reasserted? How could a new moral order be constructed out of the crisis? Indirect rule and mission welfare/education initiatives, we argue in chapter 5, were central to colonial government efforts to bring order to the chaos in gender relations that enveloped Asante during the interwar years.[102]

NOTES

1. Tashjian: Nana Osei Agyeman-Duah, Kumasi, 9 July 1990.

2. Aidoo quotes a song that well captures women's attitude toward divorce: "*Ee, fidie hwintin / fidie hwintin a/ Mɛkɔ me nkyi / Me gyae aware a / Mɛkɔ Bo-adwoo-oo* (The trap releases / when the trap releases / I shall go back home / If I am divorced / I shall go to 'The Place Called Peace-of-Mind')." Aidoo, "Women," 24.

3. Unfortunately, we have no nineteenth-century statistics with which we can compare this data, although Bowdich and Gros make it clear that divorce was common in the early nineteenth century. See Bowdich, *Mission*, 260; and Jules Gros, *Voyages, Aventures et Captivité de J. Bonnat Chez les Achantis* (Paris: E. Plon, Nourrit et Cie, 1884), 205–6.

4. Of her informants, 27 had been divorced at least once (and some of them many more times than that), while 14 said they never had a marriage end in divorce. At least 47 of the 93 marriages specifically mentioned by informants ended in divorce. With reference to the broader Akan population of southern Ghana, Christine Oppong observed that "[j]ust as conjugal relationships may be entered with a minimum of formality, so they may be, and often are, broken with comparative ease." Oppong, *Marriage*, 31 and 49.

5. The rates for Tafo and Kumasi were 34 percent and 21 percent respectively. Since these rates were derived from life histories and not from an accurate statistical sampling, it is difficult to say whether the differences are significant. They do at least suggest the possibility that during the colonial period it was easier to divorce in rural areas than in urban areas.

6. Fortes, "Kinship and Marriage," 278 and n. 3.

7. Tashjian: Adwowa Fodwo, Mamponten, 1 October 1990.

8. Tashjian: Kwadwo Paul Adum, Mamponten, 11 September 1990.

9. For a description of divorce proceedings as he found them in the 1940s, see Kyei, *Marriage*, 64–71.

10. For a discussion of the role of drinks in formalizing ties of marriage, see Akyeampong, *Drink*, 36–37.

11. Tashjian: Kwabena Boahene, Mamponten, 11 September, 1990.

12. Tashjian: Ama Akyaa, Oyoko, 23 October 1990.

13. Based on his work with the Ashanti Social Survey, Kyei provides a listing of "causes of divorce." First on the list are economic causes. See Kyei, *Marriage*, 72–73.

14. Undoubtedly lack of care was a frequent cause of divorce. However, it is also possible that not being cared for by a husband or having a disobedient wife (a common male justification) were socially acceptable, generic reasons for divorce that were sometimes given in order to avoid discussing more painful or intimate events. Kyei found that people tended to offer vague explanations when the real reason would be personally "embarrassing," "degrading," or damaging to the reputation of an ex-spouse. Kyei, *Marriage*, 73.

15. Tashjian: Aduwa Yaa Ama, Oyoko, 5 November 1990. Also Tashjian: Ama Akyaa, Oyoko, 27 November 1990.

16. Tashjian: Abena Kwa, Oyoko, 2 November 1990.

17. Tashjian: Ama Sewaa Akoto, Mamponten, 10 September 1990.

18. Kyei, *Marriage*, 62.

19. *Asɔn* means, quite literally, "bad advice." Thus, seduction is captured in the phrase *ɔbɔɔ ɔbaa nsɔn*, "he gave the woman the bad advice [to leave her husband]." See Christaller, *Dictionary*, 469 and 474.

20. Bowdich, *Mission*, 96–97. The case also has a very interesting ending. Eventually, the captain agreed to sell the woman because he had been unsuccessful in wooing her with promises of his indulgence. The woman agreed. In exchange, she promised to hand over to the captain all of the presents Quancum had given her, except for a small sum of gold that Quancum had given to her son. The woman was then sold to a "distant caboceer," but her son purchased her back with the gold and returned her to his father!

21. Bowdich, *Mission*, 369.

22. Tashjian: Aduwa Yaa Ama, Oyoko, 5 November 1990.

23. Tashjian: Abena Kwa, Oyoko, 2 November 1990.

24. Tashjian: Nana Osei Agyeman-Duah, Kumasi, 9 July 1990. Perhaps the male converse of this is the proverb "If you marry a good wife, you eat good food." Tashjian: Kwabena Manu, Mamponten, 21 September 1990.

25. Tashjian: Abena Kwa, Oyoko, 2 November 1990.

26. Tashjian: Afua Fosuwa, Oyoko, 1 November 1990.

27. Tashjian: Kofi Anto, Oyoko, 6 November 1990.

28. Mikell makes a similar point regarding divorce and the cocoa economy, though she situates her argument in the post–World War II period. See Mikell, *Cocoa and Chaos*, 120.

29. Tashjian: Abena Kwa, Oyoko, 2 November 1990, and 12 November 1990. This strong statement notwithstanding, her story is also indicative of family pressure on women to be "good" wives, which included obeying and accompanying husbands. Abena was eventually persuaded by a senior female member of her lineage to accompany her second husband to his cocoa farms, even though this was a move which her own good judgment caused her to view with suspicion.

30. Kyei, *Marriage*, 58–59.

31. Allman: Adwoa Addae, Effiduasi, 30 June 1993.

32. Tashjian: Adwowa Fodwo, Mamponten, 1 October 1990.

33. Tashjian: Akosua Nyantakyiwa, Oyoko, 24 October 1990.

34. Tashjian: Ama Akyaa, Oyoko, 23 October 1990.

35. Tashjian: Kwasi Anane, Mamponten, 5 and 8 October 1990.

36. Tashjian: Afua Dufie, Oyoko, 31 October 1990.

37. Tashjian: Adwowa Fodwo, Mamponten, 1 October 1990.

38 Tashjian: Akosua Nyantakyiwa, Oyoko, 24 October 1990.

39. NAGA, ADM 50/40/1: Juaso Civil Record Book, 1914–1917, *Emilia Boakruwa v. Emmanuel Frimpong*, dd. Juaso, 13 July 1915.

40. MRO: Ashanti Confederacy Council, Minutes of the Third Session, 7–23 March 1938. Although discussions were held in 1938, it was not until 1948 that the council actually ruled in favor of allowing a wife and children to inherit one-third of a man's property if he died intestate. See Matson, *Digest*, 26–48. For further discussion of inheritance, see chapter 3.

41. MRO: Asantehene's A Court, "The Views of Members of the Court in the case of Affua Kraah v. Kojo Tanoah," dd. Kumasi, 1 April 1947. Appended to the case of *Ama Mansah v. Afua Kraa and Kwadjo Tanoah*, Native Court of Kumawu, 16 July 1951 [typescript].

42. Ibid.

43. See, for example, MRO: Asantehene's A Court, *Ekua Bantama v. Yaw Frimpong*, dd. 1 June 1948, heard on appeal from the Native Court of Ahafo, 23 December 1947 [typescript].

44. See, for example, MRO: Kumasi Division Court B1, Abina Serwah per *Hyimanhene Kwaku Appaw v. Kwaku Druyeh*, dd. Kumasi, 12 February 1952 [typescript].

45. MRO: Native Court of Kumawu, Grade B, *Yaa Agyiwah v. Kofi Asante*, dd. Kumawu, 17 May 1954 [typescript].

46. It should be noted that sometimes couples jointly made farms on land controlled not by the husband but by the wife, and a number of court cases were brought during this period by husbands seeking a share of the output of these farms. The courts typically upheld the husband's right to a share of the harvest, and usually put his share at 50 percent, substantially larger than the one-third or less awarded to women suing for a portion of conjugally produced farms. Most of these cases involved family land rather than self-acquired property, as women found it difficult to amass the substantial cash resources needed to create cocoa farms on non-family land. See, for example, MRO: Native Court of Agona, *Akosua Anana v. Kofi Ban*, dd. Agona, 18 February 1943 [typescript]; Asantehene's A2 Court, *Ekua Bantama v. Yaw Frimpong*, dd. Kumasi 1 June 1948, heard on appeal from the Native Court of Ahafo, dd. Kanyase 1, 25 November 1947 [typescript]; Asantehene's A Court, *Kwame Attakora v. Afua Mansah*, dd. Kumasi 4 June 1951, heard on appeal from the Mampong Native Court, dd. Mampong, 7 May 1951 [typescript].

47. Ivor Wilks Papers, typescript: Kumasi Division, Native Court C, Nana Kwasi Bafuor per *Kojo Kakari v. Adjoa Adai*, dd. Kumasi, 17 November 1953.

48. Ibid.

49. For analyses of recent attempts to provide such mechanisms, see Kofi Awusababo, "Matriliny and the New Intestate Succession Law of Ghana," *CJAS* 24:1 (1990), 1–15; and Takyiwaa Manuh, "Wives, Children and Intestate Succession in Ghana," in Gwendolyn Mikell, ed., *African Feminism: The Struggle for Survival in Sub-Saharan Africa* (Philadelphia: University of Pennsylvania Press, 1997), 77–95.

50. See, for example, Barnes, "*We Women*"; Parpart, "'Where Is Your Mother?'"; Schmidt, *Peasants*; Walker, "Gender"; and Luise White, *The Comforts of Home: Prostitution in Colonial Nairobi* (Chicago: University of Chicago Press, 1990).

51. White, *Comforts of Home*, especially 29–50.

52. As those familiar with Ghanaian history will note, there was a massive migration of laborers from the Northern Territories into Asante during this period and consistent, concerted attempts by the colonial authorities to control that movement. By and large, however, Asante men were not labor migrants, nor was their labor subject to influx or outflow control. For a superb discussion of the role of Northern labor in the development of the south, see Nicholas Van Hear, "Northern Labour and the Development of Capitalist Agriculture in Ghana" (Ph.D. thesis, University of Birmingham, 1982).

53. The etymology of the term '*baasi*' is not clear. It may be a compound word, *ɔbaa* (woman) + *si* (to stand), thus a "standing woman." It may be a derivative of *ɔbaasimma*, "a low, humble, simple unpresuming woman, not entitled to much respect or esteem." See Christaller, *Dictionary*, 9.

54. In "Sexuality," especially 164–66, Akyeampong argues for the precolonial origins of prostitution in the Gold Coast through an examination of "public women." Although the *Baasi* Community was clearly a twentieth-century organization, it sought chiefly recognition in much the same way as had the "public women" of old along the coast.

55. NAGK, ARA/2339: Atta Baasi, Head-Woman of the Baasi Community to CCA, dd. Kumasi, 19 July 1943.

56. Victoria Tashjian, "'You Marry to Beget': Menopause and Non-Marriage in Asante," paper presented at the Annual Meeting of the African Studies Association, Boston, 4 December 1993.

57. Fortes, "Kinship and Marriage," 278.

58. Sarpong, *Ghana*, 78. The discussion which follows first appeared in Jean Allman, "Rounding Up Spinsters: Gender Chaos and Unmarried Women in Colonial Asante," *JAH* 37:2 (1996), 195–214.

59. NAGK, ARA/1286: "Report on Native Affairs, Mampong District for Two Quarters Ending . . . 31 March 1933." It is worth underscoring here the wide-ranging autonomy enjoyed by native authorities in Asante and other parts of the Gold Coast, particularly as compared to the limited powers allotted to chiefs by colonial authorities in areas with a substantial white settler population and/or a large African migrant labor force. See, for example, Richard Rathbone's discussion of the "remarkably indirect Indirect Rule" that characterized the State Council in colonial Akyem Abuakwa, in his *Murder and Politics in Colonial Ghana* (New Haven, CT: Yale University Press, 1993), 54–67; and Jean Allman, "Of 'Spinsters', 'Concubines' and 'Wicked Women': Reflections on Gender and Social Change in Colonial Asante," *Gender and History* 3:2 (1991), 179–80. Cf. Chanock, *Law*, 25–47 and *passim*; and Chanock, "Making Customary Law," 53–67.

60. To date, we have found written evidence of arrests occurring in the Asante towns of Adansi, Asokore, Bekwai, Edweso, Effiduasi, and Mansu Nkwanta.

61. Allman: Eponuahemaa Afua Fom, Effiduasi, 30 June 1993.

62. Christaller defines *osigyani* (pl. *asigyafo*) as "an unmarried person, i.e. a man or woman who has either not been married at all, or a man who has sent away his wife, or a woman who has forsaken her husband, in general one who is not in the state of regular marriage." See Christaller, *Dictionary*, 456.

63. See NAGK, ARA/1907: Assistant Chief Commissioner, Ashanti, to Chief Commissioner, Ashanti, dd. Kumasi, 19 July 1932; District Commissioner, Bekwai, to Assis-

tant Chief Commissioner, Ashanti, dd. Bekwai, 23 July 1932; Bekwaihene to District Officer, Bekwai, dd. Bekwai, 23 July 1932; Mansu Nkwantahene to District Commissioner, Bekwai, dd. Mansu Nkwanta, 26 July 1932; Chief Commissioner to Assistant Chief Commissioner, dd. 18 July 1932. The fees involved in these arrests, though not exorbitant, were not inconsequential. As Rathbone indicates for the 1930s, a blacksmith earned roughly 3/- per day, while a day-laborer earned about 1/6. One yam could cost as much as 1/- and six plantains about 1 d. Rathbone, *Murder*, 19 n. 50; and N. A. Cox-George, *Studies in Finance and Development: The Gold Coast (Ghana) Experience, 1914–1950* (London: Dobson, 1973), 79.

64. The recently reopened Colonial Secretary's Office [CSO] collection at the National Archives of Ghana, Accra includes a file entitled "Kwahu State Unmarried Women Movement Control Bye-Laws." The contents of this file suggest that events in Asante were not unique. In Nana Kofi Akuamoa VI to D.C. Kwahu District, dd. Mpraeso, 25 August 1930, Akuamoa explains,

> It is an old custom of the State that as soon as [a] maiden attained the age of puberty it becomes incumbent on her parents to give her in marriage. This custom in the olden days was strictly observed until recent times when means of travelling to abroad became accessible, that the custom started to be ignored. In the year 1916 or thereabout, during the reign of Nana Kwaku Akuamoa V, the State Council met and revived this Custom. Gongong was beaten throughout the State prohibiting spinsters from travelling outside the State to foreign countries and a penalty of £5 and two sheep provided against the infringement of this gongong order. . . . This gongong order is repeated once every two years throughout the State requesting parents to give their marriageable daughters in marriage within an appointed time. Such time being generally 40 days. During these "days of grace" the inordinate customary expenses generally attendant upon the marriage, are reduced to a maximum of 16/- and the payment [of] dowry or head money protracted to the Cocoa season next following. This concession is made to enable the average youngman to avail himself of the opportunity with less burden.
>
> Every spinster resisting marriage before the expiry of the 40 days allowed, is deemed to have violated the custom and her parents too are charged as accomplices to the neglection of the custom. Those women to become implicated are seldom mulcted in a heavy fine but instead are usually tossed here and there until she proposed love to a man and such named person is bound according to the custom to accept and engage such wooer as his wife. This custom, strangely queer, as it may appear to a European, has the effect of restraining the immoral conduct of our women and it is practised in many States throughout this Province with little variations compatible with local circumstances.

65. Meyer Fortes Papers, "Marriage Prestations" [no date]. Unfortunately, Fortes gives no indication of the sources upon which his description is based. This makes it particularly difficult, for example, to ascertain how much the fees involved in "captured spinster" marriages differed from those paid in other circumstances. Rattray wrote in the 1920s that the *tiri aseda* (money and wine payments) marking the marriage of commoners was usually 10/-, with an additional 6d. for rum or wine. Fortes, presumably with reference to the 1940s, remarked that *tiri nsa* (as *aseda* was increasingly termed) "was said to have been as much as £3 at one time, but in most of the descriptions spirits and

a few shillings are referred to." Fortes, "Marriage Prestations"; and Rattray, *Religion and Art*, 81.

66. Vellenga, "Who is a Wife?" 150. Vellenga's reference was to a sub-file in the "Ghanaian archives," entitled "Forced Marriage of African Girls, Prevention of, 12 June 1939," and a letter to the editor, *Gold Coast Independent*, 15 January 1930. Unfortunately, Vellenga did not name the archive in which the sub-file was located, and we have not come across it in the national archive collections in Accra or in Kumasi.

67. Roberts, "The State," 61. Roberts's pioneering work on gender, colonialism, and indirect rule in Sefwi Wiawso has shaped the discussion here in profound ways.

68. Ibid. For the postcolonial period, Carmel Dinan cites a *Mirror* article from 1975, which reports on a "local traditional council" ordering that "'all unmarried girls should get married within six months and submit particulars of their husbands to the council.' A customary fine of 'one live sheep, ten cedis, two bottles of schnapps and a pot of palm wine' would be levied on all the girls who disobeyed this ruling." See Dinan, "Sugar Daddies and Gold Diggers: The White-Collar Single Women in Accra," in Oppong, ed., *Female and Male*, 363 n. 2.

69. NAGK, ARA/1907: Chief Commissioner, Ashanti, to Assistant Chief Commissioner, Ashanti, dd. Kumasi, 18 July 1932.

70. NAGK, ARA/1907: District Commissioner, Bekwai, to Assistant Chief Commissioner, Ashanti, dd. Bekwai, 23 July 1932.

71. The Mansu Nkwantahene reported that "the object of beaten gong-gong is to prevent venereal diseases and etc. prevalent within the Division." NAGK, ARA/ 1907: Mansu Nkwantahene to District Commissioner, Bekwai, dd. Mansu Nkwanta, 26 July 1932.

72. While the chiefs spoke of a new tendency for women not to marry, it is virtually impossible to ascertain, with quantitative data, whether it was actually the case that women were staying unmarried at rates far greater than before. Unfortunately, sources simply are not available to judge whether the chiefs' fears were well grounded or simply articulated a general concern over women's "uncontrollability" during this period.

73. NAGK, ARA/1907: Bekwaihene to District Officer, Bekwai, dd. Bekwai, 23 July 1932.

74. Ibid.

75. NAGK, ARA/1907: District Commissioner, Bekwai, to Assistant Chief Commissioner, Ashanti, dd. Bekwai, 23 July 1932. It should be noted that during this same period numerous Asante chiefs faced destoolment charges, often for impotence or sterility. Included among them was the chief responsible for the rounding up of unmarried women in Effiduasi, Kwame Owusu. MRO: "Mampong Native Affairs," Queen Mother Kwami Asreh and Loyal Elders to D.C. Mampong, dd. 15 May 1931. (I am grateful to Thomas C. McCaskie for this reference.) It is, of course, exceedingly difficult to ascertain whether there was any direct connection between the destoolment charges and the actions taken against unmarried women in the town.

76. Meyer Fortes Papers, *Kwaku Afram v. Afuah Buo*, Native Tribunal of Asokore, 13 August 1929, mimeographed.

77. Vellenga, "Who Is a Wife?" 145. Lovett has discussed the fluidity of marriage arrangements in the urban townships of the Copperbelt during the same period, noting how these arrangements "posed an especially powerful threat to the authority of the el-

ders and to the maintenance of rural social relations. They also increased women's autonomy." See Lovett, "Gender Relations," 31. For a fascinating discussion of the dynamics of marriage today, see Clark, *Onions*, chapter 9, especially 344–48.

78. While none of the women with whom Allman spoke in Kumasi and Tafo recalled the capture of unmarried women, many in Effiduasi and Asokore could remember the episode in some detail. Of these, nearly all were willing to talk about it generally or as something that happened to certain other women. In some cases, however, it was fairly obvious that the reminiscences were those of someone who had herself been captured, even though the story was told in the third person. Because of the stigma attached to being from "among those caught," however, Allman did not ask women directly whether they had been arrested or not. Only Eponuahemaa Afua Fom volunteered that information, and she did so nearly a year after their first discussions.

79. Allman: Akosua Atta (a.k.a. Sarah Obeng), Asokore, 26 August 1992.

80. Allman: Mary Oduro, Effiduasi, 25 August 1992; and Rosina Boama, Effiduasi, 24 August 1992.

81. Again, we are hampered by the dearth of demographic information for this period. Certainly, no such imbalance appears in the 1948 *Census,* and the *Censuses* for 1921 and for 1931, although admittedly unreliable, in fact suggest that the male population in Asante was growing faster than the female population during this period as a result of immigration from the Northern Territories. See Gold Coast, *Census of Population, 1948.* For an excellent overview of population trends and census data in Ghana from the mid-nineteenth century to the postindependence era, see Engman, *Population of Ghana,* especially 92 and 100–105, for data on sex ratios. It is far more likely that Boama's assertion of men outnumbering women reflected the fact that young men were delaying marriage longer than they had before. That is, women outnumbered men in terms of availability, if not in statistical terms. Why this may have been the case is open to speculation. Although far more local research is required before any conclusions can be drawn, it is not improbable that, during the late 1920s and early 1930s, young men were finding it far more difficult than their fathers or uncles to successfully enter the colonial cash economy. The Bekwaihene's assertion that men could not afford the marriage payments certainly substantiates such a hypothesis, as does Afua Fom's recollection that "in those days, the women were able to get money faster than the men." Allman: Eponuahemaa Afua Fom, Effiduasi, 30 June 1993.

82. Allman: Rosina Boama, Effiduasi, 24 August 1992.

83. Allman: Beatrice Nyarko, Effiduasi, 24 August 1992; and Jean Asare, Effiduasi, 30 June 1993.

84. Allman: Yaa Dufie, Effiduasi, 25 August 1992.

85. Allman: Beatrice Nyarko, Effiduasi, 24 August 1992.

86. Allman: Akosua So, Effiduasi, 28 August 1992.

87. Eponuahemaa Afua Fom, Effiduasi, 1 September 1992.

88. It is difficult to retrieve the numbers involved in these arrests. Most of the women talked of "many" or "not many." The written sources provide no statistics. Afua Fom recalled that there were "maybe 60. . . . But there may be more than that because they were going to the farms. The 60 is what I saw. But we were more than 60 because they went far." We are accepting Fom's figure for the time being, because she is the only woman we have encountered who has identified herself as among those captured. Allman: Eponuahemaa Afua Fom, Effiduasi, 30 June 1993.

89. Allman: Adwoa Addae, Effiduasi, 28 August 1992.

90. Allman: Adwoa Addae, Effiduasi, 30 June 1993. Adwoa subsequently established her own farm on land given to her by her grandfather and reported, "right now I am enjoying from the fruits of that cocoa farm."

91. Ibid.

92. Ibid.

93. See chapter 2. See also Rattray, *Ashanti Law*, 25–26; and Rattray, *Religion and Art*, 81–82.

94. Certainly, this incident must be understood in light of the broader contest within Asante over the meaning of marriage and the reciprocity of conjugal obligations.

95. Allman: Eponuahemaa Afua Fom, Effiduasi, 30 June 1993. We have found no written evidence of this order.

96. Ibid.

97. See NAGA, ADM.52/5/3: Mampong District Record Book, 1931–1946, 11.

98. A two-session panel was devoted to "Wicked Women" at the 1994 Annual Meeting of the African Studies Association in Toronto. Several of the papers presented at these sessions were subsequently published in a special issue of the *CJAS*. See, for an introduction, Dorothy Hodgson and Sheryl McCurdy, "Wayward Wives, Misfit Mothers, and Disobedient Daughters: 'Wicked' Women and the Reconfiguration of Gender in Africa," *CJAS* 30:1 (1996), 1–9.

99. Hunt, "Noise," 471.

100. Vaughan, *Curing Their Ills*, 144. Jeater's recent work on Southern Rhodesia also does an excellent job of disentangling women's economic agency and independence from moral discourses regarding promiscuity and perversion. See Jeater, *Marriage,* especially 119–40.

101. Roberts, "The State," 49. See also Allman, "Of 'Spinsters,'" 176–89. Perceptions of a "moral crisis" were not unique to Asante. Women's economic or social autonomy was often interpreted as sexual uncontrollability. See, for example, Hunt, "Camouflaged Polygamy," 471–94; and Hunt, "Domesticity and Colonialism in Belgian Africa: Usumbura's *Foyer Social*, 1946–1960," in Jean O'Barr, Deborah Pope, and Mary Wyer, eds., *Ties That Bind: Essays on Mothering and Patriarchy* (Chicago: University of Chicago Press, 1990), 149–77, especially 155–56; Summers, "Intimate Colonialism," 787–807; Schmidt, *Peasants*, especially 98–106; and Jeater, *Marriage*, especially 119–69.

102. See also Allman, "Making Mothers."

5

MAKING PROPER MOTHERS
AND DUTIFUL WIVES:
CHIEFS, MISSIONS, AND
ORDER OUT OF CHAOS

I think you will all agree with me that the women of these days have
no character.[1]

—Drobohene, 1938

INTRODUCTION

We have seen the multiple ways in which the introduction of cash and
cocoa dramatically transformed the conjugal and parental landscapes of
colonial Asante, and we have explored the varied strategies women employed in their efforts to secure autonomy in the midst of rapid economic
change. In this chapter, we are concerned with how those efforts sparked
the creation or reformulation of measures to control women's productive
and reproductive power. Certainly the small number of British government agents—chief commissioners, district commissioners, or even assistant district commissioners—were in no position to intervene directly
in matters of marriage, morality, and mothering. Such intervention required the collaboration of others, and it is no mere coincidence that the
onset of indirect rule in Asante coincided with a solidification of the partnership between colonial authorities and mission societies in the development of women's education and maternal/child welfare initiatives. The
empowerment of chiefs (via indirect rule) and of missions (via their partnership with government in education and welfare work) in the 1920s
and 1930s worked as twin efforts to address the crisis in gender relations

that had sprung from Asante's expanding cash economy. It is to those twin efforts that we now turn.

THE POWER OF CHIEFS THROUGH THE PRISM OF *AYEREFA*

If in the first years of colonial rule little was said officially about women because, as Carol Summers has written, they were deemed by the colonial power "irrelevant to knowledge, production and war," they were at the very center of colonial policymaking from the 1920s on.[2] One of the most studied outcomes of that policymaking was, of course, indirect rule, and it is important that we now explore in more depth the specific implications of indirect rule for mediating gender conflict, shaping gendered boundaries, and reformulating gender subordination. While indirect rule in Asante served the obvious ends of providing administration on the cheap and legitimating colonialism, it also facilitated direct, though not uncontested, access to the private realm, to the domestic world of marriage, divorce, inheritance, adultery, childbirth, and parenting. In short, one might argue, it facilitated the formal colonization of the first colonized generation of Asante women.[3]

The fact that indirect rule was conceived by British administrators and chiefs alike as a mechanism specifically effective for reinforcing gender subordination was evident well before the 1935 restoration of the Asante Confederacy Council. In a strikingly frank discussion between Kumasi's D.C., Major Gosling, and members of its council of chiefs in 1926, Chief Kuffuor expressed concern to Gosling regarding the "great number of prostitutes going about in our villages giving disease to all the young men." When Gosling asked Kuffuor what he wanted him to do about this problem, Kuffuor replied: "We want a law." At this point, Gosling reassured Kuffuor that the recently passed Native Jurisdiction Ordinance would serve just this purpose. "In the villages," he explained, "this can easily be controlled as soon as the Native Jurisdiction Ordinance is applied. If any woman spreads disease in your village the NJO gives you the power to deal with such cases." The chiefs and the D.C. were in agreement that measures had to be taken. "Nowadays," remarked Chief Kofi Owusu, "we cannot force a woman to marry unless she chooses whom she likes. If she is forced by the family to marry, in due course there will be a great trouble." The D.C. concurred: "Every woman should have a husband. Only last week I reported to the Chief Commissioner of Ashanti that the proper marriage is dying out and concubinage is increasing. This leads to women becoming prostitutes."[4] Through indirect rule, then, Asante chiefs, as the arbiters of "customary law" through executive order and native tribunals, would be well positioned to manipulate the boundary between domestic and public and thereby transform private concerns into political issues.[5]

Indeed, one cannot help but be struck by the near obsession of Asante's chiefs with women's roles, with women's sexuality, and with women's challenges to existing definitions of marriage and divorce from 1924 on, but particularly after the formal commencement of indirect rule restored the Asante Confederacy Council in 1935.[6]

In our earlier discussions, we have seen how native courts and chiefs' councils provided forums for and determined victors in contests waged over the meanings and makings of marriage, divorce, inheritance, and childrearing. Yet those discussions only hinted at the importance of situating indirect rule in the gender chaos of the interwar years and of understanding its centrality to the process of creating order, especially after 1935. That the picture so far has been a fragmentary one reflects, in many ways, the fragmentary encounters of Asante's first generation of colonized women with native courts and chiefs. In this section, we attempt to bring some of these fragments together in order to present a more cohesive narrative of the evolution of chiefs' power and of the ways in which that power was aimed at controlling productive and reproductive power. *Ayerefa* (which can roughly be translated as "adultery") provides a perfect lens through which to construct this narrative. The chronological breadth and the profusion of sources on *ayerefa* make it possible to trace the evolution of chiefly power across the intellectual deadzone, from the nineteenth century to the end of the colonial period, and to see the ways in which that power was specifically aimed, particularly during the chaos of the interwar years, at restoring order and at asserting control over women's productive and reproductive power.[7]

While there is little variation in the definitions of *ayerefa* offered in most sources, precolonial and colonial, including the judgments of colonial courts and tribunals, there was much disagreement, as we have seen, over what constituted a fully recognized marriage between a man and a woman. Once that had been determined, however, there was always general concurrence that a husband's chief prerogative was the exclusive right to sexual relations with his wife.[8] Adultery, therefore, was *ayerefa* (the taking of someone's wife). It was the theft, "the taking away," of a husband's sexual rights in his wife. The theft usually occurred as a result of a sexual connection and, in such cases, was specifically called *di obi yere* (to make use of someone's wife). However, both Rattray and Danquah listed a number of other actions that were considered tantamount to *di obi yere*. These included sleeping on the same mat as a woman, handling a woman's waistbeads, attempting to verbally seduce a woman (*asombo* or *asommo*, literally, "to burn a hole in her ear") or "to pull, or play with, a woman's nose, ears, breasts or any part of her body."[9]

As with the definition of *ayerefa*, there is much concurrence in the sources across a broad span of time on the general procedures for initiating a case. In addition to eyewitness discovery by the husband or a third party, the most common means by which adultery was revealed was by a wife's confession or *wiakyere* (revealing the theft). Such a confession generally came as a result of the husband asking that the wife "'take fetish' before her relatives as to her fidelity and past conduct." As Danquah wrote in the 1920s, "The best opportunity for knowing the truth from one's wife is considered to be the time of illness or of confinement. The doctor or fetish man is most likely to ascribe her illness or indisposition to some sin she had committed, and she must now confess and get cured, or Death, once so near, will not leave empty-handed."[10] After a wife had confessed, the husband was required to inform his family head or his father, who, in turn, would report the matter to the father of the adulterer (*ayerefafɔ*) and ask for the appropriate compensation. Compensation was termed *ayefare*, derived from *oyere fa deɛ* (the thing given for taking someone's wife).[11] For *ayefare* to be collected, it was essential that charges of adultery be submitted through proper channels.

Although it was the wife, by her confession, who often set an adultery case into motion, she was never a central figure in the proceedings. Adultery remained, from the precolonial period onward, a suit, a transaction between men. Indeed, in its gender specificity, the Akan term for adulterer (*ayerefafɔ*, "one who takes another's wife") precluded women assuming a central role in a case unless it was through a claim of subrogation. What Danquah wrote of Akyem Abuakwa is pertinent to Asante as well:

> It would have been thought that rather than allow her to give evidence as a witness on behalf of her husband the wife who accuses a person with an offence should be made a principal party in an action for or in a defence against a charge of adultery. The custom, however, is plain on the point and the husband being the real person wronged—for, in fact, the fidelity of his wife is exclusively his own concern—it stands to reason that he and not the woman must seek redress at law.[12]

Indeed, it was immaterial, in terms of the wife's role in an adultery case, whether she consented to a sexual connection or was forced. Consent did not mitigate the basic charge of *ayerefa*, even when, as Rattray writes, "the woman had pretended that she was unmarried."[13] The use of force could compound the penalties faced by the nineteenth-century offender, resulting in execution should it involve *ahahantwe* (sex in the "bush"), but it did not transform the wife's position in the case. The husband, not the woman herself, was considered the person wronged.[14]

Both historically and across social classes in a given epoch, a number of features—*ayerefa's* basic definition, the means by which it was revealed, the initial procedures for collecting compensation, and the marginality of wives to the case—have been relatively constant. However, the factors determining both compensation (*ayefare*) and the sphere(s), public and/or private, in which a case has been played out have shifted dramatically across time. These shifts render *ayerefa* a perfect prism through which to view, over the longue durée, contests over control of productive and reproductive power in Asante. For example, *ayefare* was always determined by, among other things, the rank and status of the husband and of the offender.[15] In the nineteenth century, a commoner found guilty of committing adultery with the wife of an *ɔmanhene* was generally executed. Had he committed adultery with the wife of someone of his own rank, he would only have been liable for paying a small fine.[16] What distinguished these two offenses, and thus accounted in large degree for the disparity in damages, was the sphere in which each was legally positioned. The first case was viewed as *ɔman akyiwadeɛ*—a crime or taboo against the state, which had to be addressed in the public realm. The second case was seen as *efiesɛm*—a household or domestic matter to be settled by the parties concerned, in consultation with their elders.[17] It was always possible, however, for a domestic matter to be transformed into *ɔman akyiwadeɛ* by the swearing of an oath (*ntam*).[18] In this way, as K. A. Busia wrote, "It was possible . . . to get the chief and elders to inquire into a private cause."[19] How *efiesɛm* and *ɔman akyiwadeɛ* were distinguished is of central importance to our argument, for the line separating the public and the private in Asante did not hold firm through the colonial period. It was drawn and re-drawn in the shifting sands of power and subordination.

The most striking feature of nineteenth-century *ayerefa* cases, as McCaskie has written, is the "evident distinction of power and status between those men who paid physical compensation for adultery, and those who paid for their transgressions with money."[20] Equally striking, one might add, were the vast differences in the amounts of money offenders were obliged to pay, if they were not among those who paid compensation with their lives. For example, T. E. Bowdich, writing in the early nineteenth century, observed that "A captain generally gives a periguin to the family on taking a wife, a poor man two ackies: the damages for intrigue in the former case are ten periguins; in the latter, one ackie and a half and a pot of palm wine. . . . [I]ntrigue with a wife of the King's is death."[21] Brodie Cruickshank, in the mid-nineteenth century, noted similar variations of between £1 and £10 based on rank, while the cases recorded by de Heer at the court of the Asantehene in the 1860s included not only death sentences for adultery with a chief's wife but monetary damages as high as 25 ounces of gold (over £85).[22] During the 1920s, Rattray interviewed a number of individuals concerning compensation for *ayerefa* in the precolonial period, including one of the Asantehene's former executioners.[23] Aware that his informants may have been "inspired by political . . . motives" because who was entitled to collect what compensation was hotly debated during much of the colonial period, Rattray nonetheless produced a precolonial "table of damages" for officeholders in Kumasi that corresponded closely with nineteenth-century sources. For ordinary cases not involving officeholders, "the damages," Rattray wrote, "amounted to about the value of 6s. in gold-dust."[24] For these men, as a common maxim explained, *Ayefare sika ntua poka ka* (Adultery compensation does not pay off a debt).[25]

One cannot help but be struck by the differences in damages, compensation, and punishment between the nineteenth-century cases falling into the category of *ɔman akyiwadeɛ* and the case of Bowdich's "poor man" who claimed his one and a half *ackies* and some palm wine in a private, domestic matter. Not only is there no question of "physical compensation" to be paid by the male offender in the latter case, but the *ayefare* is actually less than the marriage fees paid by the husband. In the *ɔman akyiwadeɛ* cases, husbands appear to have collected sums 10 to 11 times their initial investment at marriage.[26] There was also great disparity in the treatment of the offending wife depending on the status of her husband—penalties ranging from death to a token pacification.[27] Bowdich and A. B. Ellis both maintained that a chief had the right to put his wife to death, though he was "expected to accept a liberal offer of gold from the family, for her redemption." Rattray's accounts echo these remarks.[28] In adultery cases treated as *ɛfiesem*, however, the husband's right to punish his wife was strictly limited. Though Ellis offhandedly remarked that the "wife is usually beaten," it appears that in most cases the husband's only recourse was to divorce his wife or to accept a small pacification and remain married. If the wife and the offender "prefer to live together," wrote Cruickshank, "the latter may obtain her as his wife, by the payment of the husband's expenses on her account, without any additional compensation for the injury." As Rattray concluded, "Very often . . . the offence will be condoned and the couple will continue to live together."[29]

The picture that emerges from these precolonial sources is a complex one indeed—one in which class and gender constructions are impossible to disentangle. For those who controlled the Asante state, *ayerefa* obviously served to reinforce and reproduce relationships of power and subordination. This is nowhere more apparent than in the range of compensation available to men based upon their rank. At the same time, the class dynamics of *ayerefa* produced and differentiated gender relationships in very specific ways. For example, adultery constituted one of the primary mechanisms by which chiefs controlled and exploited the sexuality of their wives. Wives of chiefs could be killed for having sexual connections with other men. At the same time, some chiefs encouraged their wives, so the sources contend, to "intrigue" with other men in order that they might collect compensation.[30] In contrast to Asante's chiefs, men among the commoner ranks could not inflict serious penalties upon their offending wives, nor could they collect substantial compensation from their wives' lovers. *Ayerefa*, therefore, was not, nor could it be, a means by which common men (*mmerante* or *nkwankwaa*) exploited their wives' sexuality. It was simply a domestic matter—*ɛfiesɛm*—involving two men.

CHAOS AND CONTESTS IN THE COLONIAL COURTS

During the first two decades of British colonial rule in Asante, the customs surrounding *ayerefa* survived remarkably intact. Although corporal punishment and death were no longer sanctioned as penalties, British officials in countless district courts applied *ayefare* in ways nearly indistinguishable from precolonial courts, recognizing and enforcing the ranked differences in *ayefare sika*.[31] In the decade following the Native Jurisdiction Ordinance of 1924,[32] however, *ayerefa* was tried, tested, and challenged largely by women who sought to secure or defend their economic autonomy. Not only did they struggle for a more central position in *ayerefa* cases, they contested *ayerefa*'s very gender specificity. The cases in the post-1924 tribunals—much like those involving divorce, inheritance, and child maintenance—thus revealed the crisis in conjugal relations that engulfed Asante after World War I. In contrast, the cases heard in the native courts assembled after the restoration of the Asante Confederacy Council in 1935 revealed concerted attempts by Asante's chiefs—those empowered by a fully formulated system of indirect rule—to reassert control over women's productive and reproductive power and thereby consolidate a new moral order.

Because the 1924 Ordinance placed all adultery cases within the civil jurisdiction of the native tribunals, whether they involved commoners or chiefs, whether an oath was sworn or not, the line dividing the private realm from the public in Asante was immediately and dramatically redrawn. Thus, the contests waged by women in the late 1920s were very much public contests waged on a playing field, one might add, that was not always very even. During the chaotic period from 1924 to 1934, women appeared before Kumasi's native tribunals in *ayefare* cases, much as they did in the divorce and inheritance cases discussed in earlier chapters, seeking to challenge definitions, to assert their centrality to a case, or to contest gendered boundaries, despite the unevenness of the playing field. What most of these *ayerefa* cases had in common was a female plaintiff whose suit was based on some reformulation of *ayefare*. For example, in 1928, Clara Pomah, a sanitary inspectress, appeared before the Kumasihene's Tribunal having accused the defendant, Abenah Adutwimah, of having been her husband's lover. She swore the Great Oath in support of her accusation. The defendant denied the allegation and responded by swearing the Great Oath himself. Pomah's husband testified on behalf of his wife. The court gave judgment for the plaintiff, with costs but no damages, and then reminded the defendant's husband that he could "deal with the witness" if he so chose.[33] Pomah's accusation of adultery against a woman was thus quickly reformulated as a typical *ayefare* case between the two women's husbands.

Although Pomah's case ended up in court because it was an oath case, not because it involved adultery, some women came to the tribunals prepared to turn the whole notion of *ayerefa* on its head, with or without an oath having been sworn. Amina Badenda appeared before the Kumasihene in 1934 in an attempt to claim a £5 adultery fee from Bekoka Hausa, who, Badenda claimed, had a sexual connection with her husband. Badenda told the court that her claim was in "accordance with Mohammadan customary law of marriage." After calling in Malam Mahama as an expert witness, the court ruled against Badenda, concluding that "the fact that the Plaintiff's husband has known carnally the Defendant cannot be questioned, but this does not, however, entitle the Plaintiff to sue for an adultery fee which is quite repugnant to both the Mohammadan and the Asante custom, as well as to the English custom."[34]

Some women had better luck convincing the courts of the merit in their rather unorthodox claims during these chaotic years. In 1931, for example, Yaa Kwaryie sued her husband, Kwaku Mensah, before the civil court of the Kyidomhene, claiming that Mensah refused to pay her a pacification fee after having a sexual connection "with a certain woman." In what would have been treated as a private marriage dispute in previous years, Kwaryie maintained in the civil tribunal that her husband had claimed £4 pacification from her when she committed adultery and now it was her turn to be pacified. That Mensah did not appear in court that day may go some way toward explaining the court's decision. Kwaryie won her suit, the court ordering Mensah to pay her £2.7.0, the standard commoner adultery fee, as well as the standard pacification fee for spouses.[35]

In another rather unorthodox case, Ama Jan-Yiadu sued a Mr. Jonsan for £50 damages for having a sexual connection with her daughter. Previously, Mr. Jonsan had been married to the daughter, but he had since divorced her and received all of the marriage expenses from Jan-Yiadu. The daughter was about to marry another man but, at the time of the incident, was single. Jan-Yiadu's claim challenged the gender specificity of *ayefare* in very fundamental ways, in its contention that adultery fees should be collectible on an unmarried woman by the person (temporarily) "owning" or controlling sexual access to that unmarried woman—in this case, her mother. The defendant, Mr. Jonsan, did not appear in court, and the tribunal, in an unparalleled judgment, ruled in favor of Jan-Yiadu, awarding her an adultery fee of £7.4.0, damages of £5, and costs of £3.12.0.[36]

If some women were challenging constructions of adultery in this chaotic decade by reformulating *ayefare* in customary suits, others simply refused to play their assigned role in the proceedings—that of the third party confessor. In precolonial and early colonial cases, a woman could refuse to confess the name of the adulterer if she were willing to assume responsibility for paying her husband's *ayefare*. Case after case appears in the civil record books of this period in which women refused both to name the adulterer and to pay the *ayefare*—a refusal not looked upon sympathetically by the tribunals. In *Kofi Boaten v. Yaa Korankyewa*, the defendant refused to name the two men, to pay the *ayefare*, or to attend the court session to which she had been summoned.[37] In *Yaw Fohuo v. Atta Ya*, the defendant refused to name the man with whom she had a child, refused to pay the fee, and then defended her actions by arguing that her husband had not provided for her subsistence and therefore was not entitled to *ayefare*. Atta Ya told the court she would not name the adulterer until her husband paid her eight years' worth of subsistence. The court ruled against Atta Ya, ordering her to pay her husband's adultery fee of £9.6.0. According to the court, Atta Ya should have approached her husband for dissolution of the marriage if she were not being maintained.[38] But failure to provide subsistence could in no way abrogate the collection of *ayefare*.

Clearly, the decade following the Native Jurisdiction Ordinance of 1924 was one of intense change in Asante—change highlighted through the prism of *ayefare* cases. Colonial officials had virtually erased the boundary between *efiesɛm* and *ɔman akyiwadeɛ* in adultery cases so that all could now be brought to the public realm as civil suits in native tribunals, with or without an oath being sworn. Thus, adultery, regardless of class or rank, was now a public concern. In the confusion that followed, women and men appeared before tribunals and contested, sometimes successfully and sometimes not, the social construction of *ayerefa*. At times, women were quite successful in their efforts to recast *ayefare* compensation, though this was more likely to be the outcome if their suit was against another woman or if a male defendant failed to appear than if the case involved a chief or disputed the definition of marriage. Nonetheless, 1924 to 1934 was undoubtedly a period in which the meaning of *ayefare*, like marriage, divorce, inheritance, and parenting, was widely contested in the public realm, and class and gender subordination was challenged. In the decade that followed, these challenges, like so many others, were met head-on by Asante's chiefs.

REFORMULATING A MORAL ORDER:
CHIEFS AND INDIRECT RULE

For the chiefs who sat in Asante's colonial tribunals, much of the gender chaos of the late 1920s and early 1930s—from contested definitions of marriage and adultery to a perceived increase in prostitution and venereal disease—was attributable to uncontrolled women. By the early 1930s, a "moral crisis," as Roberts has called it, had erupted, and one of the many ways that chiefs and elders responded to this crisis and attempted to reassert control over women's sexuality was through systematic reformulations of *ayefare*. In the nineteenth century and, indeed, well into the colonial period, *ayefare* had provided a mechanism by which Asante's chiefs could both control and exploit their own wives' sexuality. *Ayefare*, now fully within the public realm, was easily adapted to the requirements of the 1930s, that is, to the need to (re)establish control over *all* women's sexuality, not just that of chiefs' wives. Informally and often subtly, the imposition of constraints is evident in the circumstances surrounding post-1935 *ayefare* cases, in the testimony of women, and in the judgments of the courts. Formally, it is apparent in the series of official rules and orders under which the native courts operated— orders that criminalized adultery, strictly regulated wives' fidelity and adultery fees, and extended special *ayefare* compensation to Asante soldiers.

The colonial government's restoration of the Asante Confederacy Council in 1935 and its recognition of the Asantehene as the head of Asante created a context not only for marriage to be rigorously defined and rules of inheritance delimited but also for *ayefare* to be systematically reformulated and then implemented as a mechanism of social/sexual control. Because *ayefare* had always been intimately connected to state power, it could also be wielded as an instrument for reasserting Asante's hegemony in the region after the "restoration" of the council. Indeed, one of the first acts of the newly restored Asantehene was to dispatch messengers throughout the Gold Coast— from Sefwi Wiawso, to Saltpond, Winneba, Oda, and Kwahu—to collect satisfaction fees on behalf of his *nhenkwaa* (servants). In each case, the messenger collected £16, two sheep, and two bottles of gin. One of the Asantehene's messengers reported to the Sefwi Wiawso D.C. that in every town he delivered a letter, passed through the local D.C., to the local ɔhene. The money collected, he further reported, went to the Asantehene, although if the Asantehene "liked to give some of it to the husband he could do so."[39] A representative letter from July 1935, addressed to the ɔmanhene of Sefwi Wiawso, announced:

> It has been reported to me that one of your subjects by name Attah Affukah residing at Essakrome in the Wioso District, has had sexual intercourse

with the wife of one of my Nhinkwas by name Kofi Nkuan (my soul washer). The wife's name is called Abina Aduah now residing at Essakrome. Under the circumstances, I will be very grateful if you will kindly assist my bearer, Kwabena Gyanfi to collect £16.0.0, two sheep and two bottles gin from the adulterer. My bearer will give you two bottles of gin according to native custom. Many thanks for your assistance please.[40]

The D.C. for Sefwi Wiawso concluded that the "wives of the Asantehene's *nhinkwas* are distributed round the country and . . . whenever one of them is 'seduced,' £16 is claimed and goes to form part of the Asantehene's revenue." In one case at Bibiani, the accused adulterer had already paid the local satisfaction fee of £4.13.0, but the Asantehene sent messengers anyway, requesting the amount of £16, as well as a sheep and four bottles of gin, on the grounds that the husband was his *ahenkwaa*. The accused refused to pay more than the local fee. The Asantehene's rather conciliatory reply was most telling: at least £2 for a sheep should be added to the local fee, but "in future cases where the aggrieved husband was an Ashanti, the claim for satisfaction was to be referred to him for settlement."[41] Indeed, what the D.C. failed to appreciate was that the Asantehene was not simply adding to his revenue by collecting adultery compensation throughout the Gold Coast. He was, through the mechanism of *ayefare*, reclaiming (and even extending) Asante's precolonial borders. He was reasserting Kumasi's hegemony over the outlying divisions, as well as Asante hegemony over portions of the Colony.[42]

Within the borders of Asante, *ayefare* was no less important as a mechanism for restoring *social* control. Under the Native Courts (Ashanti) Ordinance of 1935, courts were established for Asante in four grades—A, B, C, D—with civil and criminal jurisdiction.[43] The Asante Confederacy Council itself served as a criminal court for hearing major constitutional cases and, after 1936, was empowered to make orders and rules on a number of topics, including so-called "native custom."[44] But even before the council was so empowered, a governor's order of 1935, the Native Courts (Offences Under Native Law and Custom) Order, rendered adultery a criminal offence triable in Asante's B and C grade criminal courts, with criminal action not prejudicing civil action to collect *ayefare*.[45]

While adultery thus remained an economic transaction between two men, the order added a new dimension of social control by permitting the criminal prosecution of a male adulterer, with the native court sanctioned to impose fines and exact penalties including imprisonment with hard labor. Criminal prosecution could thus serve to control the sexuality and, thereby, the options (economic and otherwise) of wives, by deterring men from having sexual connections with the wives of other men. *Ayerefa*, whether *ɛfiɛsem* or *ɔman akyiwadeɛ*, whether civil or criminal, was now fully in the public realm.[46]

Other orders aimed at the specific control of sexuality were passed by the Confederacy Council in the decade and a half after restoration. Of direct relevance to this discussion were the council's 1942 resolution (followed by a 1946 order) allowing Asante soldiers who fought in World War II to collect an adultery fee of £9.6.0, not only for the duration of the war but for their entire lives. The measure was aimed at encouraging "Ashanti youths to enlist . . . and to discourage any further desertions," but it was also aimed very directly at controlling soldiers' wives. Section 2 of the order required a soldier's wife to pay a pacification fee of £4.13.0 to her husband for "every case of adultery proven against her." If the woman did not pay the fee after a civil summons, she was to be imprisoned "for the appropriate number of days."[47]

In 1944, the council standardized a schedule of adultery fees that were subsequently embodied in the Ashanti (Declaration of Native Customary Law) Order of 1946. The lengthy schedule listed adultery fees according to rank for everyone from a Grade I *ɔmanhene*, who could collect £111.12.0, to Kumasi's Grade III Gyasehene (£74.8.0), to the Asantehene's *nhenkwaa* (£7.0.0), to commoners (£2.7.0). In ranking, it differed little from what we know of precolonial *ayefare* or from the 1911 scale utilized by the chief commissioner.[48] Certainly, the purpose was the same: to reinforce social status differentiation and broaden social control through *ayefare* compensation.[49] The same committee of the council that standardized adultery fees also ultimately recommended that "it should be made an offense, by Ordinance, for women to commit adultery." The Asante Confederacy Council agreed to the recommendation, but no subsequent action was taken. Nonetheless, the fact that the option of criminalizing adultery for women was seriously contemplated in 1944 only shows the length to which the council was prepared to go in order to deter what it perceived as women's uncontrollability. Though adultery was never criminalized for Asante women—this would have necessitated the complete regendering of *ayerefa*—the council did take a very direct shot at uncontrollability with its 1949 Wives' Fidelity Declaration Order. The order made it the duty of every woman married under customary law, "when so required by her husband . . . to make a declaration upon oath of her fidelity." Any woman who failed to carry out her duty was "liable to a fine of twenty-five pounds or to imprisonment for two months or to both such fine and imprisonment."[50] That such an order was considered necessary in 1949 at least suggests that some women were refusing to swear an oath. By not revealing the theft (*wiakyere*) or providing the confession upon which all *ayefare* cases were based, wives could undermine the very process of *ayefare* collection. The Wives' Fidelity Declaration Order, with both civil and criminal repercussions, was aimed at reinforcing the essential step between a wife's uncontrolled, extramarital activities and her husband's compensation—the confession.

If the orders passed by the Asante Confederacy Council go a long way toward illustrating the formal actions taken by Asante's chiefs in order to use *ayefare* as an instrument of social control, the treatment of testimony and the judgments of courts during the period provide glimpses of informal, subtle efforts to limit women's options for autonomy by reinforcing relationships of power and subordination. Unfortunately, we do not have material from the nineteenth century with which to compare these domestic cases, but certainly when compared to early colonial cases they show a marked tendency for the courts to undervalue women's testimony and to deflate the responsibilities of men in conjugal relationships. For example, Kwaku Boakyi brought his wife before the Asantehene's D-Grade Court in 1935, charging that she refused both to swear an oath of fidelity and to announce the name of the adulterer. Yaa Mansah responded to her husband: "Do you not remember that you have failed to maintain me for the past six years and hence I offered myself to another man to deal with me and hence I object to point out the particular man . . . to you?" When the court asked Yaa Mansah if her marriage had been dissolved, she said that it had been, in the presence of Chief Kwasi Boakyi. The chief later testified in court that the marriage had not been dissolved before him. The court finally ruled against Yaa Mansah, reasoning that her "contention is rather immaterial to justify her case." She was ordered to swear an oath of fidelity and either reveal the adulterer to her husband or pay the *ayefare* herself.[51]

In a very different sort of case, a similar judgment on men's obligations to provide subsistence for wives was made. In the Asantehene's B-Grade Court, Ama Manu sued her brother-in-law for the amount of £8.5.0 representing subsistence for herself and her two children for a period of eleven months. Ama Manu's husband had been sick for some time and was not contributing to her subsistence or to that of their children. The defendant, her husband's brother, did not assist either. Eventually the husband died, and Ama Manu technically became the defendant's wife. She was forced to confess the names of the men with whom she had sexual connections during the previous months. This she did, and then she pacified the defendant with £8. Subsequently, the defendant refused to continue the marriage with Ama Manu, and so Manu demanded to be reimbursed for the eleven months of subsistence owed to her by the defendant as her husband. The court ruled against Ama Manu on the grounds that by "her behaviour towards her sick husband and her conduct after the death of her husband, she is customarily not entitled to any subsistence by the Defendant."[52]

The rulings in these two cases provide a good sense of the predicament in which some Asante women found themselves when post-restoration native courts ruled on spousal obligations with regard to subsistence and adultery. A man's refusal to provide subsistence for his wife, even for as long as six years, did not affect his right to collect *ayefare*. However, even if that wife were willing to cooperate in the collection of *ayefare*, that is, "to reveal the theft" and pay pacification, she was still not entitled to demand what was once a husband's primary obligation to his wife—to provide for her subsistence. In other words, for a husband, a wife's extramarital affair was an excuse *not* to fulfill subsistence obligations in marriage, but a husband's failure to provide subsistence for his wife gave her *no* excuse for refusing to cooperate in her husband's collection of *ayefare*. The reciprocity and fluidity that had been hallmarks of marrying[53] in Asante for generations were thus fundamentally undermined in post-1935 *ayefare* cases.

Subtle shifts in judgments in *ayefare* cases after 1935 at least partly reflected the courts' changing attitudes toward women's testimony. In the nineteenth and early twentieth centuries, a woman's testimony concerning sexual encounters was considered incontestable: *ɔba na ɔka nokware* (a woman speaks the truth). Those days were now long gone.[54] For example, in the oath case *Yaw Brenyah v. Effuah Frimpoma*, Brenyah swore the Great Oath to deny Frimpoma's charge that he had a sexual connection with her. Frimpoma swore the Great Oath in response. The court ruled that "wherein the Defendant prefers a serious charge of adultery . . . the court is not satisfied with the unsupported statement of the Defendant and therefore enters judgement against the Defendant."[55] In a similar oath case, Akua Aframkuma, a boiled corn seller, accused Henry Kusi, a cocoa weighing clerk, of having a sexual connection with her in a cocoa shed. Kusi swore the Great Oath to deny the accusation and Aframkuma swore an oath to support it. Aframkuma first confessed the incident to her husband when she was in labor, and both the plaintiff (Kusi) and the defendant (Aframkuma) had witnesses testify on their behalf, though neither witness actually saw what occurred in the cocoa shed. In the end, the court ruled against Akua Aframkuma on the grounds that it was "not possible for any sane man to have a sexual connection with a woman in a cocoa shed in a cocoa season and in the broad day light, at 1 o'clock as alleged by the Defendant."[56] Case closed.

Ayerefa in Asante was always about power and subordination: chiefs over commoners, Kumasi over Asante's periphery, and husbands over wives. It was also remarkably consistent in the ways it differentiated status and class and marginalized women. That *ayefare* survived not only Asante's final tumultuous century as an independent power but over half a century of British colonial rule certainly testifies to its resilience as an articulator of power differentials and as an instrument of social control. This is not to argue that it was an immutable social construct, a stable constant in Asante's social past that seamlessly crosses the intellectual deadzone. Rather it is to underscore that its consistence rested largely on its adaptability to economic, political, and social change. In 1850, *ayerefa* was either a private, domestic matter handled by two men and their respective families or it was a crime against the state, punishable by heavy fines or death. In the first case, women's sexuality was certainly regulated, though not controlled. In the second it was regulated, controlled, and exploited. In the 1920s and early 1930s, *ayefare* was placed under the civil jurisdiction of native tribunals, and there women and men contested its meanings, as part of broader struggles over conjugal rights and obligations. By 1935, *ayerefa* was fully within the public realm and punishable in all cases as a crime against the colonial state, though penalties were far less severe than in the nineteenth century. It was constructed, moreover, to regulate and control all women's sexuality, not just that of chiefs' wives. In other words, *ayefare* compensation continued to reinforce the class and rank of Asante men, but it no longer differentiated among wives; all women's sexuality could now be subject to state control. This is not to say that *ayerefa*'s meaning was uncontested after 1935 or that Asante's chiefs managed, with a few blows, to solve the problem of "uncontrollable" women. Certainly, the meaning not only of *ayerefa* but of marriage, divorce, and inheritance would continue to be contested at every turn. But the women of the first colonized generation, who had struggled throughout the interwar years to secure places for themselves in the expanding cash economy and to defend those spaces in both public and private forums, were faced after 1935 with a centralized and increasingly hegemonic state power set on reasserting control over wayward women and establishing a colonial moral order.

MISSIONARIES, MEDICAL OFFICERS, AND WOMEN'S WORK

If indirect rule worked, in part, as British colonialism's political response to the gender crisis of the 1920s and 1930s, then women's education, mothercraft, and maternal and child welfare initiatives must be considered colonialism's social responses. And as Summers reminds us, "social programs . . . were not mere sideshows to the public politics and the economic maneuvering of imperialism. They were integral to the holding of power."[57] Missionaries—medical, educational, and evangelistic—were no less important than chiefs in attempts to control "uncontrollable" women, in efforts to stabilize colonial rule. They, too, were empowered by the colonial government to intervene in spheres untouchable by colonial officers. At times the connections between the two—indirect rule chiefs and missionaries intent on making "proper" mothers—were extremely intimate. Tafohene Yaw Dabanka, for example, collaborator chief *par excellence*, worked very closely with the British in their efforts to implement indirect rule in the Kumasi Division of Asante.[58] Although he did not convert to Christianity, Dabanka was also responsible for granting the Wesleyan Missionary Society the large parcel of land upon which the very first girls' boarding school was built in Kumasi. In recognition of his efforts, the mission permitted up to six of his children (who numbered about 105) to attend without paying fees. Two of his daughters were enrolled in the boarding school in the 1930s.[59] At this girls' school and others, at child welfare centers, and at weighing clinics, Europeans considered themselves entitled, by their "expertise" and in the name of their "civilizing mission," to enter directly the private world of Asantes—the world where children were born, the sick were healed, meals were cooked, babies were bathed, marriages were negotiated, deaths were mourned, and the next world was pondered.

While it is possible to point to the broad outlines of an imperial discourse on maternal and child welfare in the first three decades of the twentieth century, how, why, and when this general discourse was transformed into imperialist practice was largely determined by the specific dynamics of the colonial enterprise in a given historical context, not by decree from the center. For example, Belgian attempts to socially engineer motherhood in the Belgian Congo, as Nancy Hunt has shown, must be situated in the context of the 1920s "panic . . . over fertility levels, depopulation, and labor requirements."[60] Colonial intervention in breast-feeding and birth-spacing was specifically aimed at increasing women's fertility. In the context of Uganda, Carol Summers examines similar efforts by the British to "reform motherhood" in response to a drastic increase in sexually transmitted diseases and a perceived crisis in population growth.[61] In Asante, by comparison, there were no fears of a dramatic population decline, and, though there was certainly official concern over the spread of sexually transmitted diseases, it did not reach the fever pitch it did in Uganda.

In fact, until the mid-1920s, neither the colonial government, nor the missions, nor Asante's chiefs appeared very interested at all in women's education or maternal and child welfare.[62] Making mothers or dutiful wives was simply not a part of the initial imposition of colonial rule. The first government girls' school in Kumasi was not opened until 1914, and then only a third of the girls attending, approximately 21, were Asante.[63] Missions focused primarily on boys' education, though there was some early concern about the need to provide good Christian wives as companions for male converts, especially catechists. In the mid-1920s, however, an explosion of interest in female education and child welfare efforts was evident at almost every level. For example, the Government Girls' School in Kumasi was enlarged and the "Domestic Training Subjects . . . received considerable attention." These included cookery, laundry, sewing, domestic hygiene, and child welfare.[64] On a broader level, the Gold Coast government appointed a committee in 1926 to examine welfare work among women and children throughout the colony, and the committee decided that Kumasi should be the site of one of three maternal and infant welfare centers.[65] There was considerable debate over who should run these centers—government medical officers or mission workers—with Governor F. Gordon Guggisberg arguing that the welfare work could be "dealt with more satisfactorily by the missions than by the appointment of medical officers." In the end, the government funded the construction of the buildings and met the expenses of the center's medical and nursing staff, but it relied on the Wesleyan Methodist Mission to cover the costs of maintaining and managing the center in Kumasi.[66] Similar arrangements between the government and missions in the mid-1920s were made concerning girls' education. For example the Methodists' proposal to set up a boarding school for girls in Kumasi was enthusiastically endorsed by the governor with promises to provide £12,000 of the £20,000 needed for construction.[67] In other words, the mid-1920s witnessed the colonial government's empowering of missionary societies as junior partners in maternal/child welfare work and girls' education.

Virtually all of the colonial government's initiatives in women's education and maternal and infant welfare in Asante during the two decades before World War II were undertaken via partnerships with nongovernmental organizations like missionary societies and the Red Cross.[68] In fact, it is virtually impossible to disentangle the efforts of one from the efforts of another, to figure out where government initiative left off and nongovernmental initiatives picked up. But no matter how blurred the boundary, colonial officials insisted that the appearance of separateness be maintained. As Selwyn-Clarke wrote of the Red Cross in 1933, "It was extremely important . . . not to give the impression that the new *voluntary* organisation was a sub-department of the Government, designed to obtain free services and funds to finance government activities from the general public who were already paying taxes in various forms for government service."[69] Appearances in this case, however, were seldom deceiving. In the 1920s and 1930s, Asante women encountered welfare and/or education initiatives not as government or nongovernment efforts but as the integrated, lived experience of colonialism. The main factor that differentiated how Asante women initially experienced what can best be described as "colonization of the maternal" was age. Those of Asante's first colonized generation, when and if they encountered government/nongovernment initiatives, did so as wives and mothers who were taught the finer points of mothercraft and conjugal duty. Their daughters encoun-

tered initiatives in mission and government schools where, as mothers of
the future, they studied hygiene, cookery, and infant care.[70]

SANITATION, WELFARE, AND
STATE APPROACHES TO MOTHERCRAFT

Let us begin by looking at the first type of encounter. Like many of the earliest, broad-based efforts to make proper mothers and dutiful wives in colonial
Africa, those initiated in Kumasi were put forward in the name of public health,
in this case by Kumasi's Sanitation Office in 1925.[71] It was in that year that the
first health week was organized by Dr. Selwyn-Clarke, who was then the senior
sanitary officer in Kumasi. Activities included neighborhood clean-ups, the inspection of pupils' personal hygiene, exhibits, and an essay contest. But the big-
gest event, by far, was the baby show. Selwyn-Clarke initially hoped that 200
babies would be entered, but "as many as five hundred were brought to the Baby
Show."[72] In the following year, Selwyn-Clarke decided to refuse admission to
babies whose names had not been entered in the Register of Births. The result
was nearly a threefold increase in the number of births registered between September and October of 1926.[73] By 1929, the baby show had been transformed
completely into a mechanism of social regulation, if not social control, as women
were encouraged to enter and then rewarded for entering the world of colonial
motherhood. The baby show was open only to children who had regularly attended the newly opened Welfare Centre and whose births had been registered.
In the judging of the baby contestants, extra points were given to children who
had received vaccinations.

If the first efforts to reconstruct motherhood in Asante fell under the general rubric of public health, were often biomedical, and were largely based
on voluntary cooperation, subsequent efforts aimed at mothers in the late
1920s and early 1930s were increasingly social, often intrusive, and failed to
recognize the boundary between private and public. They sought to address
specific medical and environmental problems with a rather ambiguous, yet
nonetheless invasive, discourse on mothercraft and hygiene. In other words,
efforts encouraging a mother, via a baby show, to have her child vaccinated
were succeeded by unannounced visits to women's homes where recommendations concerning hygiene and infant feeding were made to a captive audience. The Gold Coast League for Maternity and Child Welfare played an
important role in bringing mothercraft initiatives directly into women's homes.
Founded in Accra in 1927 by Governor Ransford Slater's wife and active in
Asante by 1929, the league brought together European women (primarily the
wives of government officials) and some African women in attempts to popularize maternal and child welfare schemes.[74] The league, according to Selwyn-
Clarke, had four main objects:

(1) to dispel the suspicion with which the welfare centres were regarded by the less informed and poorer section of the population—resulting in a failure to make use of the facilities for advice, treatment and teaching in mothercraft available at the centres; (2) to popularize skilled obstetrical aid for mothers whose medical history pointed to the necessity for such assistance or whose homes were unsuitable for confinements . . . (3) to carry the doctrine of good personal and domestic hygiene into the compounds of the less fortunate and in this way assist in the prevention of disease and premature death . . . (4) to assist in the breaking down of the barrier between the two races which mars progress by the association of a European and African in work for the common good.[75]

Members of the league sought to achieve these objects through house-to-house visits. At the Kumasi league inauguration, volunteers for house visiting were told how they could "combat the evil" of infant mortality through "voluntary endeavor." They were cautioned, however, not to "worry the women, but first gain their friendship. Ask for the rectification of one or two obvious errors and do not ask far too much at once."[76] By 1930, the Gold Coast "Report on the Medical and Sanitary Department for the Year 1929—1930" claimed that the "propaganda work carried out by the members of the Gold Coast League for Maternity and Child Welfare is of the greatest utility and has gone a long way toward the popularising of both antenatal and infant welfare work."[77]

The springboard for much of these efforts was the Kumasi Child Welfare Centre, which began operations in its permanent quarters in September 1928. In many ways its opening marked the beginning of a formal maternal and infant welfare scheme in Asante. It not only provided a much needed locus for a variety of initiatives, but it gave direction to the activities of government and nongovernment groups in Asante, particularly in Kumasi. Though funded primarily by the government, the center relied heavily on the support of services from missions and voluntary organizations.[78] Its presence meant that antenatal care could now be coordinated with postnatal care, weighing-in clinics, domiciliary visits, and instructional sessions in mothercraft. Government, mission, and other voluntary efforts could be more closely integrated. When the center opened its (temporary) doors in 1927 under the supervision of Dr. M. C. Chapel, woman medical officer in charge, its primary objectives were to provide antenatal care to expectant mothers and to offer postnatal, well-baby care to infants. Its main agenda, then, was preventive treatment, not care of the sick. In addition to its regular clinics, the center held weighing clinics to which mothers were supposed to bring their infants on a monthly basis in order to assess the children's development. It also helped to coordinate the house-to-house visitations conducted by the Maternity

League after its founding in 1927. It was not equipped, however, to provide services to parturient mothers or those immediately postpartum. (The African Hospital in Kumasi was similarly ill-equipped, though it did handle emergency cases, particularly those requiring surgery.)[79] In its first full year of operation, according to the "Report on Ashanti," attendance at the center was 24,019, and the success of its work was due "to the great confidence and trust which the Ashanti mother reposes in the Women Medical Officers." In addition to running the center's clinics, the medical officers also visited neighboring villages, "inspected 617 children and gave simple advice to the mothers on hygiene.[80] By 1930–31, there were 30,897 visits by children to the clinic and 12,070 visits by expectant mothers. "At times," wrote the woman medical officer, "it has been difficult to cope with the number of women attending this clinic, but the charge of a small medicine fee has reduced the numbers."[81]

By 1931–1932, however, after only a few years in operation, maternal and child welfare schemes throughout the Gold Coast suffered serious setbacks as a result of the Depression. Alice Piegrome, a former woman medical officer, reported to the Colonial Office in 1932 that infant welfare schemes had been the hardest hit of all social services. Five women medical officers were retrenched and three infant centers were closed in 1931–1932 alone.[82] While the Kumasi Centre was not closed, it faced operation with a reduced staff and with far less funding than before. It was at this juncture, in 1932, that the colonial government turned to the Red Cross to bolster and in some instances resuscitate its fledgling welfare programs. Basically, under the guidance of Selwyn-Clarke, the Maternity and Child Welfare League, after the addition of several male members, became the nucleus for the new Gold Coast Branch of the British Red Cross, with Selwyn-Clarke serving as director and the colonial secretary, G.A.S. Northcote, serving as president.[83] In a letter to Asante's chief commissioner in 1932, requesting him to serve as director of the Asante Branch of the Red Cross, Selwyn-Clarke explained, "Now that the Government is unable to afford social services on such a large scale, it seems to me to be up to the African to do what he or she can do in the way of tangible support for the services from which they alone derive benefit."[84] While the new Red Cross branch assumed complete responsibility for several infant centers, including those at Accra and Sekondi, its work in Kumasi was limited to fund-raising for a maternity wing for the center, staffing the infant weighing centers throughout the district, and organizing domiciliary visits.[85] The Junior Red Cross Links—youth groups sponsored by the society—were launched in 1933 and assisted the parent group in fund-raising activities, in addition to offering assistance at welfare centers, running village dispensaries, training members in hygiene and first aid, and organizing town clean-ups.[86] In its published reports, the colonial government frequently expressed its hope that "those centres in which setback will take place may enter on a fresh career of usefulness under organised voluntary effort."[87]

While the Depression clearly resulted in cutbacks, it is important to recognize that there was not that much to cut back in 1932. Most social welfare efforts aimed at women were limited almost entirely to Kumasi and the surrounding villages. Asante's rural areas were virtually ignored, with the exception of limited mission work in a few key towns like Agogo and Mampon. As Steven Feierman wrote generally of medical care in the British colonies, "facilities (of both government and missions) rarely reached more than 20 percent of the population."[88] From their beginnings in the mid-1920s, most womens' and infants' programs were conceived by the government as low cost social welfare initiatives whose limited financial and staffing burdens could be shared by missions and voluntary organizations. The economic straits of the Depression years did not challenge this conception but simply reinforced it. This was largely because welfare schemes were viewed not as supplements to broad-based medical programs but as substitutes for them. Prevention, largely on the cheap and organized by volunteers, was offered instead of curative measures requiring well-equipped facilities and expertise. For example, the city of Kumasi, throughout the 1930s, had no maternity ward in its Child Welfare Centre or obstetrical wing in its African Hospital. (The first fully-equipped maternity unit opened in 1949.) And yet this was the very decade in which weighing centers flourished (with their reams of associated paperwork), mothercraft lectures abounded, and hygiene posters were plastered from one end of town to another by Junior Links volunteers.

It was also the period during which indirect rule took shape in Asante, and it is important to situate the welfare schemes within that specific political context. While most chiefs enthusiastically endorsed welfare initiatives, some were less cooperative. Asante's chief commissioner reported in 1929 that the wards of the Child Welfare Centre had been visited "by many African mothers, including the Queen Mother of Ashanti."[89] However, the acting chief commissioner wrote in his diary several months later that he and his wife had visited the queen mother at her new estate to "enlist her sympathy . . . for the Child Welfare Visiting Committee" and found their suggestion of child welfare visiting met "with a rather cold and suspicious reception."[90] On the subject of the center itself, the commissioner recorded that Asante's former king, exiled in 1896 and repatriated in 1924 as a private citizen, believed that its unpopularity with many women had much to do with the fact that men were employed as "houseboys" and cleaners. He suggested that replacing these men would

considerably enhance the center's image among women.[91] Nongovernmental groups also solicited the support and advice of chiefs in implementing
maternal and infant welfare initiatives. The Red Cross launched a massive appeal for associate and life members in 1933 and was delighted
with the "magnificent response . . . to join the Society . . . led by Nana
Osei Agyeman Prempeh II, Kumasihene, and his chiefs." Prempeh's private secretary, J.W.K. Appiah, served as an honorary secretary of the
Asante Division of the society from 1933 until after World War II.[92] In
fact, the society saw its fortunes in Asante as being tied directly, in no
uncertain terms, to Prempeh's restoration as Asantehene and to the formal implementation of indirect rule. "In this Division," according to a
1934 published report of the Red Cross, "expenditure exceeded income,
but it is hoped that more funds will be forthcoming once the new Ashanti
Confederation with the revival of a Kingdom of Ashanti has come to
pass."[93]

But how did Asante women negotiate this terrain of mother-making in
the 1920s and 1930s, aimed as it was toward addressing not only a host
of biomedical and environmental problems but also women's very recal-
citrance or uncontrollability? Though no archive of minutes and reports
exists to provide a direct answer to this question, the oral reminiscences
of Asante women, as well as the recorded concerns and frustrations of
colonial officials regarding women's reception of welfare schemes, have
much to tell. They suggest that Asante mothers responded in a variety of
ways. Some became enthusiastic participants in the schemes. They attended antenatal clinics at the Welfare Centre, had their babies delivered
by one of the two registered midwives in Kumasi, and brought their children to the weighing clinics on a regular basis. These women lived almost exclusively within Kumasi and tended to be active in mission
churches and even to have married in a Christian ceremony. They were
also more likely than women who did not frequent the center to have a
husband who worked in an occupation closely linked to the requirements
of an expanding colonial economy—as driver, typist, store clerk, or mason. In a matrilineal society in which it was not uncommon to stay with
your matrikin after marriage, they appear to have been more likely to
share a residence with their husbands.[94]

At the other extreme were the women about whom we know very
little—the ones who by choice or because of lack of funds for travel and
medicine avoided the center, the league, the missions, and the Red Cross
entirely. The government, for example, lamented on occasion the "large
numbers of women who continued to rely on the unqualified woman"
rather than the registered midwife.[95] Indeed, that continued reliance might
explain the rather insubstantial Midwives Ordinance of 1931. The ordi-

nance did not restrict the practice of midwifery to "properly qualified" midwives, as was the case in Uganda, but instead provided for the enrollment of local midwives on a "List of Unqualified Midwives if they had been engaged in the practice of midwifery for a period of not less than two years . . . [and were] of good character."[96] The government justified this decision by claiming that "there is not as yet so great a confidence in scientific methods of obstetrics as to warrant such a course and if there were such confidence there will not be for some time a sufficiently large number of properly trained midwives to meet the public demands."[97] One has to do very little reading between the lines to glean from this statement that the majority of women preferred being attended by local midwives and that the colonial legislation signified, more than anything, the government's inability to fully regulate, much less redefine, midwifery. It remained, for the time being, firmly in the hands of local practitioners.

But between these two extremes—of full participation or complete avoidance—most women negotiated their way through maternal decisions and colonial encounters on a daily basis, participating at one moment, avoiding at another. As one Kumasi resident recalled of the births of her three children, "Sometimes I would take some herbs and sometimes I would go to the hospital."[98] Indeed, the medical officer in charge of the Kumasi Centre in 1931 explained women's attendance at the antenatal clinic in a strikingly similar way. She attributed it to the fact that "it is customary to take medicine during pregnancy," and so attending the clinic was not considered a radical departure in the care of pregnant women.[99] Moreover, those who did attend clinics and those who did participate in the various infant and maternal welfare schemes did so on terms that were not simply dictated by the colonial agent. Rather, many, by the way they *chose* to participate, by the way they structured the encounter, sought to transform the making of colonial mothers into something else entirely.

The very statistics gathered by the Gold Coast government provide evidence of this process. Kumasi's Child Welfare Centre was set up to provide antenatal care and well-child care, yet in its first decade of operation its officers in charge found it virtually impossible to limit its function to welfare issues. With no maternity hospital available to cope with high-risk deliveries, the center found itself delivering babies even though it had no maternity beds. In 1936, 84 women delivered their babies at the center; in 1937, 109 delivered there. Indeed, in the first full annual report on the center, the medical officer revealed that the facility was, in fact, focusing on curative, not preventive, medicine:

The popularity of the Kumasi Clinic has continued. . . . During the latter part of 1930 the numbers were too large for one Medical Officer to deal with efficiently; the charge of a small medicine fee during the last three months has reduced attendances to more reasonable numbers. An over-crowded clinic means that the Medical Officer cannot give the necessary individual attention to each case, thus diminishing the value of welfare work. As the Clinic becomes better known to the Ashantis the difficulty of confining the activities of the Centre to welfare work becomes greater.

Most telling, perhaps, were the medical officer's remarks concerning the activities of the clinic. "Nearly every child is suffering from some definite disease," she reported, and of the more than 10,000 new children seen by the clinic, only 9 percent came for well-child care, that is, "for inspection and advice."[100] If the Kumasi Child Welfare Centre was envisioned as the site for the making of colonial mothers, many of the Asante mothers who visited appear to have had a very different vision. In those early years, they suc-ceeded in transforming the very locus of maternal and infant welfare schemes in Asante into what they *did* want—affordable and convenient curative health care alternatives in a rapidly changing and often confusing colonial urban environment. And in their quest to transform colonial initiatives, Asante women did not always encounter opposition from those nurses, medical of-ficers, and volunteers who had been entrusted with the task of colonizing the maternal in Asante.

That the women medical officers had collaborated, wittingly or not, in the process of transformation was one of the charges made by Director of Gold Coast Medical Services J. B. Kirk in his 1942 report on his tour of inspection.[101] According to Kirk, "so-called welfare clinics have been al-lowed to degenerate into treatment clinics and educative and welfare work has been completely swamped by the huge wave of suffering childhood which has inundated them." The Kumasi Centre, he wrote, "is being used as a combined maternity and sick children's hospital." He blamed this state of affairs, first and foremost, on the medical officers, their failure to provide direction, and their "desire to ensure the popularity of these clin-ics so far as it may be expressed in the number of attendances year by year." While Kirk also blamed the "absence of adequate hospital accom-modation" and the "low standard of living of those who are most in need of instruction and guidance," he believed that the centers, given proper management, could have fulfilled their original purpose. He used the weighing clinics as an example of how the teeth had been taken out of infant welfare measures:

In Europe the weighing centre is generally the place where demonstrations in the care and management of infants are conducted, cookery lessons given, dress-making classes organised and the general welfare of children impressed upon all who attend there for these purposes. Here the weighing centre appears to be merely a weighing centre and the mothers have to be continually pestered to bring their children there to be weighed.

If the women who worked on a daily basis at the Kumasi Centre—the nurses, medical officers, and volunteers—were willing to collaborate in transforming a maternal and infant welfare center into a curative medical clinic by abandoning hygiene lectures and mothercraft talks for treatment of yaws or placenta previa, Kirk was not. He believed that if African women insisted on frequenting the center for curative procedures and refused to visit for welfare advice, then the only way to "help mothers in the raising of their children," whether they liked it or not, was organized house visiting. "If the mothers will not bring the babies regularly to the weighing machine," he wrote, "the weighing machine must be brought to the house." Moreover, he continued, "while the visit is being made those features of the home life of the child which may militate against its welfare should be noted and the mother's attention drawn to them." But even Kirk, in some ways, appreciated the not-so-subtle contradictions in what he advocated, suggesting at one point that the "welfare of children should logically await the establishment of the general measures affecting the whole community." But he was not so "logical" in his final recommendations. He simply advised the "discontinuance of work in the slum areas and its concentration in new layouts or model villages where the environment is suitable for the profitable establishment of such special measures as are necessary," in other words in areas where welfare work would not be muddied by the nagging problems of overcrowded housing and disease. In Kirk's view, "the principal obstacles to the attainment of a healthy childhood" remained "dirt and unsuitable diet."[102] Both could be blamed on untrained mothers, and both could be addressed by making new mothers, whether those mothers wanted "making" or not.

Kirk's report is significant not only in that it points to the contradictions, the bankruptcy, and the hypocrisy of colonial social welfare schemes but for the light it sheds on the encounter between Asante mothers of the first colonized generation and maternal imperialists. It suggests that that encounter was shaped as much, if not more, by the actions of Asante women as by a transnational discourse on maternal and child welfare. Asante mothers, for the most part, exhibited a profound lack of interest in the mothercraft agenda with which the Kumasi Centre began operations. They were not ambivalent, however, concerning their access to medical care alternatives. Using the pressure of their numbers at the health care clinics and the absence of their numbers at weighing clinics and mothercraft lectures, they fundamentally transformed the agenda of the

Photo 5.1 Our first pupils, Mbofraturo, 1931. (From *Woman's Work*, April 1931. Courtesy of MMS Archives, Methodist Church of Great Britain. Reprinted with permission.)

center, and there is little evidence to suggest that those who staffed the centers on a daily basis offered any effective opposition to the transformation. That the director of Gold Coast Medical Services essentially called for the abandonment of social welfare initiatives by welfare centers evidenced the strength with which Asante mothers daily negotiated the terrain of colonial motherhood. Having observed this strength (though he preferred to describe it as a "wave of suffering childhood"), Kirk concluded in 1942 that the colonial government must change the field of battle, take the struggle for "motherhood" right into Asante homes. Would colonization of the maternal fare any better there? To answer that question, let us turn to the Women's Work section of the Methodist Mission, which began actively working in Asante in the late 1920s. Its program focused not just on making proper mothers out of the first colonized generation through home visits and village demonstrations, but on educating their daughters in the science of mothercraft and then leading those girls back into the villages. There they could instruct their own mothers in the finer points of motherhood.

BASINS, BIBLES, AND NEEDLEPOINT:
IT'S WOMEN'S WORK MAKING MOTHERS

The introduction of Methodist women missionaries to Asante in the late 1920s was portrayed by the mission and by the colonial government as nothing less than a gender-specific response to the moral crisis born of colonial rule.[103] As Reverend E. W. Thompson wrote in the *Woman's Work* magazine of the mission:

> In former times, which, after all, is no farther off than yesterday, some sort of sexual morality was upheld and enforced by barbarous ordeals. . . . But with the introduction of a humane and civilised code of laws, ancient sanctions and restraints have been removed without a higher sanction of equal potency taking their place. A most experienced district official made complaint to me of the increasing and wide-spread laxity of morals under modern conditions. Young men and women formed irregular connections, and thought little of sin, because physical fear had been abolished.

Though the language was different, Thompson's words echo the same concerns as those expressed by Asante's chiefs. But Thompson believed the only way to counter this moral crisis was for women missionaries to "introduce and make real the Christian ideal of marriage and the family" in Asante. Motherhood, of course, was central to that ideal and key to the civilizing mission. The "most beautiful feature of . . . [West African] life," Thompson concluded, "is the piety of the 'Mammies.' One comes across many a motherly happy soul with a simple belief in God and Heaven and God's Christ. Such women will be the truest friends and helpers of the missionary when she goes to work in their midst."[104] That women missionaries were absolutely essential to this enterprise constituted the basic premise upon which the missionary efforts of the 1920s and 1930s were based. "Slowly—all too slowly," F. Deaville Walker wrote,

> it came at last to be realised that although African women might be evangelised by men, they needed women to lead and instruct them in the Christian life. If African homes are to be truly Christian homes, if African women are to become truly Christian, they must have women missionaries who can be among them as women among women and teach them about the intimate things of a woman's life in a way that no man can possibly do.[105]

In short, making colonial mothers was women's work.

While the government's maternal and infant welfare efforts in Kumasi focused mainly on reconstructing contemporary motherhood, the Methodist

Mission's first goal in Kumasi and in Asante generally was to shape the mothers of the next generation through educational initiatives. Early in 1927, the mission's district chair, Harry Webster, wrote to Governor Guggisberg about Methodist plans for a boarding school in Kumasi. "It is our intention," he wrote, "to place the emphasis on domestic and home training subjects— native cooking, laundry work, needle work, and gardening." Whether because of the severity of the "moral crisis" in Asante or because of Asante's relatively recent experience with European missions, the Methodists viewed education for Asante women as requiring a different agenda from the one utilized in the mission's coastal schools. "There is no thought of training the girls for English Examination," wrote Webster, "such as is attempted at Accra and Cape Coast."[106]

In 1928, for the first time in the history of the Methodist Mission in the Gold Coast, a meeting of women missionaries was held. It coincided with the beginnings of construction of the Kumasi school. Known as Mmofraturo (literally, "the children's garden"), the school was modeled on an African village, though "not necessarily an African village as it is," a 1928 report added, "but an African village as it might be under ideal conditions. Small houses are grouped around the Kindergarten block, which is approximately the size of a village school."[107] In 1930 Mmofraturo opened its doors, with Sister Persis Beer in charge. The school began with six children, "of whom two dropped out almost right away."[108] In the following year, a training college for women was added to Mmofraturo's program, with women taking some courses at neighboring Wesley College, but the problem with attendance continued. In fact, the school failed to receive its government grant for 1932 because the average daily attendance in 1931 was only 17.4, and the mission's headquarters seriously considered closing the school because "the belief in education has not yet gone deep enough to induce the African people to make personal sacrifice to secure it for their girls."[109] Not wanting, however, to take any "ill-considered action," the mission kept the school open. By 1932, enrollment was up to 22 and it climbed steadily throughout the decade, reaching 27 training college students and 89 pupils by 1940.[110]

From its inception, the school sought to mold proper Christian women and mothers through daily routine. The original campus consisted of three small houses containing two bedrooms and a dining room. One bedroom was for the training college students and the other was for the children. They were to interact as a family, eating together and dividing up specific chores, with the training college students serving as "mothers" to the pupils.[111] Everyone was to be up and bathed by six, and students and pupils prepared their own breakfasts and did their own cleaning, laundry, and ironing.[112] In classes, pupils focused on letters and numbers and general domestic skills,

Photo 5.2   Persis Beer, Mmofraturo School, ca. 1930s. Photograph by Jean Allman.

including needlecraft. The training college students took courses in cooking, housewifery, and domestic science, and what was taught in class was practiced outside of class. While this type of "home life" education, as Nancy Hunt called it, was quite common throughout Africa, Mmofraturo seems to have put an unusual twist on the model.[113] From the very beginning, while stressing domesticity and Christian motherhood, it also emphasized self-activity and empowerment in ways that appear almost inimical to the broader domestic agenda. For example, in 1931, Persis Beer reported that every week students and staff "meet in a 'Mother's Council' to discuss matters affecting the training of the children and anything that concerns our common welfare."[114] By 1934 the "Mother's Council" had become simply the "Mbofraturo Council," and Beer was reporting that "the aims of self-government and the freedom which comes of service continue to be carried out in the children's democratic assembly, the Mbofraturo Council, and in the whole life of the school."[115]

Mmofraturo's unusual combination of participatory democracy and domestic training was, in part, a reflection of Persis Beer's missionary feminism, if we can call it that. Beer, during her nearly 20 years in the Gold Coast and Asante, spent a good deal of time negotiating her own autonomy within the Methodist Mission movement in the colony. While her philosophy of education and of women's emancipation was not unproblematic, unburdened by racism, or free of the contradictions that riddled maternal imperialism, it did represent a fairly successful and long-term challenge to the prevailing missionary discourse on domesticity. From her correspondence and her reports, it is obvious that Beer considered domestic training to be only one part of a multifaceted education for girls, which should include academic subjects as well as agriculture. Certainly her views contrasted sharply with those of mission leaders like Harry Webster. In a 1933 article in *Woman's Work*, Beer attacked the second-class status of women in the church, the "assumption of women's inferiority [that] results in lack of opportunity for girls and women," and the assumptions of male teachers concerning female students in the higher standards. "Nearly all the teachers are men," she wrote, "and most of them assume that girls are intellectually inferior."[116] Beer considered education, not just domestic training, as key to women's advancement. "For this country," she proclaimed in 1933, "an educated Christian womanhood! Is that not our ideal?"[117] During World War II, Beer found herself in frequent conflict with male church members. For example, in a 1942 letter to the Women's Department in London, she complained about disciplinary cases involving Mmofraturo women training college students being heard by the Wesley College committee, "all of whom are men except two . . . and quite likely young men." In the same letter she complained of one of the church's "prominent African laymen [who] . . . spoke and made a fierce attack on women's work. He said some extreme things (I think he fears where the emancipation of women will lead!) and in a way it was to our advantage . . . that he went too far and the African ministers did not go with him."[118]

While Persis Beer's personal approach to education goes some distance toward explaining Mmofraturo's particular brand of democratic/domestic education, it does not tell the whole story. Asantes were active participants in the making of their world, even when it was a colonial world, and Mmofraturo, democratic assembly and all, was as much a product of the daily realities of life in Asante as it was of the ambiguous missionary feminism of Persis Beer. Indeed, the ways in which Beer was able to negotiate the missionary terrain of domestic education can only be explained by specific reference to the society in which she was situated and to the ways in which Beer herself interpreted that society. For example, from the outset, Beer was impressed by what she considered to be the extraordinary power women in Asante wielded within their matrilineal families, and she recognized that women were often economically independent of their husbands. In a 1933 article, rather than presenting this power as an obstacle to the creation of a solid Christian nuclear family, she directly contrasted it with Asante women's inferior status in the Methodist Church and in mission education. Beer's approach to education for women in Asante, therefore, was rooted in her perception that "in family matters, [Asante] women have power."[119] How to extend that influence into the church and into education was Beer's starting point, and, in large part, the Mmofraturo Council and the school's combined agenda of participatory democracy and domestic training can be seen as her efforts to reproduce the domestic power of Asante women in the mission school context. It is in this rather complex way that domesticity and Asante women's power mingled in seeming harmony at Mmofraturo. It was in this way that the children's garden became a "negotiated settlement," not just between Sister Persis and her mission's leaders, but among her students and pupils, their mothers and fathers, and Asante's chiefs.

Certainly, the vast majority of Asantes had no contact with Mmofraturo or with any similar institutions throughout this period, and of those who did and of those who wanted to educate their daughters, many must have found the costs prohibitive. (Mmofraturo's tuition per term in 1932 was £5.)[120] Yet despite their very limited impact in this period, schools like Mmofraturo are important as microcosms of the colonial encounter. They did not simply drop from the sky, as prefabricated colonial mission schools; they embodied, in various ways, the very struggle over how Asante's colonial mothers were to be made—a daily struggle whose outcomes were never predictable.

Two life stories provide some insight into the various and complex ways Asante women encountered this contested process as schoolgirls. Mary Anokye, one of the younger daughters of Tafohene Dabanka, was enrolled in Mmofraturo's first class. "I was one of the pioneers," she recalls, and by all evidence Mmofraturo profoundly affected her life's course. Persis Beer "saw to" her marriage or, more literally, "stood at her back" (*ɔgyina n'akyi*) for the ceremony. Mary Anokye was married in the church to a young catechist and spent most of her adult life traveling with him from mission school to mission school. She and her husband had two children, delivered by a registered midwife in Kumasi, and they always lived together. Mary Anokye worked as a seamstress in her home—a skill she had acquired at Mmofraturo—and relied on none of her matrikin, male or female, in the raising of her children. Her first child is named Persis.[121]

Mary Anokye's life seems to suggest that an early missionary education profoundly shaped the next generation of Asante mothers—creating a group of young women who lived with their husbands in monogamous marriages, remained in the home during the day (rather than going out to trade or to farm), and did not share childcare responsibilities with others.[122] However, Ama Dapah's story suggests a very different outcome. Ama attended the small Methodist school in Tafo, not far from Mmofraturo, and reached about the same stage as Mary Anokye before leaving. Her father was a servant (*ahenkwaa*) to the Asantehene in Kumasi, and Ama lived with her mother, a farmer, in the matrilineal family house in Tafo. At about the age of 12, Ama was taken out of school by her mother because her mother believed that "if you kept going to school you would be unable to have children." Ama eventually had her first child, but she did not marry the father. Nor did she marry, according to Asante custom or according to the Methodist Church, the fathers of her other 12 children. She explained that "in those days, the women were trusted by their husbands, so when he took you, he would decide not to do the rites because he trusted you not to go to any other man apart from him." Ama claims that she preferred this arrangement because of the flexibility it gave her: "if you kicked me, I would just leave you! That's it. . . . If they weren't any good, I just left." Ama Dapah supported her children, including paying their school fees, through her work as a trader. She always lived in her family house and her mother looked after the children when she was out. She never lived with any of her husbands.[123]

The point of telling these two stories is not to draw conclusions as to which was a more typical outcome of missionary mother-making. Neither woman was more or less "colonized" than the other; each simply negotiated the colonial map in a different way. Their stories illustrate how impossible it is to speak of a "missionary impact" when the "mission" constituted contested terrain and when so many factors external to the school itself came to bear on the making of Asante's first generation of colonized mothers. For example, in both cases here the class and status of the father (particularly relative to that of the mother) played a significant role in mediating the woman's encounter with mission education. In short, while future mothers were certainly being made at Mmofraturo and other girls' schools during this period, it was not always in the way that advocates of girls' education and mothercraft training had intended.

In fact, one of the major concerns of women missionary educators in the late 1930s was that girls' education seemed to be producing the opposite of what was intended—good Christian mothers and wives, skilled in domestic science and mothercraft. "A very distressing condition is increasing each year as girls leave school," Beer wrote in a "Memorandum on Women's Work in the Gold Coast":

This is the growth of prostitution in a way we have not known it before. . . . the number of girls attending school has increased tremen-

dously. These girls acquire a taste for European dress and for amuse-
ments. They will not go home to the heavy manual work of the farm.
There is little economic outlet for them. Some get accepted to train as
nurses or teachers. A few get work at the Post Office or Telephone
Exchange. But great numbers fail to find any wage earning occupation.
Of these it is grievous to know that many are coming to our large towns,
or to the mining centres, or roam from village to village, town to town
as prostitutes. It is our problem in a special sense because it is in one
way a result of the education we have given.[124]

While it is doubtful that prostitution was as rampant as Beer imagined, it
is significant that her report cast girls' education—one of the proposed
solutions to Asante's "moral crisis"—as contributing to that crisis. The
economic changes that underlay the gender chaos of the late 1920s and
early 1930s were obviously not mitigated by mothercraft or needlework.
Perhaps some of the products of schools like Mmofraturo were actually
working the streets of mining towns as "Corner-Side Women." Perhaps
many, like Ama Dapah, were simply negotiating the zone between marriage and nonmarriage in search of economic security in an expanding
cash economy. The fact remained that mission schools proved no more
effective than Kumasi's Welfare Centre in manufacturing the ideal: a
Christian colonial motherhood that could, in its pure and uncontested form,
not just lower infant mortality and reduce disease but eradicate the very
moral crisis that had so concerned Asante's chiefs and colonial administrators for over a decade.

While the Methodist Women's Work that went into education did not
always result in the intended harvest, there were other efforts not bounded
by the walls of the school. From the very beginning, an important aspect
of girls' education entailed outreach programs aimed at the mothers of
the next generation's mothers. From Mmofraturo's first year, its students
and staff went out to nearby villages on weekends. At first these visits
were rather informal, envisioned as efforts at "making friends" with village women. "Clad in their native 'ntama,'" Elsie Lince wrote of the
Mmofraturo students in the early 1930s, "they wear an air of distinction
and gracefulness that is lacking when they put on European dress and as
they pass from compound to compound, greeting the women, admiring
their babies, advising them to seek treatment for yaws and other diseases,
they create a general atmosphere of friendliness and good will that is
delightful to witness."[125] By 1934, these friendly visits were far more
organized and had gained a specific maternal and infant welfare agenda.
"With added zest due to an increased interest in Red Cross work," reported Beer, the students were visiting the neighboring town of Tafo and

bathing babies.[126] Beer's 1939 report detailed the extensive nature of the students' village work:

> On Sundays they visit Christian and heathen women in their compounds, teach classes of women and children and sometimes do dispensary work. During the week the students go to Tafo. The second year [they] do Infant Welfare work and hold a play hour for children up to eight or nine years of age. To this enjoyable hour only well-bathed children are admitted! The third year students also go to Tafo each week, and have worked with some of the women in the compounds, teaching them clean ways of cooking, helping them to clean kitchens and compounds and giving health talks, and trying to arouse their interest in improving their homes.[127]

In many ways, outreach programs such as these constituted the most intimate of Asante women's encounters with colonialism. Daughters became targets of and agents in the colonization of the maternal in an ambiguous process of indirect social reconstruction. But did the intimacy of this particular colonial encounter render school outreach programs more successful in creating an uncontested colonized motherhood than, for example, welfare clinics? Let us look briefly at the encounter from the perspective of the mother whose baby was being bathed. In 1992, Allman spoke to many women in the towns of Tafo, Effiduasi, and Asokore who had direct experience of these outreach programs in the 1930s and early 1940s. The majority of them had had their babies bathed by the Methodist outreach groups and all described very similar scenes, including Mary Anokye, who served in the Mmofraturo outreach program. They recall the missionaries arriving in town with a group of their students. Often the group was equipped with soap, sponges, powder, and basins and, at times, brought bandages and clothes made by the students and medicines for various skin ailments. Sometimes the group's arrival was formally announced by the chief through the beating of a gong-gong, but more often it was informally announced by the women singing a welcoming song to the missionaries as they went to fetch water for the baths.[128] As Yaa Pokuaa recalls, "When they came, they asked us to bring them the children so they could show us how to bathe them. We took them to the outside of the house. There, they showed us how to bathe them well and then powder them. They advised us to do that every day when we got up."[129]

But how did Asante women perceive this encounter—as a welcomed instructional session or as a coercive intrusion into their private worlds? Allman expected to hear one or the other of these responses when she

asked women what they thought of the bathing sessions. She heard neither. When asked what they thought of this bathing of their babies, virtually every woman responded quite simply that it was good. When asked
if it was good because it changed or improved the ways that women
washed their babies, only a few could point to any differences at all. Mary
Oduro suggested that the only differences were that the missionaries used
a basin to bathe the children and that they powdered them when finished:
"They told us to use a basin and not to bathe them like we were doing,
just pouring water over them."[130] However, most could think of no difference and responded like Efuah Nsuah, who said, "No, it did not change
anything."[131] Only after encountering several responses like Efuah Nsuah's
did Allman realize that there was no contradiction in the reminiscences,
that the sessions could be perceived, at once, as non-coercive, non-in-
structional, and yet somehow "good." For many women, the bathing sessions were simply a means of gaining access to various imported items,
including powder and medicated skin ointments. Rose Afrakoma remembers the encounter as follows:

RA: We would line up under a tree with our children. The ones who had
sores, they would treat them. They would bathe the children and powder
them.

JA: You didn't consider that to be interfering in your business?

RA: . . . No, it was good because some of the children had these sores
called *doee* [yaws].

JA: . . . I would find it rather strange if people from another country
came to my house and said they were going to teach me how to bathe my
children!

RA: Well, it didn't bother us. They were teaching us something.

JA: Did the things that they taught you change the way in which you
cared for your children?

RA: It didn't change at all.

JA: Then why was it good?

RA: Because they were helping us. We were getting powder free and all
of that!

JA: So, it didn't change anything?

RA: No, nothing.[132]

Adwoa Mansah recalls receiving clothes for her babies, in addition to medicine and powders.[133] But many women seemed to have no underlying agenda

for attending the sessions; nor did they perceive any particular cultural significance in these baby baths.

When asked why she thought the missionaries wanted to bathe the children, Ama Dapah simply replied, "They were dirty!" She did not consider the bath to be an intrusion. "We were not bothered [by it]," she recalled, "because the children could be dirty, so they just came to help us."[134] This perception of the session as a culturally uncluttered bit of assistance to busy mothers was not uncommon. After having been asked if the missionaries and students knew anything about bathing children that the mothers did not, Akua Kankroma replied, "We were doing it ourselves, but when they came they would ask if they could do it, so we just said yes."[135] Indeed, some women found the whole spectacle rather amusing—a bit of entertainment to break the routine of daily life. When Adwoa Tana was asked why she thought the bathing sessions were good, she replied with a hearty chuckle, "It is good to have a white woman bathing your children. . . . You are just lucky to have whites who are bathing your children for you!"[136] While Adwoa Tana obviously imputed some cultural significance to the bathing sessions, it was not the significance intended. She was struck not by the instruction she had received in mothercraft but by the irony of having someone from among the colonizers bathing the babies of the colonized. And as Adwoa Nsiah recalled, once the maternal colonizers went on their way, they left little in their wake: "It was whites who came to bathe the children, so it was good. But, as for my child, I bathed her myself! I bathed my children before they came. I bathed my children after they came!"[137] Indeed, some women recalled attending only out of courtesy. As Afua Manu explained, "when someone comes to tell you something, you definitely have to listen to them. You have to honor the invitation, even if you already know what they are saying."[138]

The reminiscences of women whose babies were objects in bathing demonstrations point to a fascinating, textured colonial encounter that defies simple categorization. It was neither one of coercion and resistance nor one of imparting and receiving instruction. It was a social occasion, at times even festive, that brought daughters to villages to instruct mothers through the medium of missionary outreach. Though the students came bearing some of the cultural baggage of their teachers, that baggage was not as heavily loaded as many might assume. It did not dominate the encounter; it did not structure that encounter in incontestable ways. As Mary Anokye recalled of those bathing sessions, "We didn't teach things that would contradict customs. . . . They always received the message happily. But I couldn't tell if they turned deaf ears to it when we returned back home."[139] Anokye understood that Asante women participated in mothercraft exercises largely on their own terms. They did not come because they wanted to learn a "better" way. They came because it facilitated access to powder, or to baby clothes made from imported cottons, or to medicine. Perhaps it was simply something to do, an expression of courtesy, a bit of entertainment on a Saturday afternoon.

This is not to suggest that the bathing encounter was wholly without social meaning but to argue that its meanings were many and contested. For example, recollections of how the boundary between private and public in Asante fared during these bathing sessions provide striking evidence of multiple and embattled definitions. In recent reminiscences, most Asante women, like Rose Afrakoma, recalled bringing their children *out* of the house and into public space in order to take part in the bathing festivities.[140] In contrast, much of the correspondence of the Methodist Women's Department describes women missionaries *entering* the homes of Asante women in order to bathe their babies. These conflicting accounts are not about truth and falsehood, nor are they necessarily about what constitutes the "inside" of a house and what constitutes "outside." They are about the very meaning of the colonial encounter. In the first, the colonized mother leaves her private space and makes the decision to participate in the encounter on her own terms. In the second version, the colonizer, empowered by the state, by Christianity, and by domestic science expertise, enters on her own terms the private sphere of Asante women. In the first version, the boundary between private and public is not violated; in the second it is. In Tafo, Effiduasi, and a host of other towns throughout Asante, missionaries, mothers, and student-daughters crossed and recrossed, mapped and remapped this boundary of contested colonial terrain while they engaged in a dialogue of basins, bathwater, powder, and bandages. Motherhood was certainly invented through this process, but it was nothing like the ideal Christian motherhood of Persis Beer's dreams.

WOMEN'S FELLOWSHIP GROUPS AND CHRISTIAN VALUES

Nor was that ideal realized through the Methodist Women's Fellowship groups that spread throughout Asante in the late 1930s and early 1940s. These groups were spearheaded by the first evangelical women missionaries sent to the area—women who often delivered elaborate sermons on motherhood and Christian values. Heavily laden with the imperialist discourse of proper motherhood, these lectures were far more about western nuclear family values and parental responsibility than they were about bath powder or basins. The lectures delivered by Irene Mason in the mid-1930s were not atypical. Mason, according to her notes, always highlighted the importance and responsibilities of motherhood, the need for fathers to take an active role in disciplining their children, and the "importance of unity in the home" for training and proper discipline. The only way this unity could be attained, Mason warned her listeners, was through the "marriages of two people who love one another and choose one another in the sight of God and who are prepared to build up together a home according to the laws of Christ."[141]

Yet Asante women who became active participants in these fellowship groups in the 1930s and 1940s do not recall any significant differences between their homes and marriages and those of non-Christians. Indeed, only a few of the members had their customary marriages blessed in the church, while fewer still went through the Christian ceremony.[142] They tend to recall missionaries not for their spiritual guidance but for very specific and practical reasons. For example, Kathleen White arrived in Asante in 1941 as an evangelical missionary whose program included the setting up of fellowship groups. From the beginning, she saw the groups as forums for reconstructing motherhood. In one of her first reports to London she wrote: "I used this initial visit to talk to the women on cleanliness in their homes and in most of the villages I bathed babies and washed sores. . . . in the villages one is faced with illiteracy and all the things which go with it, such as dirty homes, sickness amongst the children, lack of desire and initiative."[143] Several months later, White was bringing unmarried young women into her home for weeks at a stretch in order to "teach them a few rules of cleanliness, and also to learn to read, sew, cook and such things." She referred to these women as her "family" and closed one letter with this apology: "Please excuse more news now, but my family is needing attention. I am going to talk to them about the care of their babies and try to show them how to feed them. If only they could realise that if they began to train their babies from birth it would be much easier for their children when they grew up. Half the trouble in Africa is the absolute lack of physical control."[144]

White's message was a strong one, certainly far more burdened with maternal racism (for lack of a better term) than Persis Beer's and with far less room for negotiation. Yet White is fondly remembered, but not so much for her message on Christian motherhood. When Victoria Adjaye was recently asked what kind of work the women missionaries like White were doing in the early 1940s, she replied, "They taught us how to make pancakes, but I knew how already. . . . They taught us how to give a sick person food to eat when s/he has no appetite."[145] Most of the women in Effiduasi, the town in which White eventually based herself, echoed similar memories of food preparation: "White taught us how to cook—semolina, biscuit, pancake."[146] Others recall detailed lessons on making soup: "When our mothers were cooking, they would just put the foodstuffs in

Photo 5.3   Kwadaso Training Centre, 1992. Photograph by Jean Allman.

the cooking pot. . . . They would have added the garden eggs and pepper on to the yams and cassava. But we weren't taught that way. We were taught to keep it separate. We prepared the fufu separate and the soup separate."[147] Though White came on a "civilizing" mission as burdened as any could be with European notions of godliness, cleanliness, and discipline, it was a mission with which Asante women interacted largely on their own terms, much as they did with welfare clinics and outreach programs. Their encounter with Women's Work missionaries like White was mediated not so much by Bibles and hymns as by the practical, even the mundane —by pancakes, biscuits, and stews. In these ways, through daily choices, by taking some and leaving the rest, Asante women continued to actively shape their colonial world. By 1948 that world was changing quickly. Persis Beer had returned to England.[148] Kathleen White's mission had been given a permanent home with the construction of the women's training center at Kwadaso, a center designed to provide instruction to rural women in infant welfare, hygiene, religion, and morality, as well as in reading and simple arithmetic. Yet for White's and Beer's successors, the making of colonial mothers remained a difficult battle. As Gwen Ash reported of a group that attended the center in 1948: "They don't seem as keen on child welfare . . . but are tremendously keen on the reading."[149] "Women's Work," it seems, was never done.

But what can we make of these welfare efforts aimed at Asante women? Did missionaries address the gender chaos of the expanding cash economy with pancakes and needlework? When put into action, did missionary and government rhetoric on social welfare and girls' education come down to baby shows and baby baths? In a discussion of domesticity and hegemony, Jean and John Comaroff have written that this was precisely what colonialism was all about, that "colonization . . . entailed the reconstruction of the ordinary, of things at once material, meaningful, and mundane."[150] Certainly, in Asante, colonization of the maternal did not take place, at least with any success, on the level of mothercraft lectures by women like White and Mason or through weighing clinics like the one in Kumasi. Rather, it occurred through the medium of ordinary objects and daily routines, through bathing basins and biscuits. But if the "seeds of cultural imperialism were most effectively sown along the contours of everyday life," [151] as the Comaroffs have written, Asante women's encounters with colonial efforts to make them proper mothers and dutiful wives raise important questions of control and of agency in the imperialist enterprise. They suggest not only that there were few other places to sow those seeds but that women of the first colonized generation determined in large part how and where the seeds could be sown. For maternal colonizers to sow the seeds of cultural imperialism in the "contours" of Asante "daily life," then, was to sow in ground they did not own, in a climate they could not predict, and at intervals they did not determine. What eventually took root and thrived in that ground was something barely recognizable as imperialism's own.

CONCLUSION: ASANTE WOMEN IN THE MAKING OF A COLONIAL WORLD

If indirect rule and government/mission welfare initiatives worked as twin efforts to address the gender chaos of the interwar years—chaos sparked in no small part by the movement of women into the cash economy as producers in their own right—how then do we judge the success of these efforts? What do they tell us about the ways in which colonialism shaped women's lives and the ways in which Asante women themselves shaped the colonial world? The answers are not simple. Certainly, mission and government welfare efforts aimed at making proper mothers and dutiful wives were actively shaped and, at times, completely recast by Asante women who, as active agents, negotiated the terms of their own participation in the "civilizing mission." More often than not, they chose to participate through the medium of baby contests, basins, and pancakes and not through the medium of mothercraft lectures or social welfare projects—those non-negotiable and non-negotiating initiatives that demanded the complete reconstruction of the private domain. That the Kumasi clinic, that Persis Beer, that Kathleen White agreed, wittingly or not, to these terms of participation was an acknowledgment of Asante women's power and autonomy, as well as a silent admission of the shallowness of the "civilizing mission." Government agents, missionaries, and medical officers set out to make mothers and dutiful wives in colonial Asante, but in the end they could not make them just as they pleased. They did not, to recall Marx's celebrated observation, make them "under circumstances chosen by themselves, but under circumstances directly encountered, given and transmitted from the past" and on terms largely defined by Asante women themselves.[152]

And if mission and government welfare initiatives did not and could not effectively address the gender chaos of the interwar years, what of the formal political structures of indirect rule from which women, commoner and royal alike, had been excluded? Certainly in their daily rulings, chiefs were able to articulate and enforce definitions of marriage, adultery, and divorce that often undercut ordinary women's struggles to control their own productive and reproductive power, although we have ample evidence of women persuading native courts to accept the legitimacy of particular claims. But what of the chiefs' direct attempts to assert control over those women they viewed as "uncontrollable"? Here, too, we find that chiefs' efforts were not particularly successful or enduring. For example, many today remember the capture of "spinsters" as solving the crisis in marriage only momentarily. As Beatrice Nyarko recalled, "People became afraid. It put fear in them,"[153] but in the long run "it didn't help at all."[154] The impact was minimal and short-lived in no small part because of the success of women in subverting the entire process from the outset. Afua Fom, one of those captured, recalled that once women entered the room where they were to be kept, some immediately mentioned a man's name—"any man's name." This was not necessarily out of fear or desperation, however. Many women arranged to give their release fee to a particular man in advance of their arrest, so, once arrested, the woman named that man; he came, he paid the fee, and she was set free, supposedly to marry her suitor. Granted, even in this scenario chiefs still collected 5/- for every unmarried woman, thus making the exercise a "money making proposition," but they did not succeed in securing firm and uncontested control over women's productive and reproductive labor or, in their own words, in encouraging "conjugal marriages among our womenfolk." At best, they had succeeded merely in implementing, for a very short time, a kind of "nonmarriage tax" by making women pay 5/- for not marrying.

That many women were able to continue to circumvent chiefs' efforts to regulate their productive and reproductive power even after 1935 underscores their ongoing ability to actively shape the colonial world. There is certainly no shortage of evidence on this score—from the life stories of women who chose divorce or periods of nonmarriage, to the petition of *Baasifɔɔ*, to the court testimonies of women who relentlessly pursued their rights to conjugally produced properties. Asante women, in short, refused to "eat stone." Even the careful reformulations of *ayefare* undertaken by the Asante Confederacy Council do not seem to have had an enduring impact. Indeed, that *ayefare* today is something about which you consult the historical memories of the oldest inhabitants is some indication that the contest over meaning was not won by Asante's ruling chiefs. When an 82-year-old Effiduasi woman was asked why *ayefare* had disappeared, she simply answered: "The men don't take care of the women and the women don't even allow their husbands to come and do the marriage rites! So, who will pay it?"[155]

NOTES

1. MRO: Asante Confederacy Council, Minutes of the Third Session, 7–23 March 1938.

2. Carol Summers, "Intimate Colonialism," 806. Nakanyike Musisi's work on education and domesticity suggests a similar chronology for the colonization of women. See her "Colonial and Missionary Education: Women and Domesticity in Uganda," in Hansen, ed., *African Encounters*, 182–83. Rattray was a crucial figure in directing colonial government attention to the roles and status of Asante women. He wrote of women in his first lengthy volume on Asante: "a woman, besides suffering from periodical disability, cannot go to war; but for these two facts the Ashanti woman under a matrilineal system, would, I believe, eclipse any male in importance." See Rattray, *Ashanti*, 81–82.

3. Mamdani has recently argued that the "'world historic defeat' of the female gender was experienced in Africa not as much with the onset of state organization as with the consolidation of the colonial state." *Citizen and Subject,* 41.

4. NAGK, ARA/463: "Minutes of Meeting of the Kumasi Council of Chiefs Held in the D.C.'s Court, Kumasi on Thursday morning, the 6th of May 1926."

5. As Hansen described it, colonization was essentially an "act that turned the organization of household activity and sexuality into political matters." Karen Tranberg Hansen, "Introduction," in *African Encounters*, 5.

6. See Matson, *Digest*, passim.

7. For a fuller historical discussion of *ayerefa*, see Allman, "Adultery."

8. See, for example, Rattray, *Ashanti Law*, 317; Rattray, *Religion and Art*, 76–77; Ellis, *Tshi-Speaking Peoples*, 281–89; and John Mensah Sarbah, *Fanti Customary Laws* (London: W. Clowes, 1897), 41–56. For a discussion of what constitutes a marriage in the postcolonial period, see Vellenga, "Who is a Wife?" 144–55.

9. Rattray, *Ashanti Law*, 317–18; Danquah, *Gold Coast*, 166. See also the discussion of seduction in chapter 4.

10. Danquah, *Gold Coast*, 155 and 166.

11. Rattray, *Ashanti Law*, 322; Christaller, *Dictionary*, 587; Danquah, *Gold Coast*, 177.

12. Danquah, *Gold Coast*, 167–68.

13. Rattray, *Ashanti Law*, 318.

14. The punishments for sexual assault are far more difficult to trace historically than those for adultery. It is virtually impossible to trace them for the precolonial period, although the heavy penalties for having a sexual connection "in the bush" suggest that *ahahantwe* virtually implied force because no one would voluntarily commit such an offense. For the colonial period, the picture is quite complex. Certainly, many of the obvious sexual assault cases in the colonial record books were tried in native courts as cases of sexual connection "in the bush," with the male offender receiving a stiff fine or imprisonment. The husband of the woman concerned could also collect *ayefare* compensation from the offender. In the British colonial courts, rapes were treated as sexual assaults under criminal law. See Rattray, *Ashanti Law*, 308.

15. Ibid., 304–8 and 317–23.

16. Rattray, *Religion and Art*, 87–93; Bowdich, *Mission*, 259–60; Ellis, *Tshi-Speaking Peoples*, 282–83. For a detailed discussion of the many factors that differentiated *ayefare* among commoner classes, see Rattray, *Ashanti Law*, 317–23.

17. Rattray viewed *ɛfiesɛm* and *ɔman akyiwadeɛ* as nearly replicating the British legal distinction between "civil" and "criminal." There were, however, several important differences, some of which are discussed in *Ashanti Law*, 286–88. For the purposes of historical reconstruction, it is important to keep the categories distinct in order to understand what happens when Asante notions of *ɛfiesɛm/ɔman akyiwadeɛ* collide with British notions of "civil" and "criminal." See also Busia, *Position of the Chief*, 65.

18. For full discussions of oath-swearing, see Rattray, *Religion and Art*, chapter 22; Rattray, *Ashanti Law*, 379–80; Busia, *Position of the Chief*, 75–77.

19. Busia, *Position of the Chief*, 75.

20. McCaskie, "State and Society," 491.

21. Bowdich, *Mission*, 259–60. A *periguin* or, more commonly, *peredwan* was equivalent to 16 *ackies* or £8.2.0.

22. See Brodie Cruickshank, *Eighteen Years on the Gold Coast: Including an Account of the Native Tribes and Their Intercourse with Europeans*, 2 vols. (London: Hurst and Blackett, 1853), 199–225. For de Heer's figures, see McCaskie, "State and Society," 490–91, citing the original text: Instituut voor Taal-, Land-, en Volkenkunde, Leiden, MS H-509, P. de Heer, Aanhangsel: Journale gehouden te Comassee door eenen tapoeier (1866–67).

23. Rattray, *Religion and Art*, 86–93; and Rattray, *Ashanti Law*, 307–8.

24. Rattray, *Ashanti Law*, 323. Six shillings is roughly equivalent to one and a half *ackies*—Bowdich's figure for a common man's compensation in the early nineteenth century. Bowdich, *Mission*, 259.

25. Rattray, *Ashanti Law*, 322–23; and Rattray, *Religion and* Art, 96.

26. McCaskie, "State and Society," 490.

27. With regard to the different penalties faced by men and women, McCaskie explains: "the woman was killed as *punishment* for participation while the man surrendered his life in *compensation* to the offended husband." "State and Society," 489.

28. Bowdich, *Mission*, 260; Ellis, *Tshi-Speaking Peoples*, 283. Ellis wrote that if a wife of a chief was from a family "too powerful to admit of the husband putting her to death, he usually cuts off her nose as punishment." See Rattray, *Religion and Art*, 87–91.

29. Ellis, *Tshi-Speaking Peoples*, 282; Cruickshank, *Eighteen Years*, 199; Rattray, *Religion and Art*, 98.

30. Joseph Dupuis, *Journal of a Residence in Ashantee* (London: Frank Cass, 1966; orig. pub., London: Henry Colburn, 1824), 37. Also see Cruickshank, *Eighteen Years*, 199.

31. See Allman, "Adultery," 37–45.

32. Gold Coast, Native Jurisdiction Ordinance, No. 4 of 1924.

33. MRO: Native Tribunal of Kumasihene, Civil Record Book 4, *Clara Poma v. Abena Adutwimah*, dd. Kumasi, 5 September 1928, 426.

34. MRO: Native Tribunal of Kumasihene, Civil Record Book 24, *Amina Badenda v. Bedoka Hausa*, dd. Kumasi, 21 December 1934, 410.

35. MRO: Native Tribunal of Kyidomhene, Civil Record Book 3, *Yaa Kwaryie v. Kwaku Mensah,* dd. Kumasi, 8 December 1931, 327. It was common practice for spouses to pacify each other in cases of adultery. The fee for commoners was generally £2.7.0. See, for example, Native Tribunal of Gyasehene, Civil Record Book 1, *Yaw Fohuo v. Atta Ya*, dd. Kumasi, 23 March 1928, 124.

36. MRO: Native Tribunal of Kumasihene, Civil Record Book 4, *Ama Jan-Yiadu v. Mr. Jonsan*, dd. Kumasi, 24 December 1928, 231.

37. MRO: Native Tribunal of Kumasihene, Civil Record Book 20, *Kofi Boaten v. Yaa Korankyewa*, dd. Kumasi, 6 September 1933, 45.

38. For a listing of grounds for divorce, see Rattray, *Religion and Art*, 97-98.

39. Rhodes House Library, Oxford: Mss.Afr.s.713, AFL. Wilkinson Papers, D. C. Wiawso to Commissioner of Western Province, Sekondi, dd. Wiawso, 30 July 1935.

40. Rhodes House Library, Oxford: Mss.Afr.s.713, AFL. Wilkinson Papers, Asantehene Osei A. Prempeh II, Asantehene to Omanhene of Sefwi Wioso, dd. Kumasi, 19 July 1935.

41. Rhodes House Library, Oxford: Mss.Afr.s.713, AFL. Wilkinson Papers, Asantehene Osei A. Prempeh II, Asantehene to Omanhene of Sefwi Wioso, dd. Kumasi, 19 July 1935; Memorandum, District Commissioner's Clerk to District Commissioner, Wiawso, dd. 30 July 1935; D.C. Wiawso to Commissioner of Western Province, Sekondi, dd. Wiawso, 30 July 1935.

42. For a pre-restoration case in which a man is accused of using the Kumasihene's name in order to demand adultery fees, see MRO: Native Tribunal of Kumasihene, Criminal Record Book 6, *Native Tribunal v. Attah Kwabinah, Kwabena Jaimfie, and Akwasi Chaye*, dd. Kumasi, 12 May 1923, 203.

43. Gold Coast, Native Courts (Ashanti) Ordinance, No. 2 of 1935. For a summary of the structure of Asante's post-restoration native court system, see Hailey, *Native Administration III*, 244–45.

44. See Matson, *Digest*, 32.

45. Gold Coast, Native Courts (Offences under Native Law and Custom) Order, No. 7 of 1935. Amended by Order 24 of 1943. See also Matson, *Digest*, 42–45. For a similar discussion of the criminalization of adultery in Zimbabwe, see Schmidt, *Peasants*, 104–6.

46. In 1943, the council amended its original order on the criminalization of adultery so that prosecutions were limited to marriages that had been registered. The civil remedy for adultery compensation was not affected. Thus, in civil adultery suits well into the 1940s, a main source of contention continued to be whether or not the husband and wife were *really* married. Increasingly, as we saw in chapter 2, the only criterion used by the courts was the payment or nonpayment of *tiri nsa* (*tiri aseda*).

47. The order is discussed and reproduced in full in Matson, *Digest*, 25 and 40–41. Suits filed under this order can be found in MRO: Asantehene's Appam Court D, Civil Record Books 27–31, 1943–1946. In Ex-GC 54341, *John Mensah v. Gariba Hausa*, Civil Record Book 31, dd. Kumasi, 17 May 1946, 552, the court ruled against the plaintiff because it suspected that he "and his wife entered into a mutual arrangement between themselves to put the Defendant in trouble."

48. For the 1911 Chief Commissioner's "Scale of Adultery Fees," see NAGK, ARA/848. The scale closely approximates what we know of precolonial fees, with one important exception. Kumasi's "clan heads," as the British termed them (of Kronti, Adonten, Akwamu, Oyoko, Kyidom, Gyase, and Ankobea), were entitled to compensation equal to that of *amanhene*—a reward, no doubt, for their collaboration with British colonial rule.

49. The order is reproduced in full in Matson, *Digest*, 45–48. While one cannot help but be struck by the continuities in *ayefare* over so many decades, the order did differ from the 1911 scale in two important ways. First, the 1946 order held that no husband could claim adultery compensation more than twice "in respect of any one wife." This is, perhaps, the only evidence of a significant British impact on the reformulation of *ayefare*, outside of the elimination of death and corporal punishment as legitimate sanctions. Secondly, the 1946 scale returned Kumasi's "clan heads" to their precolonial rankings. They were no longer entitled to the same compensation as *amanhene*—a reflection perhaps of changed power relations after the restoration of the council and the stabilization of indirect rule. Certainly, the order was a response to the seemingly endless number of cases in which men claimed higher fees than the adulterers believed they were entitled to. For example, in *Akua Brago v. Kwaku Appaw* (MRO: Asantehene's Appam Court D, Civil Record Book 10, dd. Kumasi, 23 Aug. 1937, 353), Akua Brago confessed two counts of adultery to her husband. One of the adulterers could not be located, so Brago was liable for the *ayefare*. Her husband told her that in his status as an ex-*odikro* (village chief) and a "royalist to the linguist Nantwi of Bantama," he was entitled to £11.6.0. Brago paid this and then became convinced her husband was only due £2.7.0. The court ruled in Brago's favor, and her husband had to refund the difference.

50. The order is reproduced in full in Matson, *Digest*, 44. Women who were members of the royal family of one of the stools scheduled in the order were excluded from the requirement, as were women for whom swearing an oath was "repugnant" to their "religious beliefs."

51. MRO: Asantehene's Appam Court D, Civil Record Book 3, *Kwaku Boakyi v. Yaa Mansah*, dd. Kumasi, 23 December 1935, 370, and Native Tribunal of the Gyasehene, Civil Record Book 1, *Yaw Fohuo v. Atta Ya*, dd. Kumasi, 12 March 1928, 124.

52. MRO: Asantehene's Native Court B, Civil Record Book 20, *Ama Manu v. Kwasi Buo*, dd. Kumasi, 25 September 1940, 180.

53. The erosion of reciprocity in marrying is discussed in full in chapter 2.

54. An interesting exception is Yaw Amoah's statement in MRO: Asantehene's Native Court B, Criminal Record Book 1, Native Authority Police per *Kojo Nimo v. Yaw Amoah*, dd. Kumasi, 14 February 1936, 210. After several witnesses testified against him, Amoah switched his plea to guilty, saying, "What a woman has said in connection with adultery or sexual connection is always correct and I do not wish to prolong this matter."

55. MRO: Asantehene's Native Court B, Civil Record Book 4, *Yaw Brenyah v. Effua Frimpoma*, dd. Kumasi, 13 February 1936, 38.

56. MRO: Asantehene's Native Court B, Civil Record Book 20, *Henry Kusi v. Akua Aframkuma*, dd. Kumasi, 19 October 1940, 278.

57. Summers, "Intimate Colonialism," 807. Parts of this section also appear in Allman, "Making Mothers," 24–47.

58. See Tordoff, *Ashanti*, 159 n. 2, 239, 240.

59. Dabanka also donated the land upon which Wesley College was built. Allman: Mary Anokye, Old Tafo, 19 June 1992; Efua Nsuah, Tafo, 24 June 1992; and Akua Senti, Old Tafo, 19 June 1992.

60. Hunt, "'Le Bébé en Brousse,'" 411.

61. See Summers, "Intimate Colonialism," 787–807.

62. Relying solely on archival sources, one could easily be convinced that there were no women in Asante until 1925!

63. PRO, CO 98/24: Ashanti Report on the Blue Book for 1914.

64. PRO, CO 98.40: Gold Coast Report on Ashanti for 1923–1924.

65. PRO, CO 96/665/9: J. C. Maxwell, Officer Administering the Government, to L. S. Amery, M.P., Colonial Office, dd. Accra, 1 May 1926. The other two centers were to be situated in Accra and Sekondi.

66. Ibid. See also PRO, CO 96/665/9: "Report of Committee Appointed to Consider Welfare Work amongst Women and Children," Accra, 1926; "Minutes of Conference Held at Christiansborg on the 26 March 1926 to Consider the Taking Over by the Missionary Societies of the Welfare Work among Women and Children in the Gold Coast"; and CO 96/674/4: J. C. Maxwell, Officer Administering the Government, to L. S. Amery, Colonial Office, dd. Accra 4 May 1927; Harry Webster, WMMS, to Colonial Secretary, dd. Accra, 9 February 1927; E. O. Thompson, WMMS, to Secretary of State for the Colonies, dd. London, 12 July 1927.

67. PRO, CO 96/673/8: Harry Webster, WMMS, to Governor F. Gordon Guggisberg, dd. Accra, 15 February 1927. Normally, a mission was entitled to only one-third of the cost of a school building provided certain conditions were observed. Guggisberg wanted to give more in this case because "now the government could abandon any idea of a Government Girls' Boarding School in Kumasi and entrust this section of . . . education policy to the Mission."

68. Many tend to view the pervasive role of nongovernmental organizations (NGOs) in the political and economic life of African states as a recent, postcolonial phenomenon. Even a brief look at the role of the Red Cross and the missionary societies in education and welfare initiatives suggests otherwise.

69. British Red Cross Society [BRCS] Archives, Guildford, England, Correspondence: P. S. Selwyn-Clarke, "A Red Cross Branch on the Gold Coast," n.d. [1933?]. Also excerpted in BRCS, Eleventh Annual Report of Gold Coast Branch of the British Red Cross Society for the Year 1943.

70. This two-pronged strategy mirrored efforts in Britain that targeted both schoolgirls and mothers. See Anna Davin, "Imperialism and Motherhood," *History Workshop Journal* 5 (1978), 26 and 30; and Jane Lewis, *The Politics of Motherhood: Child and Maternal Welfare in England, 1900–1939* (London: Croom Helm, 1980), 90.

71. As Summers writes of the population crisis in Uganda, the first response "began as a straightforward attempt to treat the ill. After the World War, though, 'social hygiene' became an important therapeutic tool." See "Intimate Colonialism," 788.

72. NAGK, ARA/1741: P. S. Selwyn-Clarke, "Kumasi Health Week, 1925."

73. Ibid.

74. See BRCS, Eleventh Annual Report of Gold Coast Branch; PRO, CO 98/55: Report on the Medical and Sanitary Department for the Year 1929–1930; and CO 98/50: Gold Coast, Report on Ashanti for the Year April, 1927–28. The league was inaugurated in Asante in 1927 but did not begin serious work until 1929.

75. PRO, CO 96/705/10: P. S. Selwyn-Clarke, Secretary of BRCS, Gold Coast Branch, to Colonial Secretary, dd. Accra, 28 June 1932.

76. NAGK, uncatalogued item 1454, League of Maternity and Child Welfare, Kumasi Branch: "Memorandum: Inauguration of the League of Maternity and Child Welfare, Kumasi Branch," 6 October 1927.

77. PRO, CO 98/55: Gold Coast, Report on the Medical and Sanitary Department for the Year 1929–1930.

78. As noted above, the center's operation was originally based on an agreement between the government and the Methodist Mission. The mission agreed to provide the doctor and nurses in charge, while the government covered all other expenses. PRO, CO 96/674/4: J. C. Maxwell, Officer Administering the Government, to L. S. Amery, Colonial Office, dd. Accra 4 May 1927; Harry Webster, WMMS, to Colonial Secretary, dd. Accra, 9 February 1927; E. O. Thompson, WMMS, to Secretary of State for the Colonies, dd. London, 12 July 1927. To this day, the center continues to rely heavily on non-governmental support to carry out its day-to-day operations. Allman: Dr. Irene Des Bordes, Principal Medical Officer in Charge of the Maternal and Child Health Clinic, Kumasi, 18 June 1992.

79. Note, for example, that in the year 1930–1931, of the 150 maternity cases treated at the African Hospital, 50 required surgery and the maternal mortality rate was 14 percent. There was no special accommodation for obstetrical work in the hospital. There was no labor ward. PRO, CO 98/58: Gold Coast, "Reports on the Eastern and Western Provinces of Ashanti for 1930–1931."

80. PRO, CO 98/53: Gold Coast, "Report on Ashanti for the Year 1928–1929." The figure for visits records the total number of attendances, not the number of women who attended.

81. PRO, CO 98/58: Gold Coast, "Report on the Medical Department for the Year 1930–1931."

82. PRO, CO 96/705/10: Alice Piegrome to Dr. Stanton, Colonial Office, dd. Accra, 16 June 1932.

83. PRO, CO 96/705/10: "Minutes of the First Meeting of the Central Committee of the Gold Coast Branch, British Red Cross Society," dd. Accra, 11 June 1932.

84. NAGK, ARA/2053: P. S. Selwyn-Clarke to Chief Commissioner H. S. Newlands, dd. Accra, 13 February 1932. Newlands declined to become director because he felt the organization should be "based on and controlled by persons mainly representative of the people who would be benefitted by and directly concerned in it." He argued that an "official organisation in which . . . holders of high office appear in varied ranks in the controlling body at once awakens among the Africans a feeling that it is but a new form of governmental activity and therefore one in which private effort is not the factor which can, alone, command the success of the venture." See NAGK, ARA/2053: Newlands to Selwyn-Clarke, dd. Kumasi, 20 February 1932. Major F.W.F. Jackson, Newlands' assistant, became the Asante branch president.

85. BRCS, Eleventh Annual Report of the Gold Coast Branch and *Reports of the British Red Cross Society* (published), 1934; PRO, CO 96/705/10: "Minutes of the First Meeting of the BRCS," and P. S. Selwyn-Clarke, Secretary of BRCS, Gold Coast Branch to Colonial Secretary, Accra, dd. Accra 28 June 1932; CO 98/60: "Annual Report on the Social and Economic Progress of the People of the Gold Coast, 1931–1932; Report on the Medical Department for the Year 1931–32"; CO 98/62 and 65: Gold Coast, "Report on the Medical Department for the Year 1932–1933 and Report on the Medical Department for the Year 1933–1934." The Christiansborg Welfare Centre was handed over to a private physician in 1931, and the medical officers in charge of the clinics in Sekondi and Cape Coast were retrenched in that same year. The Red Cross subsequently took over management of both of these clinics. The government continued to maintain the centers at Accra, Kumasi, and Koforidua but relied on the Red Cross for voluntary and salaried workers in connection with domiciliary visiting and baby weighing in Kumasi and Accra.

86. BRCS, Third Annual Report of the Gold Coast Branch for the Year 1935. There were 33 Links groups in the Gold Coast by 1935.

87. PRO, CO 98/60: "Report on the Medical Department for the Year 1931–1932." The Red Cross Society continued to maintain these clinics long after the end of World War II. On several occasions, the BRCS leadership in Britain expressed concern that maternal and child welfare work had not been returned to the government. The transfer, in fact, did not occur until after independence. See BRCS, Correspondence: Lady Limerick to L. G. Eddey, Chief Medical Officer, dd. London, 6 April 1954; L. G. Eddey to Lady Limerick, dd. Accra, 11 June 1954; and Lady Limerick to Dr. G. Watt, Acting Chair of the Gold Coast BRCS, dd. London 28 June 1955.

88. Steven Feierman, "Struggles for Control: The Social Roots of Health and Healing in Modern Africa," *ASR* 28:2/3 (1985), 123. In 1938, the government began to consider the extension of some maternal and infant welfare programs to rural areas. See PRO, CO 96/752/12: W. M. Howells, Acting Director of Health Service, "Welfare Work among Women and Children in the Backward Rural Areas," dd. 12 August 1938 (enclosed in Gold Coast No. 540 of 12 August 1938).

89. PRO, CO 98/53: Gold Coast, "Report on Ashanti for the Year 1928–1929."

90. NAGK, ARA/134: Acting Commissioner, Eastern Province, Ashanti, Kumasi, "Confidential Diary for May 1929."

91. Ibid.

92. BRCS, First Annual Report of the Gold Coast Branch for the Year 1933.

93. BRCS, *Reports of the British Red Cross Society* (published), 1933.

94. Allman: Mary Antwi, Kumasi, 8 June 1992; Adwoa Brago, Kumasi, 2 June 1992; Adwoa Poku, Kumasi, 3 June 1992; Efua Samata, Kumasi, 3 June 1992. Based upon his research during the 1945–46 Ashanti Social Survey, Fortes wrote that "only about a third of all married women reside with their husbands." See Fortes, "Kinship and Marriage," 262.

95. PRO, CO 98/82: Gold Coast, "Report on the Medical Department for the Year 1947."

96. Gold Coast, Midwives Ordinance, No. 8 of 1931. Paragraph 5 deals with "unqualified midwives." Cf. Summer's description of the training, registration, and regulation of midwives in Uganda in "Intimate Colonialism," 799–807 passim.

97. PRO, CO 96/700:12: "Report on the Midwives Ordinance, 1931." For example, in 1937 12,489 antenatal visits were made to the center, yet only 405 babies were delivered by certified midwife (that is, by one of the two!). Although we do not know how many attendances represented repeat visits by the same woman, it is obvious that most women who attended the antenatal clinic did not or could not be delivered by certified midwife. See PRO, CO 98/71: Gold Coast, "Report on the Medical Department for the Year 1937."

98. Allman: Ama Konadu, Kumasi, 9 June 1992.

99. PRO, CO 98/58: Gold Coast, "Report on the Medical Department for the Year 1930–1931."

100. Ibid.

101. Rhodes House Library, Oxford: Mss.Afr.s.1402, J. B. Kirk Papers, "Some General Considerations Arising out of the Tours of Certain Parts of the Gold Coast, Made by the Director of Medical Services between 5 January and 23 September 1942."

102. Ibid.

103. Clearly this response was not unique to Asante. Most recently, see Carol Summers, "'If You Can Educate the Native Woman . . .': Debates over the Schooling and Education of Girls and Women in Southern Rhodesia, 1900–1934," *History of Education Quarterly* 36:4 (1996), 449–71.

104. MMS, WW, E. W. Thompson, "The West African Adventure," *Woman's Work* (July 1928), 341–42.

105. MMS, WW, F. Deaville Walker, "Africa's Womanhood—Then and Now," *Woman's Work* (October 1934), 176.

106. PRO, CO 96/673/8: Harry Webster to F. Gordon Guggisberg, dd. Accra, 15 February 1927.

107. MMS, Women's Work Collection [hereafter, WW], "Annual Report of the Women's Auxiliary, 1928."

108. MMS, WW, Correspondence, Africa, Missionaries: P. Beer to D. Leith, dd. Kumasi, 6 April 1930.

109. MMS, WW, Correspondence, Africa, Chairman: H. Webster to D. Leith, dd. Accra, 3 March 1932 and D. Leith to H. Webster, dd. London, 14 December 1931.

110. MMS, WW, Reports, Africa: "Mmofraturo Report, 1940." According to this report, in its first ten years Mmofraturo trained 70 students. Over the same period, 186 children attended the primary school.

111. MMS, WW, Correspondence, Africa, Chairman: "Official Report upon the Kumasi Mmofraturo Girls' School," Kumasi, 6 June 1932; and MMS, West Africa Synod, Gold Coast: "Report of Sub-Committee on Women's Work, 1931."

112. MMS, WW, Correspondence, Africa, Chairman: "Official Report upon the Kumasi Mmofraturo Girls' School," Kumasi, 6 June 1932.

113. See, for example, Nancy Hunt, "Colonial Fairy Tales," 158–59; LaRay Denzer, "Domestic Science Training in Colonial Yorubaland, Nigeria," in Hansen, ed., *African Encounters*, 118–20; Musisi, "Colonial and Missionary Education," 174–75 and 181–82; Schmidt, *Peasants,* 134; Summers, "'If You Can Educate.'"

114. MMS, WMMS, West Africa Synod, Gold Coast: "Report on Mbofraturo, Kumasi, Synod 1931."

115. MMS, WW: "Annual Report of the Women's Department, 1934."

116. MMS, WW, Persis Beer, "Beginnings," *Woman's Work* (October 1933), 82.

117. MMS, WMMS, West Africa Synod, Gold Coast: "Official Report on Mbofraturo, Kumasi, 1933."

118. MMS, WW, Correspondence, Africa, Missionaries: P. Beer to Miss Walton, dd. Mmofraturo, 29 January 1942.

119. Beer, "Beginnings," 82.

120. MMS, WW, Correspondence, Africa, Chairman: "Official Report upon the Kumasi Mbofraturo Girls' School," dd. Kumasi, 6 June 1932.

121. Allman: Mary Anokye, Old Tafo, 19 June 1992.

122. As Christine Oppong and Katharine Abu have written, "a notable feature of Ghanaian motherhood is the extent to which childcare responsibilities are delegated to non-parental kin and others, thus alleviating the potentially heavy burdens of care which might otherwise need to be borne by the biological mother." See "The Changing Maternal Role of Ghanaian Women: Impacts of Education, Migration and Employment," *Working Paper 143* (Geneva: International Labour Office, 1984), 45–46. For a broader discussion of nonparental caregivers and biological motherhood, see Faye Ginsburg and Rayna Rapp, "Politics of Reproduction," *Annual Review of Anthropology* 20 (1991), 327–29.

123. Allman: Agnes Ama Dapah, Tafo, 22 June 1992.

124. MMS, WW, Correspondence, Africa, Missionaries: Persis Beer, "Memorandum on Women's Work in the Gold Coast" (no date, but probably September 1938). The mission was quite concerned with the fate of its young women graduates in the late 1930s and early 1940s. Beer recommended the establishment of "post-standard VII classes for domestic and vocational work" and "of educational centres of the YWCA type." In 1940 the Women's Work Committee of the synod recommended special training in laundry or cooking so that graduates could work in institutions. In 1941, the synod appointed a subcommittee to examine the question of women's work in the Gold Coast; the subcommittee further recommended additional training to prepare young women to become domestic workers. See MMS, WW, Reports, Africa: Women's Work Committee, Synod 1940, "Extract from the Minutes," and "Report of Women's Work Sub-Committee, 1941." The fear that educated girls would become prostitutes was not limited to the Gold Coast. See, for example, Schmidt, *Peasants,* 140–41.

125. MMS, WW, Correspondence, Africa, Missionaries: Elsie Lince, "Work among the Women of Ashanti," 1932.

126. MMS, WW, Reports, Africa: "Report on Women's Work for 1934."

127. MMS, WW, Reports Africa: "Mmofraturo Report, 1934." Schmidt describes a similar scene in *Peasants*, 149.

128. Allman: Afua Manu, Tafo, 25 June 1992; Rose Afrakoma, Tafo, 25 June 1992.

129. Allman: Yaa Pokuaa, Tafo, 25 June 1992.

130. Allman: Mary Oduro, Effiduasi, 25 August 1992.

131. Allman: Efuah Nsuah, Tafo, 24 June 1992.

132. Allman: Rose Afrakoma, Tafo, 25 June 1992.

133. Allman: Adwoa Mansah, Tafo, 25 June 1992.

134. Allman: Agnes Ama Dapah, Tafo, 22 June 1992.

135. Allman: Akua Kankroma, Tafo, 23 June 1992.

136. Allman: Adwoa Tana, Tafo, 23 June 1992.

137. Allman: Adwoa Nsiah, Tafo, 29 June 1992.

138. Allman: Afua Manu, Tafo, 25 June 1992.

139. Allman: Mary Anokye, Old Tafo, 19 June 1992.

140. Allman: Rose Afrakoma, Tafo, 25 June 1992.

141. WMMS, WW, Correspondence, Africa Missionaries: I. Mason to Miss Walton, dd. Mmofraturo, 24 October 1937.

142. According to the 1933 report of its marriage committee, the synod recognized both native and ordinance marriages, but it expected all marriages to be Christian. While ministers were required to be married under the ordinance, other officers of the church could be married according to custom, but they had to have a "Public Marriage Blessing Service." However the marriage was "contracted," it was "a condition of Church membership that the Scriptural principle of monogamy and lifelong fidelity be obeyed." WMMS, West Africa Synod, Gold Coast: "Report of Marriage Sub-Committee, 1933." Of the 80 women Allman interviewed in 1992, many of whom had been married more than once, only four had had church weddings, while six had had a marriage that was blessed in the church. Margaret Etwiano's experience suggests that some Asantes viewed a "blessed" marriage as one that was Christian and yet not monogamous. Etwiano described the blessing as a formal ceremony in which her husband insisted "that he came to marry me and he was solely concerned with marrying me, but he had the right to marry more. . . . Initially, I was the only wife, and after my delivery I went to church and thanked God and I gave out some money and it was then that I received the blessing. . . . One other reason, too, why I received the blessing at church was I was then promoted in the church, and it was required that my husband always stand by me for them to realize that I actually didn't engage in premarital sex, that I had a clean record. That's why my husband was there." After Etwiano's marriage was blessed and she had become an active member of the church, her husband left the church and took several other wives. Etwiano's position in the church was not affected by this turn of events. Allman: Margaret Etwiano, Asokore, 26 August 1992.

143. MMS, WW, Correspondence, Africa, Missionaries: K. White to Miss Walton, dd. Kumasi, 17 June 1941.

144. MMS, WW, Correspondence, Africa, Missionaries: K. White to Miss Walton, dd. Kumasi, 31 January 1942. Cf. Davin, "Imperialism and Motherhood," 54.

145. Allman: Victoria Adjaye, Effiduasi, 25 August 1992. The third person singular in Akan does not differentiate gender.

146. Allman: Jean Asare, Effiduasi, 24 August 1992; Kate Baa, Effiduasi, 21 August, 1992; Rosina Boama, Effiduasi, 24 August 1992.

147. Allman: Kate Baa, Effiduasi, 21 August, 1992.

148. Persis Beer's final departure from the missionary service is somewhat mysterious. She was placed on "special leave" in Accra in August 1942 but never returned to Mmofraturo after that time. Her name does not appear among those listed as retiring in issues of *Woman's Work* (from 1945 to 1960).

149. MMS, WW, Chairman's Correspondence, Gold Coast: G. Ash to Miss Walton, dd. Kumasi, 18 July 1948.

150. Jean and John Comaroff, "Home-Made Hegemony: Modernity, Domesticity, and Colonialism in Southern Africa," in Hansen, ed., *African Encounters*, 67.

151. Ibid.

152. Karl Marx, "The Eighteenth Brumaire of Louis Bonaparte," in Marx and Frederick Engels, *Selected Works* (New York: International Publishers, 1977), 97.

153. Allman: Beatrice Nyarko, Effiduasi, 24 August 1992.

154. Allman: Adwoa Addae, Effiduasi, 28 August 1992.

155. Allman: Adwoa Addae, Effiduasi, 28 August 1992.

BY WAY OF CONCLUDING

In chapter 5 we witnessed the ways in which indirect rule and Christian missions worked as twin forces to address the chaos in gender relations that shook Asante in the interwar years. It was chaos born of an expanding cash economy and of women's concerted efforts to secure and defend a place for themselves in that economy. But for us to end on such a note seems discordant. The life stories embedded in that same chapter, as well as those recounted in preceding ones, were certainly not stories of Asante women's historic defeat[1] but of a generation's economic and political acumen, its tenacity, strength, and resilience. As we consider these two narrative counter-strands and the texture they bring to the social fabric of Asante's past, we must recall Frederick Cooper's important admonition, "[t]hat the violence of colonizers" can be considered "no less violent for the narrowness of its range and the limits of its transformative efficacy."[2] This generation's stories of resilience and struggle remain, at one and the same time, stories of shifting obligations and growing responsibilities. Women of Asante's first colonized generation did not simply walk away from fidelity ordinances, from episodes like the "spinster round-ups," from their divorces (however arbitrated), or from the host of native courts set up by British colonial rule as long-term victors in the struggle for control over their labor, especially their labor as wives and mothers. As we have seen, the spaces they negotiated for themselves in the colonial economy were narrow at best, fleeting at worst and required constant, ever-evolving strategies of defense. Indeed, in the course of one generation, despite those careful strategies, women found the burden of social reproduction—a burden their mothers and grandmothers had earlier shared via a complex web of fluid social relationships between matrilineal and conjugal

units—falling increasingly on their shoulders alone. Perhaps this is why
so many from the first colonized generation, as they reflected with us on
their lives as wives and mothers, concluded that the roads they had traveled were far more treacherous than those trodden by their own mothers
and grandmothers. "Mine was more difficult," remembered Akosua Addae.
"In my mother's day, they were taking things free of charge. They weren't
buying anything. You didn't need money."[3]

And yet the life stories of Asante women who came of age with cocoa and
colonial rule defy not only the totalizing narratives of the state and of political elites but also the chronologies that have dominated much of the historiography of this part of West Africa—chronologies of production and reproduction, of trade, of travel and urbanization, of politics, state power, and
Christian conversion. They certainly challenge notions of a singular "colonial moment" or a monolithic "colonial impact." Indeed, "colonialism" seems
to fracture when it is reflected as lived experience in the reminiscences of
old women and men. It appears disaggregated—episodic and uneven, gendered
and generational. But it is precisely because colonialism is rendered non-
totalizing in these life stories that we are better able to understand its meanings, the ways it was refracted in people's daily lives. We can more effectively perceive just how broader economic and political forces—for example,
cash cropping, production for the market, monetization, native courts, mission schools—recast the domestic terrain of conjugal production and reproduction, both before and after 1900, and how, in turn, ordinary women and
men negotiated, sometimes successfully, sometimes not, that ever-shifting
landscape.

By looking across the great divide between a "precolonial" and "colonial"
past, we traverse the intellectual deadzone. We are able to detect continuity
where, by appearances and labels anyway, there appears to be dramatic change,
and to locate change in apparent continuity. Thus, for example, we find the
subordinate categories of "slave" and "pawn"—rather than being effectively
abolished—simply rendered invisible, collapsed into the categories of "wife"
and "child," as the power of the husband/father was remade in ways that
eerily mirrored the authority of the nineteenth-century Asante pawn-holder.[4]
At the same time, we are able to see how the historic mutability of Asante
custom or customary law, wherein continuity embodied change, gave way in
the interwar years to stasis—but again, in patterns that were uneven and
unpredictable.

It is the stories of this first colonized generation, stories that disaggre-
gate "colonialism" and upset its pervasive chronologies, that present a
number of challenges to historians of Asante and Ghana. Perhaps above
all, they challenge us to flesh out the alternative chronologies embedded
in the life stories of commoners—women and men alike. We have only

hinted at some of those broader alternative chronologies here. Much remains to be done. We need to consider in far greater detail, for example, the gendered meanings of the abolition of the slave trade and the rise of legitimate commerce—meanings that clearly reverberated in the lives of those born nearly a century later. We need to gender chronologies of conversion and Christianity, which for men of this generation seemed intimately connected, initially anyway, to concerns regarding employment and upward mobility, and for women to concerns surrounding health and fertility. And perhaps most crucially, we need to consider the long-term consequences of women's marginalization from colonial politics and political discourse. If the historical record is beginning to more accurately reflect the centrality of women to economic change in the nineteenth and twentieth centuries, women's crucial roles in reshaping the productive, reproductive, and distributive landscape of Asante, it has not even begun to measure the social and political costs of an indirect rule that pushed women to the margins, an indirect rule that, aiming at restoring moral order, remapped the terrain of patriarchal power in colonial Asante.

But as we begin to address questions like these, historians of women and gender in Asante and Ghana will have much to contribute to broader efforts, both in Africa and in the West, that are aimed at understanding transnational processes of exploitation, subordination, and marginalization. We will begin to draw some meaningful conclusions about the ways in which these processes—whether of imperialist economic exploitation or of Eurocentric discourses of conjugality and domesticity—have worked over the course of the last two centuries to erode women's economic autonomy and increase women's work burdens across the African continent.[5]

When the historical focus is limited to male political elites, the common, transnational processes often remain obscure. The story of European colonialisms in Africa becomes one of striking contrasts—the fate of Asantehene Agyeman Prempe I, for example, measured against that of Lobengula or Mirambo. But when one aims the historical spotlight on commoner women, on work obligations, on the shifting burdens of social reproduction, one cannot help but be struck by the commonalities in experiences. Whether Shona, Asante, Luo, Igbo, or Zulu, despite the range of "colonialisms"—whether there was intensive labor migration or not, whether there were white settlers and plantations or peasant cash cropping, whether there was matrilineal or patrilineal descent—African women's status declined, work burdens increased, and safety nets disappeared, as women bore increasing responsibility, across the continent, for social reproduction.

Indeed, it is striking that one of the most powerful recent statements on colonial commonalities, on the salience of "a decentralized despotism" across the continent and the myth of South African exceptionalism, has very little to say about women or gender.[6] Yet if the work of women's historians over the past decades has anything to contribute to this compelling argument—an argument that has important ramifications in terms of both theory and praxis[7]—it is that gender is absolutely fundamental to transcolonial/transnational/globalizing processes. This is no small point. These are not processes that ended with decolonization. Indeed, many would argue that, with structural adjustment and IMF-sponsored privatization schemes, they have actually accelerated. That was certainly the opinion of many in that first colonized generation who shared their stories with us. If they were nearly unanimous in arguing that they faced more difficulties and uncertainties than did their mothers and grandmothers, they were equally convinced that their own daughters and granddaughters now faced nearly insurmountable odds. As Adwoa Addae explained, "Those days are better than these days. In those days women could work hard and get a lot of things they wanted. But today it is not like that. Even if you try to assert some form of independence, it doesn't work like it used to work."[8]

But to their daughters and granddaughters, women of this first colonized generation have bequeathed an invaluable legacy—a legacy with which subsequent generations face those near insurmountable odds. Through their ongoing struggles to secure and defend their economic autonomy, that first generation made an indelible imprint on the historical record—despite colonizing discourses aimed at erasing them. They have left no doubt that women made history in colonial Asante; they were not just victims of it. The stories we have heard here—of marriages and divorces, of parents and children, of spinsters and widows, of pancakes, biscuits, and bathing basins—do not simply evidence the gendered authority of commoner men, the power of colonial chiefs, or the mundane salience of a colonial "civilizing mission." They also stand as testament to the success and resourcefulness of a generation of Asante women in negotiating the harsh terrain of cash, cocoa, and colonialism.

NOTES

1. On the "historic defeat" of women, see Mamdani, *Citizen and Subject*, 41; and Amadiume, "Gender, Political Systems and Social Movements." See also Ifi Amadiume's *Reinventing Africa: Matriarchy, Religion and Culture* (London: Zed Books, 1997).

2. Frederick Cooper, "Conflict and Connection: Rethinking African Colonial History," *American Historical Review* 99:5 (1994), 1545.

3. Allman: Akosua Addae, Asokore, 26 August 1992.

4. Not to mention the nineteenth-century British patriarch.

5. In this regard, the publication by CODESRIA [Council for the Development of Economic and Social Research in Africa] of the proceedings of its 1991 conference on gender marks a significant watershed, as it posits an agenda for gendered research in the coming millennium. See Ayesha Imam, Amina Mama, and Fatou Sow, eds., *Engendering the African Social Sciences* (Dakar: CODESRIA, 1997).

6. Mamdani, *Citizen and Subject*.

7. This is powerfully demonstrated in Ifi Amadiume's recent collection. See Amadiume, *Reinventing Africa*, especially 1–26 and 109–43.

8. Allman: Adwoa Addae, Effiduasi, 30 June 1993.

BIBLIOGRAPHY

PUBLISHED WORKS

Abu, Katharine. "The Separateness of Spouses: Conjugal Resources in an Ashanti Town." In *Female and Male in West Africa*, ed. Christine Oppong, 153–68. London: Allen and Unwin, 1983.

Adomako-Sarfoh, J. "Migrant Asante Cocoa Farmers and Their Families." *Legon Family Research Papers* 1 (Legon, Ghana: Institute of African Studies, University of Ghana, 1974), 129–44.

Afshar, Haleh, ed. *Women, State, and Ideology: Studies from Africa and Asia*. Albany: State University of New York Press, 1987.

Agbodeka, Francis. *Ghana in the Twentieth Century*. Accra: Ghana Universities Press, 1972.

Agyeman-Duah, Joseph. *Mamponten Stool History*. Legon, Ghana: Institute of African Studies, University of Ghana, 1963.

Aidoo, Agnes Akosua. "Asante Queen Mothers in Government and Politics in the Nineteenth Century." In *The Black Woman Cross-Culturally*, ed. Filomina Chioma Steady, 65–77. Rochester, VT: Schenkman, 1981.

———. "Women in the History and Culture of Ghana." *Research Review* (new series) 1:1 (1985), 14–51.

Akyeampong, Emmanuel. *Drink, Power and Cultural Change: A Social History of Alcohol in Ghana, c. 1800 to Recent Times*. Portsmouth, NH: Heinemann, 1996.

———. "Sexuality and Prostitution among the Akan of the Gold Coast c. 1650–1950." *Past and Present* 156 (1997), 144–73.

Akyeampong, Emmanuel, and Pashington Obeng. "Spirituality, Gender, and Power in Asante History." *International Journal of African Historical Studies* 28:3 (1995), 481–99.

Allman, Jean M. "Adultery and the State in Asante: Reflections on Gender, Class and Power from 1800 to 1950." In *The Cloth of Many Colored Silks: Papers on History and Society, Ghanaian and Islamic, in Honor of Ivor Wilks*, ed. John Hunwick and Nancy Lawler, 27–65. Evanston, IL: Northwestern University Press, 1996.

———. "Be(com)ing Asante, Be(com)ing Akan: Thoughts on Gender, Identity and the Colonial Encounter." In *Ethnicity in Ghana*, ed. Carola Lentz and Paul Nugent. London: Macmillan, forthcoming.

———. "Fathering, Mothering and Making Sense of *Ntamoba:* Reflections on the Economy of Child-Rearing in Colonial Asante." *Africa* 67:2 (1997), 296–321.

———. "Making Mothers: Missionaries, Medical Officers and Women's Work in Colonial Asante, 1924–1945." *History Workshop Journal* 38 (1994), 23–48.

———. "Of 'Spinsters,' 'Concubines' and 'Wicked Women': Reflections on Gender and Social Change in Colonial Asante." *Gender and History* 3:2 (1991), 176–89.

———. "Rounding Up Spinsters: Gender Chaos and Unmarried Women in Colonial Asante." *Journal of African History* 37:2 (1996), 195–214.

Allott, Anthony. "The Development of the East African Legal Systems during the Colonial Period." In *History of East Africa*, ed. D. A. Low and Alison Smith, 348–82. Oxford: Clarendon Press, 1976.

Alpers, Edward. "The Story of Swema: Female Vulnerability in Nineteenth Century East Africa." In *Women and Slavery in Africa*, ed. Claire Robertson and Martin Klein, 185–219. Madison: University of Wisconsin Press, 1983.

Amadiume, Ifi. "Gender, Political Systems and Social Movements: A West African Experience." In *African Studies in Social Movements,* ed. M. Mamdani and E. Wamba-dia-Wamba. Dakar: CODESRIA, 1995.

———. *Reinventing Africa: Matriarchy, Religion and Culture*. London: Zed Books, 1997.

Ampofu, Akosua Adomako. "Controlling and Punishing Women: Violence against Ghanaian Women." *Review of African Political Economy* 56 (1993), 102–10.

Ardayfio-Schandorf, Elizabeth, and Kate Kwafo-Akoto. *Women in Ghana: An Annotated Bibliography*. Accra: Woeli Publishing Services for United Nations Population Fund, 1990.

Arhin, Kwame. "The Ashanti Rubber Trade with the Gold Coast in the Eighteen-Nineties." *Africa* 42:1 (1972), 33–43.

———. "Aspects of the Ashanti Northern Trade in the Nineteenth Century." *Africa* 40:4 (1970), 363–73.

———. *The City of Kumasi: Past, Present and Future*. Legon, Ghana: Institute of African Studies, University of Ghana, 1992.

———. "The Economic and Social Significance of Rubber Production and Exchange on the Gold and Ivory Coasts, 1880–1900." *Cahiers d'Etudes Africaines,* 57/58 (1980), 49–62.

———. *The Expansion of Cocoa Production: The Working Conditions of Migrant Cocoa Farmers in the Central and Western Regions*. Legon, Ghana: Institute of African Studies, University of Ghana, 1985.

———. "Gold-mining and Trading among the Ashanti of Ghana." *Journal des Africanistes* 48:1 (1978), 89–100.

———. "Market Settlements in Northwest Ashanti: Kintampo." *Research Review, Ashanti and the North-west Supplement* (1965), 135–55.

———. "Monetization and the Asante State." In *Money Matters: Instability, Values and Social Payments in the Modern History of West African Communities*, ed. Jane Guyer, 97–110. Portsmouth, NH: Heinemann, 1995.

———. "A Note on the Asante *Akonkofo*: A Non-Literate Sub-Elite, 1900–1930." *Africa* 56:1 (1986), 25–31.

———. "On the Hwesoni, Caretaker, Category of Land Holding in Ahafo Land Tenure." *Research Review* 2:1 (1965), 68–72.

———. "Peasants in 19th-Century Asante." *Current Anthropology* 24:4 (1983), 471–80.

———. "The Political and Military Roles of Akan Women." In *Female and Male in West Africa*, ed. Christine Oppong, 91–98. London: Allen and Unwin, 1983.

———. "The Pressure of Cash and Its Political Consequences in Asante in the Colonial Period." *Journal of African Studies* 3:4 (1976), 453–68.

———. "Rank and Class Among the Asante and Fante in the Nineteenth Century." *Africa* 53:1 (1983), 2–22.

———. "Savannah Contributions to the Asante Political Economy." In *The Golden Stool: Studies of the Asante Centre and Periphery*, ed. Enid Schildkrout, 51–59. New York: Anthropological Papers of the American Museum of Natural History, 1987.

———. "Some Asante Views of Colonial Rule: As Seen in the Controversy Relating to Death Duties." *Transactions of the Historical Society of Ghana* 15:1 (1974), 63–84.

———. "State Intervention in the Asante Economy." *Universitas* (new series) 3:3 (1970), 33–44.

——— "The Structure of Greater Ashanti (1700–1820)." *Journal of African History* 8:1 (1967), 65–85.

———. "Succession and Gold Mining at Manso-Nkwanta." *Research Review* 6:3 (1970), 101–12.

———. "Trade, Accumulation and the State in Asante in the Nineteenth Century." *Africa* 60:4 (1990), 524–37.

Austin, Dennis. *Politics in Ghana, 1946–1960*. London: Oxford University Press, 1964.

Austin, Gareth. "Between Abolition and *Jihad*: The Asante Response to the Ending of the Atlantic Slave Trade, 1807–1896." In *From Slave Trade to "Legitimate" Commerce: The Commercial Transition in Nineteenth Century West Africa*, ed. Robin Law, 93–118. Cambridge: Cambridge University Press, 1995.

———. "Capitalists and Chiefs in the Cocoa Hold-Ups in South Asante, 1927–1938." *International Journal of African Historical Studies* 21:1 (1988), 63–95.

———. "The Emergence of Capitalist Relations in South Asante Cocoa-Farming, c. 1916–33." *Journal of African History* 28:2 (1987), 259–79.

———. "Human Pawning in Asante, 1800–1950: Markets and Coercion, Gender and Cocoa." In *Pawnship in Africa: Debt Bondage in Historical Perspective*, ed. T. Falola and P. Lovejoy, 121–59. Boulder, CO: Westview Press, 1994.

———. "Indigenous Credit Institutions in West Africa, c1750–c1960." In *Local Suppliers of Credit in the Third World, 1750–1960*, ed. Gareth Austin and Kaoru Sugihara, 93–159. New York: St. Martin's Press, 1993.

———. "Mode of Production or Mode of Cultivation: Explaining the Failure of European Cocoa Planters in Competition with African Farmers in Colonial Ghana." In *Cocoa Pioneer Fronts since 1800*, ed. W. Clarence-Smith, 154–75. Basingstoke, England: Macmillan, 1996.

———. "'No Elders Were Present': Commoners and Private Ownership in Asante, 1807–96." *Journal of African History* 37:1 (1996), 1–30.

Austin, Gareth, and Kaoru Sugihara, eds. *Local Suppliers of Credit in the Third World, 1750–1960*. New York: St. Martin's Press, 1993.

Awusababo, Kofi. "Matriliny and the New Intestate Succession Law of Ghana." *Canadian Journal of African Studies* 24:1 (1990), 1–15.

Barnes, Teresa. "The Fight for Control of Women's Mobility in Colonial Zimbabwe, 1900–1939." *Signs* 17:3 (1992), 586–608.

———. *"We Women Worked So Hard": Social Reproduction in Colonial Harare, Zimbabwe, 1930–1956.* Portsmouth, NH: Heinemann, 1999.

Beecham, John. *Ashantee and the Gold Coast.* London: John Mason, 1841.

Beneria, Lourdes, ed. *Women and Development: The Sexual Division of Labor in Rural Societies.* New York: Praeger, 1980.

Bening, R. B. "Evolution of Administrative Boundaries of Ashanti, 1896–1951." *Journal of African Studies* 5:2 (1978), 123–49.

Berger, Iris, and Claire Robertson, eds. *Women and Class in Africa.* New York: Africana Publishing Company, 1986.

Berry, Sara. *No Condition Is Permanent: The Social Dynamics of Agrarian Change in Sub-Saharan Africa.* Madison: University of Wisconsin Press, 1993.

———. "Unsettled Accounts: Stool Debts, Chieftaincy Disputes and the Question of Asante Constitutionalism." *Journal of African History* 39:1 (1998), 39–62.

Bledsoe, Caroline. *Women and Marriage in Kpelle Society.* Stanford, CA: Stanford University Press, 1980.

Bleek, Wolf. "Did the Akan Resort to Abortion in Pre-Colonial Ghana? Some Conjectures." *Africa* 60:1 (1990), 121–31.

Bosman, William. *A New and Accurate Description of the Coast of Guinea, Divided into the Gold, the Slave, and the Ivory Coasts.* London: J. Knapton, 1705.

Bowdich, T. Edward. *Mission From Cape Coast Castle to Ashantee.* London: John Murray, 1819.

Bozzoli, Belinda, with Mmantho Nkotsoe. *Women of Phokeng: Consciousness, Life Strategy, and Migrancy in South Africa, 1900–1983.* Portsmouth, NH: Heinemann, 1991.

Bradford, Helen. "Women, Gender and Colonialism: Rethinking the History of the British Cape Colony and Its Frontier Zones, c. 1806–70." *Journal of African History* 37:3 (1996), 351–70.

Brydon, Lynne. "Women at Work: Some Changes in Family Structure in Amedzofe-Avatime, Ghana." *Africa* 49:2 (1979), 97–111.

Busia, K. A. *The Position of the Chief in the Modern Political System of Ashanti.* London: Frank Cass, 1968. First published 1951.

Casely-Hayford, J. E. *Gold Coast Native Institutions.* London: Sweet and Maxwell, 1903.

Chanock, Martin. *Law, Custom, and Social Order: The Colonial Experience in Malawi and Zambia.* Cambridge: Cambridge University Press, 1985.

———. "Making Customary Law: Men, Women and Courts in Colonial Northern Rhodesia." In *African Women and the Law: Historical Perspectives*, ed. Margaret Jean Hay and Marcia Wright, 53–67. Boston: Boston University Papers on Africa VII, 1982.

Chaudhuri, Nupur, and Margaret Strobel, eds. *Western Women and Imperialism.* Bloomington: Indiana University Press, 1992.

Christaller, J. G. *Dictionary of the Asante and Fante Language Called Tshi (Twi).* 2nd ed. Basel, Switzerland: Basel Evangelical Missionary Society, 1933.

Clark, Gracia. "Colleagues and Customers in Unstable Market Conditions: Kumasi, Ghana." *Ethnology* 30:1 (1991), 31–48.

———. "Money, Sex and Cooking: Manipulation of the Paid/Unpaid Boundary by Asante Market Women." In *The Social Economy of Consumption,* ed. Benjamin Orlove and Henry Rutz, 323–48. Lanham, MD: University Press of America, 1989.

———. *Onions Are My Husband: Survival and Accumulation by West African Market Women.* Chicago: University of Chicago Press, 1994.

———. "Separation Between Trading and Home for Asante Women in Kumasi Central Market, Ghana." In *The Household Economy: Reconsidering the Domestic Mode of Production,* ed. Richard R. Wilk, 91–118. Boulder, CO: Westview Press, 1989.

Colson, Elizabeth. "The Resilience of Matrilineality: Gwembe and Plateau Tonga Adaptations." In *The Versatility of Kinship: Essays Presented to Harry W. Basehart,* ed. Linda S. Cordell and Stephen Beckerman, 359–74. New York: Academic Press, 1980.

Comaroff, Jean, and John Comaroff. "Home-Made Hegemony: Modernity, Domesticity, and Colonialism in South Africa." In *African Encounters with Domesticity,* ed. Karen Tranberg Hansen, 37–74. New Brunswick, NJ: Rutgers University Press, 1992.

———. "The Management of Marriage in a Tswana Chiefdom." In *Essays on African Marriage in Southern Africa,* ed. Eileen Krige and John Comaroff, 29–49. Cape Town: Juta and Company, 1981.

Comaroff, John. "Preface." In *Essays on African Marriage in Southern Africa,* ed. Eileen Krige and John Comaroff. Cape Town: Juta and Company, 1981.

Cooper, Barbara. *Marriage in Maradi: Gender and Culture in a Hausa Society in Niger, 1900–1989.* Portsmouth, NH: Heinemann, 1997.

———. "Women's Worth and Wedding Gift Exchange in Maradi, Niger, 1907–1989." *Journal of African History* 36:1 (1995), 121–40.

Cooper, Frederick. "Conflict and Connection: Rethinking Colonial African History." *American Historical Review* 99:5 (1994), 1516–45.

Cordell, Linda S., and Stephen Beckerman, eds. *The Versatility of Kinship: Essays Presented to Harry W. Basehart.* New York: Academic Press, 1980.

Cox-George, N. A. *Studies in Finance and Development: The Gold Coast (Ghana) Experience, 1914–1950.* London: Dobson, 1973.

Cruickshank, Brodie. *Eighteen Years on the Gold Coast of Africa: Including an Account of the Native Tribes and Their Intercourse with Europeans.* 2 vols. London: Hurst and Blackett, 1853.

Daaku, Kwame Y. "Trade and Trading Patterns of the Akan in the Seventeenth and Eighteenth Centuries." In *The Development of Indigenous Trade and Markets in West Africa,* ed. Claude Meillassoux, 168–81. London: Oxford University Press, 1971.

Danquah, J. B. *Gold Coast: Akan Laws and Customs and the Akim Abuakwa Constitution.* London: Routledge, 1928.

Davin, Anna. "Imperialism and Motherhood." *History Workshop Journal* 5 (1978), 9–66.

Davison, Jean, and the women of Mutira. *Voices from Mutira: Lives of Rural Gikuyu Women.* Boulder, CO: Lynne Reinner, 1989.

de Moraes Farias, P. F. and Karin Barber, eds. *Self Assertion and Brokerage: Early Cultural Nationalism in West Africa.* Birmingham, England: Centre of West African Studies, 1990.

Denteh, A .C. "Birth Rites of the Akans." *Research Review* 3:1 (1966), 78–81.

———. "*Ntoro* and *Nton.*" *Research Review* 3:3 (1967), 91–96.

Denzer, LaRay. "Domestic Science Training in Colonial Yorubaland, Nigeria." In *African Encounters with Domesticity,* ed. Karen Tranberg Hansen, 116–42. New Brunswick, NJ: Rutgers University Press, 1992.

Dewey, Clive, and A. G. Hopkins, eds. *The Imperial Impact: Studies in the Economic History of Africa and India.* London: Athlone Press, 1978.

Dickson, K. B. "Origins of Ghana's Cocoa Industry." *Ghana Notes and Queries* 5 (1963), 4–9.

Dinan, Carmel. "Sugar Daddies and Gold Diggers: The White-Collar Single Woman in Accra." In *Female and Male in West Africa,* ed. Christine Oppong, 344–66. London: Allen and Unwin, 1983.

Douglas, Mary. "Is Matriliny Doomed in Africa?" In *Man in Africa,* ed. Mary Douglas and Phyllis M. Kaberry, 123–37. Garden City, NY: Anchor Books, 1971. First published 1969.

Douglas, Mary, and Phyllis M. Kaberry, eds. *Man in Africa.* Garden City, NY: Anchor Books, 1971. First published 1969.

Dumett, Raymond. "Precolonial Gold Mining and the State in the Akan Region: With a Critique of the Terray Hypothesis." *Research in Economic Anthropology* 2 (1979), 37–68.

———. "The Rubber Trade of the Gold Coast and Asante in the Nineteenth Century: African Innovation and Market Responsiveness." *Journal of African History* 12:1 (1971), 79–101.

Dumett, Raymond, and Marion Johnson. "Britain and the Suppression of Slavery in the Gold Coast Colony, Ashanti, and the Northern Territories." In *The End of Slavery in Africa,* ed. Suzanne Miers and Richard Roberts, 71–116. Madison: University of Wisconsin Press, 1988.

Dunn, John, and A. F. Robertson. *Dependence and Opportunity: Political Change in Ahafo.* Cambridge: Cambridge University Press, 1973.

Dupuis, Joseph. *Journal of a Residence in Ashantee.* London: Frank Cass, 1966; orig. pub., London: Henry Colburn, 1824.

Ekow-Daniels, W. C. "Problems in the Law Relating to the Maintenance and Support of Wives and Children." *Legon Family Research Papers* 1, (1974), 285–91.

Eldredge, Elizabeth. *A South African Kingdom: The Pursuit of Security in Nineteenth-Century Lesotho.* Cambridge: Cambridge University Press, 1993.

Ellis, A. B. *The Tshi-Speaking Peoples of the Gold Coast of West Africa.* London: Chapman and Hall, 1887.

Emecheta, Buchi. *The Joys of Motherhood.* London: Allison and Busby, 1979.

Engman, E.V.T. *Population of Ghana, 1850–1960.* Accra: Ghana Universities Press, 1986.

Falola, T., and P. Lovejoy, eds. *Pawnship in Africa: Debt Bondage in Historical Perspective.* Boulder, CO: Westview Press, 1994.

Feierman, Steven. "Struggles for Control: The Social Roots of Health and Healing in Modern Africa." *African Studies Review* 28:2/3 (1985), 73–147.

Field, M. J. *Akim-Kotoku: An Oman of the Gold Coast.* Accra: Crown Agents, 1948.

Fortes, Meyer. "The Ashanti Social Survey: A Preliminary Report." *Rhodes-Livingstone Journal* 6 (1948), 1–37.

———. "A Demographic Field Study in Ashanti." In *Culture and Human Fertility*, ed. Frank Lorimer. Paris: UNESCO, 1954.

———. *The Family: Bane or Blessing?* Accra: Ghana Universities Press, 1971.

———. "Kinship and Marriage among the Ashanti." In *African Systems of Kinship and Marriage*, ed. A. R. Radcliffe-Brown and Daryll Forde, 252–84. London: Oxford University Press, 1950.

———. "The Structure of Unilineal Descent Groups." *American Anthropology* 55 (1953), 17–41.

———. "The 'Submerged Descent Line' in Ashanti." In *Studies in Kinship and Marriage*, Occasional Papers of the Royal Anthropological Institute, ed. I. Schapera, 58–67. London: Royal Anthropological Institute, 1963.

———. "Time and Social Structure: An Ashanti Case Study." In *Time and Social Structure*, ed. Meyer Fortes, 1–32. New York: Humanities Press, 1970. Previously published in *Social Structure: Studies Presented to A.R. Radcliffe-Brown,* ed. Meyer Fortes, 54–84. Oxford: Oxford University Press, 1949.

Fortes, Meyer, R. W. Steel, and P. Ady. "Ashanti Survey, 1945–1946: An Experiment in Social Research." *Geographical Journal* 110 (1947), 149–79.

Fortes, Meyer, ed. *Social Structure: Studies Presented to A. R. Radcliffe-Brown.* Oxford: Oxford University Press, 1949.

———, ed. *Time and Social Structure.* New York: Humanities Press, 1970.

Freeman, Thomas B. *Journal of Two Visits to the Kingdom of Ashanti, in Western Africa.* London: J. Mason, 1844.

Friedman, J., and M. J. Rowlands, eds. *The Evolution of Social Systems: Proceedings of a Meeting of the Research Seminar in Archaeology and Related Subjects, London University.* Pittsburgh: Duckworth, 1977.

Fynn, John. *Asante and Its Neighbours, 1700–1897.* London: Longman, 1971.

Gaitskell, Deborah. "Devout Domesticity? A Century of African Women's Christianity in South Africa." In *Women and Gender in Southern Africa to 1945*, ed. Cherryl Walker, 251–72. Cape Town: David Philip, 1990.

Garrard, Timothy F. *Akan Weights and the Gold Trade.* London: Longman, 1980.

———. *Gold of Africa.* Geneva: Barbier-Mueller Museum and Munich: Prestel-Verlag, 1989.

Geiger, Susan. *TANU Women: Gender and Culture in the Making of Tanganyikan Nationalism, 1955–1965.* Portsmouth, NH: Heinemann, 1997.

———. "Women's Life Histories: Method and Content." *Signs* 11:3 (1986), 334–51.

Ginsburg, Faye and Rayna Rapp. "Politics of Reproduction." *Annual Review of Anthropology* 20 (1991), 311–43.

Gocking, Roger. "British Justice and the Native Tribunals of the Southern Gold Coast Colony." *Journal of African History* 34:1 (1993), 93–113.

———. "Competing Systems of Inheritance before the British Courts of the Gold Coast Colony." *International Journal of African Historical Studies* 23:4 (1990), 601–18.

Goody, Esther. *Parenthood and Social Reproduction: Fostering and Occupational Roles in West Africa.* Cambridge: Cambridge University Press, 1982.

Goody, Jack. *The Developmental Cycle in Domestic Groups.* Cambridge: Cambridge University Press, 1958.

Goody, Jack, and Joan Buckley. "Inheritance and Women's Labour in Africa." *Africa* 44:1 (1974), 108–21.

Gould, P. R. *The Development of the Transportation Pattern in Ghana.* Evanston, IL: Northwestern University Press, 1960.

Greene, Sandra. "A Perspective on African Women's History: Comment on 'Confronting Continuity.'" *Journal of Women's History* 9:3 (1997), 95–104.

Greenstreet, Miranda. "Social Change and Ghanaian Women." *Canadian Journal of African Studies* 6:2 (1972), 351–55.

Grier, Beverly. "Pawns, Porters, and Petty Traders: Women in the Transition to Cash Crop Agriculture in Colonial Ghana." *Signs* 17:2 (1992), 304–28.

———. "Underdevelopment, Modes of Production and the State in Colonial Ghana." *African Studies Review* 24:1 (1981), 21–47.

Gros, Jules. *Voyages, Aventures et Captivité de J. Bonnat Chez les Achantis.* Paris: E. Plon, Nourrit et Cie, 1884.

Gunnarsson, Christer. *The Gold Coast Cocoa Industry 1900–1939: Production, Prices and Structural Change.* Lund, Sweden: Economic History Association, 1978.

Guyer, Jane I. "Household and Community in African Studies." *African Studies Review* 14:2/3 (1981), 87–137.

———. "Wealth in People, Wealth in Things: Introduction." *Journal of African History* 36:1 (1995), 83–90.

———. "Women and the State in Africa: Marriage Law, Inheritance, and Resettlement." *Working Papers in African Studies 129.* Boston: Boston University, African Studies Center, 1987.

———. ed. *Money Matters: Instability, Values and Social Payments in the Modern History of West African Communities.* Portsmouth, NH: Heinemann, 1995.

Hailey, W. M. *Native Administration in the British African Territories: Part III, West Africa.* London: HMSO, 1951.

Hansen, Karen Tranberg, and Margaret Strobel. "Family History in Africa." *Trends in History* 3:3/4 (1985), 127–49.

Hansen, Karen Tranberg, ed. *African Encounters with Domesticity.* New Brunswick, NJ: Rutgers University Press, 1992.

Hay, Margaret Jean. "Luo Women and Economic Change during the Colonial Period." In *Women in Africa: Studies in Social and Economic Change,* ed. N. Hafkin and E. Bay, 87–109. Stanford, CA: Stanford University Press, 1976.

———. "Queens, Prostitutes and Peasants: Historical Perspectives on African Women, 1971–1986." *Canadian Journal of African Historical Studies* 22:3 (1988), 431–47.

Hay, Margaret Jean, and Marcia Wright, eds. *African Women and the Law: Historical Perspectives.* Boston: Boston University Papers on Africa VII, 1982.

Herskovits, Melville J. "The Ashanti *Ntoro*: A Re-Examination." *Journal of the Royal Anthropological Institute* 67 (1937), 287–96.

Hill, Polly. *Migrant Cocoa-Farmers of Southern Ghana.* Cambridge: Cambridge University Press, 1963.

———. "The West African Farming Household." In *Changing Social Structure in Ghana,* ed. Jack Goody, 119–36. London: International African Institute, 1975.

Hilton, Anne. "Family and Kinship among the Kongo South of the Zaire River from the Sixteenth to the Nineteenth Century." *Journal of African History* 24:2 (1983), 189–206.

Hobsbawm, Eric, and Terence Ranger, eds. *The Invention of Tradition*. Cambridge: Cambridge University Press, 1983.

Hodgson, Dorothy, and Sheryl McCurdy. "Wayward Wives, Misfit Mothers, and Disobedient Daughters: 'Wicked' Women and the Reconfiguration of Gender in Africa." *Canadian Journal of African Studies* 30:1 (1996), 1–9.

Hughes, Heather. "'A Lighthouse for African Womanhood': Inanda Seminary, 1869–1911." In *Women and Gender in Southern Africa to 1945*, ed. Cherryl Walker, 197–220. Cape Town: David Philip, 1990.

Hunt, Nancy. "'Le Bébé en Brousse': European Women, African Birth Spacing and Colonial Intervention in Breast Feeding in the Belgian Congo," *International Journal of African Historical Studies* 21:3 (1988), 401–32.

———. "Colonial Fairy Tales and the Knife and Fork Doctrine in the Heart of Africa." In *African Encounters with Domesticity*, ed. Karen Tranberg Hansen, 143–71. New Brunswick, NJ: Rutgers University Press, 1992.

———. "Domesticity and Colonialism in Belgian Africa: Usumbura's *Foyer Social*, 1946–1960." In *Ties That Bind: Essays on Mothering and Patriarchy*, ed. Jean O'Barr, Deborah Pope, and Mary Wyer, 149–77. Chicago: University of Chicago Press, 1990.

———. "Introduction," special issue on "Gendered Colonialisms in African History." *Gender and History* 8:3 (1996), 323–37.

———. "Noise over Camouflaged Polygamy, Colonial Morality Taxation, and a Woman-Naming Crisis in Belgian Africa." *Journal of African* History 32:3 (1991), 471–94.

———. "'Single Ladies on the Congo': Protestant Missionary Tensions and Voices." *International Women's Studies Forum* 13:4 (1990), 395–404.

Hunwick, John, and Nancy Lawler, eds. *The Cloth of Many Colored Silks: Papers on History and Society, Ghanaian and Islamic, in Honor of Ivor Wilks*. Evanston, IL: Northwestern University Press, 1996.

Imam, Ayesha, Amina Mama, and Fatou Sow, eds. *Engendering the African Social Sciences*. Dakar: CODESRIA, 1997.

Jeater, Diana. *Marriage, Perversion and Power: The Construction of Moral Discourse in Southern Rhodesia, 1894–1930*. Oxford: Oxford University Press, 1993.

Johnson, Marion. "The Slaves of Salaga." *Journal of African History* 27:3 (1986), 341–62.

Jones-Quartey, P. W. "The Effects of the Maintenance of Children Act on Akan and Ewe Notions of Paternal Responsibility." *Legon Family Research Papers* 1 (1974), 292–303.

Kay, G. B., ed. *The Political Economy of Colonialism in Ghana*. Cambridge: Cambridge University Press, 1972.

Kaye, Barrington. *Bringing Up Children in Ghana*. London: George Allen and Unwin, 1962.

Kea, Ray A. *Settlements, Trade and Polities in the Seventeenth Century Gold Coast*. Baltimore: Johns Hopkins University Press, 1982.

Kimble, David. *A Political History of Ghana: The Rise of Gold Coast Nationalism 1850–1928*. Oxford: Clarendon Press, 1963.

Kyei, Thomas E. *Marriage and Divorce among the Asante: A Study Undertaken in the Course of the Ashanti Social Survey (1945)*. Cambridge African Monographs 14. Cambridge: African Studies Centre, 1992.

Landau, Paul. *The Realm of the Word: Language, Gender, and Christianity in a Southern African Kingdom.* Portsmouth, NH: Heinemann, 1995.

Law, Robin, ed. *From Slave Trade to "Legitimate" Commerce: The Commercial Transition in Nineteenth Century West Africa.* Cambridge: Cambridge University Press, 1995.

Lentz, Carola, and Paul Nugent, eds. *Ethnicity in Ghana.* London: Macmillan, forthcoming.

Lerner, Gerda. "Motherhood in Historical Perspective." *Journal of Family History* 3:3 (1978), 297–301.

Lewin, Thomas. *Asante before the British: The Prempean Years, 1875–1900.* Lawrence: University of Kansas Press, 1978.

Lewis, Jane. *The Politics of Motherhood: Child and Maternal Welfare in England, 1900–1939.* London: Croom Helm, 1980.

Lovejoy, Paul E. "Concubinage and the Status of Women Slaves in Early Colonial Northern Nigeria." *Journal of African History* 29 (1988), 245–66.

Lovett, Margot. "Gender Relations, Class Formation and the Colonial State." In *Women and the State in Africa,* ed. Jane Parpart and Kathleen Staudt, 23–46. Boulder, CO: Lynne Rienner, 1989.

MacMillan, Allister, ed. *The Red Book of West Africa: Historical and Descriptive Commercial and Industrial Facts, Figures and Resources.* London: Frank Cass, 1968. First published 1920.

Mamdani, Mahmood. *Citizen and Subject: Contemporary Africa and the Legacy of Colonialism.* Princeton, NJ: Princeton University Press, 1996.

Mandala, Elias. "Peasant Cotton Agriculture, Gender and Inter-generational Relationships: The Lower Tchiri (Shire) Valley of Malawi, 1906–1940." *African Studies Review* 25:2/3 (1982), 27–44.

Mann, Kristin. *Marrying Well: Marriage, Status, and Social Change among the Educated Elite in Colonial Lagos.* Cambridge: Cambridge University Press, 1985.

Mann, Kristin, and Richard Roberts, eds. *Law in Colonial Africa.* Portsmouth, NH: Heinemann, 1991.

Manuh, Takyiwaa. "Changes in Marriage and Funeral Exchanges in Asante: A Case Study from Kona, Afigya-Kwabre." In *Money Matters: Instability, Values and Social Payments in the Modern History of West African Communities,* ed. Jane Guyer, 188–201. Portsmouth, NH: Heinemann, 1995.

———. "Wives, Children and Intestate Succession in Ghana." In *African Feminism: The Struggle for Survival in Sub-Saharan Africa,* ed. Gwendolyn Mikell, 77–95. Philadelphia: University of Pennsylvania Press, 1997.

Marks, Shula, and Richard Rathbone. "The History of the Family in Africa: Introduction." *Journal of African History* 24:2 (1983), 145–61.

Martinson, A.P.A. *Reverend Benjamin A. Martinson, 1870–1929.* Accra: Presbyterian Press, 1965.

Marx, Karl. "The Eighteenth Brumaire of Louis Bonaparte." In Karl Marx and Frederick Engels, *Selected Works.* New York: International Publishers, 1977.

Marx, Karl, and Frederick Engels. *Selected Works.* New York: International Publishers, 1977.

Matson, J. N. *A Digest of the Minutes of the Ashanti Confederacy Council from 1935 to 1949 Inclusive and a Revised Edition of Warrington's "Notes on Ashanti Custom*

Prepared for the Use of District Commissioners." Cape Coast, Ghana: Prospect Printing Press, n.d., but ca. 1951.

McCaskie, Thomas C. "Accumulation, Wealth and Belief in Asante History. I: To the Close of the Nineteenth Century." *Africa* 53:1 (1983), 23–43.

———. "Accumulation, Wealth and Belief in Asante History II: The Twentieth Century." *Africa* 56:1 (1986), 3–23.

———. "*Ahyiamu*—'A Place of Meeting': An Essay on Process and Event in the History of the Asante State." *Journal of African History* 25:2 (1984), 169–88.

———. "Anti-Witchcraft Cults in Asante: An Essay in the History of an African People." *History in Africa* 8 (1981), 125–54.

———. "Inventing Asante." In *Self Assertion and Brokerage: Early Cultural Nationalism in West Africa*, ed. P. F. de Moraes Farias and Karin Barber, 55–67. Birmingham, England: Centre of West African Studies, 1990.

———. "*Konnurokusεm*: Kinship and Family in the History of the *Oyoko Kɔkɔɔ* Dynasty of Kumase." *Journal of African History* 36:3 (1995), 357–89.

———. *State and Society in Pre-Colonial Asante*. Cambridge: Cambridge University Press, 1995.

———. "State and Society, Marriage and Adultery: Some Considerations toward a Social History of Pre-Colonial Asante." *Journal of African History* 22:4 (1981), 477–94.

Meillassoux, Claude, ed. *The Development of Indigenous Trade and Markets in West Africa*. London: Oxford University Press, 1971.

Meredith, David. "The Colonial Office, British Business Interests and the Reform of Cocoa Marketing in West Africa, 1937–1945." *Journal of African History* 29:3 (1988), 285–300.

Merry, Sally Engle. "The Articulation of Legal Spheres." In *African Women and the Law: Historical Perspectives*, ed. Margaret Jean Hay and Marcia Wright, 68–89. Boston: Boston University Papers on Africa VII, 1982.

Miers, Suzanne, and Richard Roberts, eds. *The End of Slavery in Africa*. Madison: University of Wisconsin Press, 1988.

Miescher, Stephan. "Of Documents and Litigants: Disputes on Inheritance in Abetifi, a Town of Colonial Ghana." *Journal of Legal Pluralism and Unofficial Law* 39 (1997), 81–119.

Mikell, Gwendolyn. *Cocoa and Chaos in Ghana*. New York: Paragon House, 1989.

———. "Filiation, Economic Crisis, and the Status of Women in Rural Ghana." *Canadian Journal of African Studies* 18:1 (1984), 195–218.

———. "Pleas for Domestic Relief: Akan Women and Family Courts." In *African Feminism: The Struggle for Survival in Sub-Saharan Africa,* ed. Gwendolyn Mikell, 96–126. Philadelphia: University of Pennsylvania Press, 1997.

———. "Sexual Complementarity in Traditional Ghanaian Society." *Canadian Journal of African Studies* 22:3 (1988), 656–61.

———. "The State, the Courts, and 'Value': Caught between Matrilineages in Ghana." In *Money Matters: Instability, Values and Social Payments in the Modern History of West African Communities*, ed. Jane Guyer, 225–44. Portsmouth, NH: Heinemann, 1995.

Mikell, Gwendolyn, ed. *African Feminism: The Struggle for Survival in Sub-Saharan Africa*. Philadelphia: University of Pennsylvania Press, 1997.

Miles, John. "Rural Protest in the Gold Coast: The Cocoa Hold-Ups, 1908–1938." In *The Imperial Impact: Studies in the Economic History of Africa and India*, ed. Clive Dewey and A. G. Hopkins, 152–70. London: Athlone Press, 1978.

Mirza, Sarah, and Margaret Strobel. *Three Swahili Women: Life Histories from Mombasa, Kenya*. Bloomington: Indiana University Press, 1989.

Moore, Sally Falk. *Law as Process: An Anthropological Approach*. London: Routledge and Kegan Paul, 1978.

———. *Social Facts and Fabrications: "Customary" Law on Kilimanjaro, 1880–1980*. New York: Cambridge University Press, 1986.

Musisi, Nakanyike. "Colonial and Missionary Education: Women and Domesticity in Uganda, 1900–1945." In *African Encounters with Domesticity*, ed. Karen Tranberg Hansen, 172–94. New Brunswick, NJ: Rutgers University Press, 1992.

O'Barr, Jean, Deborah Pope, and Mary Wyer, eds. *Ties That Bind: Essays on Mothering and Patriarchy*. Chicago: University of Chicago Press, 1990.

Odamtten, S. K. *The Missionary Factor in Ghana's Development (1820–1880)*. Accra: Waterville Publishing, 1978.

Ofei-Aboagye, Rosemary Ofeibea. "Altering the Strands of Fabric: A Preliminary Look at Domestic Violence in Ghana." *Signs* 19:4 (1994), 924–38.

Okali, Christine. *Cocoa and Kinship in Ghana: The Matrilineal Akan of Ghana*. London: Kegan Paul International, 1983.

———. "Kinship and Cocoa Farming in Ghana." In *Female and Male in West Africa*, ed. Christine Oppong, 169–78. London: Allen and Unwin, 1983.

Oppong, Christine. "From Love to Institution: Indications of Change in Akan Marriage." *Journal of Family History* 5:2 (1980), 197–209.

———. *Middle Class African Marriage: A Family Study of Ghanaian Senior Civil Servants*. London: George Allen and Unwin, 1981. Originally published as *Marriage among a Matrilineal Elite*. Cambridge: Cambridge University Press, 1974.

———. "Notes on Cultural Aspects of Menstruation in Ghana." *Research Review* 9:2 (1973), 33–38.

Oppong, Christine, and Katharine Abu. "The Changing Maternal Role of Ghanaian Women: Impacts of Education, Migration and Employment," Geneva: International Labour Office, 1984.

Oppong, Christine, ed. *Female and Male in West Africa*. London: Allen and Unwin, 1983.

———. ed. *Sex Roles, Population and Development in West Africa*. Portsmouth, NH: Heinemann, 1987.

Oppong, Christine, G. Adaba, M. Bekombo-Priso, and J. Mogey, eds. *Marriage, Fertility and Parenthood in West Africa*. Canberra: Australian National University Press, 1978.

Orlove, Benjamin and Henry Rutz, eds. *The Social Economy of Consumption*. Lanham, MD: University Press of America, 1989.

Owusu-Ansah, David. *Islamic Talismanic Tradition in Nineteenth Century Asante*. Lewiston, NY: Edwin Mellen Press, 1991.

Parpart, Jane. "'Where is Your Mother?' Gender, Urban Marriage and Colonial Discourse on the Zambian Copperbelt." *International Journal of African Historical Studies* 27:2 (1994), 241–71.

Parpart, Jane, and Kathleen Staudt, eds. *Women and the State in Africa*. Boulder, CO: Lynne Rienner, 1989.

Patterson, K. David. *Health in Colonial Ghana: Disease, Medicine and Socio-Economic Change, 1900–1955*. Waltham, MA: Crossroads Press, 1981.

———. "The Influenza Epidemic of 1918–19 in the Gold Coast." *Journal of African History* 24:3 (1983), 485–502.

Pederson, Susan. "National Bodies, Unspeakable Acts: The Sexual Politics of Colonial Policy-making." *Journal of Modern History* 63 (1991), 647–80.

Pellow, Deborah. *Women in Accra: Options for Autonomy*. Algonac, MI: Reference Publications, 1977.

Personal Narratives Group. *Interpreting Women's Lives: Feminist Theory and Personal Narratives*. Bloomington: Indiana University Press, 1989.

Phillips, Anne. *The Enigma of Colonialism: British Policy in West Africa*. London: Currey, and Bloomington: Indiana University Press, 1989.

Poewe, Karla O. "Matrilineal Ideology: The Economic Activities of Women in Luapula, Zambia." In *The Versatility of Kinship: Essays Presented to Harry W. Basehart*, ed. Linda S. Cordell and Stephen Beckerman, 333–57. New York: Academic Press, 1980.

Potash, Betty, ed. *Widows in African Societies*. Stanford, CA: Stanford University Press, 1986.

Radcliffe-Brown, A. R., and Daryll Forde, eds. *African Systems of Kinship and Marriage*. London: Oxford University Press, 1950.

Ranger, Terence. "The Invention of Tradition in Colonial Africa." In *The Invention of Tradition*, ed. Eric Hobsbawm and Terence Ranger. Cambridge: Cambridge University Press, 1983.

Rathbone, Richard. *Murder and Politics in Colonial Ghana*. New Haven, CT: Yale University Press, 1993.

Rattray, Robert S. *Ashanti*. London: Oxford University Press, 1923.

———. *Ashanti Law and Constitution*. London: Oxford University Press, 1929.

———. *Ashanti Proverbs (The Primitive Ethics of a Savage People)*. Oxford: Clarendon Press, 1916.

———. *Religion and Art in Ashanti*. London: Oxford University Press, 1927.

Rhodie, Sam. "The Gold Coast Cocoa Hold-Up of 1930–31." *Transactions of the Historical Society of Ghana* 9 (1968), 105–18.

Roberts, Penelope. "The State and the Regulation of Marriage: Sefwi Wiawso (Ghana), 1900–40." In *Women, State, and Ideology: Studies from Africa and Asia*, ed. Haleh Afshar, 48–69. Albany: State University of New York Press, 1987.

Robertson, Claire. "Changing Perspectives in Studies of African Women, 1976–85." *Feminist Studies* 13:1 (1987), 87–136.

———. "Post-Proclamation Slavery in Accra: A Female Affair." In *Women and Slavery in Africa*, ed. Claire Robertson and Martin Klein, 220–45. Madison: University of Wisconsin Press, 1983.

———. *Sharing the Same Bowl: A Socioeconomic History of Women and Class in Accra, Ghana*. Bloomington: Indiana University Press, 1984.

Robertson, Claire, and Martin Klein, eds. *Women and Slavery in Africa*. Madison: University of Wisconsin Press, 1983.

Sabean, David Warren. "The History of the Family in Africa and Europe: Some Comparative Perspectives." *Journal of African History* 24:2 (1983), 163–71.

Sarbah, John Mensah. *Fanti Customary Laws.* London: W. Clowes, 1897.

Sarpong, Peter. *Ghana in Retrospect: Some Aspects of Ghanaian Culture.* Tema, Ghana: Ghana Publishing Corporation, 1974.

———. *Girls' Nubility Rites in Ashanti.* Tema, Ghana: Ghana Publishing Corporation, 1977.

Schapera, Isaac, ed. *Studies in Kinship and Marriage.* London: Royal Anthropological Institute, 1963.

Schildkrout, Enid. "Changing Economic Roles of Children in Comparative Perspective." In *Marriage, Fertility and Parenthood in West Africa,* ed. C. Oppong, G. Adaba, M. Bekombo-Priso, and J. Mogey, 289–306. Canberra: Australian National University Press, 197.

———, ed. *The Golden Stool: Studies of the Asante Centre and Periphery.* New York: Anthropological Papers of the American Museum of Natural History, 1987.

Schmidt, Elizabeth. *Peasants, Traders, and Wives: Shona Women in the History of Zimbabwe, 1870–1939.* Portsmouth, NH: Heinemann, 1992.

Smock, Audrey. "Ghana: From Autonomy to Subordination." In *Women, Roles and Status in Eight Countries,* ed. J. A. Giele and A. Smock, 173–216. New York: John Wiley and Sons, 1977.

Southall, Roger J. "Farmers, Traders and Brokers in the Gold Coast Cocoa Economy." *Canadian Journal of African Studies* 12:2 (1978), 185–211.

Starr, J., and J. F. Collier, eds. *History and Power in the Study of Law: New Directions in Legal Anthropology.* Ithaca, NY: Cornell University Press, 1989.

Steady, Filomina Chioma, ed. *The Black Woman Cross-Culturally.* Rochester, VT: Schenkman, 1981.

Strobel, Margaret. *European Women and the Second British Empire.* Bloomington: Indiana University Press, 1991.

Summers, Carol. "'If You Can Educate the Native Woman . . .': Debates over the Schooling and Education of Girls and Women in Southern Rhodesia, 1900–1934." *History of Education Quarterly* 36:4 (1996), 449–71.

———. "Intimate Colonialism: The Imperial Production of Reproduction in Uganda, 1907–1925." *Signs* 16:4 (1991), 787–807.

Tashjian, Victoria B. "The Diaries of A. C. Duncan-Johnstone: A Preliminary Analysis of British Involvement in the 'Native Courts' of Colonial Asante." *Ghana Studies* 1 (1998), 137–53.

———. "'It's Mine' and 'It's Ours' Are Not the Same Thing: Changing Economic Relations between Spouses in Asante." In *The Cloth of Many Colored Silks: Papers on History and Society, Ghanaian and Islamic, in Honor of Ivor Wilks,* ed. John Hunwick and Nancy Lawler, 205–22. Evanston, IL: Northwestern University Press, 1996.

Tordoff, William. *Ashanti under the Prempehs, 1888–1935.* London: Oxford University Press, 1965.

Vaughan, Megan. *Curing Their Ills: Colonial Power and African Illness.* Stanford, CA: Stanford University Press, 1991.

———. "Which Family? Problems in the Reconstruction of the Family as an Economic and Cultural Unit." *Journal of African History* 24 (1983), 275–83.

Vellenga, Dorothy Dee. "Matriliny, Patriliny, and Class Formation among Women Cocoa Farmers in Two Rural Areas of Ghana." In *Women and Class in Africa,* ed. Claire Robertson and Iris Berger, 62–77. New York: Africana Publishing Company, 1986.

————. "Who is a Wife? Legal Expressions of Heterosexual Conflicts in Ghana." In *Female and Male in West Africa*, ed. Christine Oppong, 144–55. London: Allen and Unwin, 1983.

————. "The Widow among the Matrilineal Akan." In *Widows in African Societies*, ed. Betty Potash, 220–40. Stanford, CA: Stanford University Press, 1986.

Vercruijsse, Emile V. W. *The Dynamics of Fanti Domestic Organisation: A Comparison with Fortes' Ashanti Survey*. Cape Coast, Ghana: University of Cape Coast Research Report Series, Paper No. 12, 1972.

Walker, Cherryl. "Gender and the Development of the Migrant Labour System c. 1850–1930: An Overview." In *Women and Gender in Southern Africa to 1945*, ed. Cherryl Walker, 168–96. Cape Town: David Philip, 1990.

————, ed. *Women and Gender in Southern Africa to 1945*. Cape Town: David Philip, 1990.

White, Luise. *The Comforts of Home: Prostitution in Colonial Nairobi*. Chicago: University of Chicago Press, 1990.

Wilk, Richard R., ed. *The Household Economy: Reconsidering the Domestic Mode of Production*. Boulder, CO: Westview Press, 1989.

Wilks, Ivor. "Asante: Human Sacrifice or Capital Punishment? A Rejoinder." *International Journal of African Historical Studies* 21:3 (1988), 443–52.

————. *Asante in the Nineteenth Century: The Structure and Evolution of a Political Order*. Cambridge: Cambridge University Press, 1975.

————. *Forests of Gold: Essays on the Akan and the Kingdom of Asante*. Athens: Ohio University Press, 1993.

————. "The Golden Stool and the Elephant Tail: An Essay on Wealth in Asante." *Research in Economic Anthropology* 2 (1979), 1–36. Subsequently published as "The Golden Stool and the Elephant Tail: Wealth in Asante," in his *Forests of Gold: Essays on the Akan and the Kingdom of Asante*, 127-67. Athens: Ohio University Press, 1993.

————. "Land, Labor, Gold, and the Forest Kingdom of Asante: A Model of Early Change" in Ivor Wilks, *Forests of Gold: Essays on the Akan and the Kingdom of Asante*, 41–90. Athens: Ohio University Press, 1993. Originally published as "Land, Labour, Capital and the Forest Kingdom of Asante: A Model of Early Change." In *The Evolution of Social Systems: Proceedings of a Meeting of the Research Seminar in Archaeology and Related Subjects, London University*, ed. J. Friedman and M. J. Rowlands, 487–534. Pittsburgh: Duckworth, 1977.

————. *One Nation, Many Histories: Ghana Past and Present*. Accra: Anansesem Publications, 1996.

————. "She Who Blazed a Trail: Akyaawa Yikwan of Asante." In *Life Histories of African Women*, ed. P. Romero, 113–39. London: Ashfield Press, 1988. Republished in Ivor Wilks, *Forests of Gold: Essays on the Akan and the Kingdom of Asante*, 127–67. Athens: Ohio University Press, 1993.

Wright, Marcia. "Technology, Marriage and Women's Work in the History of Maize-Growers in Mazabuka, Zambia: A Reconnaissance." *Journal of Southern African Studies* 10:1 (1983), 71–85.

Yanagisako, Sylvia Junko. "Family and Household: The Analysis of Domestic Groups." *Annual Review of Anthropology* 8 (1979), 161–205.

Yarak, Larry. *Asante and the Dutch, 1744–1873*. Oxford: Clarendon Press, 1990.

PAPERS, THESES, AND UNPUBLISHED MANUSCRIPTS

Arhin, Kwame. "The Political Economy of a Princely City." Paper presented at the Institute of African Studies Symposium on "The City of Kumasi: Past, Present and Future," 13–16 December 1990.

Chanock, Martin. "Crimes Created and Wrongs Experienced: Perspectives on the Social History of Crime in Colonial Africa." Unpublished paper, Herskovits Library, Northwestern University, 1983.

Clark, Gracia. "The Position of Asante Women Traders in Kumasi Central Market, Ghana." Ph.D. dissertation, Cambridge University, 1986.

Hansen, Karen Tranberg. "Local Court, Custom and Gender Relations in Post-Colonial Lusaka." In "The Cloth of Many Colored Silks: Essays in Honor of Ivor Wilks." Unpublished *Festschrift* edited by John Hunwick and Nancy Lawler and presented to Ivor Wilks on 22 May 1993.

Hunwick, John and Nancy Lawler, eds. "The Cloth of Many Colored Silks: Essays in Honor of Ivor Wilks." Unpublished *Festschrift* presented to Ivor Wilks on 22 May 1993. A copy is available in the Northwestern University library.

LaTorre, Joseph R. "Wealth Surpasses Everything: An Economic History of Asante, 1750–1874." Ph.D. dissertation, University of California, Berkeley, 1978.

Opoku, Alfred Kwasi. "The Population of Kumasi: A Retrospect and Prospect." Paper presented at the Institute of African Studies Symposium on "The City of Kumasi: Past, Present and Future," 13–16 December, 1990.

Tashjian, Victoria B. "It's Mine and It's Ours Are Not the Same Thing: A History of Marriage in Rural Asante, 1900–1957." Ph.D. dissertation, Northwestern University, 1995.

———. "'You Marry to Beget': Menopause and Non-Marriage in Asante." Paper presented at the Annual Meeting of the African Studies Association, Boston, 4 December 1993.

Van Hear, Nicholas. "Northern Labour and the Development of Capitalist Agriculture in Ghana." Ph.D. thesis, University of Birmingham, England, 1982.

Vellenga, Dorothy Dee. "Changing Sex Roles and Social Tensions in Ghana: The Law as Measure and Mediator of Family Conflicts." Ph.D. dissertation, Columbia University, 1975.

PUBLISHED GOVERNMENT SOURCES

Gold Coast, *Census of the Population, 1948*. Accra: Government Printer, 1950.

Gold Coast, *Report of Commission on Native Courts*. Accra: Government Printer, 1951.

Gold Coast, *Report on the Census of the Population, 1911*. Accra: Government Printer, n.d.

ARCHIVAL SOURCES

[Documents are cited in full in endnotes.]

Ghana
Manhyia Record Office, Kumasi

Ashanti Confederacy Council [later, Asanteman Council]

Files
Minutes of Sessions

Court Records

Akyempemhene's Court, Record Book, 1915–1926
Asantehene's Appam Court D, Criminal Record Books *1–5*, 1935–1937
Asantehene's Appam Court D, Civil Record Books *1–61*, 1935–1960
Asantehene's Native Court A and A2, typescripts of misc. cases.
Asantehene's Native Court B, Civil Record Books *1-81*, 1936-1960
Asantehene's Native Court B, Criminal Record Books *1–96*, 1935–1960
Asantehene's Native Court B3, Criminal Record Books *1–16*, 1947–1952
Asantehene's Native Court B4, Civil Record Books *1–14*, 1950–1953
Asantehene's Native Court C, Civil Record Book *1–26*, 1946–1953
Asantehene's Divisional Court B Appeal, Record Books *1–9*, 1935–1949
Bompatahene's Court, Record Books, 1915-1922
Kumasi Divisional ("Clan") Courts:
   Kyidom, Civil Record Books *1-19*, 1928–1935
   Kyidom, Criminal Record Books *1–4*, 1928–1945
   Kronti, Civil Record Books *1–22*, 1925–1945
   Kronti, Criminal Record Books *1–12*, 1928–1945
   Gyasi, Civil Record Books *1–24*, 1928–1945
   Gyasi, Criminal Record Books *1–5*, 1935–1941
   Ankobia, Civil Record Books *1–32*, 1928–1945
   Ankobia, Criminal Record Books *1–3*, 1928–1943
   Oyoko, Civil Record Books *1–21*, 1926–1945
   Oyoko, Criminal Record Books *1–5*, 1935–1944
   Benkum, Civil Record Books *1–6*, 1938–1945
   Akwamu, Civil Record Books *1–24*, 1928–1945
   Akwamu, Criminal Record Books *1–8*, 1924–1944
   Adonten, Civil Record Books *1–12*, 1928–1945
Native Appeal Tribunal of Kumasihene, Record Books *1–2*, 1930–1934
Native Tribunal of Kumasihene, Civil Record Books [second series] *1–26*, 1926–1935
Native Tribunal of Kumasihene, Civil Record Books *1–25*, 1926–1935
Native Tribunal of Kumasihene, Criminal Record Books *1–19*, 1926–1935
Native Tribunal of Kumasihene, Criminal Record Books *16–21*, 1933–1935
Palaver Book, 1907–1910
Supreme Native Tribunal of Bompata, Record Books, 1922–1926

Kumasi State Council

Files
Minutes Book, 1952–1957
Record Books 1–11, 1932–1965
Secretary's Correspondence Book, 1934

National Archives of Ghana, Accra [NAGA]

ADM 5: Reports (Departmental)
ADM 11: Secretary of Native Affairs
ADM 45: Administrative Records, Chief Regional Officer
ADM 46: District Records, Obuasi
ADM 50: District Records, Juaso
ADM 51: District Records, Kumasi
ADM 52: District Records, Mampong
CSO 21: Colonial Secretary's Office, Native Affairs

National Archives of Ghana, Kumasi [NAGK]

[Please note: all reference numbers to Asante Regional Administration reflect the listing system in use prior to 1997. In 1997–1998, the archive underwent a massive reorganization and new classes and listings have been created. Most files, however, will be easily identifiable under the new improved system.]

ADM 175: Kumasi District Commissioner's Court, Civil Record Books, 1907–1935
ADM 176: Kumasi District Commissioner, Palaver Book, 1910–1913
ARA: Ashanti Regional Administration Files
SCT 24: Chief Commissioner's Court, Record Books, 1897–1942
SCT 204: Magistrate's Court, Civil Record Books, 1897–1956
SCT 205: Juvenile Court, Kumasi, Criminal Record Books, 1948–1955

Great Britain

African Studies Centre, Cambridge

Meyer Fortes Papers

British Red Cross Society Archives [BRCS], Guildford

Correspondence, Gold Coast, 1932–1957
Reports of the British Red Cross Society (published), 1933–1957
Annual Report of Gold Coast Branch of the British Red Cross Society, 1933–1952

National Library of Scotland, Edinburgh

Church of Scotland, Foreign Mission Papers, 1918–1953

Public Record Office [PRO], Kew

Colonial Office Files

CO 96   Gold Coast, Original Correspondence, 1900–1951
CO 97   Gold Coast, Acts, 1900–1907
CO 98   Gold Coast, Sessional Papers, 1900–1956
CO 343   Gold Coast, Original Correspondence Register, 1900–1951
CO 554   Africa, West, Original Correspondence, 1951–1957
CO 843   Ashanti, Acts, 1920–1934
CO 859   Social Service, Original Correspondence, 1939–1963
CO 997   Colonial Social Welfare Advisory Committee, 1943–1952
CO 1018 Lord Hailey's Papers

International Missionary Council Archives, School of Oriental and African Studies Library, London

Africa, General.

Methodist Missionary Society Archives, School of Oriental and African Studies Library, London

Wesleyan Methodist Missionary Society [WMMS]

Correspondence, Gold Coast, 1835–1950
Correspondence, West Africa, Miscellaneous
Special Series, Biography, West Africa: Rev. T. B. Freeman Journals
Special Series, Photographs
West Africa, Synod Minutes, 1842–1945

Women's Work Collection [WW]

Africa, 1928–1945
Africa, Reports, 1934–1941
Correspondence, 1928–1952
Correspondence, Africa, Chairman, 1928–1945
Correspondence, Africa, Missionaries, 1928–1942
Correspondence, Gold Coast, Chairman, 1946–1950
Correspondence, West Africa, Missionaries, 1928–1933
Minutes, 1917–1939
Annual Report of the Women's Auxiliary, 1923–1934
Women's Work, Annual Report, 1935–1965
Woman's Work (On the Mission Field), 1922–1969

Rhodes House Library, Oxford

J. Banks Elliott Photographs, Mss.Afr.s. 1956
J. B. Kirk Papers, Mss.Afr.1402
A.F.L. Wilkinson Papers, Mss.Afr.s.713

Switzerland
Basel Mission Archive [BMA], Basel
D-1:   Incoming Correspondence from Ghana to the Outbreak of the First World War
D-4-2:   Jahresberichte/Annual Reports, 1926–1947
D-4-4:   Korrespondenz mit Missionaren, 1926–1950
D-4-7:   Ghana Mission Correspondence, 1918–1948
D-10:   Miscellaneous Mss. Concerning Ghana in European Languages
D-30:   Photographs
QD-30:   Photographs

USA

The Melville J. Herskovits Library of African Studies, Northwestern University Library,
      Evanston

Polly Hill Papers
Ivor Wilks Papers

INTERVIEWS

Victoria Tashjian

All of the interviews cited below were conducted in Twi and translated by Nana Osei Agyeman-Duah. English transcriptions are on deposit at the Melville J. Herskovits Library of African Studies, Northwestern University Library, Evanston.

Kumasi

Agyeman-Duah, Joseph: 21 November 1990
Agyeman-Duah, Joseph: 29 November 1990
Agyeman-Duah, Nana Osei: early 1990
Agyeman-Duah, Nana Osei: early 1990
Agyeman-Duah, Nana Osei: 6 February 1990
Agyeman-Duah, Nana Osei: 11 February 1990
Agyeman-Duah, Nana Osei: 27 April 1990
Agyeman-Duah, Nana Osei: 9 July 1990
Agyeman-Duah, Nana Osei: 9 November 1990
Agyeman-Duah, Nana Osei: 28 November 1990
al-Hassan, Baba: 23 October 1990
al-Hassan, Suleiman: 26 October 1990
al-Tayyib: 21 October 1990
Amanfihene: 10 July 1990
Kesi, al-Haji Mustafa: 22 September 1990
Sarkin Zongo: 22 September 1990

Juaben

Juabenhene Nana Otuo Serebour II: 29 May 1990

Mamponten

Ababo, Akua: 10 September 1990
Adum, Kwadwo: Paul 11 September 1990
Afe, Abena: 28 September 1990
Afra, Akua: 6 August 1990
Akom, Yaa: 11 October 1990
Akoto, Ama Sewaa: 10 September 1990
Akyaa, Abena: 24 September 1990
Akyaa, Abena: 25 September 1990
Akyaa, Ama: 10 October 1990
Amankwa, Kwasi: 8 October 1990
Anane, Kwasi: 5 October 1990
Anane, Kwasi: 8 October 1990
Anokye, Theresa: 24 September 1990

Atta, Ama: 25 September 1990
Atta, Ama: 2 October 1990
Boafowa, Adwowa: 2 October 1990
Boahene, Kwabena: 11 September 1990
Bra, Ama: 10 October 1990
Brago, Ama: 24 July 1990
Dankwa, Yaw: 27 September 1990
Dware, Kofi: 14 September 1990
Eson, Nana Adwowa: 12 September 1990
Fodwo, Adwowa: 14 September 1990
Fodwo, Adwowa: 1 October 1990
Fodwo, Adwowa: 9 October 1990
Fodwo, Adwowa: 23 November 1990
Kawie, Yaa, and Nana Osei Agyeman-Duah: 10 October 1990
Konadu, Akua: 3 August 1990
Kro, Obaa: 7 August 1990
Kwandu, Nana Ama: 23 July 1990
Kwatema, Abena: 3 August 1990
Kyere, Akua: 8 August 1990
Manu, Kwabena: 21 September 1990
Mininowoso, Yaa: 13 September 1990
Ntim, Kofi: 3 October 1990
Ntim, Kofi: 8 October 1990
Nyame, Afua: 24 July 1990
Nyamekye, Akua: 6 August 1990
Owusu, Kofi: 18 September 1990
Pokua, Afua: 25 July 1990
Sekye, Afua: 3 August 1990
Sikafo, Abena: 15 October 1990
Tawia, Barima: 15 October 1990
Tawia, Barima: 16 October 1990
Twetwe, Panin Kwabena: 25 July 1990

Oyoko

Akyaa, Ama: 23 October 1990
Akyaa, Ama: 20 November 1990
Akyaa, Ama: 27 November 1990
Ama, Aduwa Yaa: 5 November 1990
Anto, Kofi: 6 November 1990
Asamoa, Kwame: 9 November 1990
Asamoa, Kwame: 27 November 1990
Boakye, Panin Anthony Kofi: 22 October 1990
Danso, Peter: 25 October 1990
Dapaa, Kwame: 8 November 1990
Dapaa, Kwame: 9 November 1990
Dufie, Afua: 31 October 1990
Dufie, Afua: 26 November 1990

Foku, Akua: 7 November 1990
Fosuwa, Afua: 1 November 1990
Fosuwa, Afua: 28 November 1990
Kwa, Abena: 2 November 1990
Kwa, Abena: 12 November 1990
Nyantakyiwa, Akosua: 24 October 1990

Jean Allman

Unless otherwise indicated, the interviews listed below were conducted in Twi by Allman, with the assistance of Nana Osei Agyeman-Duah. English transcriptions of the interview tapes are on deposit at the Library, Institute of African Studies, University of Ghana.

Agogo

Amokoa, Maame Yaa: 24 August 1995
Acheampong, Peter: 25 August 1995
Boateng, Adolph: 10 August 1995
Gyamera, Thompson Kwabena: 10 August 1995
Nkansah, Kwame: 25 August 1995
Sewaa, Agogohemaa Abena: 10 August 1995
Twumwaa, Christiana: 24 August 1995

Asokore

Addae, Akosua: 26 August 1992
Afra, Adwoa: 26 August 1992
Atta, Akosua (a.k.a. Sarah Obeng): 26 August 1992
Boateng, Mary Osei: 26 August 1992
Etwiano, Margaret: 26 August 1992

Effiduasi

Addae, Adwoa: 28 August 1992
Addae, Adwoa: 30 June 1993 [assisted by Ivor Agyeman-Duah]
Addae, Akua: 28 August 1992
Adjaye, Victoria: 25 August 1992
Amoam, Adwoa: 21 August 1992
Asare, Jean: 24 August 1992
Asare, Jean: 30 June 1993 [assisted by Ivor Agyeman-Duah]
Baa, Kate: 21 August 1992
Boama, Rosina: 24 August 1992
Dufie, Yaa: 25 August 1992
Edwubi, Efua: 24 August 1992
Fom, Eponuahemaa Afua: 1 September 1992
Fom, Eponuahemaa Afua: 30 June 1993 [assisted by Ivor Agyeman-Duah]
Henewah, Ellen: 21 August 1992
Nyarko, Beatrice: 24 August 1992
Nyarko, Beatrice: 30 June 1993 [assisted by Ivor Agyeman-Duah]

Oduro, Mary: 25 August 1992
Sekyiwaa, Afua: 24 August 1992
So, Akosua: 28 August 1992

Kumasi

Addai, Akua: 3 June 1992
Adjaye, Elizabeth: 8 June 1992
Afriyie, Akua: 9 June 1992
Agyewaa, Adwoa: 9 June 1992
Akoto, Nana Osei Baffuor: 29 August 1995
Antwi, Mary: 8 June 1992
Banahene, Nana Kyeame Owusu: 22 August 1995
Boadie, Mary: 8 June 1992
Boakye, Comfort: 8 June 1992
Boakye, Grace: 27 May 1992
Boateng, Grace [Mmofraturo Headmistress]: 24 June 1992
Brago, Adwoa: 2 June 1992
Brefi, Adwoa: 2 June 1992
Breyie, Yaa: 5 June 1992
Des Bordes, Dr. Irene [Chief Medical Officer, Maternal and Child Health Clinic]: 18 June 1992
Ditwi, Yaa: 2 June 1992
Dufie, Yaa: 25 August 1992
Durowaa, Akua: 1 June 1992
Dutuwaa, Abenaa: 5 June 1992
Dwumo, Abenaa: 5 June 1992
Esobontin, Afua: 9 June 1992
Foku, Akua: 1 June 1992
Frakoma, Abena: 9 June 1992
Frima, Adwoa: 8 June 1992
Gyimah, K.A.M.: 26 August 1995
Konadu, Ama: 9 June 1992
Kusiwaa, Akua: 27 May 1992
Kusiwaa, Akua: 22 August 1995
Kwabena II, Mmagyegyefohene Nana Osei: 21 September 1992
Kyaa, Ama: 1 June 1992
Kyaa, Yaa: 2 June 1992
Kyei, Thomas: 11 June 1992
Mansah, Afua: 8 June 1992
Mansah, Akosua: 3 June 1992
Mansah, Akosua: 9 June 1992
Nsia, Nana Okyeame Kwaku: 10 June 1992
Ntomu, Abena: 1 June 1992
Nyamesem, Abena: 22 May 1992
Nyarko, Akosua: 3 June 1992
Nyarko, Ama: 8 June 1992
Pokua, Adwoa: 3 June 1992

Samata, Efua: 3 June 1992
Sewaa, Ama: 5 June 1992
Sewaa, Ama: 22 August 1995
Twereboaa, Adwoa: 1 June 1992

Tafo

Abebrese, Yaa: 22 June 1992
Addae, Akosua: 22 June 1992
Addae, Akua: 23 June 1992
Afrakoma, Rose: 25 June 1992
Akyaa, Yaa: 24 June 1992
Akyima, Adwoa: 23 June 1992
Amfum, Grace: 22 June 1992
Anokye, Mary: 19 June 1992
Anokye, Mary: 29 June 1993 [assisted by Selina Opoku-Agyeman]
Dapah, Agnes Ama: 22 June 1992
Dapah, Agnes Ama: 29 June 1993 [assisted by Selina Opoku-Agyeman]
Forduah, Adjoa: 23 June 1992
Forduah, Adjoa: 29 June 1993 [assisted by Selina Opoku-Agyeman]
Gyamfia, Akosua: 26 June 1992
Kankroma, Akua: 23 June 1992
Mansah, Adwoa: 25 June 1992
Mansah, Akosua: 23 June 1992
Manu, Afua: 25 June 1992
Nkromah, Ama: 25 June 1992
Nsiah, Adwoa: 29 June 1992
Nsiah, Adwoa: 29 June 1993 [assisted by Selina Opoku-Agyeman]
Nsiah, Ama: 26 June 1992
Nyarko, Akua: 25 June 1992
Nsuah, Efua: 24 June 1992
Pokua, Afua: 26 June 1992
Pokuaa, Yaa: 25 June 1992
Senti, Akua: 19 June 1992
Sewaa, Efua: 25 June 1992
Tana, Adwoa: 23 June 1992

INDEX

About the Authors

JEAN ALLMAN is an Associate Professor in the History Department at the University of Minnesota.

VICTORIA TASHJIAN is an Associate Professor in the History Department at St. Norbert College.

ISBN 0-325-07001-6